OXFORD TEXTBOOKS IN LINGUISTICS

Series editors

Keith Brown, Eve V. Clark, Jim Miller, Lesley Milroy,
Geoffrey K. Pullum, and Peter Roach

Principles and Parameters

Principles and Parameters

An Introduction to Syntactic Theory

Peter W. Culicover

OXFORD UNIVERSITY PRESS
1997

Oxford University Press, Great Clarendon Street, Oxford OX2 6DP

Oxford New York

Athens Auckland Bangkok Bogota Bombay
Buenos Aires Calcutta Cape Town Dar es Salaam
Delhi Florence Hong Kong Istanbul Karachi
Kuala Lumpur Madras Madrid Melbourne
Mexico City Nairobi Paris Singapore
Taipei Tokyo Toronto

and associated companies in
Berlin Ibadan

Oxford is a trade mark of Oxford University Press

Published in the United States
by Oxford University Press Inc., New York

British Library Cataloguing in Publication Data
Data available

Library of Congress Cataloging in Publication Data
Culicover, Peter W.
Principles and parameters : an introduction to syntactic theory /
Peter W. Culicover.
p. cm. — (Oxford textbooks in linguistics)
Includes bibliographical references and index.
1. Grammar, Comparative and general–Syntax. 2. Principles and
parameters (Linguistics) 3. Government–binding theory (Linguistics)
I. Title. II. Series.
P291.C79 1997 415—dc20 96–22237

ISBN 0–19–870015–6
ISBN 0–19–870014–8 (pbk.)

1 3 5 7 9 10 8 6 4 2

Typeset by Graphicraft Typesetters Ltd., Hong Kong
Printed in Great Britain
on acid-free paper by
Bookcraft (Bath) Ltd.

To the memory of Adrian Akmajian

A NOTE ON THE EXERCISES

The relative difficulty of the exercises at the end of each chapter is indicated by the use of asterisks (least difficult: no asterisk; most difficult: three asterisks). The section of the chapter most relevant to each exercise is given below the exercise in square brackets. Asterisks are also used to grade the degree of difficulty of the 'further readings' for each chapter and finally, following the usual linguistic convention, to indicate when an example is ungrammatical.

PREFACE

When I made the happy transition from academic administration back to teaching and research some years ago I found myself in the position of co-teaching an introduction graduate course on government-binding theory. Naturally there were many (in fact, far too many) things that I felt that I did not have a firm command of, and more being published every day. In order to relieve the burdens on my memory, I wrote down as much as I could, in the form of lecture notes. This book is the result.

While I did not set out originally to write a textbook, I did want to do certain things in my teaching that I thought were not emphasized in the published materials that were available at the time. I wanted to inquire into how the theory would be different if certain assumptions were relaxed or changed. I wanted to focus on the motivations for these assumptions, and on the conceptual and methodological foundations of the theory. I wanted to take the students from arguments for the standard analyses all the way to the limits of these analyses. And I wanted to provide the students with an understanding of the fact that the development of this (or any) theory is very much a work in progress.

Thus, I have developed this text with emphasis on understanding how specific methodological assumptions constitute the basis for certain important core analyses that have played a central role in the development of the theory. A large number of exercises are also provided that take the student from the point of applying the mechanics of the theory to developing and organizing new data, providing analyses, and exploring alternative hypotheses. A schematic 'roadmap' is provided in Appendix 1 at the end of the book in order to show how the components of the theory relate to one another. Technical terms appear in boldface the first time they occur in the text, and all terms are defined in Appendix 2.

As much as possible I have tried here to address some of the most recent developments in the development of the theory, recognizing that by the time this book appears in print certain things will be out of date. On the other hand, the field of theoretical linguistics has shown time and again its ability to forget and then rediscover earlier observations, problems, and solutions. I hope to have chosen the concepts, phenomena, and problems sufficiently well that most of them will retain their significance in spite of any theoretical changes that may occur. Some special topics that are covered in this text include: the relationship between language learning and linguistic theory, alternatives to Exceptional Case Marking, 'quirky' Case, binding theory for non-pronominals, VP-internal subjects, the DP analysis, the theory of branching, parasitic gaps, Relativized Minimality and the theory of Move α, long distance anaphora, antecedent-contained deletion, weak and strong crossover, reconstruction and anti-reconstruction, head movement, leftward and rightward movement and antisymmetry, and the Minimalist Program. In addition, where possible I have pointed towards alternative formulations of certain phenomena in other theories, although space limitations did not allow me to explore these alternatives in detail in the text.

ACKNOWLEDGMENTS

The writing of a book such as this inevitably owes much to many people, above to all the students who must suffer through generations of imprecise explanations, obscure examples, impenetrable exercises, and insidious typos. I thank them deeply for their patience. I am particularly indebted to Svetlana Vasina for working through an earlier version of the manuscript, and to Nick Cipollone for picking apart the final manuscript with great gusto and accuracy.

The manuscript has also benefited markedly from careful scrutiny by Jim Miller and Paul Postal. They each made innumerable suggestions about form, content, and presentation; I have tried to respond to as many as possible, and I hope I have not left too many loose ends. I would like to thank them here once again for their help.

The manuscript was also read and commented on by a number of anonymous reviewers at various stages of its development. I know that I have not been able to satisfy all of their concerns and respond to all of their suggestions. But I want to thank them for their time and effort and to express the hope that the final product approaches in some respects what they wanted to see.

I am very grateful to friends and colleagues Michael Rochemont, Shigeru Miyagawa, Ray Jackendoff, Bob Levine, and Carl Pollard. Michael kept me going when it was hard to do much linguistics, and has been a constant source of support and inspiration. Shigeru co-taught with me a few years and helped to make my transition back into teaching easier. My recent collaboration with Ray has been both a pleasure and an education. Bob and Carl have proven to be an endless source of intellectual stimulation and discovery as we have explored together the foundations of syntactic theory.

And finally, thanks to my family, Diane and Daniel, whose patience, love, and good nature have prevailed throughout.

P. W. C.

Columbus, Ohio
4 January 1996

CONTENTS

9. Binding and Logical Form   315

10. Head Movement and Minimalism   337

1

Foundations and Methods

In this chapter we introduce the study of language as part of the study of the human mind, draw distinctions between what is in the mind and what people say, and relate the theory of language to the innate human capacity to learn language.

1. Language and the mind

Language is a creation of the human mind, and is the mental capacity that most clearly makes us 'human'; it is the one that distinguishes us from other creatures. The goal of linguistic theory is to understand the nature of this mental capacity. There are two fundamental empirical concerns: what knowledge of language consists of, and how the mind is structured so that we are able to acquire knowledge of language. These concerns typify the Principles and Parameters approach to linguistic theory.

The mind is not subject to direct examination. Thus, indirect methods must be found to investigate the nature of linguistic knowledge and how language is acquired by the mind. The methodology that has proven most productive in the development of linguistic theory has been to examine closely selected sentences and phrases that native speakers of a language judge to be possible, impossible, and marginal. By studying these external manifestations of linguistic knowledge, we seek to arrive, indirectly, at an understanding of the mental apparatus that gives rise to them.

Application of this methodology may give the incorrect impression that the objective of the Principles and Parameters approach, as well as earlier versions of linguistic theory in the same tradition, is to provide complete descriptions of human languages, conceived of as sets of linguistic expressions (i.e. words, phrases, and sentences). But these expressions are simply the data that are used in the investigation, and are not themselves the object of the theory. The overriding concern on this approach is not with what a speaker or group of speakers say ('E-language' in the terminology of Chomsky 1986a), but with the character of what is in the human mind that accounts for our ability to acquire, speak, and understand language ('I-language', in Chomsky's terms). Suppose, following Chomsky (1986a), that we define 'language' as the set of words, phrases, and sentences that a speaker or group of speakers can produce, while 'grammar' is the internal linguistic knowledge. Then 'language' in this sense is E-language, while 'grammar' is I-language.

Two more terms that draw a very similar distinction are competence and performance.[1] **Competence** is the linguistic knowledge that a native speaker has, idealized away from actual situations of use; that is, I-language. **Performance** is what a native speaker does, which in essence produces E-language.

These distinctions are summarized in (1).

(1)

what is in the mind	what people say
grammar	language
I-language	E-language
competence	performance

In studying grammar/I-language/competence by looking at language/E-language/performance we are in effect trying to look beyond the superficial manifestations of linguistic knowledge to the deeper principles, structures, and mechanisms that account for the organization of this knowledge in the mind.

This approach to linguistic theory proceeds with the presumption that what people say reflects what they know, but that the relationship between the two is somewhat inexact. In the mind of the speaker is his or her knowledge of language, which is used by the speaker to produce and understand the language. What people actually say does not reflect simply competence, but competence as it is revealed and distorted through performance.

For example, people make mistakes or speak in a peculiar manner when they are drunk or tired. This is something that we (some of us) are familiar with. The mistakes that people make should not be included as part of 'knowledge of language'. We should not require that our linguistic theory treat such mistakes in precisely the same way as it treats our correct utterances.

This difference between correct utterances and mistakes is theoretically significant. It presumes that there is a body of knowledge that the speaker has that is only imperfectly revealed in the speaker's normal linguistic activities. It is the task of the linguist to figure out what this knowledge is, and by means that may go beyond listening to what people say in normal discourse.

It is a corollary of this approach to linguistic theory that there are infinitely many linguistic 'facts', but not all of them serve as evidence regarding the linguistic faculty. E-language in some sense may constitute the primary evidence for I-language, but in principle so may other types of facts (e.g. psychological experiments, electrophysiology, neuroscience, language impairments, language development, etc.), to the extent that they shed insight on the nature of the linguistic faculty. It is not possible to say in advance which facts will and will not constitute such evidence. And of course, the relevance of particular facts depends in part on the state of the theory at a given time.

2. Language learning and linguistic theory

A fundamental perspective in generative grammar is the recognition that the form and content of linguistic theory are intimately related to the phenomenon of language acquisition. How do we acquire the knowledge that allows us to relate sounds to meanings, that is, to give expression to thoughts and to interpret what is uttered by others? Where do the representations of phonology, syntax, and semantics come from? How do we learn how the different representations are related to one another? Is it possible that knowledge of language is built into human beings, in that these representations are present at birth or develop over time without particular experience? Or do we acquire them in all their complex detail through general mechanisms of learning?

It is hard to suppose that knowledge of a given language, such as English, is present at birth. Why wouldn't everyone grow up speaking the same language, then? On the other hand, no one has yet been able to demonstrate that general learning mechanisms that are not specific to language acquisition could acquire human languages in all their richness. One main reason for this is that there are many things that we know, as native speakers, for which there appears to be no evidence in the experiences that we have as language learners. For instance, we know that the question in (2b) is ungrammatical, while the question in (2a) is grammatical.

(2)   a. Who did you buy a picture of?
        b. *Who did you buy Mary's picture of?

It does not appear that children are provided with specific information during the course of language learning that will indicate to them the relative grammaticality of such examples. In fact, it does not appear that children are provided with *any* systematic information about the ungrammaticality of particular examples.

The Principles and Parameters view is that much of this knowledge is not learned, but an intrinsic part of the human mind. But if some knowledge of language is built into the human mind, it must be built into all human minds, and must therefore be universal. On this view, languages are not all that different, deep down, and what we may perceive as profound variations are just minor ones: different words, different sets of sounds, differences in the order of words within phrases, and so on. The universal knowledge concerns the *principles* that determine the basic architecture of any linguistic system, and the *parameters* that govern the range of variation that this architecture may display.

We take it that the invariant core of linguistic principles and parameters is what a linguistic theory should account for. It is the content of the *linguistic faculty* that is built into the human mind. Its existence allows us to account for the fact that languages have so much in common, and that they are acquired relatively easily and directly by children. In fact, we can even go further, and argue that the existence of such a core not only facilitates learning, in many cases it is necessary if learning is to occur at all. The problem for the learner of acquiring a very complex, intricate body of knowledge, such as a language, can be proven to be impossible unless the learner is assumed to begin the task of learning with a very specific and highly detailed initial state, with a very restricted set of possible alternatives available to it. Such a proof of course requires that the final state of knowledge or range of final states be precisely specified, as part of the linguistic theory. Certain assumptions as to what the final states are can be shown to lead to **unlearnability**, in the sense that we prove that the learner cannot determine the right answer in a finite amount of time. Other initial assumptions about what the final states can be lead to unlearnability unless we cut down further on the set of possible final states.

The learner is presented with data from a language, and has to make a decision as to what the grammar is. Because the language is infinite, the learner can never encounter all of the data. But the learner is nevertheless able to construct or otherwise arrive at a grammar that will correctly account for all of the sentences in the language. How is this possible?

A theory of grammar says what is necessary and what is possible in a natural language. Suppose that this information is expressed as a set of possible grammars. The maximally restrictive theory of grammar would be that there is just one possible language, call it L^1, generated by the one possible grammar, G^1. In this theory, the set of grammars consists of one member.

(3)   Theory of Grammar A: $\{G^1\}$

Consider the problem of choosing the correct grammar in this circumstance. If in fact there was only one possible grammar of a language, there would be no real learning problem. 'Acquiring a language' would be of the same order of difficulty as 'acquiring a heart'; the particular grammar would be an intrinsic component of our biological endowment, and our linguistic behavior, like our hearts and other organs, would emerge and develop in the normal course of events as our minds and our bodies grew.

In a sense Theory of Grammar A is an extreme and simplified version of the Principles and Parameters theory. This view is that in some sense there *is* just one grammar and one language, that the variations that we observe in reality (since we do not all speak the same language) are relatively minor divergences from this idealized view.

But the fact remains that there actually is more than one human language, and so more than one possibility that the learner must choose among. If the grammars are closely related and differ along one or more dimension, then the learner must 'fix' the properties along each dimension of the grammar of the language to be learned. We may imagine the learner exposed to sequences of utterances from the language spoken in the environment, and, on the basis of this experience, determining which of the possibilities is the one he/she is faced with.

So let us suppose, slightly more realistically, that the set of possibilities consists of two members, as in (4). $\{G^1, G^2\}$ are two distinct grammars that generate two distinct languages L^1 and L^2, evidenced by two different sets of linguistic expressions.[2]

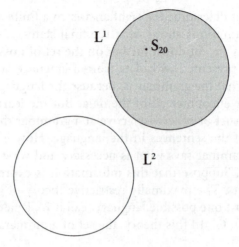

Figure 1. Disjoint languages

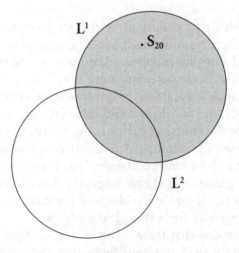

Figure 2. Intersecting languages

(4)   Theory of Grammar B: $\{G^1, G^2\}$

There are three possible relationships between the two languages. First, L^1 and L^2 may be totally *disjoint,* in the sense that there is no sentence that is in both languages. This situation is illustrated in Figure 1.

Second, L^1 and L^2 may *intersect,* in that there is at least one sentence that is in both languages, but not all sentences of one language are in the other. We see this in Figure 2. And Figure 3 illustrates the **subset relation,**

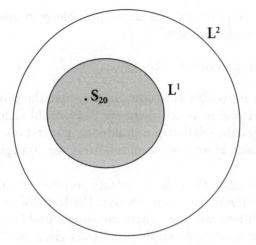

Figure 3. The subset relation

in which one language, say L^1, is properly included within the other language.

For the disjoint and intersection cases, learning is straightforward. In both cases, there are sentences in L^1 that are not in L^2, and vice versa. Encountering such a sentence constitutes immediate evidence for the learner regarding what grammar is producing the sequence. For example, the sequence in (5) can only be produced by G^1 in either case.

(5) ..., S_{20}, ...

The subset situation is somewhat more problematic. If the learner encounters S_{20}, either G^1 or G^2 would be a correct hypothesis. If the language to be learned is L^2, and the learner guesses the subset language L^1, then sooner or later the learner will encounter some sentence that is in L^2 that is not in L^1. As before, the choice will be clear. But suppose that the learner's first guess is L^2, while the target language is L^1. Then the learner's guess will be in error, but there will be no way of correcting it.

This is the Subset Problem, and there are two solutions. Either we assume that the theory of grammar does not allow for the subset relation to occur, or the learner has a strategy of always choosing the smaller language, by adopting the most restrictive hypothesis consistent with the data. With either of these assumptions, the learning problem again becomes straightforward. Of course, in the second case the question arises as to how the learner knows which is the smaller language. Such knowledge must be universal and wired into the learning mechanism.

Now let us suppose that the set of possible grammars consists of a finite number *n* of members.

(6)   Theory of grammar C: $\{G^1, G^2, \ldots, G^i, \ldots, G^n\}$

There are now *n* possible languages. In principle the problem is no different from the one in which there are two possible languages: for any pair of languages, the relation of disjointness, intersection, or subset holds. Learning proceeds as we have seen, following the strategies that we have laid out.

Suppose now that there is an infinite number of grammars in the set from which the learner must choose. The learnability problem is not quite so straightforward now. There are simple problems of the infinite type, and difficult ones. A simple problem is given in (7).[3]

(7)   Theory of grammar D: The (infinite) class of grammars
      $\{G^1, G^2, \ldots, G^i, \ldots\}$, where
      $L^1 = \{a\}$
      $L^2 = \{a, aa\}$
      $L^3 = \{a, aa, aaa\}$
      and so on.

In other words, L^1 is a finite language with just one 'sentence' in it, namely the 'sentence' *a*. L^2 has two 'sentences', *a* and *aa*, and so on. The task before the learner is to guess, given a sequence of 'sentences', what the correct grammar is that is producing those sentences.

There exists an adequate learning procedure for this class. Notice that this set of languages possesses the subset property. Given that this relation is allowed to exist, the learner's strategy is to pick the grammar of the smaller of the two languages consistent with any data encountered. Since every language is finite, every language has a longest 'sentence', and this 'sentence' occurs in no smaller language. So the learner may employ the same strategy, generalized to this situation in which there is an infinite number of languages. Namely, pick the grammar of the smallest language consistent with the evidence.

To see how this works, consider the sequence in (8).

(8) $\ldots, a^i, \ldots$

When the learner encounters the 'sentence' consisting of *i* a's, it checks to see if this sentence is already in the language that it has guessed. If so, then nothing needs to be done, but if not, the learner must guess a language that contains this 'sentence'. Following the logic of the subset relation, it should guess the grammar of the smallest such language, namely G^i. At some point, the learner will guess the correct grammar, and from that time on, all 'sentences' that it encounters will be consistent with the grammar that it has guessed.[4] The largest sentence of the language serves as an 'index'; in effect, it tells the learning procedure what the target language is.

The point of these artificial examples is to illustrate the interaction between the class of grammars presupposed by a particular theory of grammar, and the extent to which the class is learnable in the sense that there exists a learning procedure that converges on a correct answer at some point. We conclude by considering a class of grammars that is not learnable by any procedure.

(9)   Theory of Grammar E: The (infinite) class of grammars:
        $\{G^1, G^2, \ldots, G^i, \ldots\} + G^\infty$, where
          $L^1 = \{a\}$
          $L^2 = \{a, aa\}$
          $L^3 = \{a, aa, aaa\}$
        and so on, and L^∞ contains *all* sentences of the form a^i, $0 < i < \infty$.

This theory of grammar is the same as Theory of Grammar D, with the addition of the infinite language L^∞. There exists no effective learning procedure for this class, that is, no procedure that inevitably converges on a correct solution. The reason for this is that the infinite language contains every 'index' sentence for all of the finite languages. So, whenever a sentence is encountered, it could be the index sentence for some finite language, or it could be in the infinite language. If the language to be learned is a finite language, the learner could just as well guess the infinite language. But the learner cannot guess the infinite language as a general rule, because of the Subset Problem. Each finite language is a subset of the infinite language, and the strategy for the subset relation is to guess the *smaller* of the two possibilities. So there is no effective learning procedure for the class of languages that Theory of Grammar E makes available.

The intuition that this example exemplifies is that learnability is impossible unless the set of alternatives available to the learner is sufficiently restricted that the experience will serve to 'index' the proper choice of grammar. This situation exists in the case of Theory of Grammar D, but not Theory of Grammar E. We can imagine a *constraint* on the correct theory of grammar, call it Theory of Grammar H(uman), to the effect that the finite/infinite subset relation shown in the latter case is imposs-ible. By means of such a constraint, we restrict the class of grammars so that it is learnable.

Now let us consider the case of real languages, not artificial examples. Suppose that it can be shown that natural languages are not learnable unless they are formally restricted in certain ways. What we will find, if this is the case, is that certain imaginable grammatical relations or certain logically possible linguistic constructions will not occur in any natural language. What we will find, then, is that native speakers will demonstrate particular 'knowledge of language' that was not acquired through experience. This knowledge will determine their judgements of the grammaticality and meaningfulness of sentences just as knowledge acquired through experience will, since both types of knowledge are ulti-mately incorporated into the mental representations that speakers use in order to be able to speak and understand. But the knowledge that was not acquired through experience reflects the principles that form a part of Theory of Grammar H in the human mind.

At this point the general approach should be clear. We examine the native speakers' linguistic ability, and try to determine what aspects of their knowledge they could have acquired through experience, and what aspects they could not have. The latter, we presume, are directly or in-directly the consequence of general principles, and such principles are good candidates for Theory of Grammar H. This is the general thrust of the Principles and Parameters approach.

3. Methodological foundations

3.1. Idealization

In § 1 we noted that the linguistic facts are central to the development of the theory of grammar to the extent that they constitute evidence that bears on the theory. The very richness of linguistic experience requires that we idealize, in the sense that we ignore certain facts at certain times in the interest of articulating the theory. Among the two most significant idealizations that are made are (i) the notion 'competence of the native speaker' and (ii) autonomy.

(i) *Competence of the native speaker*. It is generally accepted that the goal of a linguistic description is to provide an account of the linguistic knowledge possessed by the native speaker of a language. Such a description involves a double idealization, in that we (falsely) treat all native speakers as exactly the same, and we assume that there is some stable and well-defined store of knowledge of language in the mind of the native speaker. The methodological assumption is that by ignoring differences between individuals and imprecision in the knowledge of individuals we may nevertheless discover something substantive and correct about natural language.

(ii) *Autonomy*. One strategy for idealization is to ignore certain facts that do not naturally fit. Another, more refined, approach is to decompose phenomena into components, such that it is (potentially) more feasible to come up with simple theories of the parts than to come up with a theory of the undifferentiated whole. The classical components are *syntax* (phrase and sentence structure), *semantics* (meaning), *morphology* (word structure), and *phonetics/phonology* (sound and sound structure). The notion that a linguistic theory can be organized into such components is called **autonomy**. There are various views of autonomy, depending on how strict one wants to be about the distinctness of components.

The assumption that we will make is that the components are strictly autonomous, in the sense that the principles and primitives that make up one component of a grammar are unique to that component. This is sometimes called the Autonomous Systems view (Hale, Jeanne, and Platero 1977) or the Modularity Thesis. On this view, generalizations about syntactic structure are statable independently of considerations about interpretation or use. It is important to recognize that this a methodological principle of linguistic research, corresponding to the other sorts of idealization that we have been discussing. The Autonomous Systems view bears a close relationship to the Autonomy Thesis of Chomsky (1975), which holds that meaning plays a limited role or no role in formal grammar (i.e. syntax).

The Autonomous Systems view has been articulated particularly clearly by Jackendoff (1983). According to this view, a grammar consists of a set of components, each of which characterizes well-formed representations at one or more levels. Each component of the grammar has its own primitives, rules of combination, and well-formedness conditions. Syntactic representations are composed of syntactic primitives, e.g. words and phrases of particular syntactic categories like Noun and Verb, organized into some sort of hierarchical structure. Meanings are composed of semantic primitives, e.g. concepts like 'banana' and 'eat', that are members of particular conceptual categories like Thing and Action. Moreover there are correspondence rules that map representations at one level into representations at another. On this view the primitives of one component are not completely reducible to the primitives of any other and the well-formedness conditions at one level do not make reference to aspects of representations at any other level.

3.2. Syntacticization, uniformity, and configuration

There are three other central methodological premises that form the basis for the Principles and Parameters approach and are essential to an understanding of the development of and motivation for theories within this framework. These are (i) **Syntacticization**, (ii) **Uniformity**, and (iii) (the **Primacy of**) **Configuration**. These particular terms are introduced here for expository purposes and are not widely used in the field, although the ideas that they express are implicit throughout the Principles and Parameters approach.

It is important to recognize that these premises cannot and should not be used to justify analyses. They are to be properly understood as guides that point researchers to the formulation of hypotheses. We articulate them here in order to understand the reasoning through which particular analyses have been arrived at in Principles and Parameters theory. It cannot be stressed too much that the analyses themselves must be justified on the basis of how well they account for the phenomena.

(i) Syntacticization is the tactic of taking every phenomenon that is plausibly tied to syntactic structure and characterizing it in syntactic terms. At the very least, Syntacticization is a way of rendering complex linguistic material amenable to analysis and of producing clear hypotheses and predictions. Syntactic structures are explicit, more or less well understood, and relatively easy to specify and manipulate. It is possible to state generalizations, both true and false ones, in terms of the properties of the syntactic representation. If the phenomenon is properly syntactic, totally or in part, Syntacticization will turn out to have been the correct move. Where the correct generalizations cannot in fact be captured in terms of the categories available to us in our syntactic descriptions, the mismatches will become clear over time, and the proper formulation at the proper level of representation will be (ideally) more perspicuous.[5]

A particularly clear example of Syntacticization is the treatment of infinitival complements, as illustrated by (10).

(10)   Mary expects to win.

It is intuitively clear that use of the verb *win* commits us to some notion of a winner, the person who wins. By Syntacticization, there is an empty noun phrase that occupies the subject position of *win* in the syntactic representation of sentence (10). On this view, (10) has exactly the same syntactic structure as *Mary expects herself to win*.

There are syntactic mechanisms for representing the subject of the infinitive that do not posit an empty NP at some level of syntactic representation.[6] That there is an empty NP subject follows from the next premiss, Uniformity.

(ii) Uniformity is the general view that two phenomena that share some properties are the same phenomenon, in part at least, at some level of analysis. For example, suppose that two sentences share some aspects of meaning. Applying Syntacticization, we postulate that syntactic structure determines meaning. Applying Uniformity, we hypothesize that sameness in meaning with a difference in form (roughly, word order) reflects sameness in syntactic representation at some abstract level.[7]

In the case of control, Uniformity leads us to posit an NP subject of the infinitival complement, on a part with overt NP subjects of main clauses and finite complements, as in *Mary will win* and *Mary expects that she will win*.

A particularly important example of Uniformity concerns the complement structure of verbs like *believe*. As shown in (11), *believe* takes a sentential complement.

(11)   Mary believes that John won.

Believe also takes an infinitival complement, as in (12).

(12)   Mary believes John to have won.

Under Uniformity, the complement structure of *believe* must be the same in these two cases. This leads to the hypothesis that *John to have won* has the same syntactic structure as *that John won*.

There are of course many specific questions that we may raise with respect to the hypothesis that sameness of meaning correlates with sameness of form, which as formulated is rather vague. What aspects of meaning are relevant to determining 'sameness of meaning'? What aspects of form are relevant to determining 'difference in form'? For example, does sameness in meaning with a difference in derivational morphology constitute a suitable case? If it does, then Uniformity leads to a type of syntactic theory exemplified by Generative Semantics.[8] On such a theory, syntactic transformations produce related or synonymous lexical items with different morphological properties.[9] Along similar lines, if two sentences have the same logical properties, Uniformity leads us to postulate that they have the same syntactic structure as well.

In current practice, the Uniformity approach is restricted to morpho-logical differences on the order of inflectional variation (e.g. declension and conjugation), not derivational morphology. Is it possible to give this approach some foundational substance, and what are the principles that would justify it? The answer to this question is not yet known.

(iii) By (the Primacy of) Configuration we refer to the assumption that all syntactic phenomena can be accounted for in terms of the min-imal configurational properties of the syntactic structure. The strongest position is that only the hierarchical organization of the syntactic struc-ture, expressed in terms of the relation **dominates**, is needed to capture syntactic generalizations.[10] The left-to-right organization of a sentence, on this view, is a derived property; notions such as 'subject' and 'object' are not primitive but defined in terms of the domination relation.[11]

In spite of their informal quality, Syntacticization, Uniformity, and Configuration are highlighted here because by recognizing where they have been applied, we can understand in many cases why Principles and Parameters theory takes the form that it does. The questions raised here about precisely how and when to apply these methodological strategies are not answerable in the absence of real analyses. To the extent that the outcomes constitute genuine progress in our understanding of the nature of the human language faculty, we will have some justification of the general approach and perhaps a more precise idea of how to proceed in specific circumstances.

FURTHER READING

(Note: The number of asterisks before a reference indicates its level of technical difficulty. You should be able to follow much if not all of what is in those references that lack asterisks.)

Chomsky has written extensively on language and the mind; see, for example, Chomsky (1965; 1968; 1975; 1986a; 1991). Jackendoff (1993) and Pinker (1994) contain accessible non-technical introductions to this subject matter.

A non-technical introduction to the relationship between language learnability and linguistic theory is Lightfoot (1982). Early learnability results for grammars can be found in **Gold (1967), *Hamburger and Wexler (1973), *Wexler and Hamburger (1973), and **Hamburger and Wexler (1975). The formal approach to language learnability of *Wexler and Culicover (1980) explicitly relates learnability theory to linguistic theory; *Morgan (1986), *Culicover and Wilkins (1984), and *Lightfoot (1991) propose modifications and elaborations of this approach. A more abstract and technical approach to the learnability of formal systems can be found in **Osherson, Stob, and Weinstein (1986). Pinker (1989) is concerned with the acquisition of properties of lexical items from available evidence.

*Berwick (1985) shows that the subset relation poses a general learnability problem. A linguistically relevant learnability problem involving the subset relation is discussed in considerable technical detail by *Manzini and Wexler (1987) and *Wexler and Manzini (1987). The reader should complete at least Chapter 3 of this book before attempting to tackle these latter works.

Arguments, Government, and Case

In this chapter we consider the properties of **arguments** of a sentence. Arguments are most commonly associated with verbs, but they are also associated with nouns and adjectives. Verbs and adjectives, and some nouns, express properties of things (e.g. *John is sleeping*) or relationships between things (e.g. *John sees Bill*). The arguments are the phrases that denote the things that have such properties or are involved in such relationships. Arguments are able to bear case marking, and they express semantic roles associated with some head. We will develop an account in which the assignment of case and semantic roles is mediated by a configurationally defined relation of **government**, and we will explore some of the technical issues that such an account raises.

1. Argument structure

1.1. Arguments

In general, there are two kinds of arguments. First, there is the subject, whose presence in a sentence is for the most part independent of the particular verb. So in a language like English, every sentence will have a subject. (Sometimes the subject position is filled by a dummy element that is not, strictly speaking, an argument.) Second, there are the arguments associated with a particular verb. A verb like *give* has two arguments besides the subject, e.g. *give Bill the newspaper*. A verb like *see* has one argument, e.g. *see Bill*. And a verb like *sleep* takes no arguments. Some verbs take sentential arguments, as in *believe that it is raining*. The arguments of a verb are said to be selected by the verb. A verb that selects a particular type of argument is said to be *subcategorized* for that type of argument. The set of arguments selected by the verb, including the subject argument, constitutes its **argument structure**. Nouns and adjectives also have argument structure.

A fundamental question that a syntactic theory must address in accounting for argument structure is how the argument structure is represented. Consider the example of *John sees Bill*. The noun phrase *Bill* has many properties, any one of which could be assumed to be the one that defines it as the argument of the verb, the others being in some sense secondary or derived. For example, *Bill* is the direct object of *see*, it is assigned the objective case (which is explicitly expressed on a pronoun, as in *John sees him/*he*), it is the THEME (i.e. what is seen), and it is immediately adjacent to and follows *see*. Let us call the elements that make up a phrase the constituents of the phrase. If we assume that *see Bill* is a verb phrase with two constituents, *see* and *Bill*, then *Bill* is also the **sister** of *see*.

In Principles and Parameters theory (PPT) it is assumed that the primary relation is a configurational one (the principle of Primacy of Configuration discussed in Chapter 1). It follows from this assumption that the fact that *Bill* is the sister of *see* in a phrase structure configuration determines all of the other properties of *Bill* in this expression. That is, the objective case of *Bill*, the fact that it is the direct object, the fact that it bears the role THEME, and the fact that it is adjacent to the verb and follows it are all consequences of this sisterhood relation.

Notice now that the subject of a sentence is also an argument, and has the same types of properties as do arguments of the verb. That is, it has a case, it receives a particular interpretation, and it appears in a particular position in the sentence. Assuming Uniformity (see Chapter 1, § 2.2), the subject of a sentence must bear the same type of relationship to some element of the sentence as the arguments of the verb bear to the verb; the relationship must be expressed in configurational terms. This relationship, which we will explore in some detail in this and subsequent chapters, is called government. We say, for example, that the verb governs its arguments, that a particular case is assigned under government, and so on.

1.2. Preliminaries of X'-theory

Before we can develop the nature of government, we must make certain assumptions regarding the syntactic structures in which arguments, verbs, and other elements appear. The following defines some terminology and establishes some specific assumptions about phrase structure that will be motivated in Chapter 5.

To begin, consider the following sentences.

(1) *a.* The President believes that he was arrested.
     b. The President believes himself to have been arrested.
     c. The President believes that someone arrested him.
     d. The President believes him to have been arrested.
(2) The President believes someone to have arrested him.

Let us take *he, him, himself,* and *the President* to refer to the same individual. Native speaker intuitions about these sentences include the following:

(A) What the President believes, in all sentences of (1) except (1*d*),
     can be that someone arrested him (the President).
(B) It is impossible to substitute *him* for *himself* or *himself* for *him*
     in these sentences while preserving both grammaticality and
     meaning.

Let us refer to the person arrested as the ARRESTEE. The paraphrase in (A) shows that the person denoted by the object of *arrest* in (1*c*) is the ARRESTEE. By Syntacticization, we assume that this is a syntactic fact. That is, the property that the person denoted by the object has of being the ARRESTEE is a consequence of the syntactic relationship of the object to the verb *arrest*. Therefore, we must formulate a theory of such a syntactic relationship. The theory of the possible syntactic relationships is called X'-theory (read as 'X-bar theory').

X'-theory specifies what constitutes a phrase. Every phrase has a **head**; the verb *arrest(ed)* is the head of a verb phrase (VP), the noun *President* is the head of a noun phrase (NP), and so on. A phrase such as *him* in *arrest him* that bears a close relationship to the head is called the **complement**. Determiners such as *the* are called **specifiers**.[1] A constituent that is neither a complement nor a specifier is an **adjunct**.

The fundamental relation of X'-theory is dominates. Given a head and its associated phrase, the phrasal category dominates the head, as illustrated in (3) and (4). It also dominates all the specifiers, complements, and adjuncts of the head. VP and V are called nodes; the configuration is called a tree. (3*a*) and (3*b*) are equivalent ways of representing the same tree.

(3)   *a.*

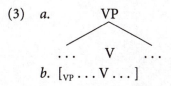

   b. [$_{VP}$ ... V ...]

The complement of a head is dominated by the same node as the head; the two are sisters. A node is said to immediately dominate those nodes that are directly beneath it in the tree. Hence VP immediately dominates V in (3) but not in (4).

Nodes of the same categorial type as a head are called projections of the head. In (4) the projections of V are V′ and VP.

(4)

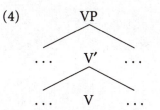

The highest phrasal node in a series of projections of a head is the **maximal projection**; it is VP in (4). It is crucial in this theory that all categories have maximal projections associated with them. This includes the familiar **lexical categories**, such as N(oun), V(erb), A(djective) and P(reposition), but also **functional categories**, such as complementizer (a word like *that*), Tense and other inflectional elements, and so on. A crucial assumption in many versions of PPT is that the verbal inflection is the head of the sentence, roughly as illustrated in (5).

(5)

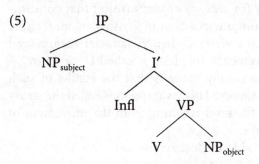

More generally, in X′-theory all phrases have the following structure, called the **X′ schema**, ignoring linear order.

(6)

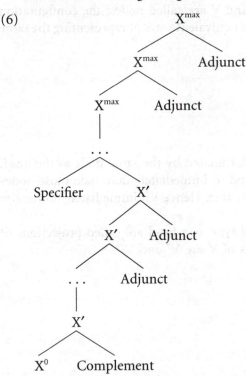

X is a variable that ranges over the syntactic categories N, V, A, etc. It is generally assumed that all branching is binary. See Chapter 5, Appendix A for a comparison of various branching possibilities.

The grammatical relations, e.g. subject and direct object, are defined in terms of the structures provided by X′-theory. As a first approximation, the direct object is the complement of the head; the subject is the specifier of the head.

Principles and Parameters theory is a variant of transformational grammar, which assumes (primarily for reasons of Uniformity) that constituents of a sentence can move from one position to another in conformity with certain principles. On such a view, X′-theory characterizes the level of structure prior to such movements; this level is called D-structure. A restrictive assumption that is generally made is that the results of such movements also conform to X′-theory. This assumption is called the **structure-preserving principle**, and the level resulting from the movement of constituents is called S-structure.

At this point you should be able to do Exercise 2-1.

1.3. θ-*theory*

The general theory of how the syntactic structure mediates the relationship between the syntactic constituents of a sentence on the one hand and the thematic argument structure of a head on the other is called θ-theory. Roles such as the one that we have called ARRESTEE are θ-**roles**; more familiar and general terms are PATIENT (the thing affected by the action), AGENT (the individual initiating the action), and so on.

We use the term **Lexicon** to refer to the component of the grammar that contains all linguistic information associated with words, or **lexical items**.[2] For each lexical item there is a **lexical entry** that itemizes the information associated with that lexical item: its syntactic category, its meaning, its sounds, and the particular ways in which it combines with other lexical items and phrases. The θ-roles assigned by a given lexical item form a part of the lexical entry of that item in the Lexicon. We have already seen that the complement of *arrest*, or more precisely, the entity denoted by the complement, bears a particular θ-role with respect to the verb; the subject of *arrest* bears a different θ-role, and the subject of *believe* bears yet another.

The question of what these θ-roles are, how they differ from one another, and what the possible θ-roles are is not generally taken to be the responsibility of θ-theory in a narrow sense. The function of θ-theory is to explain the syntax of θ-roles, that is, to explain how syntactic structure determines the assignment of θ-roles to particular constituents of the sentence. For example, θ-theory seeks to show how the object θ-role of a verb is assigned to the direct object, without accounting for the fact that the object θ-role of one verb (say *arrest*) is different from that of another verb (say *resemble*).

The θ-roles assigned to constituents within the VP are called **internal θ-roles**; these constituents are called internal arguments. The θ-role assigned to the subject is called the **external θ-role**, and the subject of a sentence is called the external argument, on the assumption that the subject is external to VP. As already noted, the set of arguments, their properties, their relationships to one another, and their role in the syntax is called argument structure.

It is crucial for the analysis of the examples in (1) that the verb *believe* takes as its complement something that expresses a proposition, namely, that someone arrested him (the President). In terms of θ-theory, we would say that *believe* assigns a θ-role to the sentential complement *that someone arrested him* in (1c), for example. By Syntacticization, there must be a constituent of this sentence that can be associated with this θ-role. The obvious candidate is the sentence *that someone arrested him*. Since the three sentences have the same meaning, by Uniformity we assume moreover that in all three sentences there is a constituent to which this θ-role can be assigned. The complement of *believe* in (1*a*) is clearly the sentence *that he was arrested*; in (1*b*) it must be *himself to be arrested*. By Uniformity, if the *that*-complement of *believe* has the syntactic category S (for example), the constituent *himself to be arrested* has the syntactic category S.

Looking at the infinitive internally, we find that the methodology of Uniformity and Syntacticization yields the same conclusion. In (2), for example, we find the same θ-roles assigned to *someone* and *him* as we find in (1*c*). By Syntacticization, θ-role assignment is determined by syntactic configuration. By Uniformity, if the θ-role assignment is the same, the syntactic configuration must be the same at some level of representation. So, in the infinitive the NP that is understood as the AGENT of *arrest* must be the subject of *arrest*, just as it is in the finite clause. So, the infinitive must have essentially the same clausal structure as the finite clause, i.e. it must be an S.

The uniform factor in these cases is that there is a verb that has a number of θ-roles associated with it. When these θ-roles are associated with particular NPs, the result is a (more or less) complete 'propositional' interpretation, that is, an interpretation that can be paraphrased as a complete declarative sentence.

This last step of the analysis of infinitives is one of great significance in the development of the PPT approach to the theory of grammar, and its specific consequences will be closely tracked and highlighted in subsequent chapters. It is sufficiently important that we spell out the general conclusion as follows in the form of a principle.

(7)   **Clausal Principle:** Any part of a sentence that has a complete
       propositional interpretation is represented as a clause at some
       level of syntactic representation.

Here, we understand 'complete propositional interpretation' as 'thematically complete.'

By assumption, the lexical entry of a verb contains only information that is not predictable from general principles. Certainly the meaning of a verb, and, in particular, the semantic roles assigned to the arguments, is not predictable. In (8)–(10) we give preliminary lexical entries for the verbs *sleep*, *see*, and *give*.

(8) *sleep*: V, [_THEME_]
(9) *see*: V, [_EXPERIENCER_, THEME]
(10) *give*: V, [_SOURCE_, GOAL, THEME]

As seen, one of the θ-roles in each entry is underlined. This role is the external θ-role, the one that is assigned external to the VP.

2. Case

Next we consider the use of case in natural language. Many languages have case systems in which every NP in a sentence bears a particular phonological form that denotes its grammatical or thematic function in that sentence.[3] One such language is Russian, exemplified in (11).[4]

(11) *a.* Ja   čital   knigu.
       I-NOM read-PAST book-ACC
       'I read a/the book.'
      b. Kniga   v komnate.
       book-NOM in room-PREP
      c. Ja   dal   knigu   Ivan'e.
       I-NOM give-PAST book-ACC Ivan-DATIVE
      d. On   ždet   podrugu.
       he-NOM wait-for-PRES friend-ACC
       'He is waiting for a (female) friend.'
      e. On   ždet   otveta.
       he-NOM waits-for-PRES the answer-GEN
       'He is waiting for the answer.'
      f. Ja   govorila   s   nim.
       I-NOM speak-PAST with him-INSTR[5]
       'I spoke with him.'
      g. Ona vošla   v   komnatu.
       she go-PAST into room-ACC
       'She went into the room.'
      h. Ona vyšla   iz   komnaty.
       she go-PAST out-of room-GEN
       'She went out of the room.'
      i. On ne zanimalsja russkim   jazykom.
       he not study-PAST Russian-INSTR language-INSTR
       'He studied Russian.'

These examples show that some verbs determine which case will be assigned to particular arguments. For example, while normally the direct object will appear in the ACCUSATIVE case, the direct object of *ždet* appears in the GENITIVE case when it is inanimate (cf. (11*e*)). In addition, a preposition also determines the case that its complement takes: *v* 'into' in (11*g*) takes the ACCUSATIVE case, while *s* 'with' in (11*f*) takes the INSTRUMENTAL case.[6]

Other languages, such as English, show overt case marking only for a restricted class of NPs, typically the pronouns.

(12)   *a.* I/we/you/*me/*us/you saw John.
       b. John saw *I/*we/you/me/us/you.
(13)   *a.* he/she/they/*him/*her/*them saw John.
       b. John saw *he/*she/*they/him/her/them.
(14)   *a.* It/they/*them hit me.
       b. I hit it/*they/them.

These examples show that in English overt case marking is in fact restricted to a subset of the pronouns, since *it* and *you* lack different forms for subject and object. Under the principle of Uniformity, the differences between Russian and English are taken to be superficial ones, just as the difference between the overtly marked NPs in English and the unmarked NPs in English is taken to be a superficial one. The view that we will adopt is that all NPs are marked for case in comparable syntactic configurations whether or not they display case overtly in their phonological form.

This uniform marking of case is called Abstract Case, or simply **Case**. The NP *John* in (12*a*) is marked with the same Case as are *me/us/you* in (12*b*). Let us call this Case ACCUSATIVE, abbreviated as ACC. Due to various accidental factors, ACCUSATIVE Case is realized overtly in English on these pronouns, but not on non-pronominal NPs. In Russian, on the other hand, ACCUSATIVE Case is realized on NPs in object position through a systematic morphological marking.

Pursuing this line of reasoning, it follows that Abstract Case must also be assigned in a language like Chinese, which entirely lacks overt case marking.

(15)   Mali chi pingguo.
        Mary eat apple
(16)   *a.* Wo chi pingguo.
        I   eat apple
       b. Xiansheng jiao   wo.
        teacher   teaches me

It is sometimes thought that the notion of Abstract Case poses a paradox for the language learner, since in languages such as Chinese and English there is little, if any, overt indication regarding which NP receives which Case, hence no data for the learner to use. This paradox is an illusion, however, because it presumes that the principles under which Abstract Case are assigned are acquired in the course of language acquisition. The actual assumption is that the system of Abstract Case is universal, and hence is not learned. What is learned is the mapping between Abstract Case and overt morphological case, which as we have seen takes on different forms in different languages. Overt morphological case, where it appears, may then be used as a clue as to how Abstract Case is assigned in general. We turn to this question next.

3. Canonical government and Case assignment

We will assume that, other things being equal, the assignment of overt morphological case reflects the assignment of Abstract Case. On this basis, the prototypical instances of **Case assignment** are those illustrated in (12)–(14) above. NOMINATIVE Case is assigned to the subject NP, while ACCUSATIVE Case is assigned to the direct object.

In a strictly syntactic theory of Case assignment, the conditions under which these Cases are assigned must be syntactic, and on the PPT approach, configurational. The classical intuition is that the verb in some sense 'governs' the direct object, and thereby assigns ACCUSATIVE case to it. Developing this intuition, we will assume that there is a well-defined relation of government, and investigate its formal properties as they are revealed through the assignment of Case and through other syntactic relations.

Let us consider ACCUSATIVE Case first. It is assigned by the verb to the direct object in the following configuration.

(17)

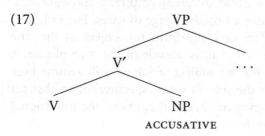

There are in fact several different syntactic relations that would serve to uniquely identify the NP in this configuration. Some of the more obvious ones are summarized in (18). For (17) the Case assigner is understood to be V.

(18)   a. In the linear ordering of constituents, the NP is strictly adjacent to V.
       b. The NP is dominated by the node in the tree that immediately dominates the Case assigner.
       c. The NP is immediately dominated by the node in the tree that immediately dominates the Case assigner (i.e. the Case assigner and the NP are sisters).
       d. The NP is dominated by the lowest maximal projection that dominates the Case assigner.

The relation expressed in (18b) is a special case of what is called c-command (c for constituent), defined as follows.

(19) α c-commands β if and only if the lowest branching node that immediately dominates α also dominates β.

The sisterhood relation in (18c) is one of mutual c-command. The relation expressed in (18d) is called m-command (m for maximal projection), defined more generally as follows.

(20) α m-commands β if and only if, for all γ, γ a maximal projection that dominates α, γ dominates β.

Simply on the basis of (17) it is impossible to determine which of the relations in (18) is the correct one, or if there is some other relation that is to be preferred. Each relation has different empirical consequences, which can be seen if we consider a broader range of cases. For example, the subject of a sentence differs crucially from the object in that the subject is not the sister of the verb, but is outside of the verb phrase. A commonly accepted structure for the subject which we will assume here and justify in Chapter 5 is that the subject is the 'specifier' of an abstract head **Infl** (also called I), as shown in (21). Infl contains the inflectional morphology realized on the verb.

(21)

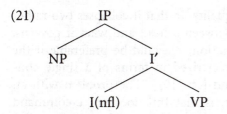

Infl assigns NOMINATIVE Case to the subject. The important point about the structure in (21) is that the node that immediately dominates Infl is I', which does not dominate the NP. Taking the Case assigner in this structure to be Infl, neither (18*b*) nor (18*c*) will do for the assignment of NOMINATIVE Case. The NP is neither a sister of Infl nor c-commanded by Infl. The only options in (18) that will suffice for the assignment of NOMINATIVE are (18*a*), adjacency, and (18*d*), m-command.

For reasons of uniformity we seek to develop an account of Case assignment under government that covers both ACCUSATIVE and NOMINATIVE Case assignment. Assume that VP is a maximal projection. VP dominates V and NP in (17), and there is no maximal projection that dominates V but not NP. Hence V m-commands NP. Similarly, IP is a maximal projection that dominates Infl and NP in (21), and there is no maximal projection that dominates Infl that does not dominate NP. Hence Infl m-commands NP. Since Infl m-commands the subject and V m-commands the direct object, the following would appear to be the minimal definition of government that accounts for the cases thus far.

(22)   *Government*: α governs β if and only if
    (i) α is a head,
    (ii) α m-commands β.

M-command is required here because the subject is assigned Case by Infl but is not a sister of Infl.

It is important to recognize the key assumptions that are being adopted here, so that the basis for the subsequent theoretical developments will be clear. Crucially, we assume that the configuration under which the assignment of ACCUSATIVE takes place is that of (17). We assume that NOMINATIVE is assigned to the subject NP in the Specifier position of IP (that is, the position immediately dominated by IP). Hence in some sense Case is assigned under two different structural configurations. One way to ameliorate this consequence and impose a uniform condition on Case assignment is to adopt m-command as the basis for a uniform government relation that is statable on precisely these two structural configurations.

M-command has a 'disjunctive' quality, in that it collapses two rather different configurational relations between a head and what it governs. Assuming Uniformity and Configuration, it would be preferable if the government relation could be characterized in terms of a single configurational relation, e.g. c-command (cf. (19)). The problem with an approach on these lines, of course, is that Infl does not c-command the subject. Another possibility is that NPs are assigned Case when they are in the specifier position of a phrase; then government *per se* would not be relevant. Then the problem would be that the direct object is not in a specifier position. So in order to pursue such alternative analyses, we will have to make different assumptions about what the structures are under which Case assignment occurs.

We postpone discussion of alternatives until we have developed additional technical apparatus. We will assume for now that Case is assigned under government according to the formulation in (22). At this point you should be able to do Exercise 2-2.

Another potential branching point to keep in mind is the distinction between Case assignment and **Case checking**. In the first instance we have in mind some notion that the Case is associated with the head and is copied onto the assignee, as in (23).

(23)

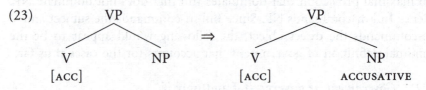

In the second instance, we assume that the NP is introduced into the structure with Case, and in the course of a derivation there is a checking relation that determines whether or not the right Case is in the right location. For instance, the Case feature could have a '*' that is erased when the NP is in the domain of the head. The head that carries out this checking must be neutralized so that it cannot continue to check off the same case for other NPs.

(24)

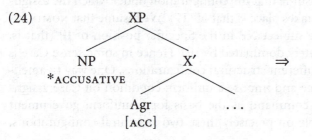

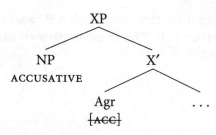

This checking off and neutralization of the feature is called **feature discharge**; we illustrate it by striking out the neutralized feature.

It may be that nothing depends on the choice of formal mechanism for Case. But if we assume for independent reasons that feature checking operations apply only when the specifier and the head agree, that is, under **Spec-head agreement**, the alternative discussed above of reducing all Case assignment to Spec-head agreement is preferred. We must then presume, of course, for uniformity, that there are no direct verb-object agreement relations in natural language, hence that all such apparent agreements are mediated by Spec-head agreement. We outline in Chapter 10, § 4 how a generalized Spec-head agreement analysis would be implemented.

In what follows, we will treat Case as assigned by the verb or Infl to the relevant NP. At this point you should be able to do Exercise 2-3.

4. Exceptional Case Marking

Consider the following sentence.

(25)   I believe her to speak French well.

This sentence has the same θ-role assignments and more or less the same meaning as (26).

(26)   I believe that she speaks French well.

On the basis of this identity of θ-roles we draw the following two conclusions, assuming crucially that identical θ-role assignment indicates identical syntactic structure in the relevant respects. First, the NP *her* bears the syntactic relation Subject to the predicate *speak French well* in both sentences. Second, the proposition that she speaks French well is expressed by the constituent *that she speaks French well* in (26) and by the constituent *her to speak French well* in (25). Both are of the same syntactic category. Presupposing for now the development of X′-theory for functional (non-lexical) categories, this category is CP, where C is the category of the complementizer *that*. The relevant parts of the two structures are then as given in (27).

(27)   *a.*

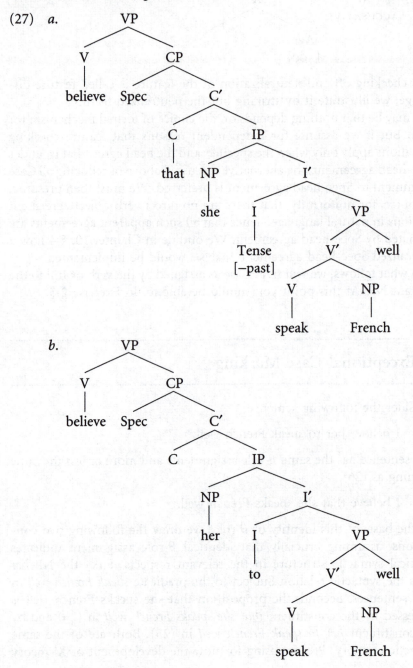

    b.

Let us focus on the Case of the subject NP. When the complement is tensed, as in (27a), NOMINATIVE Case is assigned. When the complement is untensed, as in the infinitive in (27b), ACCUSATIVE Case is assigned. We have seen that in English, ACCUSATIVE Case is assigned by a V under government. The conclusion then follows that the verb *believe* assigns ACCUSATIVE Case to *her* in (27b), but of course not to *she* in (27a). From this it follows that *believe* must govern the subject NP in (27b), but not in (27a). Apparently, *believe* must govern across the maximal projections CP and IP in (27b), a phenomenon referred to as **Exceptional Case Marking (ECM)**.

Comparing the two structures, there are several possible explanations for why there would be a difference in government. First, we note that the complementizer is empty in (27b), but it is overt in (27a). This difference is not sufficient to explain the difference in government, however, because the complementizer in (28a) is empty, but the subject is assigned NOMINATIVE Case.

(28)   *a.* I believe she speaks French well.
       b. *I believe her speaks French well.

Thus, either the empty complementizer is irrelevant, or the complementizer is overt at the point at which Case is assigned after which it is deleted. We will not pursue the consequences of a complementizer-deletion analysis.

Second, we note that the subject of the tensed clause is assigned NOMINATIVE Case, in both (27a) and (28a). This fact suggests that perhaps the existence of a governor that is capable of assigning Case to an NP pre-empts assignment of Case by another governor. Comparing the two structures in (27) we see that Infl is the closest governor of $NP_{subject}$, in the sense that Infl and $NP_{subject}$ are within the same maximal projection IP, while all other potential governors are external to IP. On this basis we may form the following hypothesis.

(29)   Case is assigned by the nearest governor. If α governs β and γ governs β, γ is the nearer governor of β if every node that dominates α dominates γ, but there is at least one node δ that dominates γ and does not dominate α.

It would be possible in this analysis to maintain the assumption that there is an empty complementizer in the infinitival construction, if we assume in addition that an empty complementizer is not a governor in the relevant sense. By the same token, the infinitival head [$_{INFL}$ *to*] in the ECM construction would have to be excluded from governing the ACCUSATIVE subject, so that the higher verb would be the nearest governor.

Another alternative is the following. While the tensed complement and the infinitival complement have essentially the same internal structure, the infinitival complement is not a CP but simply a projection of IP. The selection of the IP complement is determined by the lexical entry of *believe*. The structure for the infinitival complement is given in (30).

(30)

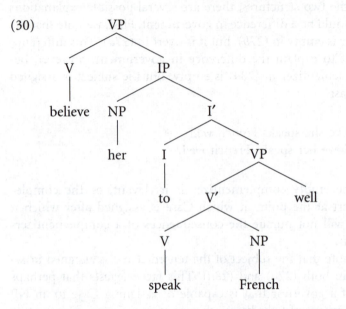

Taking this perspective, we could say that the failure of the verb to govern the subject of the tensed clause may be attributed to the presence of the CP node or of the complementizer, regardless of whether or not the complementizer is overt.

The major shortcoming of this last approach is that it assumes two distinct complement structures for propositional complements, which is a significant deviation from Uniformity. A variant of this last approach often found in the literature avoids this problem by assuming that there is a mapping, called **pruning**, from (27*b*) into (30). The *ad hoc* character of this mapping (it is only needed for this particular construction) casts some doubt on this alternative, also.

Summing up, we have seen that there are several possible explanations for ECM constructions, even if we make the Uniformity-based assumptions about the structure of the complement clause. On each alternative account, different principles must be invoked in order to yield the desired difference. All of these accounts share a common core, however, which is the notion that government from the outside of a maximal projection can be blocked by a closer governor within the maximal projection. In a sense, then, the closer governor makes its maximal projection a 'barrier' to government from a more distant governor. This intuition forms the basis for the 'Barriers' framework and the 'Relativized Minimality' framework summarized in Chapter 7. We incorporate it into the following revised definition of government, leaving the formal characterization of barrier open for the present.

(31)   *Government:* α governs β if and only if
    (i) α is a head,
    (ii) α m-commands β,
    (iii) there is no barrier γ between α and β.

For the purpose of discussion and subsequent development we will adopt the theory of ECM embodied in structure (30) and the theory of government in (31), leaving open the question of whether there is in fact pruning or whether the particular complement structure is lexically selected. It is important to see that all variants of this approach to ECM are founded on the core assumption that the complement of *believe* is clausal (i.e. CP or IP). It is because of this assumption that the NP that we call the 'subject' must function like a direct object with respect to Case assignment, which in turn raises the question of which maximal projections are barriers to government and when they are, and so on. We will return to this point in later chapters, because the subject in the ECM infinitive behaves like the direct object of the verb with respect to *virtually all* properties that are syntactically determined, with the exception of θ-role assignment. On the view that the subject of the infinitive acts like the direct object because it is governed by the verb, the general conclusion is that all of these other object properties are also determined by government.

The standard ECM analysis must be contrasted with alternatives in which the subject of the infinitival complement acts like a direct object because it is a direct object. We discuss some of these alternatives in Appendix A at the end of this chapter.

5. The Case Filter

5.1. *Case assigners*

Let us consider now a fuller set of Case assignment possibilities. It is a striking fact about English that only verbs and prepositions take NP complements. The examples in (32) and (33) illustrate.

(32)   *a.* I envied/resented/trusted her.
       b. my *envy/*resentment/*trust her
       c. I am *envious/*resentful/*trustful her.
(33)   *a.* I *envied/*resented/*trusted of her.
       b. my envy/resentment/trust of her
       c. envious/resentful/trustful of her

The verbs *envy*, *resent*, and *trust* take an NP complement, while the corresponding nouns and adjectives do not. We could represent this difference by listing the types of complements that each lexical item takes in its lexical entry, along the lines of (34).

(34)   *a. envy*: V; [____NP]
       b. envy: N; [____[PP of NP]]
       c. envious: A; [____[PP of NP]]

But we also have to indicate which θ-role is assigned to the complement in all three cases, and it turns out that in every case the same θ-role (THEME or, perhaps more precisely, TARGET (OF THE ENVY)) is assigned to the NP. Given the complement structures specified in (34), assignment of θ-roles is non-uniform, since in some cases the θ-role is assigned to the NP complement, and in some instances it is assigned to an NP within a PP complement.

There is an additional problem, even if we could render θ-role assignment uniform. Where the complement is clausal, the complement structure is uniform across all appropriate lexical categories.

(35)   *a.* I believe that she is rich.
       b. my belief that she is rich
       c. *my belief {of/in} that she is rich

(36)   *a.* I am angry (*at) that you didn't call.
      b. my anger (*at) that you didn't call
(37)   *a.* I am envious (*of) that she is rich.
      b. my envy (*of) that she is rich

So what would be maximally uniform would be to say that there is a single lexical entry ENVY with a uniform complement structure and uniform θ-role assignment; this entry has a somewhat different phonological realization depending on the syntactic category that is chosen.

(38)   ENVY: [____NP]

             |

          THEME
    V: *envy*
    N: *envy*
    A: *envious*

Similar entries would exist for RESENT, TRUST, BELIEVE, ANGER, and so on.

An even more economical lexical representation can be developed if we derive the verbs *envy, resent, trust,* and so on from the nouns, for example, but we will not pursue such details here. The point to be stressed is that by making the complement structure uniform across all syntactic categories of the head, we can maximize uniformity in the lexical representation and eliminate redundant specifications.

Of course, there is a price to pay for this uniformity. If the noun *envy* and the adjective *envious* take NP complements, why are there ungrammatical phrases in (32) and (33)? We cannot fall back on the fact that the preposition is missing in these cases, because the preposition is always missing when the grammatical clausal complement is present. So what we must conclude is that there is some property that NPs must have that clauses do not have, and this property is not assigned when the head of the maximal projection is N or A.

This last observation suggests that we are looking for a property that is assigned under government. An obvious candidate is Case. Let us say that N and A do not assign Case to their complements (although they govern their complements), and let us suppose that it is for this reason that the phrases in (32) and (33) are ungrammatical. In order for this account to go through, we must adopt a principle such as the following.

(39)   Every NP must be assigned Abstract Case.

This is called the **Case Filter**.[7]

We can see immediately that not every NP in a sentence must be assigned Case by a governor, so (39) is somewhat too strong. None of the italicized NPs in (40) are governed by a Case assigning V or P, because they are not arguments.

(40)   *a. John*, I want to see you now!
      b. This book, I think it will be made into a great movie some day.
      c. I don't think I'm going to buy it, *this book.*

A plausible restriction on the Case Filter is that it applies only to argument NPs.

Another possibility is that non-argument NPs are assigned a default Case, so that they automatically satisfy the Case Filter as it is stated in (39). Since we do not want default Case to be assigned to the offending NPs in (32) and (33), we must assume that default Case is assigned only to non-argument NPs. Let us assume that this is so; the generalization then appears to be the following.

(41)   *a.* An argument NP must be assigned Case by the governor.
      b. A non-argument NP is assigned default Case.

The obvious question that arises regarding the Case Filter is *why* it should be that an argument NP must have Abstract Case. If we compare the italicized NPs in (40) with the NPs in (32) and (33), we notice a suggestive difference. The italicized NPs are not assigned a θ-role, while those in (32) and (33) are. For example, in (40a) the NP *you* is assigned the object θ-role of *see*, and the NP *John* is not. The fact that a verb (and preposition) assigns θ-roles to NPs that it governs may underlie an explanation for the Case Filter.

5.2. Case and θ-roles

There are two ways to view the relation between Case and θ-role. On the one hand, it might be that without Case, an NP cannot be assigned a θ-role; it is 'invisible' with respect to θ-role assignment. Since only argument NPs receive θ-roles, the Case Filter would be relevant only to argument NPs. We would then reduce the requirement that every argument NP be assigned Abstract Case to the following.

(42) *a.* Every argument NP must receive a θ-role.
      b. In order to receive a θ-role, an NP must have Case.

We will call (42*b*) the **Visibility Condition** and the analysis in (42) the Visibility Thesis.[8] (42*a*) follows from the θ-Criterion, which requires a one-to-one matching between θ-roles and arguments. We state the θ-Criterion informally as (43).

(43) *a.* Every argument must receive a θ-role.
      b. Every θ-role must be assigned to an argument.

We will provide additional motivation for the θ-Criterion in Chapter 3.
   On the other hand, it might be that Case is a reflection of the assignment of θ-role. Continuing to assume the θ-Criterion, with (42*a*) as a special case, we would have an account along the following lines.

(44) *a.* Every governed NP must receive a θ-role.
      b. Abstract Case is a realization of θ-role assignment.

We will call this analysis the **Thematic Case Thesis**. It can be shown directly that this thesis cannot be maintained in its strongest form, although there is a basis for thinking that some Case assignment is determined by θ-role assignment.
   The basic idea of the Thematic Case Thesis is that a given Case, say DATIVE, shows that the NP bears a particular θ-role, say GOAL, with respect to the governing verb. The key phrase here is 'the governing verb.' A counterexample to the Thematic Case Thesis would consist of a construction in which the Case assigner is not a θ-assigner; the Case could not then be seen as 'realizing' the θ-role.
   In the ECM construction, Case is assigned to an NP by a V that does not assign a θ-role to it. (45) illustrates how this works.

(45)

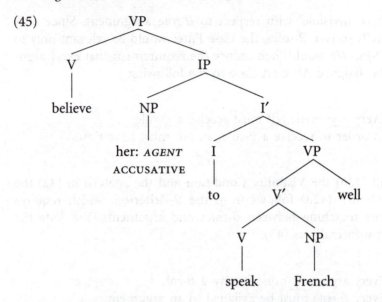

Now, if the accusative Case of *her* were due simply to the assignment of AGENT by *speak*, we would expect Case assignment in the ECM construction to be quite independent of the proximity of *her* to a governing Case assigner such as *believe*. But the following examples show that the presence of such a Case assigner is crucial.

(46)   *a.* *my belief her to have left early
       b. *Her to leave early would be unfortunate.

Let us call the subject and object positions **A-positions** (for argument-positions). As far as the A-positions are concerned, the Thematic Case Thesis is false; Case must be assigned to these positions based purely on syntactic structure, and not on θ-role assignment. It is for this reason that the Case assigned to A-positions is called **structural Case**. The question of how Case is assigned to non-A-positions is not resolved, however; we take it up in § 6.

   A crucial fact to keep in mind is that A-positions are reserved for structural Case. If for some reason structural Case cannot be assigned to an A-position, it is impossible to assign a Case on the basis of θ-role or to assign default Case. This fact forms the basis for several important aspects of Case theory.[9]

   Let us turn now to the Visibility Thesis. A counterexample to the Visibility Thesis would be an NP that does not receive a θ-role, but that nevertheless must be in a position where it is assigned Case. A good candidate is the expletive *there*, which does not receive a θ-role.

(47)   There was a dog in the basement.

In (47) *a dog* receives the θ-role THEME of the predicate *be in the basement*.

ECM constructions show that *there* may appear in a position where it receives ACCUSATIVE Case even though it does not receive a θ-role.

(48)   I believe there to have been a dog in the basement

The fact that *there* can get Case does not mean that it *must* get Case, of course. A crucial fact about the ECM construction is that it cannot appear in the complement of a non-Case-assigner, such as *belief*. (49) illustrates for the non-expletive subject.

(49)   a. I believe a dog to have been in the basement
         b. *my belief a dog to have been in the basement

Now compare (48) with (50).

(50)   *my belief there to have been a dog in the basement

This last example shows that even an NP like *there* that does not receive a θ-role must be in a Case position. Thus it seems that the Visibility Thesis is not sufficient to account for the Case Filter.

5.3. *Case assignment to chains*

The conclusion at the end of the preceding section is premature. When we consider a sentence with an expletive, we notice that the expletive appears in subject position precisely because there is some other phrase in non-subject position that receives the subject θ-role. For example, compare (51) with (47).

(51)   A dog was in the basement.

In both sentences, *a dog* receives the THEME θ-role from the predicate *be in the basement*. Similar observations hold for instances of *it*-expletives.

(52)   a. *It* is quite striking *that you didn't realize the problem before this.*
   b. *That you didn't realize the problem before this* is quite
      striking.

The clause *that you didn't realize the problem before this* is assigned the
THEME θ-role by the predicate *be quite striking* in both examples.

This connection between the expletive and the 'extraposed' constituent
suggests that there may be a formal linking relation between the two such
that the expletive counts as an argument that receives a θ-role in the
sense relevant to the Visibility Thesis. Suppose that the expletive and
the extraposed constituent form a **chain**, which we define as follows for
the situation in which only two elements are involved.[10]

(53)   <α, β> form a chain if and only if
   (i)   α and β are coindexed,
   (ii) α c-commands β.

Chains must meet additional conditions. For example, an NP-chain must
be assigned a θ-role and it turns out that the θ-role must be assigned to
the chain on the basis of the lowest position in the chain. Each element
in a chain except the top of the chain (what is usually called the head of
the chain) must be locally c-commanded by another member of the chain,
where the precise definition of local needs to be made precise. We will
discuss these conditions at various points as we proceed.

The structures in (54) illustrate the chains for the *there* construction
and for *it* extraposition.

(54)   *a.*

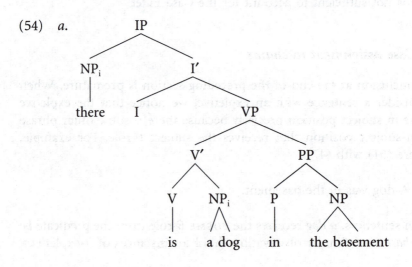

b.

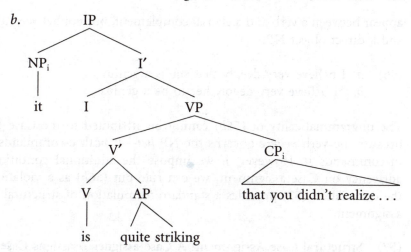

If we assume the existence of chains, we may say that the θ-role and the Case is assigned not to the individual NP position, but to the entire chain. So, in (54*a*) the chain <[*there*], [*a dog*]> is assigned the θ-role THEME and the NOMINATIVE Case, and in (54*b*) the chain <[*it*], [*that you didn't realize* ...]> is assigned the same θ-role and Case. A pair of expletive and NP or CP can form a legitimate chain only under certain conditions, it turns out; for further discussion see Exercise 2-4. There are also chains formed by movement; see Chapters 4 and 6.

Recall now the Case Filter, which we introduced in § 5.1: every NP must be assigned Abstract Case. Another application of the Case Filter is seen in the examples in (55).

(55)   *a.* *Her to leave early would be unfortunate.
       b. For her to leave early would be unfortunate.

In (55*a*) there is no governor for the NP *her*, Case cannot be assigned, and the Case Filter is violated. In (55*b*) *for* is the Case assigner.[11]

5.4. Adjacency

An additional possible condition on Case assignment is that the assigner and the NP that it assigns Case to should be adjacent to one another. As we will see, there are reasons to believe that such a condition may not be correct.

Evidence that supports the adjacency condition is exemplified by the following examples. The first shows that an adverb may in principle appear between a verb and a clausal complement, but not between a verb and a direct object NP.

(56)   *a.* I believe very deeply that she is a genius.
       b. *I believe very deeply her to be a genius.

The ungrammaticality of (56*b*) cannot be attributed to the Case Filter because the verb *believe* governs the NP *her*—it both c-commands and m-commands it. However, if we impose the additional condition of adjacency on Case assignment, we can rule out (56*b*) as a violation of the Case Filter. (57) provides a standard formulation of structural Case assignment.

(57)   **Structural Case Assignment:** A Case assigner α assigns Case to β if α governs β and α and β are adjacent.

The adverb may intervene between the verb and CP in (56*a*) because the CP does not receive Case.

The adjacency condition has the immediate consequence of ruling out examples such as (58).

(58)   *a.* *I saw yesterday her/John.
           (cf. I saw her/John yesterday.)
       b. *I ate quickly the banana.
           (cf. I ate the banana quickly.)
       c. *John caught certainly the flu.

However, there are several reasons to question whether adjacency is the correct account of the ungrammaticality here and in (56*b*).

1. The adjacency condition complicates Case assignment, since without it we could formulate Case assignment strictly in terms of government.

2. With the adjacency condition, it is not clear how to assign Case to NPs that are not adjacent to the verb, such as the NP *a present* in the English double object construction exemplified in (59).

(59)   John gave Susan a present.

We return to this question in § 6.

3. There can be an adverb between the subject and Infl, but Case assignment is not affected.

(60)   John probably will call later.

4. There are restrictions on the distribution of adverbs similar to those exemplified in (56*b*) and (58) that cannot be attributed to the assignment of Case because they do not involve NPs. Consider the following examples.

(61)   *a.* John was angry yesterday.
       b. *John was yesterday angry.
(62)   *a.* John probably lives in an apartment.
       b. *John lives probably in an apartment.

The adverb cannot precede the AP or the PP in the VP, just as it cannot precede the directly object NP.

In spite of these difficulties, we accept the analysis just given and assume it in what follows. In particular we adopt the adjacency condition on Case assignment provisionally, with the expectation that a more principled account can be given for the distribution of adverbs in VP. See Chapter 10, § 2 and Further Readings for some proposals along these lines. Exercise 2-5 deals with the problem of assigning Case in the double object construction.

6. Inherent Case

Thus far we have considered only structural NOMINATIVE and ACCUSATIVE Case. Particularly if we adopt the adjacency condition on Case assignment discussed in § 5.4, we need to consider how other NPs receive Case. There are three possibilities to consider.

1. The NP is not overtly case-marked, and is not adjacent to the V. This is the situation in the double object construction shown in (59).

2. The NP bears an overt morphological case and is not adjacent to the V. This is the situation in languages such as Margan^y and Russian, as illustrated at the beginning of this chapter.

3. The NP is governed by a preposition yet bears a θ-role associated with the lexical head. Some typical examples are given in (63). The NP in question in each example is notated with its θ-role.

(63)   *a.* my envy of Susan:*THEME*
    b. I am angry at John:*THEME*
    c. John looks at Susan:*THEME*
    d. Susan will give a book to John:*GOAL*
    e. Susan will buy a book for John:*BENEFACTEE*
    f. Susan stole a book from John:*SOURCE*

We may take possibilities 1 and 2 to be more or less equivalent; the only difference is whether there is overt marking of case. The verb governs all of the arguments within the VP under m-command, a natural consequence. But the adjacency condition prevents structural Case from being assigned. And even when adjacency is observed, there can be no structural Case assignment in NP or AP because N and A are not Case assigners.

A consequence of our analysis, then, is that Case must be assigned to certain governed NPs on some basis other than the structural Case assignment mechanism of (57). Since these NPs are governed, they are assigned θ-roles by the head; θ-role assignment lacks an adjacency condition. It is reasonable to hypothesize, then, that these NPs receive Case in virtue of being assigned a θ-role. This in turn recalls the Thematic Case Thesis in (44), repeated here.

(44)   *a.* Every governed NP must receive a θ-role.
    b. Abstract Case is a realization of θ-role assignment.

Notice, however, that the cases that we are dealing with here involve only those NPs that are not immediately adjacent to some Case assigner under (44). For the present purposes, then, it suffices if (44*b*) applies only to NPs that are not assigned structural Case. Let us refer to non-structural Case as inherent Case. We may replace (44) by (64).

(64)   **Inherent Case Assignment:** Inherent Case is a realization of θ-role.

We leave open for the moment exactly what is meant by 'realization'. While the most natural interpretation is that the Case uniquely realizes the θ-role, we will see that the notion of Inherent Case in the literature is the weaker one in which the Case expresses the fact that the NP has a θ-role, but does not uniquely correspond to a particular θ-role.

For the cases 1 and 2 above we now have the following scenario. The

verb or noun does not assign structural Case to some NP that it governs.
But, since it governs the NP, it assigns a θ-role to it. This θ-role is then
overtly realized through the assignment of inherent Case, presumably
through a mapping that identifies certain Cases with certain θ-roles. Let
us illustrate with the English double object construction.

(65)   *a.* John gave Susan a present

       b.

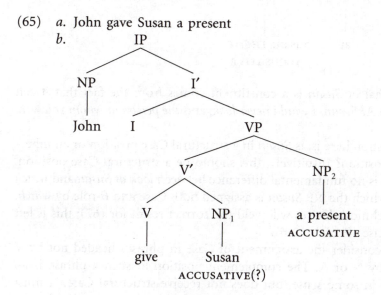

Assuming the structure in (65*b*), *give* assigns structural Case to *Susan*,
since government and adjacency hold. We tentatively designate this
ACCUSATIVE Case, since the structural conditions appear to be the same
as those in simple direct object constructions.[12] Since *a present* is not
assigned structural Case, it must be assigned inherent Case. Since this
NP is the THEME of *give*, it will be assigned ACCUSATIVE Case. The second
NP therefore receives Case by a different route in the double object construction than does the NP in the V–NP–PP construction of (66).

(66)   John gave a present to Susan

Note moreover that the same Case is assigned to the two NPs, showing
quite clearly that particular Cases do not correspond uniquely to particular θ-roles.

     Next we consider the cases of 3 above, in which an NP that is syntac-
tically governed by a P is assigned a θ-role by a V. Assume that the
structure is as in (67).

(67)

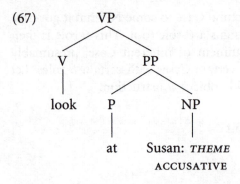

Evidence that *at Susan* is a constituent comes from the fact that it can move, as in *At Susan, I would never look,* and *the person at whom you were looking.*

The question here is, is *Susan* in a structural Case position or an inherent Case position? Intuitively, this should be a structural Case position, since there is no fundamental difference between *look at Susan* and *watch Susan,* in which the NP *Susan* is assigned both Case and θ-role by *watch.* Various technical devices will yield the correct result for (67); this is left as an exercise (Exercise 2-6).

Finally, consider the assignment of Case in phrases headed not by V or P, but by N or A. The complement position in such a phrase is an A-position in some sense, but does not receive structural Case. It must then be that *of* is inserted in the following phrases to mark inherent Case. We assume that *the city* is the complement of *destruction,* parallel to the VP *destroy the city,* and that *Susan* is the complement of *envious,* parallel to the VP *envy Susan.*

(68)   *a.* the destruction *(of) the city
       b. envious *(of) Susan

The same conclusion may hold for genitive case, as in (69).

(69)   *a.* Susan's management of the office
       b. the enemy's destruction of the city
       c. John's envy of our accomplishments

That is, we could take GENITIVE Case assignment to be the realization of the thematically marked 'subject' of the NP. Notice that it is impossible to determine uniquely the θ-role of the 'subject' of the NP simply from the fact that it has GENITIVE Case. Once again, we note that on this approach what must be meant by the statement that 'the Case realizes the θ-role' is much weaker than the too strong interpretation that the Case uniquely identifies the θ-role.

Cases such as those in (70) illustrate the difference between assignment of Case and realization of Case.

(70)   *a.* the destruction of the city
       b. the city's destruction

The NP *the city* has the same θ-role in these two expressions, and there-fore should have the same inherent Case assigned to it, that is, GENITIVE. The realization of this Case depends on the surface position of the NP. In post-nominal position GENITIVE is realized through insertion of the preposition *of*; in prenominal position it is realized by *'s*.

In summary, there are basically two systems of case in natural lan-guage. Structural Case is assigned to designated positions, in particular, to A-positions; if it is not assigned, an NP in an A-position violates the Case Filter. NPs in other governed positions are assigned inherent Case on the basis of their θ-roles. NPs not in governed positions are assigned default Case.

7. Small clauses

We extend the analysis of Case by looking at **small clauses**, exemplified by the bracketed phrases in (71). A small clause is a phrase that has a clausal (or propositional) interpretation, but lacks the full inflectional morphology of a sentence.

(71)   *a.* I consider [her intelligent].
       b. I consider [her a genius].
       c. I imagined [her in the Vatican Museum].
       d. I imagined [her solving this problem].
(72)   *a.* I consider that she is intelligent.
       b. I consider that she is a genius.
       c. I imagined that she was in the Vatican Museum.
       d. I imagined that she was solving this problem.

Since the sentences in (71) are thematically identical to those in (72), Uniformity leads us to posit the following structure for this construction, by analogy with the ECM construction.[13]

(73)

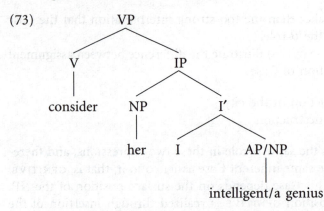

The subject of the small clause is assigned Case by the V *consider*, and a θ-role by the predicate from within the IP.

Small clauses turn out to be problematic for the standard account of ECM developed in this chapter. Examples such as the following show that small clauses, unlike infinitives, can appear in subject position. The pronouns are slightly marginal for reasons that are unclear, but they do illustrate what Case is assigned.

(74)   a.   [Susan/?Her/*She angry] is a terrible sight.
       b.   [Susan/?Her/*She in the Vatican] made history.
       c.   [Susan/Her/*She solving the problem] would be a stroke of
            luck.

If the small clause has the same structure as the infinitive, then the question arises as to why the infinitive cannot appear in subject position without *for*.

(75)   [*(For) her to leave now] would be a stroke of luck.

Any mechanism for assigning Case to the subject of the small clause would, we might presume, apply uniformly to the subject of the infinitive.

Given this observation, one plausible conclusion is that the structure of the small clause is different from that of the infinitive, in that the former contains a governor for the subject that assigns structural Case to it, while the latter does not. Within the framework of assumptions and conclusions that we have arrived at, it is difficult to see a more plausible alternative. Nevertheless, the question still remains of why the small clause structure is different from that of the infinitive.

Additional confirmation that the subject of the small clause is assigned internal structural Case is discussed in Chapter 6, § 4.3.

APPENDIX A: ALTERNATIVES TO ECM

As noted in the main text (§ 4), the subject of an infinitival behaves in virtually every respect like a direct object of the main verb. In PPT this behavior is attributed to the fact that the verb governs the complement subject. Logically possible alternatives are (i) the subject of the infinitival originates as a subject in D-structure (see § 1.2) and raises to object position, and (ii) the subject is the object of the main verb at all levels of syntactic representation.

Alternative (i) was argued for extensively by Postal (1974); see Lightfoot (1976), Bresnan (1976), Postal (1977), and Bach (1977) for various perspectives on the issue. From the current perspective, raising to object position satisfies Uniformity, since the S-structure object originates as a D-structure subject. In order to make a raising to object analysis plausible and non-redundant, we would have to redefine government so that a verb cannot govern and assign Case across IP. Suppose that we made this adjustment. It would then have to be the case that IP is not a barrier for raising of the object. The transformation is sketched in (76).

(76)

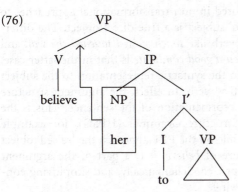

The main objection to this type of raising in PPT terms is that it is not clear what position the NP moves to. A standard assumption is that movements are structure-preserving, which is understood here to mean that there must be an independently motivated empty position into which the NP moves. On the standard analysis of the complement structure of *believe*, no such position exists; *believe* c-selects a propositional complement. For arguments against this view, see Postal and Pullum (1988).

Recent work in the Minimalist Program offers a possible solution to the problem of where the NP moves; see Chapter 10, Exercise 10-6 for some discussion.

It is important to point out that the dispute is not simply a notational one; there is also empirical evidence that weakly suggests that the subject of the infinitival is not dominated by IP at S-structure. The evidence consists of the fact that it is possible for there to be material between the infinitival subject and the infinitival VP that belongs to the higher sentence.[14]

(77)   *a.* I figured it out to be impossible to do that.
       b. I proved her all by myself to be a spy.
       c. I believe him in spite of myself to have been a good candidate.

In each of these cases, what immediately follows the subject of the infinitival is not part of the infinitive complement. The following examples show that the same material cannot follow the subject of a tensed complement, and must appear outside of the complement.

(78)   *a.* *I figured that it out was impossible to do that.
           I figured out that it was impossible to do that.
       b. *I proved that she all by myself was a spy.
           I proved all by myself that she was a spy.
       c. *I believe that he in spite of myself has been a good candidate.
           I believe in spite of myself that he has been a good candidate.

An alternative that has been explored in non-transformational approaches to grammar is one in which the 'raised' subject is a true direct object. The difference between the direct object of a verb like *touch* as in *I touched the wall* and *believe* as in *I believe him to have been a good candidate* is that in the latter case, the direct object is formally linked in the syntactic representation to the subject argument associated with the infinitival verb. In effect, the argument structure of the verb is part of the syntactic representation of the sentence. This is the approach in Head-driven Phrase Structure Grammar (HPSG), for example (Pollard and Sag 1994). Crucially, while on the PPT approach the 'raised' object is not part of the argument structure of *believe*, it is a part of the argument structure of *believe* on the HPSG approach. Schematically, and simplifying considerably, the difference is the following.

(79)   PPT: *believe x*
              x is a CP or IP,
              x is propositional, and
              x is THEME.

       HPSG: *believe x y*
              x is an NP,
              y is a VP that has the argument structure $(z, \ldots)$
              z is linked to x,

y is propositional,
y is *THEME*.

For elaboration as well as formal details, see Pollard and Sag (1994).

APPENDIX B: CASE RESISTANCE

We noted that N and A receive Case but do not appear to assign Case. The question of *why* N and A do not assign Case is an interesting one. One possibility is that in principle Case assigners cannot be assigned Case;[15] this notion can be formalized by supposing that the Case assigned to a maximal projection is copied to its head, as in (80).

(80)

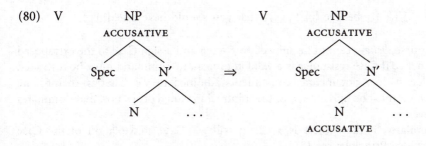

This dichotomy is attributed to an organization of syntactic features such that the Case features and the Case assigning features conflict with one another in any given lexical item.

Phrases like VP, PP, and CP 'resist' Case, in that they cannot appear in a position in which Case would be assigned to them. Stowell (1981) showed that a surprising number of facts of constituent order could be derived from this **Case Resistance Principle**, given in (81).

(81)   Case-Resistance Principle: Case may not be assigned to a category
       bearing a Case-assigning feature.

To take just one application of this principle, a tensed CP resists Case and therefore cannot appear adjacent to a Case-assigning V or P.

(82)   *a.* I thought about you calling the President.
       b. *I thought about [CP that you called the President].
(83)   *a.* John noted carefully [CP that the meeting was about to end].
       b. ?*John noted [CP that the meeting was about to end] carefully.

In (82*b*) *about* is a Case assigner.

One consequence of the Case Resistance Principle is that CPs that appear to be in Case position must actually be in a non-Case position. For example, the complement of *believe*, as in (84), cannot be a sister of the verb.

(84)   I believe [$_{CP}$ that you should have called].

Stowell proposed that in this case, the CP is 'extraposed', in the sense that it is in an adjoined position. The structure would be something like (85).

(85)   I [$_{VP}$ [$_{VP}$ believe] [$_{CP}$ that you should have called]]

The question then arises, how does the complement CP receive its θ-role? By Uniformity, it should be the governed complement of the verb. One solution to this problem is to assume that there is an empty NP in the VP that is linked to the extraposed CP through a chain, as illustrated in (86).

(86)   I [$_{VP}$ [$_{VP}$ believe [$_{NP}$ t$_i$]] [$_{CP}$ that you should have called]$_i$].

Of course, *believe* cannot be allowed to govern and assign Case to the extraposed CP; hence if Case resistance is a valid approach, m-command must be restricted so that it does not include constituents adjoined to VP. That is, in (86) the inner VP must be understood as the minimal maximal projection that dominates *believe*.

Similarly, if the subject is a CP, it will get Case, in violation of the Case Resistance Principle; see (87).

(87)   [$_{CP}$ That you should have called] is obvious.

It is possible that in this construction, the CP is not a subject but a topic that binds an empty NP in subject position, as in (88).[16]

(88)   [$_{CP}$ that you should have called]$_i$ [$_{IP}$ [$_{NP}$ t$_i$] is obvious]

Some of the evidence bearing on the correctness of these two proposals is taken up in Exercise 2-7.

EXERCISES

2-1. The nodes in the following tree have been numbered for identification purposes.

(1)

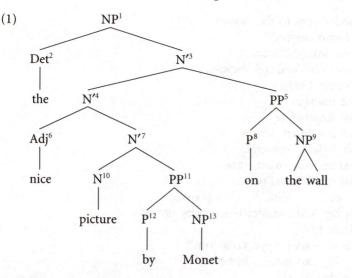

1. Indicate the nodes that N'^7 dominates.
2. What is/are the sister(s) of N'^7?
3. Name the projections of N^{10}.
4. Name the maximal projection of N^{10}.
5. Name the maximal projection of P^8.
6. What is the specifier of N^{10}?
7. What is/are the complement(s) of N^{10}?
8. What nodes does NP^1 immediately dominate?

[§ 1.2]

2-2. Consider once again the tree in (1) of Exercise 2-1.

1. What nodes are c-commanded by N^{10}?
2. What nodes are c-commanded by PP^5?
3. What nodes are m-commanded by N^{10}?
4. What nodes are m-commanded by PP^5?

[§ 3]

2-3. Discuss how each italicized NP and adjective receives Case in each of the following sentences. Assume that Case is assigned under government, and that government is defined in terms of m-command. If this set of assumptions causes problems in a particular example, indicate what they are.

(1) *English*:
   a. *Mary* is sleeping.
   b. I saw *Mary*.
   c. I gave a book to *Mary*.
   d. I gave *Mary* a book.
   e. I slept during *the class*.

(2) *a. Mary* and *I* went to the movies.
   b. It was *I* who laughed.
   c. What, *me* worry? Never.
   d. John races cars, and *Bill, bicycles.*

(3) *Russian* (Neidle 1988):
   a. Devuška umnaja.
      girl-NOM smart-NOM
      'The girl is a smart person.'
   b. Devuška byla   umnaja.
      girl-NOM be-PAST smart-NOM
      'The girl was a smart person.'
   c. On   *ee*   sčital   krasivoj.
      he-NOM her-ACC consider-PRES pretty-INSTR[17]

(4) *Walbiri* (Hale 1973):
   a. [*tyarntu wiri-ngki*] = tyu yarlki-rnu[18]
      dog   big-ERG-me   bite-PAST
      'The big dog bit me.'
   b. tyarntu-ngku = tyu yarlku-rnu *wiri*-ngki
      dog-ERG = me   bite-PAST big-ERG
      'The big dog bit me.'

(5) *Japanese* (Miyagawa 1989):
   a. Zyon-ga   nihongo-o   hanas-e-ru.
      John-NOM Japanese-ACC speak-can-PRES
      'John can speak Japanese.'
   b. Zyon-ga   nihongo-ga   hanas-e-ru.
      John-NOM Japanese-NOM speak-can-PRES
      'John can speak Japanese.'
   c. Boku-ga kono hon-o   yomi-tai.
      I-NOM   this book-ACC read-want
      'I want to read this book.'
   d. Boku-ga kono hon-ga   yomi-tai.
      I-NOM   this book-NOM read-want
      'I want to read this book.'
   e. Tanaka-no musuko-ga sinda.
      Tanaka-GEN son-NOM   die-PAST
      'Tanaka's son died.'
   f. Tanaka-ga   musuko-ga sinda.
      Tanaka-NOM son-NOM   die-PAST
      'Tanaka's son died.'

[§ 3]

*2-4. If we assume the existence of chains, we may say that the θ-role and the Case is assigned not to the individual NP position, but to the entire chain. So, in (54*a*) in the text the chain <[*there*], [*a dog*]> is assigned the θ-role THEME and the NOMINATIVE Case, while in (54*b*) the chain <[*it*], [*that you didn't realize* . . .]> is assigned the θ-role and Case.

What do the following examples suggest about the constraints on possible expletive chains? For clarity we have coindexed the elements of the crucial chains.

(1) *a.* There$_i$ is [a dog]$_i$ in the kitchen.
     b. ??There$_i$ is [your dog]$_i$ in the kitchen.
(2) *a.* A dog is howling.
     b. *There$_i$ is howling [a dog]$_i$.
     c. A problem arose.
     d. There$_i$ arose [a problem]$_i$.
(3) *a.* There$_i$ is [a problem with this analysis]$_i$.
     b. It seems [$_{CP}$ a problem has occurred with this analysis].
     c. *There$_i$ seems [$_{CP}$ [a problem]$_i$ has occurred with this analysis].
     d. That [there$_i$ was [a problem with this analysis]$_i$] was obvious.
     e. *That [there$_i$ was] was obvious [a problem with this analysis]$_i$.
(4) *a.* It$_i$ is obvious [that the analysis is in difficulty]$_i$.
     b. For [it$_i$ to be obvious [that the analysis is in difficulty]$_i$] would be very surprising.
     c. *For [it$_i$ to be obvious] would be very surprising [that the analysis is in difficulty]$_i$.

[§ 5.3]

*2-5. Suppose that the correct Case assignment for the double object construction is in general that of (1).

(1) V   NP   NP
         DATIVE   ACCUSATIVE

The DATIVE Case would appear to be an instance of inherent Case, even though it is in a structural Case position. Suppose that we had a mechanism for assigning this inherent Case. Then the ACCUSATIVE would appear to be a structural Case, even though it is not adjacent to the verb. Work out an analysis in which structural Case is assigned to this NP. It may be necessary to deviate from some of the assumptions in the text; do so as cautiously as possible.

[§ 5.4]

2-6. There are at least three ways in which to do Case assignment for verbs like *look at.*

  1. Assume that the verb is *look at,* and that this verb assigns ACCUSATIVE Case to its complement.

2. Assume that the verb *look* selects a PP headed by *at*, and that the verb *look* governs the complement and assigns Case and θ-role to it.

3. Assume that the verb *look* selects the preposition *at*, and that Case and θ-role are assigned by the preposition.

Evaluate these alternatives with respect to the following data; you may introduce your own data if you think that it is relevant, as well.

(1) *a.* What are you looking at?
     b. the person at whom I am looking
     c. At John, I would never look.
(2) *a.* I looked very closely at John.
     b. John, I was looking very closely at.
(3) *a.* I was looking at John, and Mary, at Susan.
     b. I was looking at John, and Mary, Susan.
     c. John looked at and then ignored Mary.

[§ 6]

2-7. Explain how the data in (2)–(5) below constitute evidence for the position that apparent sentential subjects in English are actually topics. Topicalization is illustrated by (1).

(1)   Such things, I would never agree to ___.
(2) *a.* ?That *for Bill to smoke* bothers the teacher is quite possible.
     b. *Although *that the house is empty* may depress you, it pleases me.
(3) *a.* *Did *that John showed up* please you?
     b. *What does *that he will come* prove?
(4) *a.* That he reads so much doesn't prove such things.
     b. *Such things, *that he reads so much* doesn't prove ___.
(5) *This book, to John I gave.

[Appendix B; Koster 1978; see also Delahunty 1982]

FURTHER READING

....

(Note: The number of asterisks before a reference indicates its level of technical difficulty. You should be able to follow much if not all of what is in those references that lack asterisks.)

X'-theory was first proposed by Chomsky (1970) and developed further by Jackendoff (1977). Subsequently there has been a progression of attempts to eliminate from the grammars of particular languages statements about phrase structure and to relocate language-specific facts into the lexicon. What is currently left is a very restricted uniform X-bar theory. See Chomsky (*1981; *1986*b*; **1994) to trace the development of this approach. For a representative range of alternative views of phrase structure, see the papers in *Baltin and Kroch (1989).

*Chomsky (1981) contains the most influential formulation of Case theory; see also Chomsky (1980). *Chomsky (1986*a*) addresses a number of problems with the original theory, including an elaboration of the notion of inherent Case. Baker (1988) presents a more recent version of Case theory of considerable elegance and broad empirical coverage. *Davis (1986) argues against the proposal that θ-assignment should be dependent on Case assignment. *Belletti (1988) deals with the assignment of PARTITIVE instead of ACCUSATIVE to direct objects, arguing that PARTITIVE is an inherent Case that is always available for assignment at D-structure. For a detailed comparison of Case assignment in English and French and the role of chains, see *Authier (1991). References to works dealing more generally with government can be found at the end of Chapter 7.

*Lasnik (1992*b*) addresses such problems as the assignment of Case to the subject under apparent non-adjacency, the role of expletives in Case assignment, the conditions for assignment of inherent Case, and visibility. His proposals assume familiarity with a number of notions that are not taken up until much later in this book.

The original motivation for the DP analysis of noun phrases appears in *Abney (1987). *Stowell (1989), and *Culicover and Rochemont (1992) provide additional evidence for this analysis of a fairly complex nature.

Williams (1975) contains the first major discussion of small clauses. Stowell (1983) contains an influential proposal within GB for the analysis of small clauses, arguing that the small clause is of the same category as its head. See also *Williams (1983), *Safir (1983), *Borer (1986*b*), and *Chung and McCloskey (1987). The notion of 'small clause' has been extended to many constructions where it would not at first glance appear to apply; see, for example, *Hoekstra and Mulder (1990).

For discussion of the syntax of case in Russian, see Babby (1980) as well as Neidle (1988); see also Brecht and Levine (1986). Blake (1987) surveys morphological case patterns in a variety of Australian languages, as do Dixon and Blake (1981). Miyagawa (1989) is an extensive survey of case phenomena in Japanese.

Binding Theory

1. Preliminaries

In this chapter we examine the long distance relation called binding. Informally, binding is a type of referential dependency, whereby the reference of the bound element is exactly the reference of the antecedent. A prototypical instance is given in (1).

(1)   Every dog loves its owner

Here, *every dog* binds *it*. As we consider each dog in the set of relevant dogs, *it* is understood as referring to that particular dog. In this sense, the reference of *it* is dependent on the reference of the antecedent. This type of binding is called variable binding, because the pronoun *it* is interpreted as a variable bound by its antecedent.

Reference is a relationship between part of a sentence and the external world. A referring expression picks out some entity in the world. As illustrated here, binding is a semantic relation, since it involves reference. In line with the general enterprise of PPT and related approaches, we syntacticize binding in order to identify and isolate those aspects that have a syntactic basis. The preliminary working assumption is that *all* aspects of binding are determined in the syntactic representation; the semantic binding relation on this view is then parasitic on the syntactic relations. That is, the working hypothesis is that referential dependency holds under those conditions where syntactic binding holds.

The particular theory based on the notion of government introduced in Chapter 2 and the theory of binding to be developed here is typically referred to as government-binding theory, or GB theory. GB theory is a precursor of Principles and Parameters theory and much of GB theory has been incorporated into PPT.

In order to represent the relation of referential dependency, we introduce the device of **indexing**. The index of an NP correlates with what the NP refers to. Informally, if two referential NPs have the same index they refer to the same thing; that is, they **corefer**. If they have different indices, this indicates that they refer to different things. Semantics interprets the indices, mapping a particular index into a particular referent in the world. However, it is important to recognize that referential dependence and coreference are different relations, as can be seen in sentences where a quantifier phrase binds a variable.

(2) [No contestant]$_i$ thought that she$_i$ would win.

In this sentence, the NP *no contestant* does not refer to anyone, yet *she* is coindexed with this NP and is (referentially) dependent on it. But *she* and *no contestant* are not coreferential.

As in the case of θ-roles, it is not crucial that we know which things an expression refers to, merely that two expressions have the same index. Binding theory concerns the syntactic conditions under which coindexing is possible, impossible, or necessary. Since syntactic coindexing is not equivalent to coreference, what is crucial to the theory of binding are the syntactic conditions on the coindexing relationship. Nevertheless, we will see that some of the crucial evidence bearing on coindexing will consist of intuitions about coreferentiality.

2. Pronominals, anaphors, and other NPs

Consider the following example.

(3) John$_i$ is here and he$_{i,j}$ is happy.

Here, the identical index *i* on *John* and *he* indicates that *John* and *he* may corefer. The different indices *i, j* on *John* and *he* indicate that coreference is possible but not necessary.

The core facts relevant to the Binding theory are (3) above and (4)–(7) below.

(4)   John$_i$ likes him$_{*i,j}$.
(5)   John$_i$ likes himself$_{i,*j}$.
(6)   John$_i$ believes that Mary likes him$_i$.
(7)   *John$_i$ believes that Mary likes himself$_i$.

What these sentences show is that there are circumstances under which the referential possibilities of elements such as pronouns and reflexives are restricted. Proceeding with the assumption that these circumstances admit of a syntactic characterization, we note that the following seems to hold.

(8)   *a.* A pronoun cannot have an antecedent in the same clause.
      b. A reflexive must have an antecedent in the same clause.

Here we provisionally understand 'in the same clause as α' as meaning something like 'an argument of the same clause of which α is an argument,' but we will refine this notion several times as we consider further examples.

Reflexives are included with reciprocals, such as *each other*, in the class of anaphors. While the terminology may be somewhat confusing, it is customary in the field to refer to the referential dependency of pronouns, reflexives, and reciprocals as anaphora, reserving the term *anaphors* for the latter two.

In addition to restricting referential dependency, Binding theory characterizes the coindexing possibilities for NPs that are not pronouns and not anaphors; these are called R-expressions (for referring expressions). An R-expression is not referentially dependent, which means that semantically it cannot have an antecedent, and syntactically it cannot be bound. Notice what happens when an R-expression is syntactically bound.

(9)   *a.* *John$_i$ likes John$_i$.
      b. *He$_i$ likes John$_i$.
      c. *John$_i$ thinks that Mary likes John$_i$.
      d. *John$_i$ can't stand John$_i$'s teacher.
      e. *He$_i$ can't stand John$_i$'s teacher.

These facts suggest the following generalization.

(10)   An R-expression must be free.

Here, free means 'not bound'. The precise conditions that determine whether an NP is bound or free will be discussed in § 3.

It should be noted that examples (9*b*) and (9*e*), in which the R-expression is bound by a pronoun, are far worse than the other examples in (9). The standard Binding theory does not address this difference, but it is something that must be accounted for in a theory of binding (see Exercise 3-4).

3. A brief history

The preliminary survey of § 2 suggests a rather simple account of syntactic binding properties for the three classes of NPs that we have introduced. Pronouns and anaphors appear to be in complementary distribution; R-expressions are always free. Historically, there have been three major complications of this simple account that have fueled the development of Binding theory. The first complication, the phenomenon of anaphoric subjects, will help us lay out the basic Binding theory of GB theory. The problem here is that reflexives and reciprocals cannot be the subjects of sentences with finite tense. The second complication is that anaphors in NPs, as in *The students bought pictures of each other*, do not have to have a local antecedent; we discuss these cases in § 5. The third complication is that in some languages there are **long distance anaphors**, in particular reflexives, that do not have to have a local antecedent. We postpone discussion of these cases until Chapter 8, § 3.

To begin with the discussion of anaphoric subjects, recall the crucial step taken in Chapter 2 to treat an infinitive in the ECM construction as a clausal complement, with the ACCUSATIVE NP as its syntactic subject, as in (11).

(11)   John believes [_{IP} Susan to be intelligent].

We find, strikingly, that although strictly speaking the ACCUSATIVE subject position is not in the clause of which *believes* is the main verb, this NP can be an anaphor.

(12)   *a.* Susan believes [_{IP} herself to be intelligent].
       b. John and Susan believe [_{IP} each other to be intelligent].

This fact suggests that the subject position of a complement is in some sense 'in the same clause' as the higher clause. However, such a relation holds only for the subject of non-finite clauses, as (13) shows.

(13)   *a.* *Mary$_i$ believes [$_{CP}$ (that) [$_{IP}$ herself$_i$ is intelligent]].
     b. *[John and Susan]$_i$ believe [$_{CP}$ (that) [$_{IP}$ each other$_i$ is intelligent]].[1]

Based on the theory developed in Chapter 2, we know that the subject of the infinitive is governed by the verb *believe*, while the subject of the tensed S is not. Presumably, a theory of what constitutes the domain in which an anaphor must be bound will make reference to its governor.

There are other restrictions on the relative syntactic positions of a referentially dependent element and its antecedent. To understand how the current theory took shape, let us look briefly at some earlier attempts to account for these restrictions.

In the *Conditions* framework of Chomsky (1973), it was proposed that in general syntactic relations that cross into a tensed S from outside are impossible.

(14)   **Tensed S Condition (TSC):** No rule can involve X, Y in the structure
$$\ldots X \ldots [_\alpha \ldots Y \ldots] \ldots$$
where α is a tensed S.

(14) blocks the movement of a constituent from position Y to position X. If X is a potential antecedent and Y is an anaphor, (14) blocks them from being coindexed. Through this technical device of coindexing the *Conditions* framework expressed the relationship of referential dependency. Thus the examples in (13) are ruled out, as well as (15).

(15)   *Mary$_i$ expects [$_{CP}$ that we like herself$_i$].

In all three examples, the node CP corresponds to α in the TSC. In (13a) X is *John$_i$* and Y is *herself$_i$*. In (13b) X is *John and Susan$_i$* and Y is *each other$_i$*. In (15) X is *Mary$_i$* and Y is *herself$_i$*.

But it turns out that even in an infinitive, if the anaphor is not the subject, it must have an antecedent within its own clause.

(16)   *a.* *Mary$_i$ expects [$_{IP}$ us to like herself$_i$].
     b. Mary expects [$_{IP}$ us$_i$ to like ourselves$_i$].

So in addition to the TSC, we must have a condition that deals with the case in which the antecedent is not the subject, regardless of whether or not the complement is tensed.

(17) **Specified Subject Condition (SSC):** No rule can involve X, Y in the structure

$$\ldots X \ldots [_\alpha \ldots Z \ldots -WYV \ldots] \ldots$$

where Z is the specified subject of WYV in α.

In (16a), the specified subject[2] is *us*, which intervenes between potential antecedent and anaphor.[3] X is *Mary$_i$*, Y is *herself$_i$*, and Z is *us*.

The effect of the TSC and the SSC is to render tensed S's and sentences with specified subjects 'local' domains for anaphor binding. Note, however, that TSC and SSC do much of the same work, in that they both will rule out a sentence such as (18).

(18) *[Mary and Susan]$_i$ believe that I like each other$_i$

In this case, the anaphor is within a tensed S while the antecedent is outside. Moreover, the anaphor is within the domain of a specified subject (the embedded sentence), while the antecedent is outside of this domain.

In order to eliminate this redundancy, subsequent reformulations of the conditions on binding focused on identifying the core distinguishing properties of the domains in which an anaphor cannot be bound. The examples considered above suggest that there are two.

(19) An anaphor cannot be bound if
    a. it is marked with NOMINATIVE Case;
    b. it is in a domain that has a subject and its antecedent is outside of the domain.

The first condition isolates what it is about a tensed S that prevents an anaphor from being its subject, while the second is an extension of the SSC to (13a) as well as (16a). The redundancy is thus eliminated.

At this point you should be able to do Exercise 3-1.

··

4. The binding conditions

··

We will now proceed to reformulate the observations captured in (19). This reformulation will have two goals. First, as noted above it will state the domain in which an anaphor must be bound in terms of the governor of the anaphor. This will allow us to explain in more abstract terms why a NOMINATIVE subject cannot be an anaphor, rather than simply to

stipulate it in the form of (19a). Ideally, the impossibility of a NOMINAT-
IVE subject should be the consequence of a more general principle that
does not specifically mention 'NOMINATIVE anaphor' in its formulation.
Second, the reformulation will seek to reduce the two parts of (19) to a
single characterization of the domain of binding, in terms of government.

To begin, consider what is wrong with (20).

(20)   *John's$_i$ mother likes himself$_i$.

Our first hypothesis might be that the antecedent of an anaphor cannot
be possessive. But this is immediately ruled out by sentences such as

(21)   [$_{NP}$ John's$_i$ picture of himself$_i$] is nice

in which the antecedent is within the same NP as the anaphor. Cases
such as these also demonstrate that our account of binding cannot be
restricted to sentences. We will use the term **domain** to refer to the set
of categories for which binding of anaphors is constrained. The domain
for binding includes at least IP and NP.

If the possessive is not responsible for (20), the only other plausible
account (within a strictly syntactic theory of the sort that we are developing here) is that the potential antecedent in (20) fails to c-command the
anaphor.[4] The structure is given in (22), with irrelevant details omitted.

(22)

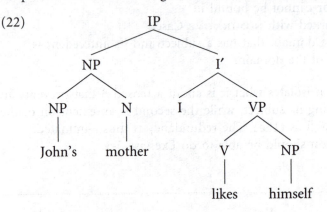

Let us therefore assume the following definition of **bind**.

(23) α binds β if and only
        (i) α c-commands β and
        (ii) α and β are coindexed.

We distinguish binding from coreference, which requires coindexing but
does not require c-command. In a sentence like (24)—

(24) Mary$_i$ was here and she$_i$ was angry

—*Mary$_i$* and *she$_i$* are not in a binding relationship. The presence of a true binding relationship is revealed when the antecedent is a quantified expression, as in (25).

(25) Every girl$_i$ thought that she$_i$ would win.

While a quantified NP can bind a pronoun, it cannot simply be coreferential with it, in general, as shown by (26).

(26) *Every girl$_i$ was here and she$_i$ was angry.

Therefore, syntactic binding entails coreference just when the antecedent is not a quantified NP, and coreference without c-command does not yield either syntactic binding or semantic binding.[5]

As discussed above, an anaphor must be bound 'in the same clause,' a notion which we must now understand more generally as 'in its domain,' in order to include IP and NP. Now consider (27).

(27) *a.* *Himself$_i$ likes John$_i$.
      b. *I expect himself$_i$ to like John$_i$.

In (27*a*), the potential antecedent *John* does not c-command the anaphor—

(28)

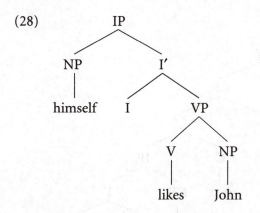

—hence the anaphor is not bound in its domain. Similarly, in (27*b*) the potential antecedent does not c-command the anaphor.[6]

Similarly a pronoun must be free 'in its domain.' The pronoun behaves as expected when its potential antecedent is within the same NP.

(29)   John's$_i$ mother likes him$_j$.
(30)   *John$_i$'s picture of him$_i$ is nice.

On the basis of these observations we may state the binding conditions as follows:

(31)   **Binding conditions**
        a. An anaphor must be bound in its domain.
        b. A pronominal must be free in its domain.
        c. An R-expression must be free.

It now remains to specify precisely what constitutes the domain.

5. Defining the local domain

As we have seen, ECM allows the clause associated with a verb like *believe* to extend into another clause, in the sense that *believe* governs not only within its own clause, but the subject of the complement. This fact suggests that the domain of an anaphor or a pronominal is the clause or NP in which its governor appears. Consider (32).

(32)   *a.* John thinks that Mary redeemed herself
        b.

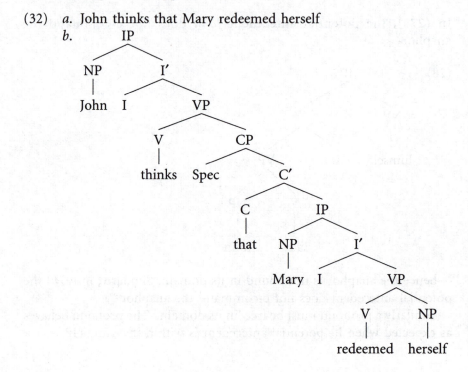

In this example, the governor of *herself* is the verb *redeemed*. The only possible antecedent is *Mary*. The domain of *herself* must contain the antecedent, but it cannot be so large that it also contains *John*, which is not a potential antecedent.[7] These considerations suggest that the domain should be defined as the **governing category**, as in (33).

(33) Governing category (GC): The governing category for α is the minimal clause or NP containing α, a governor for α, and a potential antecedent for α.

But as it stands (33) makes a false prediction. Suppose that the subject of the lower clause is not a potential antecedent. Then the next clause above it that contains a potential antecedent would be the governing category, which would be in error, as (34) shows.

(34) *John$_i$ said [that it seemed to himself$_i$ [that we were trying to speak French]]

In fact, the phrase that determines the scope of the governing category will be one that contains a subject. We revise the definition accordingly.

(35) Governing category (GC): The governing category for α is the minimal clause or NP containing α, a governor for α, and a subject.

Since *it* in (34) is a subject, the lower clause that excludes *John$_i$* will be the governing category for *himself*. This means that *himself* does not have an antecedent in its governing category; hence the sentence is ungrammatical.

We may now state the binding conditions in their final form.

(36) Binding conditions
    a. An anaphor must be bound within its governing category.
    b. A pronominal must be free within its governing category.
    c. An R-expression must be free.

These conditions are typically referred to as Condition A, Condition B, and Condition C of the Binding theory.

Examining the definition of governing category closely, we see that each component reflects an aspect of the earlier approaches to binding discussed above. The requirement that the domain must contain a subject captures the observation that a subject blocks binding from outside of its domain. The requirement that the domain be the minimal clause or

NP containing a governor for the anaphor appears to rule out the possibility that the anaphor can be a subject itself.

The definition of governing category that we have arrived at accounts also for the distribution of pronominals. In effect, the requirement that anaphors be bound and that pronominals be free in the equivalent domain yields the result that they will be in complementary distribution, a result that appears desirable in view of the data discussed thus far.

6. Anaphors in NP

6.1. Accessibility

While the generalization arrived at in the preceding paragraph is desirable, there is a class of data that suggests that anaphors and pronominals are in fact not in complementary distribution. The first example is given in (37).

(37)   Mary$_i$ thinks that [$_{IP}$ [a beautiful picture of herself$_i$] is hanging on the wall of the post office].

The IP of which *a beautiful picture of herself$_i$* is the subject is the minimal category that contains the reflexive, the governor of the reflexive (*picture*), and a subject (namely, *a beautiful picture of herself$_i$*). Since the reflexive lacks an antecedent in this domain, the sentence should violate Condition A of the Binding theory, but it does not; the sentence is grammatical. So somehow the sentence of which *Mary$_i$* is the subject must be the GC for *herself*.

The solution to this problem in GB theory is to reanalyze the structure of (37) and at the same time to reformulate the definition of GC. The essential intuition to be captured is that while the lower clause contains a subject, this subject is not accessible to *herself$_i$*, because it contains *herself$_i$*. The lowest accessible subject will be in the higher clause, and the definition of GC will be adjusted accordingly.

(38)   Governing category (GC): The governing category for α is the minimal clause or NP containing α, a governor for α, and a subject *accessible to α*.

The trick now is to define what an accessible subject is. One obvious possibility is the following.

(39) α is accessible to β if and only if α does not contain β.

While this definition will work correctly for cases in which the subject contains the anaphor, it will yield the wrong results in cases such as (40).

(40)   *John and Susan think [that each other is intelligent].

The anaphor *each other* is the subject of the lower clause. The lowest subject that is accessible to *each other* would be the subject of the higher clause, so this sentence should be grammatical.

We have two apparently conflicting cases. On the one hand, if the anaphor is contained in the subject, the subject of the higher clause should be accessible. But if the anaphor *is* the subject, the subject of the higher clause should not be accessible, even though a subject (properly) contains itself. That is, for some anaphor α we have the following options, where the lower NP is a subject in both cases.

(41) $NP_i \ldots [_\beta [_{NP} \ldots \alpha_i] \ldots]$
(42)   *$NP_i \ldots [_\beta [_{NP} \alpha] \ldots]$

Somehow we have to ensure that the governing category will be the entire sentence in the first case, and the clause β in the second. This appears to be a paradox, under the current definition.

6.2. I-within-i

To avoid the apparent paradox, we introduce the element Agr. Suppose that Agr is in some sense the 'subject' of the sentence in (37) and (40), rather than, respectively, *a beautiful picture of herself* and *each other*. The assumption that Agr functions as a subject in some sense, while imprecise, is not entirely unnatural, given that in many languages subject (and even object) agreement morphology appears to express the grammatical functions of subject and object, while the NPs are in a sense adjuncts.[8]

The structures that we have to deal with are now the following.

(43) $NP_i \ldots [_\beta [_{NP} \ldots \alpha_i]_j \; Agr_j \ldots]$
(44)   *$NP_i \ldots [_\beta [_{NP} \alpha]_i \; Agr_i \ldots]$

And for the particular examples they are as in (45).

(45) *a.* Mary$_i$ thinks that [$_{IP}$ [a beautiful picture of herself$_i$]$_j$ [Agr$_j$ [is hanging on the wall of the post office]]].

   b. [John and Susan]$_i$ think [that [$_{IP}$ each other$_i$ [Agr$_i$ [is intelligent]]]].

The agreement between Agr and the subjects is shown as coindexing.[9]

On the assumption that Agr is a subject in (45*b*), Agr is the accessible subject for the anaphor, hence IP is the GC. Lacking an antecedent in IP, the anaphor *each other* violates Condition A of the Binding theory.

Now we have a problem with (45*a*). Here, if Agr is the accessible subject, the sentence will be incorrectly ruled out. This is because IP will be the GC, and *herself* lacks an antecedent within IP, just as in (45*b*). But we can reformulate the notion of accessible subject in such a way that Agr is not accessible in this case, to yield the result that we were seeking earlier in the form of (39). The situation that we want to arrive at is described in (46).

(46) Agr is not accessible if changing the index of Agr and the index of the subject to the index of the anaphor would yield a situation in which the anaphor and the NP that contains it have the same index.

The condition described in (46) in which the anaphor and the NP that contains it have the same index is called the **i-within-i Condition**. Consider a concrete example of how it is supposed to work. In (45*a*), *a beautiful picture of herself* and Agr are coindexed with *j*. Let us change the index to the index of the anaphor.

(47) ... [$_{IP}$ [a beautiful picture of herself$_i$]$_i$ Agr$_i$ ...]

We now have a situation in which *herself* is contained in an NP with the same index. Thus Agr is not an accessible subject, and IP is not the GC for *herself*. Hence *herself* can have an antecedent outside of the clause containing the NP that dominates it.

This characterization of the i-within-i Condition appears to generalize with the condition that an NP cannot be coindexed with one of its constituents, as in (48).

(48) *a.* *[a picture of itself$_i$]$_i$

   b. *[her$_i$ friend]$_i$

But the generality of this condition may well be questioned, in view of such sentences as the following.

(49) *a.* One finds [many books about themselves$_i$]$_i$ in Borges's literary output.

　　b. You$_i$ are [your$_i$ worst enemy]$_i$.

Moreover, the particular device of changing the indices of NP and Agr in order to determine whether the i-within-i pattern exists is quite unique in the theory, and appears designed just for this particular case. Hence it appears that the i-within-i Condition is not strongly motivated beyond the specific Binding theory problem illustrated here.

We have devoted this much attention to the i-within-i solution because the complexity of this solution highlights an essential property of the reflexives in NPs headed by nouns like *picture*. While an anaphor in argument position must have a local antecedent, that is, one that is an argument of the governor of the anaphor, anaphors in *picture*-NPs may have 'long distance' antecedents. Whether there can be a single simple account of the two types of anaphors is open to question, a point to which we will return below.

6.3. SUBJECT

Continuing with the account of accessible subject, we see that it must be further revised to account for the fact that the GC is well defined for structures that lack Agr, such as infinitival clauses and NPs.[10] Assume the notion of SUBJECT defined as follows:[11]

(50) The **SUBJECT** of a clause is Agr if there is one, otherwise the [Spec, IP] or [Spec, NP].

We modify the definition of governing category accordingly.

(51) Governing category (GC): The governing category for α is the minimal clause or NP containing α, a governor for α, and a SUBJECT accessible to α.

Now we can derive the following.

(52) *a.* Susan expects [$_{IP}$ John$_i$ to help himself$_i$].

　　b. Susan stole [$_{NP}$ John$_i$'s picture of himself$_i$].

　　c. Susan$_i$ expects [$_{IP}$ herself$_i$ to win the race].

It is crucial that in the embedded IP of (52c) there is no Agr, so that the GC for *herself* will be the larger clause. Compare this case with the one in which the embedded clause is tensed.

(53)   *Susan$_i$ expects [$_{CP}$ that [$_{IP}$ herself$_i$ Agr$_i$ will win the race]].

Note that the cost of this solution is the disjunctive definition of SUB-JECT in (50). In general, the use of such disjunctive formulations is symptomatic of a failure to capture a generalization.

6.4. BT-compatibility

Another problem concerns cases like the following.

(54)   *a.* [John and Susan]$_i$ solved [$_{NP}$ [each other$_i$'s] problems].
       b. John$_i$ dislikes [$_{NP}$ his$_i$ job].

On the view that the possessive is the subject of the NP, these sentences present a paradox. On the one hand, if the GC is the NP, the pronoun and the anaphor are both free within their GC, so (54a) should be ungrammatical, by Condition A of the Binding theory. On the other hand, if the GC is the entire sentence, the pronoun and the anaphor are both bound within their GC, so (54b) should be ungrammatical, by Condition B of the Binding theory.

To solve this problem, we could try to reanalyze the pronoun, so that it may also be understood as an anaphor. If *his$_i$* is an anaphor, then it is not a problem if it is bound within the full sentence. The full sentence will be the GC, since it is the minimum domain that contains an accessible subject for *his$_i$*. Alternatively, we could reformulate the Binding theory so that the GC for the possessive pronoun is the NP that contains it while the GC for the possessive anaphor is the full sentence.

The plausibility of the first alternative is shown by the fact that there is a problematic gap in English. A reflexive cannot be possessive, although a reciprocal can be, as we have seen.

(55)   *John dislikes himself's job.

It is natural (although not necessary) to assume that this gap is filled by a form that is phonologically identical to the pronoun. Notice that it must also be possible for a true pronoun (a non-anaphor) to appear in this position, because of the grammaticality of sentences such as (56).

(56)   John$_i$ thinks [that Mary should read his$_i$ book].

Here, *his$_i$* must be free within the complement clause. The GC in fact is the complement, because it is the minimal domain that contains an accessible subject (i.e. *Mary*).

The following examples suggest there is a problem with this alternative.

(57)   *a.* Mary$_i$ lost a beautiful picture of herself$_i$ (that I had given
            her).
        b. Mary$_i$ lost a beautiful picture of her$_i$ (that I had given her).

If the GC for the anaphor is the main clause, the pronoun is bound in its GC. If the GC for the pronoun is the NP *picture of her$_i$*, the anaphor is free in its GC. We cannot suppose that what appears to be a pronoun here is actually an anaphor, since the anaphor can also appear; there is no morphological gap in this case.

This problem suggests that we should seek an account in which there are two distinct GCs, one for anaphors and one for pronominals.[12] On such an alternative, we consider that since an anaphor must be bound, it makes no sense to restrict its GC to an NP of which it is the subject (in fact, the SUBJECT). The minimal 'plausible' domain for an anaphor is some domain that contains a potential antecedent for the anaphor, some NP that could be coindexed with it. On the other hand, since a pronoun must be free, it makes sense that its GC would be the NP, since it can readily be free within that domain. A pronoun does not require an antecedent in order to be interpreted.

Let us define the notion **BT-compatible**, a more formal development of the idea that the GC for an referentially dependent expression is the minimal domain in which there exists a plausible indexing.[13] The Binding theory on this approach takes the following form. Suppose that α has some indexing I. The question is, for some local domain β, is this indexing of α BT-compatible? The answer is given in (58).[14]

(58) α under the indexing I is BT-compatible in the local domain β
        if:
        a. α is an anaphor and is bound in β under this indexing;
        b. α is a pronominal and is free in β under this indexing;
        c. α is an R-expression and is free in β under this indexing.

For (54a), taking β to be the IP, the anaphor is bound under this indexing if its indexing is such that it is coindexed with the subject NP. For

(54*b*), taking β to be the NP, the pronominal is free in NP under any indexing, even when it is coindexed with the subject.

Consider now sentence (57*a*). An optional empty subject in the NP *picture of herself*$_i$ would render this NP the GC for the anaphor.[15] This NP counts as a local domain in the sense that it is thematically complete (what Chomsky calls a 'complete functional complex' or CFC). Moreover, the subject position of the NP is not obviously occupied by something that would render the NP an impossible domain for the antecedent (such as the anaphor itself). It is therefore natural that the antecedent of the anaphor should appear in this NP, rather than more distantly.

Notice, finally, that the approach sketched out here fails to avoid the problem that led us to the unsatisfactory i-within-i Condition. If the anaphor is contained within a subject NP, its GC is simply the smallest IP that contains it that can also contain an antecedent. This IP is the sentence of which it is a subject, since the SUBJECT in this case is Agr. Coindexing the subject NP with Agr produces the i-within-i configuration, which as before must be ruled out.

6.5. Summary

While the solutions reviewed here are technically workable, it is not clear that they capture the essential character of the phenomena under investigation. The peculiar behavior of the anaphor contained within the subject in English suggests that something else may be involved besides a refinement of the definition of GC. Furthermore, a broader survey of anaphoric relations in natural language suggests that the class of anaphors is not homogeneous. In effect, there are at least two and possibly three or four kinds of anaphor. One type, the local anaphor, is found in argument position and requires a local antecedent, as in *Mary redeemed herself*. A second type, the long distance anaphor, takes an antecedent outside of the local domain. The distinction is difficult to see in English, where all anaphors have the same form, but is morphologically marked in other languages. Moreover, long distance anaphora is by and large restricted to arguments within NPs in English, while this is not the case in other languages. (That is, in some languages a long distance anaphor can be the complement of a verb.) There is also the **logophoric** use of anaphors, in which the antecedent is outside of the sentence, as in *As for myself, things are fine*. Certain cases of long distance anaphora may turn out to be special cases of logophoric anaphora.

In Chapter 8, § 3 we summarize some of the cross-linguistic phenomena and relate them to the English cases.

At this point you should be able to do Exercises 3-2 through 3-9.

7. PRO

Our examination of binding has shown that there are three types of
NPs, anaphors, pronominals, and R-expressions. If we say that [+a] is
the property of being an anaphor, and [+p] is the property of being a
pronoun, then the following picture emerges.

(59)

	[+a]	[−a]
[+p]		pronominal
[−p]	anaphor	R-expression

There is no empirical necessity behind this classification. But if this is the
correct way to view matters, we should be able to find an element to fit
into the gap [+a, +p], or prove that no such element can exist. We will
in fact find such an element.

Consider first the following sentences.

(60) a. I want [$_{CP}$ [e] to visit you].
    b. They want [$_{CP}$ [e] to visit each other].
    c. I want [$_{CP}$ Susan to visit you].

Uniformity, applied to θ-role assignment, entails that there is an empty
subject argument of the infinitive.[16] Just as *Susan* bears the subject θ-role
of *visit* in (60c), so must there be a subject of *visit* where there is no overt
subject. We will call this empty subject PRO, and try to determine its
properties. Crucially, PRO is an NP, by Syntacticization.

The most obvious property of PRO is that it is referentially dependent
on an NP in the higher clause. That is, the AGENT of *visit* in (60a) is *I* and
in (60b) it is *they*. This is the property called **control**. PRO may be controlled, or it may be **arbitrary**, as in (61).

(61)   [PRO to err] is human, [PRO to forgive], divine.

PRO occurs only as the subject of a non-finite clause in English.

(62)   *a.* I tried PRO to understand the problem.
       b. It is important PRO to understand the problem.
       c. *PRO is/are singing.
       d. *I spoke to PRO.
       e. PRO to understand the problem is important.
       f. PRO running away would be unwise.
       g. PRO sitting in my office one day, I remembered the solution.
       h. I left [PRO angry].
       i. I hammered the metal [PRO flat].

That is, only the subject of a non-finite clause can be empty. Why is this? Looking at the ungrammatical examples in (62), two possibilities come to mind: either PRO cannot have Case, or PRO cannot be governed.

We might rule out the first possibility by showing that even in non-Case positions, PRO cannot appear.[17]

(63)   *a.* *I like very much PRO. (meaning 'I like someone very much')
       b. *It was arrested PRO. (meaning 'someone was arrested')
       c. *There was arrested PRO. (meaning 'someone was arrested')
       d. *John's destruction PRO. (meaning 'John's destruction of something')
       e. *John believes very much PRO to have won.

For each of these cases it can be argued that the position occupied by PRO does not get Case assigned to it. For example, in (63a) PRO does not satisfy the adjacency condition for Case assignment. But if PRO cannot appear even in non-Case positions, the problem with the ungrammatical examples in (62) cannot be due to Case.

Consider the second possibility. Case depends on government, but it is possible for an NP to be governed without having Case. It is reasonable to suppose that in (63) PRO is governed but lacks Case. So we may conclude that the problem with PRO in these cases is that it cannot be governed, but finds itself in a governed position.

We could stipulate as a lexical property of PRO that it must be ungoverned, although this would not really explain much. But perhaps we can actually deduce that PRO must be ungoverned, if we assume the feature analysis of NPs in (59). Suppose that PRO fills the gap, and is therefore both [+p] and [+a]. If PRO is pronominal, it must be free in its GC. If it is an anaphor, it must be bound. If it is both, it must be both bound and free. This is impossible, hence PRO must lack a GC. In order to lack a GC, it must be ungoverned. This reasoning is often referred to as the **PRO Theorem**.

A consequence of PRO being ungoverned is that PRO will always lack Case. We therefore predict that there will be a complementary distribution between PRO and overt NP. PRO should occur only where overt NP cannot, and vice versa. The following evidence supports the prediction.

Direct object
(64) I saw John/*PRO.

Subject of Tensed S
(65) John thinks that he/*PRO will win.

Subject of infinitive without ECM
(66) I was wondering what $\begin{Bmatrix} \text{PRO} \\ \text{*Bill} \\ \text{*for Bill} \end{Bmatrix}$ to say next.

ECM subject position
(67) John believes $\begin{Bmatrix} \text{Mary} \\ \text{himself} \\ \text{*PRO} \end{Bmatrix}$ to be strange.

For some apparent counterexamples to the prediction, see Exercise 3-10. For considerations concerning the interpretation of the Binding conditions with respect to PRO, see Exercise 3-11.

8. Summary

In this chapter we investigated the syntactic conditions under which anaphoric elements can be referentially dependent on potential antecedents. The Binding theory contains the following conditions.

(68) Binding conditions
      a. An anaphor must be bound within its governing category.
      b. A pronominal must be free within its governing category.
      c. An R-expression must be free.

We went through a series of definitions of governing category, as follows.

(69)   Governing category (GC): The governing category for α is the minimal clause or NP containing α, a governor for α, and
   (i)   a subject.
   (ii)   a subject accessible to α.
   (iii)   a SUBJECT accessible to α.

While (i) is the simplest version, we found that we had to develop the notion of 'accessible SUBJECT' in order to explain the fact that an anaphor within a subject can take an antecedent in a higher clause, while the subject of a tensed S cannot be an anaphor. Assuming that Agr is the SUBJECT of the sentence, Agr is accessible to the subject anaphor, which therefore lacks an antecedent in its GC. But Agr is not accessible to an anaphor properly contained within the subject, hence a higher Agr must be the accessible SUBJECT.

BT-compatibility was introduced in order to account for the fact that pronoun and anaphors can appear in the same contexts in NPs. A pronoun in an NP is free within the NP, while an anaphor, which must have an antecedent, takes as its domain a larger structure in which there is a potential antecedent.

The distribution of PRO was accounted for in terms of the Binding theory. As a pronominal anaphor, it cannot be both free and bound in its governing category; hence it cannot have a governing category, from which it follows that PRO is not governed at all.

In Chapter 8 we provide evidence that long distance anaphora, of which anaphors in picture NPs are a special case, is subject to different conditions than local anaphors. Anticipating the conclusions of that discussion here, we will adopt version (i) of the definition of governing category in (69).

APPENDIX A: WHERE IS BINDING THEORY?

One of the major contributions of GB theory has been the formal treatment of such 'semantic' phenomena as binding, along the lines summarized in this chapter. On the other hand, the Binding theory of GB Theory is concerned specifically with the binding conditions for pronominal elements, including pronouns and reflexives, that occur within a single sentence. The claim is that the referential dependency of anaphoric elements can be represented by syntactic coindexing at S-structure and/or LF, a syntactic representation of meaning, and that the syntactic indices are semantically interpreted either as identity of reference or as variable binding. In this section, we consider how to extend the Binding theory to a broader range of phenomena, and the consequences of doing so.

Culicover and Jackendoff (1995) argue that binding theory is properly not a part of syntax, but of Conceptual Structure (in the sense of Jackendoff (1983; 1990)). The argument is based on the behavior of the English expression *else*. *Else*, like a pronoun, is referentially dependent on an antecedent. In some respects it behaves like a pronoun, in other respects like an anaphor.

(70) a. John$_i$ loves someone else$_{j \neq i}$.
      b. John$_i$ loves himself$_i$.
(71) a. John$_i$ carefully ignores everyone else$_{j \neq i}$ while doing yoga.
      b. Frankly, we$_i$ don't expect anyone else$_{j \neq i}$ to like this paper, but we're publishing it anyway.
(72) a. Mary$_i$ was elected President and someone else$_{j \neq i}$ was elected Vice President.
      b. John$_i$ thought that someone else$_{j \neq i}$ would win.
      c. John$_i$'s mother thought that someone else$_{j \neq i}$ would win. (*John* does not c-command *someone else*.)
(73) a. Mary was elected President and she was not elected Vice President.
      b. John thought that he would win.
      c. John's mother thought that he would win.

These examples show that *else* can have a local antecedent like an anaphor (in (70a)), and that it can have a long distant antecedent like a pronoun (in (71)–(72)).

The major peculiarity of *else* is that, unlike a pronominal, it does not show strong crossover effects (see Chapter 9, § 1).

(74) a. *Who$_i$ does he$_i$ love? [strong crossover]
      b. ??Who$_i$ does his$_i$ mother love? [weak crossover]
      c. ??Who$_i$ does someone else$_{j \neq i}$ love?
          (= Who$_i$ does someone other than α_i love?)
      d. ??Who$_i$ does someone else's$_{j \neq i}$ mother love?
          (= Who$_i$ does [someone other than α_i]'s mother love?)

This fact follows if the expression *someone else* is not a referentially dependent element, on a par with the pronoun *he*, but decomposable into an expression of the form *other than α_i*, where α_i is coindexed with the antecedent. Crucially, there is no evidence that this decomposition corresponds to the syntactic structure of *someone else*, at D-structure or at S-structure.

The possibility remains that *someone else* is translated into LF, which is a syntactic representation. The evidence that this is not correct is that for some sentences containing *else*, there is no syntactic expression that could be construed as the antecedent. Some examples from Culicover and Jackendoff (1995) are given in (75).

(75) *a.* John patted the dog, and Sam did something else to it.
  b. Mary put the food in the container, and then Susan did something else with it.

There is in fact no antecedent VP in these cases that can supply the interpretation for *something else*. Compare the ungrammatical examples in (76)–(77).

(76) *a.* *John patted the dog, and Sam did something other than pat to the dog.
  b. *. . . , and Sam did something other than pat it to the dog.
  c. *. . . , and Sam did something other than pat the dog to it.
(77) *a.* *John put the food in the container, and then Susan did something other than put the food in the container with it.
  b. *. . . , and then Susan did something other than put (it) in the container with the food.
  c. *. . . , and then Susan did something other with it than put the food in the container.

It therefore appears that the level of representation at which the interpretation of the elliptical VP is supplied is not syntactic, not even LF, but a level of semantic representation (i.e. Conceptual Structure).

Given that a referentially dependent element such as *else* must receive its interpretation at Conceptual Structure, there is no reason to suppose that the treatment of all referential dependency is not uniform. While there are clearly syntactic conditions on referential dependency, it can be argued that the Binding theory in general must be formulated in terms of Conceptual Structure representations.

EXERCISES

3-1. In the text it was claimed that the subject of a non-finite clause can be an anaphor, but the subject of a finite clause cannot be. The examples in the text (12)/(13) illustrate this claim for infinitives and tensed clauses. Extend the data by testing this claim for the other types of 'clauses' illustrated in (1). The question is, is it possible for an anaphor to appear in the position occupied by *John* in these examples?

(1) a. *small clauses, e.g.*: I consider [John intelligent].
   b. *gerundives, e.g.*: I imagined [John singing in French].
   c. *subjunctives, e.g.*: I insisted [(that) John be allowed to speak].

What do the results tell you about the syntax of the bracketed expressions in these examples?
[§ 3]

3-2. Determine whether or not the binding conditions apply as expected to the following examples. If the binding conditions apply correctly, indicate how they account for the judgement. If the binding conditions do not apply as expected, indicate what is predicted and why.

(1) a. John$_i$ expects Mary$_j$ to be angry at *himself$_i$/herself$_j$/him$_i$/*her$_j$.
   b. John$_i$ expects Mary$_j$ to prove *himself$_i$/herself$_j$/him$_i$/*her$_j$ to be honest.
(2) a. Not even his$_i$ own mother recognized John$_i$.
   b. *Not even he$_i$ recognized John$_i$.
   c. No one recognized John$_i$ in the picture; not even he$_i$ recognized John$_i$.
(3) a. *Mary$_i$ told Susan$_j$ about themselves$_{i+j}$.
   b. Mary$_i$ told Susan$_j$ that there were pictures of themselves$_{i+j}$ hanging on the post office wall.
   c. *Mary$_i$ told Susan$_j$ that there were pictures of each other$_{i+j}$ hanging on the post office wall.
(4) a. As for myself$_j$, there was nothing left to do.
   b. *As for himself$_j$, there was nothing left to do.
   c. As for himself$_j$, John$_j$ said that there was nothing left to do.
(5) a. John$_i$ let Mary$_j$ pour the water all over *himself$_i$/herself$_j$/him$_i$/*her$_j$.
   b. [John and Mary]$_i$ let the water trickle all over each other$_i$.
   c. Mary$_i$ let the water drip all over herself$_i$/her$_i$.
   d. Mary$_i$ let the water splash *herself$_i$/her$_i$ all over.
   e. Susan$_i$ splashed the water all over herself$_i$/her$_i$.
(6) a. Susan$_i$ solved the problem with her$_i$ calculator.
   b. Susan$_i$ brought a calculator with *herself$_i$/her$_i$.
   c. Susan$_i$ has a calculator with *herself$_i$/her$_i$.
   d. Susan$_i$ has a strange air about *herself$_i$/her$_i$.
(7) a. *[Mary and Susan]$_i$ suddenly realized that each other$_i$ was in trouble.
   b. [Mary and Susan]$_i$ suddenly found out what each other$_i$ was up to.

[§ 4–§ 6]

3-3. The Binding theory is a theory of syntactically determined referential dependency. In some sense, a quantified phrase in the scope of another quantifier is referentially dependent, as illustrated by the following sentence and its logical paraphrases.

(1) a. Every chapter contains a difficult problem.
     b. for every x (x a chapter) there is a y (y a difficult problem) such that x contains y.

As shown by the paraphrase in (1b), what *a difficult problem* refers to depends on the particular choice of chapter. Similarly, in (2) the subject can (but need not) be understood to depend on the object.

(2) a. Someone in the class solved every problem.
     b. for every y (y a problem) there is an x (x a person in the class) such that x solved y.

Show that this type of referential dependency does not pattern syntactically like the type of referential dependency that involves anaphors and pronouns.

[§ 4–§ 6]

*3-4. 1. Suggest an explanation for the following pattern of grammaticality. The examples in (1) are to be read without focal stress on the main subject; with such focal stress they are grammatical (e.g. *Who likes Mary? Mary likes Mary.*)

(1) a. *Mary$_i$ likes Mary$_i$.
     b. *Mary$_i$ thinks that Mary$_i$ will win.
     c. *Mary$_i$ thinks that no one likes Mary$_i$.
(2) a. Before Mary$_i$ goes out, Mary$_i$ will call.
     b. When$_i$ Mary$_i$ is ready to call, Mary$_i$ will call.
(3) a. Mary$_i$ will call before Mary$_i$ goes out.
     b. Mary$_i$ will call when Mary$_i$ is ready to call.
     c. I introduced Mary$_i$ to Mary$_i$'s future spouse.

2. Compare your answer to part 1 with what is suggested by the following pattern.

(4) a. *She$_i$ likes Mary$_i$.
     b. *She$_i$ thinks that Mary$_i$ will win.
     c. *She$_i$ thinks that no one likes Mary$_i$.
(5) a. Before Mary$_i$ goes out, she$_i$ will call.
     b. When$_i$ Mary$_i$ is ready to call, she$_i$ will call.
(6) a. *She$_i$ will call before Mary$_i$ goes out.
     b. *She$_i$ will call when Mary$_i$ is ready to call.
     c. *I introduced her$_i$ to Mary$_i$'s future spouse.

What implications do your answers have for the Binding theory as formulated in the text?

[§ 4–§ 6]

3-5. In English it is possible to use a definite NP to refer to an individual previously introduced into the discourse; in this respect, such a definite NP (called an epithet) is like a pronoun.

(1)   Mary$_i$ came into the room, but the kid$_i$/jerk$_i$/bozo$_i$/turkey$_i$/president$_i$ didn't stay very long.

What do the following sentences tell you what the status of epithets should be in the Binding theory? Can you explain why they should have this status?

(2)   *a.* Mary$_i$ claims that the *kid$_i$/*jerk$_i$/*bozo$_i$/*turkey$_i$ /*president$_i$/she$_i$ didn't stay very long.
   b. Mary$_i$ lost *the kid$_i$'s/*jerk$_i$'s/*bozo$_i$'s/*turkey$_i$'s /*president$_i$'s/her$_i$ watch.
   c. The kid$_i$'s/jerk$_i$'s/bozo$_i$'s/turkey$_i$'s/president$_i$'s/her$_i$ mother thinks that Mary$_i$ is doing a fine job.

[§ 4–§ 6]

*3-6. Discuss the status of the following examples with respect to the Binding theory. Of particular concern is the question of how the pronouns and anaphors can be 'bound' under the formal definition of 'bind' discussed in this chapter.

(1)   *a.* John$_i$ told every girl$_j$ his$_i$/her$_j$ grade.
   b. John$_i$ told every girl$_j$ about his$_i$/her$_j$ grade.
   c. John$_i$ told every girl$_j$ that he$_i$/she$_j$ would pass the course.
(2)   *a.* John$_i$ showed every girl$_j$ himself$_i$/herself$_j$.
   b. John$_i$ told every girl$_j$ about himself$_i$/herself$_j$.
(3)   *a.* [John and Mary]$_i$ showed the students$_j$ each other$_{i,j}$.
   b. [John and Mary]$_i$ told the students$_j$ about each other$_{i,j}$.

[§ 4–§ 6]

*3-7. The Binding theory as it was originally construed used indices for two purposes. First, they were used to indicate coreference and disjoint reference, as in (1).

(1)   *a.* Mary$_i$ came to the party but she$_i$ left early.
   b. Mary$_i$ is talented and Mary$_i$ is intelligent.
   c. She$_j$ likes Mary$_i$.
   d. Mary$_i$ likes her$_j$.

Second, they were used to indicate binding, as in (2).

(2)   *a.* *She$_i$ likes Mary$_i$.
   b. *Mary$_i$ likes her$_i$.

The following examples suggest that only one of these uses of indexing is possible. Explain why this is, and propose a revision of the theory to solve the problem.

(3) a. *Mary$_i$ likes Susan$_j$ and her$_i$.
　　 b. *Susan$_j$ and she$_i$ like Mary$_i$.
　　 c. *She$_i$ and Susan like Mary$_i$.
　　 d. *She$_i$ and Susan think that Mary$_i$ will win.
(4) a. ?I like us.
　　 b. ?We like me.
　　 c. I think that we will win.
　　 d. I told you that we(='you and I') will win.

[§ 4–§ 6]

**3-8. What do the following examples suggest about the analysis of *own* in English? How can these observations be integrated into the Binding theory?

(1) a. Susan$_i$ lost her$_i$ money.
　　 b. Susan$_i$ lost her$_i$ own money.
(2) a. Susan$_i$ lost her$_i$ mind.
　　 b. *Susan$_i$ lost her$_i$ own mind.
(3) a. Mary$_i$ thinks that John$_j$ lost his$_j$/her$_j$ money.
　　 b. Mary$_i$ thinks that John$_j$ lost his$_j$/*her$_j$ own money.
(4) a. Mary$_i$ thinks that her$_i$ mother wouldn't recognize her$_i$.
　　 b. Mary$_i$ thinks that her$_i$ own mother wouldn't recognize her$_i$.
(5) a. Mary$_i$ told John$_j$ that her$_i$/his$_j$ mother wouldn't recognize her$_i$/him$_j$.
　　 b. Mary$_i$ told John$_j$ that her$_i$/his$_j$ own mother wouldn't recognize her$_i$/him$_j$.

[§ 4–§ 6]

3-9. The following data illustrate the behavior of the anaphors *ton eafton tou* and *o idhios* in Modern Greek.

(1) a. Egho idha ton eafton mou ston　kathrefti.
　　　 I　　saw myself　　　　　 in-the mirror
　　　 'I saw myself in the mirror.'
　　 b. *Egho idha ton eafton tis ston　 kathrefti.
　　　 I　　saw herself　　　　 in-the mirror
(2) a. O Yanis　theli　[i Maria　na voithisi ton eafton tis].
　　　 the Yanis wants the Maria to help　　 herself
　　　 'John wants Maria to help herself.'
　　 b. *O Yanis　theli　[i Maria　na voithisi ton eafton tou].
　　　 the Yanis wants the Maria to help　　 himself
　　　 'John wants Maria to help herself.'

(3)   O Yanis   theli   [i Maria na   voithisi ton idhio]
        the Yanis wants the Maria to help   himself
        'John; wants Mary to help him;.'

(4)   O Yanis   pistevi oti   o   idhios tha kerdhisi
        the Yanis believes COMP himself will   win
        'John; believes that he; will win.'

(5) *a.* O Yanis   aghapa ton eafton tou/*ton idhio
        the Yanis loves   himself
        'John loves himself.'

     b. O Yanis   theli   na katalavi   ton eafton tou/*ton idhio
        the Yanis wants to understands himself
        'John wants to understand himself.'

(6) *a.* O Yanis   ipe ston Costa   [oti i   Maria aghapa ton idhio]
        the Yanis; said to-the Costa; C   the Maria_k loves   him_{i/j/*k}
        'John said to Costa that Mary loves him/*herself.'

     b. O Yanis   ipe stin   Katerina [oti i Maria   aghapa ton idhio]
        the Yanis said to-the Katerina C   the Maria loves   himself
        'John; told Catherine that Mary loves him;.'

     c. O Yanis   ipe stin   Katerina [oti i Costas   aghapa tin idhia]
        the Yanis said to-the Katerina C   the Costas loves   herself
        'John told Catherine; that Costas loves her;.'

State in as general form as you can the properties of *o idhios*. Does its behavior follow from the Binding theory? Explain.

[§ 4–§ 6; Iatridou (1986)]

3-10. We have proposed that PRO cannot have a governing category, and hence it cannot have a governor. Discuss how the following data call this conclusion about PRO into question.

(1) *a.* I want Mary to win.
     b. I want PRO to win.
(2) *a.* I expect Mary to win.
     b. I expect PRO to win.
(3) *a.* His running away upset Kim.
     b. Him running away upset Kim.
     c. PRO running away upset Kim.

Propose a lexical solution for the cases illustrated in (1) and (2). Discuss whether or not this solution will extend to the cases in (3).

[§ 7]

*3-11. The result that PRO cannot be governed follows from a particular interpretation of binding conditions A and B. When we say that 'an anaphor must be bound within its governing category,' we are not to understand this as requiring that an anaphor have a GC or that it must be bound. Rather, we are to understand this as saying that if the anaphor has a GC it must be governed within the GC. Similarly for pronouns. This leaves open the question of what happens with overt anaphors and pronouns that lack a GC. Show why this interpretation of the binding conditions does not create a problem for overt elements. Then consider what consequences your answer has for the assignment of a θ-role to PRO. What are the implications for the Visibility Thesis of Chapter 2?

[§ 7]

**3-12. In the text we discussed Chomsky's proposal that *picture of himself* contains an optional (empty) subject. Show that this subject has to be PRO. What implications does this conclusion have for the claim that PRO cannot be governed? How would you resolve the problem while maintaining the ungoverned status of PRO?

[§ 7]

*3-13. 1. Show that the accessible SUBJECT for *himself*$_i$ in the following example is *John*$_i$. Assume the i-within-i Condition.

(1)   *John$_i$ Agr said that his$_i$ brother Agr likes himself$_i$.

   2. What does the Binding theory that assumes the notion accessible SUBJECT and the i-within-i Condition predict about the following example?

(2)   John Agr said that his brother Agr likes him.

[§ 6.4; Bouchard 1985]

***3-14. In the text it was noted that the following sentences are not equivalent in acceptability.

(1)   *a.* *John believes (that) herself is intelligent.
      b. *John and Susan believe (that) each other is intelligent.

Sentence (1*b*) is not as bad as (1*a*).
   Along with these judgements we have the following, shared by many speakers.

(2)   *a.* [John and Susan]$_i$ were wondering exactly what each other$_i$ was going to do when the balloon hit the ground.
      b. [John and Susan]$_i$ were extremely concerned about what was going to happen to each other$_i$ when the balloon hit the ground.
      c. [John and Susan]$_i$ were extremely concerned about the dangers that each other$_i$ was facing.

    d. ?[John and Susan]ᵢ were amazed at what each otherᵢ was wearing to
       the beach.

Nevertheless, there are some cases that seem to be completely impossible.

(3)   *a.* *[John and Susan]ᵢ were wondering what you said to each otherᵢ.
     b. *[John and Susan]ᵢ were extremely concerned about what you did to
      each otherᵢ.

Explore the conditions under which this extended type of anaphora is possible. What implications do examples such as these have for the standard Binding theory?

FURTHER READING

[Note: The number of asterisks before a reference indicates its level of technical difficulty. You should be able to follow much if not all of what is in those references that lack asterisks.]

Wasow (1979) (based on Wasow 1972) exemplifies the theory of anaphora in earlier generative grammar; it contains many hints and precursors of much more recent proposals. Lasnik (1976) and Reinhart (1983) are among the most important and influential works on the general theory of anaphora in generative grammar. For a range of recent perspectives on binding and anaphora, see *Aoun (1985), *Bouchard (1984; 1985), *Williams (1989), **Chierchia (1992), among many others. Pollard and Sag (1992) contains a summary of various technical problems imposed by the attempt to extend the Binding Conditions to account for the full distribution of anaphors.

Burzio (1989) argues that Principles B and C of the Binding theory do not exist as independent principles. See also Burzio (1991), and Levinson (1991).

Enç (1989) and Saxon (1984) discuss the behavior of certain referentially dependent elements in languages other than English that are neither anaphors nor pronouns. *Carlson (1987) discusses the properties of the referentially dependent elements *same* and *different*. *Moltmann (1992) is a more recent approach to the same problem. Partee (1989) points out the existence of a large number of words that are neither pronominals nor anaphors, but that are referentially dependent.

Farmer (1987) points out problems with the use of indices to formulate both the binding relation and coreference. **Higginbotham (1980; 1982; 1985) develops a view of binding and coreference that is stated directly in terms of the antecedent/dependent relation, rather than in terms of coindexing.

Everaert (1986*a*, *b*), Giorgi (1984), Hellan (1986; 1988), Maling (1984), Napoli (1979), Rappoport (1986), and the papers in Koster and Reuland (1991) explore the behavior of anaphors with non-local antecedents in a range of languages. See Chapter 8 for additional discussion.

For discussion of the extent to which the distribution of PRO can be accounted for in terms of binding, see Koster (1984) and Lasnik (1992*a*).

Manzini and Wexler (1987) discuss the conditions on anaphora in a number of languages and consider the question of the learnability of the Binding theory, given that its conditions appear to differ in different languages.

A-Movement

1. Passive

1.1. Properties of the passive

Having developed Case theory, which concerns properties of A-positions, we are now in a position to consider the passive and other constructions that involve relations between A-positions. These constructions involve movements to A-positions, that is, **A-movements**.

Let us take the passive construction, illustrated in (1), as an exemplar.

(1)   *a.* John borrowed the car (from Susan).
       b. The car was borrowed (from Susan) by John.

A simple English passive sentence such as those given in (1) has the following properties.

(2)   *a.* The subject of the passive sentence bears the θ-role of the object adjacent to the verb in the active sentence.
      b. The object position adjacent to the verb is empty in the passive sentence.
      c. An idiom chunk, the subject of an ECM infinitive, or an expletive NP may become the subject of a passive.
      d. The structure of the passive conforms to X'-theory.

In the context of our theoretical assumptions, the first property may be understood in a number of ways. Assuming uniformity of θ-role assignment, we might conclude that at some level of syntactic representation the surface subject of a passive is the direct object. Call this level D-structure. The object is assigned its θ-role at D-structure and is then moved into the surface subject position, yielding another syntactic representation, which we will call S-structure. This has been the standard view of the passive in generative grammar, and it is the one that we will develop here.[1]

An initially plausible alternative is that what appears as the passive verb is really a verbal adjective that is derived from the active verb through a lexical relation. Such a possibility is plausible in light of the property in (2*d*). Given that there are adjectives derived from verbs, it is difficult to see how passive sentences of the form NP-*be*-Adj could *not* be generated as basic in some sense. Consider the following examples.

(3)   *a.* The thief was arrested.
      b. The thief was incompetent.
      c. the arrested thief
      d. the incompetent thief

Example (3*b*) shows an adjective in predicate position. Example (3*c*) shows that a passivized verb can be used adjectivally, parallel to the adjective in (3*d*). It therefore follows that (3*a*) could have the structure of (3*b*), and not be derived transformationally.

A lexical derivation of the passive has the consequence of assigning a thematic structure to the adjective that is related to the thematic structure of the verb in a systematic way. In particular, the θ-role assigned to the direct object by the active verb is assigned to the subject of the passive.

The crucial question is whether there *must* be movement in the derivation of the passive. Both of these approaches to the passive account for the empty object property noted in (2*b*). The third property, that expletive NPs and idiom chunks may become the subject of a passive, constitutes prima facie evidence for the movement analysis. Consider the following sentences.

(4)   *a.* They took considerable advantage of our indecision.
      b. Considerable advantage was taken of our indecision.

Idiomatic interpretation requires that at some level of representation there is a verb phrase of the form *take considerable advantage*. Such a level is D-structure in the movement analysis; on a lexical analysis along the lines outlined here, there is no obvious way to capture the idiomatic character of (4b), if we restrict the mapping between active and passive to involve just θ-roles.[2]

Similar conclusions can be drawn from examples such as the following.

(5) *a.* I expect Susan to win the race.
     b. Susan is expected to win the race.
(6) *a.* I expect there to be a solution to this problem.
     b. There is expected to be a solution to this problem.
(7) *a.* I expect it to be obvious that I can't solve this problem.
     b. It is expected to be obvious that I can't solve this problem.

In the ECM construction, the subject of the infinitive does not receive a θ-role from the higher verb. Therefore, a lexical derivation that simply maps the set of θ-roles associated with the active into a set of θ-roles for the passive cannot refer to the ECM subject.[3] The expletive subjects further complicate the matter, since they do not receive a θ-role even within their own clause. We have seen that an expletive is part of a chain, but it is difficult to see how the entire chain in the lower clause is to be related in terms of θ-roles to the subject position of the higher clause in which the expletive appears.

A traditional intuition is that passive is derived from active by turning the object into a subject. Another traditional intuition is that the subject of the ECM construction is in some sense the object of the higher verb. Both of these intuitions are mediated through the mechanism of government in the Principles and Parameters approach. ECM and the active–passive relation are not explicitly expressed in terms of the grammatical relations associated with the verb, but in terms of government. Thus, this approach avoids stating generalizations in terms of 'derived' relations such as subject and object, with rather clear consequences.

Within the current framework of assumptions, the analysis of the passive construction must involve movement between two A-positions that are present both at D-structure and S-structure. Exercise 4-1 deals with evidence that even in an analysis with a movement passive, there must be lexical passives as well.

1.2. Questions about movement

In the movement analysis of passives there are a number of questions that must be answered.

(8)   a. What moves? That is, what is the **target** of the movement?
And why is this the target?

   b. Where does the moved constituent move to? That is, what is
the **landing site** of the movement? And why is this the landing
site?

   c. Does the moved constituent have to move, and if so, why?

   d. Under what circumstances is movement allowed?

   Consider first the target. It appears that what moves is an NP that is
adjacent to the verb.

(9)   a. John put the book on the table.

   b. The book was put ___ on the table by John.

   c. *The table was put a book on ___ by John.

(10)   a. Susan gave the book to John.

   b. Susan gave John the book.

   c. The book was given ___ to John by Susan.

   d. John was given ___ the book by Susan.

   e. *John was given the book to ___ by Susan.

   f. ??The book was given John ___ by Susan.[4]

As we have seen, the NP that is adjacent to the verb has a special property
that distinguishes it from all other constituents: it is assigned structural
Case by the verb. It is natural to hypothesize that this fact is part of the
explanation for why just these NPs are targets of movement in the passive. In fact, the current theoretical framework provides us with very little
else in the way of formal mechanisms that we can use for this purpose.

The passive verb is adjectival in the sense that like an adjective it fails
to assign structural Case to its complement.[5] Nevertheless it is a verb, and
takes a complement in a structural Case position. We saw in Chapter 2
that only verbs, Infl, and prepositions assign structural Case. So, if the
direct object did not move from its D-structure position, it would fail to
get structural Case, and would violate the Case Filter. By assumption, the
direct object cannot receive an inherent Case or a default Case. (We will
see shortly that there may be reasons to modify this assumption.)

Let us say that the object of the passive lacks Case. The NP that moves
does so because it lacks structural Case. It moves to the subject position,
in which it receives structural Case, and we hypothesize that it moves
precisely in order to get Case assigned to it. The derivation of the passive
is thus more or less as follows, under the assumption that the subject
position is empty at D-structure.

(11)

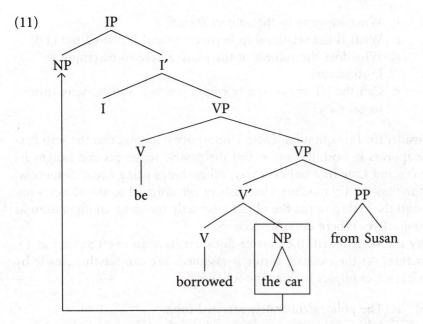

The notion that the NP moves in order to get Case is given some support by the fact that in passives whose direct objects cannot get Case, the direct object can remain in place. Compare the following examples.

(12) *a.* We believed John's story
      b. John's story was believed
      c. *It was believed [John's story].
(13) *a.* We believed that John told the truth.
      b. That John told the truth was believed.
      c. It was believed [that John told the truth].

As discussed in Chapter 2, CP cannot be assigned Case. Nevertheless, it can function as the argument of a verb. It is striking that in the passive, a CP argument remains in its θ-position while an NP does not. We attribute this difference to a difference between CP and NP with respect to Case assignment.

The movement analysis provides a unified answer to the first three questions in (8) in terms of Case theory. It raises additional questions, though.

(14) *a.* How do we explain why the object of the passive fails to get Case?

    b. What happens to the subject θ-role?

    c. What is the relationship between *be* and *borrowed* in (11)?

    d. Why does the subject of the passive have to be empty at D-structure?

    e. Can the NP move to any empty position with Case in order to get Case?

Consider the first question. From Uniformity it follows that the verb *borrow* appears in both the active and the passive sentences and assigns its θ-roles and Case in a uniform way, other things being equal. Somehow, in the passive, ACCUSATIVE Case fails to get assigned to the object, even though the verb governs the object in exactly the same configuration as in the active. Where does the Case go?

By the same token, the passive does not have an overt subject at D-structure, yet the external θ-role is assigned. We can see this clearly by comparing examples such as the following.

(15)   *a.* The police deliberately arrested John.
       b. John was deliberately arrested (by the police).
(16)   *a.* The police arrested John in order to prove a point.
       b. John was arrested (by the police) in order to prove a point.
(17)   *a.* John bought the piano to practice sonatas on it.
       b. The piano was bought (by John) to practice sonatas on it.

In (15), *deliberately* orients to the AGENT, as does the rationale clause in (16).[6] So the AGENT θ-role must be represented somehow. From Syntacticization it follows that the AGENT θ-role must be assigned to some constituent in the syntactic representation, at the level at which θ-roles are assigned in general, that is, D-structure. By Uniformity, this θ-role should be assigned to the (empty) subject position. But the *by*-phrase apparently expresses this θ-role also (or instead), which raises the question of whether it is correct to insist on strict Uniformity here.

It might be argued that knowledge of the argument structure of *arrest* is simply semantic, in that we know that there must be an ARRESTOR and an ARRESTEE. But this type of knowledge cannot in itself explain the possibility of subject-oriented adverbs or of *by*-phrases in passives. The very same kind of semantic knowledge is present in the **middle** construction, where the subject is the PATIENT and the verb is active and intransitive. Here subject-oriented adverbs and *by*-phrases are impossible.[7]

(18)   *a.* Someone bribed the bureaucrats (to keep them happy).
       b. The bureaucrats bribe easily (*by ordinary citizens).

     c. *Bureaucrats bribe easily to keep them happy.
     d. *Bureaucrats deliberately bribe easily.[8]
     e. The bureaucrats were bribed to keep them happy.
     f. The bureaucrats were deliberately bribed (by ordinary citizens).
(19) *a.* Someone burned down the buildings to collect insurance.[9]
     b. *The buildings burned down to collect insurance (by an arsonist).
     c. *The buildings deliberately burned down.
     d. The buildings were burned down to collect insurance (by an arsonist).
     e. The buildings were deliberately burned down (by an arsonist).

Even though we know that there must be a causal agent in these events, particularly when there is an agent-oriented adverb like *easily* or *deliberately*, there is no AGENT θ-role expressed in the middle sentence, hence none assigned by the verb, hence nothing for the rationale clause or *deliberately* to orient to.

    In order to account for the properties of the passive that we have reviewed here, let us suppose that the Case and the external θ-role are absorbed by the passive morphology.[10] To implement this idea, we may treat the passive morpheme *-en* literally as an argument, to which Case is assigned.[11] This move is intended to eliminate the need for the theoretically obscure notion of 'absorption'. The basic structures are shown in (20).

(20)

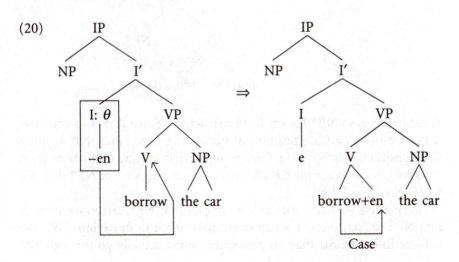

The core idea of this analysis recalls the proposal in Chapter 3 to the effect that Agr is in some sense the subject of the sentence. Analogously, suppose that the passive morpheme is also an argument, in effect the external argument of the verb. It absorbs the external θ-role. After adjunction to V, this same morpheme is in a position to be assigned structural Case by the verb, since it is now adjacent to the verb. The observed properties follow directly, and the questions in (14a) and (14b) are answered.

Now let us consider the status of the structure in (20) with respect to the auxiliary *be*. Since the verb with passive morphology immediately follows *be*, it is reasonable to assume that this IP is a complement of *be*. The structure is given in (21) after movement of the passive morpheme.

(21)

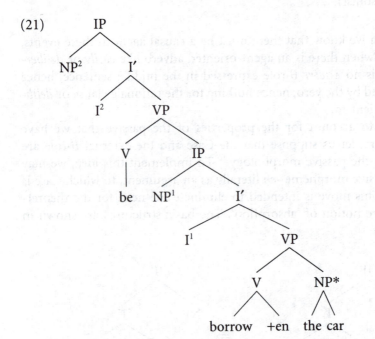

What happens to NP* *the car* in this structure? Since it fails to get Case, it must move to a Case position or violate the Case Filter. NP^1 is not a Case position, but NP^2 is a Case position if I^2 is Agr, or if there is an external Case assigner for NP^2. So there is a landing site for NP* that will satisfy the Case Filter.

Given what we have just said, it appears that NP* can move directly into NP^2; in fact, there is no apparent basis for it to move into NP^1. We will see in § 4 below that the movement must actually go through NP^1

and then to NP². This conclusion in turn raises questions about how precisely to understand the explanation given for movement of the NP, which is that it moves in order to get Case. While such an explanation can be sustained, it requires a rather different conception of 'movement' than we have been working with to this point.

You should be able to do Exercises 4-2 and 4-3 at this point.

1.3. Chains

Up to now, our discussion of the passive construction has assumed implicitly that θ-roles are assigned at D-structure, while structural Case is assigned at S-structure. On this basis, we explain how it is that the S-structure subject gets NOMINATIVE Case while it bears the direct object θ-role. The structure in (22) illustrates; some details are omitted.

(22)

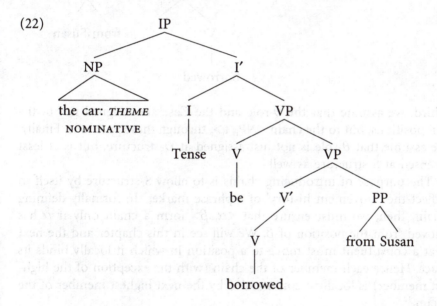

This structure contains an apparent paradox. Recall the Visibility Thesis of Chapter 2. We concluded that in order to get a θ-role an argument must be Case-marked. In order for the S-structure subject *the car* to get the θ-role THEME it must be Case-marked in the position where THEME is assigned. On the current account this position is the D-structure object, to which Case cannot be assigned. Thus the paradox.

We can eliminate the paradox while maintaining all of our other assumptions if we make several other assumptions. First, let us assume that when the NP moves it leaves behind a copy, which we will call **trace**, and represent as *t*. Second, assume that this trace is coindexed with the NP, so that the two form a chain. The structure is thus (23), not (22).

(23)

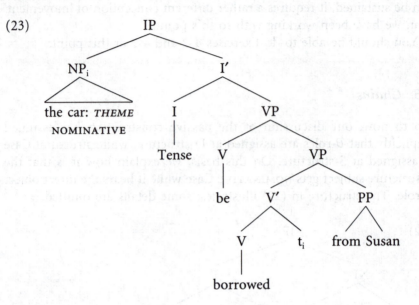

Third, we assume that the θ-role and the Case are assigned not to the NP positions, but to the chain $<NP_i, t_i>$, through these positions. Finally, we assume that θ-role is not just assigned at D-structure, but is at least licensed at S-structure as well.

The purpose of introducing chains is to allow S-structure by itself to reflect the 'movement history' of a phrase marker. In formally defining chain, then, we must ensure that $<\alpha, \beta>$ form a chain only if α has moved from the position of β. We will see in this chapter and the next that a constituent must move to a position in which it locally binds its trace. Hence each member of the chain (with the exception of the highest member) is locally c-commanded by the next highest member of the chain.[12]

(24) $C = (\alpha_1, \alpha_2, \ldots, \alpha_n)$ is a chain iff, for $1 \le i \le n$, α_i is the local binder of α_{i+1}.

This definition supplants the simpler one in Chapter 2, § 5.3.

An interesting consequence of the theory of chains is that it is no longer clear that it is necessary to assign θ-roles in D-structure at all. Since the assignment of θ-roles is in large part what defines D-structure, the possibility exists that D-structure is not an independent level of syntactic representation. In such a case, chains would be produced not through movement (that is, the D-structure/S-structure mapping), but through an operation applying to S-structures. We return to this question in Chapter 10.

The chain has a θ-role because the verb assigns a θ-role to the object position. The chain has NOMINATIVE Case because Infl assigns Case to the subject position. Notice that because of Visibility it is crucial that θ-roles and structural Case be assigned at S-structure.

On the chain analysis, the argument structure (in particular, the thematic structure) associated with a verb must be satisfied by the appropriate syntactic arguments at D-structure and at S-structure. That is, if a V selects an argument, that argument must be present at D-structure, in the form of an overt NP, and at S-structure, in the form of a trace. Without this requirement, i.e. that there is a trace, we could not guarantee that there would actually be a chain produced by movement. By Uniformity, it is natural to generalize this requirement to 'every level of syntactic representation.'[13] In this sense, the selectional requirements associated with a lexical entry are projected onto all syntactic structures. We call this the **Projection Principle**.

(25)   Projection Principle: the selectional requirements of a lexical
       item are projected onto every level of syntactic representation.

From this principle it immediately follows that if a verb selects an argument and that argument undergoes movement, there will be a trace in the argument position at the level or levels of representation in which the argument appears in its landing site. Hence all movement produces chains that contains traces. Moreover, by Syntacticization, if a lexical item projects an argument, then that argument must be present in the syntactic structure. It is not sufficient that there be an argument expressed in the semantic interpretation, for example.

Introducing chains raises important questions regarding the contribution that each link in the chain makes to the well-formedness of the chain in its entirety. Suppose, for example, that NP_i and t_i in a chain $<NP_i, t_i>$ are both in A-positions to which a θ-role can be assigned; can the chain have two θ-roles? In general the answer to this question is 'no,' and the reason typically given is that a sentence such as (26)—

(26)   John hit

—cannot mean 'John hit himself', derived as in (27).

(27)   [e]   hit   John$_i$ ⇒   John$_i$ hit   t$_i$
    AGENT   *PATIENT*   *AGENT*   *PATIENT*

The chain <John$_i$, t$_i$> in (27) has two θ-roles assigned to it, one through the subject position and one through the object position.[14]

The possibility of a derivation such as (27) depends on there being a provision in the theory for an NP with structural Case to move to another structural Case position. If this possibility exists, then (27) will have to be ruled out. The obvious way to do this is to require that a chain can have no more than one θ-role, where we understand an unmoved NP (an NP *in situ*) as being a chain with one member. Moreover, a chain must have at least one θ-role, which means that it must have Case assigned to it, so that the Visibility Condition is satisfied. These two requirements constitute the θ-Criterion.[15]

(28) θ-Criterion: Each argument α appears in a chain containing a unique visible θ-position P, and each θ-position P is visible in a chain containing a unique argument α.

Formulated in terms of chains, the θ-Criterion reduces to the requirement that a chain can have at most one θ-position, and each θ-position is visible.[16]

(29) θ-Criterion: A chain has at most one θ-position; a θ-position is visible in its maximal chain.

The term 'maximal' in (29) is required on the assumption that any set of adjacent links in a chain forms a chain; the chain of interest here is the longest chain in which the θ-position appears. Notice that the θ-Criterion rules out the possibility that in the syntactic passive the external θ-role is assigned to the subject position. This definition in terms of chains supplants the definition in Chapter 2 in terms of arguments.

Summarizing, the Projection Principle ensures that every θ-role will be assigned to some argument chain, while the θ-Criterion requires that exactly one θ-role will be assigned to any argument chain. Since the chain is assigned a θ-role, it must be visible, which means that it must be assigned Case. What is left open is whether the θ-role and Case can be assigned to the chain at any position of the chain, and whether there can be more than one Case position. If we independently rule out movement from a non-argument position to an argument position, then the position to which the θ-role is assigned must be the lowest in the chain, that is, α_n in (24). Our discussion of A-movement has already shown that Case can be assigned to the highest member of the chain, α_1; we will see in Chapter 6 that where there is movement to a non-argument position, Case will be assigned to α_n. Whether there can be more than one Case position is a more complex question to which we will return later in this chapter.

At this point you should be able to do Exercise 4-4.

2. Raising

A crucial property of our analysis of the passive is that in a certain sense there is no such theoretical entity as the 'passive construction.' What exists in the theory is government, Case, θ-role assignment, and movement chains. The passive construction arises when certain conditions are simultaneously in effect, in particular, when the Case and θ-role are 'absorbed.'

Such an approach allows for the possibility that NPs may fail to get Case in other ways. If so, we would expect that they would move (if they could) into a Case position. Such an expectation is satisfied in case of Raising, the phenomenon illustrated in (30).

(30) a. *John* seems to like beer a lot.
      b. *Susan* seems to have been elected president.
      c. *The fat* seems to be in the fire [Idiomatic].
      d. *There* seems to have been a lot of interest in that problem.
      e. *It* seems to be obvious that John will win.

In each case the subject of *seems* must be understood as the syntactic subject of the infinitive. But this fact does not show that there is A-movement. There is a familiar way in which the situation illustrated in (30) can arise: control, in which the subject of the infinitive is an empty pronominal anaphor, called PRO, that is coindexed with the subject (see Chapter 3, § 6). Compare the following.

(31) a. John$_i$ expects [$_{CP}$ PRO$_i$ to be elected president].
      b. *The fat$_i$ expects [$_{CP}$ PRO$_i$ to be in the fire].

     c. *There$_i$ expects [$_{CP}$ PRO$_i$ to be a lot of interest in that
       problem].
     d. *It$_i$ expects [$_{CP}$ PRO$_i$ to be obvious that John will win].
(32) *a.* John$_i$ managed [$_{CP}$ PRO$_i$ to be elected president].
     b. *The fat$_i$ manages [$_{CP}$ PRO$_i$ to be in the fire].
     c. *There$_i$ manages [$_{CP}$ PRO$_i$ to be a lot of interest in that
       problem].
     d. *It$_i$ manages [$_{CP}$ PRO$_i$ to be obvious that John will win].

The ungrammatical examples show that there are NPs that cannot be the
subject of a verb that appears in a Control structure. From this it is concluded that *seems* cannot be in a Control structure. The argument is as
follows.

(33)   *a.* *expects/manages* appear in a (subject) Control construction;
     b. *it, there, the fat* (Idiomatic) cannot appear with *expect*;
     c. the only reason why something cannot appear in a Control
       construction is because it cannot be the antecedent of the
       subject of the infinitive;
     d. *it, there, the fat* (Idiomatic) can appear with *seem*;
     e. therefore *seem* does not appear in a Control construction.

The tacit assumption (33c) is essential for the conclusion. If there is
another means of ruling out the ungrammatical sentences in (31)/(32),
then they could be Control structures. For example, note that *expect* and
manage impose an animacy requirement on their subjects. Since these
NPs are not animate, they cannot be subjects of *expect* or *manage*. Suppose that *seem* places no such requirements on its subject. Then anything,
including an idiom chunk and *there*, could appear as its subject.

However, it is possible to construct examples where animacy considerations do not rule out the sentence, and Control is still not possible.
These are illustrated below.[17]

(34)   You can't be kind without [$_S$ PRO being cruel first].
(35) *a.* *There can't be peace without [$_S$ PRO being war first].
     b. There can't be peace without [$_S$ there being war first].
(36) *a.* *It can't be obvious that John left without [$_S$ PRO being
      obvious that there is something wrong].
     b. It can't be obvious that John left without [$_S$ it being obvious
      that there is something wrong].

(37) a. *It can't be obvious that John left without [$_s$ PRO being regretted that John left].
   b. That John left can't be obvious without being regretted.
   c. It can't be obvious that John left without [$_s$ it being regretted that John left].

(35b) shows that *there* can be the subject of a *without*-clause. PRO controlled by *there* should also be grammatical, a prediction that is tested in (35a). The ungrammaticality of (35a) is a failure of Control: *there* cannot be a controller of PRO. Similarly for expletive *it*, as shown in (36a). Hence the Control analysis for *seems* can be ruled out, on the assumption that subject Control and the type of Control involving the *without*-clause are the same phenomenon.

If we conclude that *seems* does not involve Control, we are left with movement as the only way to explain the properties of the subject of *seems* within this framework. In order for the movement analysis to go through, we must show that the subject of *seems* fails to get a θ-role, so that the θ-Criterion is not violated. We must also show how the subject of the infinitive fails to get Case.

Examples such as the following show that the subject of *seems* is not a θ-position.[18]

(38) a. It seems that John is hungry.
   b. *John seems that he is hungry.
   c. *That John is hungry seems.

Only an expletive *it* may appear in the subject position when there is a tensed S complement. But there is no thematic chain in this construction. In contrast with extraposition, *it* here is not part of an expletive chain with the θ-role assigned to the subject position. Cf. (39).

(39) a. It is obvious that John is hungry.
   b. That John is hungry is obvious.

As far as Case is concerned, it is straightforward to say that *seems* does not assign structural Case to a complement as a lexical property. In a sense *seems* is intransitive. We now have the conditions for A-movement, which is illustrated in (40) for Raising.

(40)

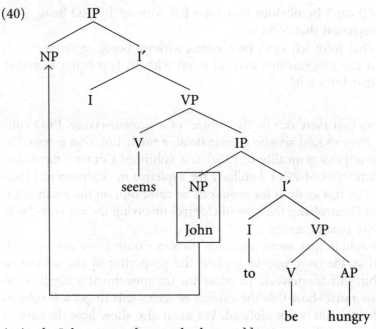

(41) [IP John_i seems [IP t_i to be hungry]].

(41) shows the trace of the raised subject *John* in S-structure.

Note that the conclusion that the subject of *seem* is not a θ-position has consequences for the applicability of the Projection Principle introduced earlier. A sentence must have a subject whether or not the predicate assigns a θ-role to the subject. The fact that every sentence must have a subject is therefore not reducible to the selectional requirements of lexical items. In addition to the Projection Principle, then, we need an additional principle requiring a subject in every clause. This requirement is often called the Extended Projection Principle.[19]

At this point you should be able to do Exercise 4-5.

3. Constraints on A-movement

Let us return now to the question of what landing sites are available to a given NP that lacks Case. To simplify the discussion, we observe first of all that the pattern that results from A-movement is remarkably like one that we have already looked at, that of binding. Both involve a discontinuous relationship between two positions that are coindexed.

(42)   a.   The car$_i$ was borrowed t$_i$.
　　　 b.   John$_i$ cut himself$_i$.
　　　 c.   John$_i$ thinks that he$_i$ will win.

Crucially, the chain in (42a) and the antecedent–anaphor link in (42b) are local, in the sense that they involve constituents of the same clause. We will see that this locality is quite systematic.

By analogy with our discussion of binding, we will consider three situations. In the first, the NP moves out of the subject position of a tensed S.

(43)   a.   [e] seems [$_{CP}$ (that) John is hungry] $\Rightarrow$
　　　　　　 *John$_i$ seems [$_{CP}$ (that) t$_i$ is hungry]
　　　 b.   [e] is believed [$_{CP}$ (that) John is hungry] $\Rightarrow$
　　　　　　 *John$_i$ is believed [$_{CP}$ (that) t$_i$ is hungry]

Here we see a pattern that is very reminiscent of the binding of anaphors. When the subject NP is the subject of an infinitival IP complement, movement is unproblematic.

(44)   a.   [e] seems [$_{IP}$ John to be hungry] $\Rightarrow$
　　　　　　 John$_i$ seems [$_{IP}$ t$_i$ to be hungry]
　　　 b.   [e] is believed [$_{IP}$ John to be hungry] $\Rightarrow$
　　　　　　 John$_i$ is believed [$_{IP}$ t$_i$ to be hungry]

The pattern noted here can be accounted for if we assume that the trace of an NP moved to an argument position is an anaphor. The moved NP must then bind its trace within the GC of the trace; this is possible in (44), but not in (43), just as with overt anaphors in comparable examples.

(45)   a.   *John believes that himself is hungry.
　　　 b.   *John and Susan believe that each other is hungry.
(46)   a.   John believes himself to be hungry.
　　　 b.   John and Susan believe each other to be hungry.

There are other principles that might also be responsible for some of the examples in (43). For instance, the movement of the subject of a tensed complement into the subject position of *seem* creates a chain that has two Case positions; moreover, movement over *that* produces a so-called *that-t* effect.[20] If the fact that trace of A-movement is an anaphor also rules these examples out, then the redundancy raises questions as to the correctness of the account.

But if NP trace is an anaphor, we predict that NP will not be able to move over the subject of an infinitive, since the subject determines the GC of the anaphor/trace. Suppose the verb of the embedded clause is passive and the subject of the infinitive is empty or expletive. Then the subject need not get Case, since there is no NP in this position that needs to be visible in order to get a θ-role.

(47)   [e] seems [$_{IP}$ {[e]/it} to be disliked Susan]

If *Susan* moves directly into the higher [e], we get the following, which is ungrammatical because of Condition A of the Binding theory.

(48)   *Susan$_i$ seems [$_{IP}$ it to be disliked t$_i$].

Notice that in this derivation, *Susan* is assigned only one Case, that assigned to the position occupied by t$_i$. But if *Susan* moves through the lower empty subject, we get the following.

(49)   Susan$_i$ seems [$_{IP}$ t$_i'$ to be disliked t$_i$].

Here, t$_i'$ is the local antecedent of t$_i$, while *Susan$_i$* is the local antecedent of t$_i'$. Neither link violates Condition A of the Binding theory, taking both of the traces to be anaphors. To the extent it is not possible to rule out (48) on other grounds, we have further evidence consistent with the claim that NP trace is an anaphor.

Finally, we predict that A-movement cannot extract an NP from any position within a tensed S, again because the tensed S defines the GC for the trace of the NP. The example in (50) confirms this prediction.

(50)   [e] seems that John dislikes Susan $\Rightarrow$
        *Susan$_i$ seems that John dislikes t$_i$

Again, in this example the chain <*Susan$_i$*, t$_i$> is assigned two Cases, which might be problematic. But let us consider an example in which the moved NP is in a Case-less position and all of the other NPs have Case.

(51) [e] seems that John is angry Susan

Here, *angry*, being an adjective, fails to assign Case to *Susan*. *John* receives Case as the subject of the tensed S. If we move *Susan*, we derive an ungrammatical sentence.

(52) *Susan$_i$ seems that John is angry t$_i$.

In this example it appears that there is no explanation for the ungram- maticality other than the fact that the NP has moved too far from its trace, or, alternatively, that the trace appears in S-structure too far from its antecedent. Thus, while there may be alternative accounts of some of the examples that we have examined, the hypothesis that the trace of A-movement is an anaphor appears to provide a comprehensive account of the phenomena.

Let us return to an issue raised in connection with (21) of § 1.3, also exemplified by (49). While the movement of the Caseless NP to its ultimate landing site can be understood as satisfying the requirement that the NP receive Case at S-structure, intermediate movements cannot themselves be understood in this sense. In particular, the movement of *Susan* to the subject position of *to be disliked* is not movement to a Case position. This is why *Susan* must move into the subject of *seems*, in fact.

The classical approach to this situation is to assume that all movements are optional and untriggered. This is the theory of Move α. A chain is the consequence of a sequence of independent movements.[21] Whether or not a movement or sequence of movements is legitimate is determined by the resulting configuration. So, (48) violates Condition A of the Binding theory, while (49) does not. By the same token, the movement of an NP to a Case position is optional; if it lacks Case and fails to move, there is a violation of the Case Filter. If it lacks Case and moves to a Case posi- tion, it satisfies the Case Filter.

But suppose that the NP has Case; can it move anyway? On one inter- pretation of the A-movement analysis, the answer would be 'no,' because the NP already has Case and does not have to move. But if movement is optional, it is not clear what will stop A-movement of a Case-marked NP, except some constraint against the assignment of more than one Case to a chain. This is a complex question and its resolution depends on a number of aspects of the theory that we have not yet discussed. We will return to it in Chapter 10, § 4.

At this point you should be able to do Exercises 4-6 through 4-8.

4. Unaccusatives

As we have seen in the case of passives and Raising, A-movement occurs if an NP lacks structural Case and there is a local Case position that is not assigned a θ-role. **Unaccusativity** concerns the fact that such a configuration can be associated with the lexical entry of a verb. In such a case, the S-structure subject originates as a D-structure direct object that lacks ACCUSATIVE Case (that is, it is 'unaccusative'); such verbs are also called ergative verbs. Passives are a class of derived unaccusatives. Verbs that lack D-structure direct objects are called **unergatives;**[22] they are true intransitives. Some of the strongest evidence for unaccusativity comes from Italian, in which the subject of intransitives may appear postverbally.

(53)   *a.* Arriva Giovanni.
         arrives Giovanni
         'Giovanni arrives.'
       b. Telefona   Giovanni.
         telephones Giovanni
         'Giovanni telephones.'

Italian also has a construction in which a clitic, *ne* 'of it/them', is moved from a direct object NP and adjoins to the verb. Crucially, *ne*-cliticization can only take place from a direct object, not from a subject, an adjunct, or a postposed subject.[23]

(54)   *a.* Gianni trascorrerà tre   settimane a Milano.
         Gianni will-spend three weeks   in Milano
       b. *Gianni trascorrerà tre   a Milano.
         Gianni will-spend three in Milano
       c. Gianni ne   trascorrerà tre   a Milano.
         Gianni of-them will-spend three in Milano
(55)   *a.* Tre   settimane passano rapidamente.
         three weeks   elapse rapidly
       b. Tre   passano rapidamente.
         three elapse   rapidly
       c. *Tre ne   passano rapidamente.
         three of-them elapse rapidly
(56)   *a.* Gianni è rimasto   tre   settimane a Milano.
         Gianni is remained three weeks   in Milano

    b. Gianni è rimasto   tre   a Milano.
        Gianni is remained three in Milano
    c. *Gianni ne   è rimasto   tre   a Milano.
        Gianni of-them is remained three in Milano

However, as the examples in (57) show, there is an exception to the last statement; the postposed subjects of certain verbs allow *ne*-cliticization.

(57)   *a.* Sono passate tre   settimane.
        are   elapsed three weeks
        'Three weeks elapsed.'
    b. *Sono passate tre.
        are   elapsed three
    c. Ne   sono passate tre.
        of-them are   elapsed three
(58)   *a.* Ne   arrivano molti.
        of-them arrive   many
        'Many of them arrive.'
    b. *Ne   telefonano molti.
        of-them telephone many
        'Many of them telephone.'

   We do not want to stipulate that certain verbs are exceptional in allowing *ne*-cliticization *per se*; this does not explain anything. Rather, let us suppose that the postposed subjects in question are direct objects at D-structure. *Ne*-cliticization applies at this point. The evidence shows that these NPs must move to subject position; therefore, we assume that they lack Case as a consequence of a lexical property of the verb. By the same token, the subject position must lack a θ-role, so that there will be no violation of the θ-Criterion. The derivation of (58*a*) is shown in (59).[24]

(59) $[_{IP}$ [e] $[_{VP}$ arrivano $[_{NP}$ molti ne$_i]_j$:θ]] $\Rightarrow$
      $[_{IP}$ [e] $[_{VP}$ ne$_i$ arrivano] $[_{NP}$ molti t$_i]_j$:θ] $\Rightarrow$
      $[_{IP}$ [molti t$_i]_j$ $[_{VP}$ ne$_i$ arrivano t$_j$:θ]] $\Rightarrow$
      $[_{IP}$ t$_j{'}$ $[_{VP}[_{VP}$ ne$_i$ arrivano t$_j$:θ]] [molti t$_i]_j]$

   This correlation of Case with θ-role has come to be known as Burzio's Generalization.[25]

(60)   A verb Case-marks its object if and only if it θ-marks its subject.[26]

Under this analysis, certain verbs have the property of unaccusativity. It is striking that in Italian, those verbs that reveal this property under *ne*-cliticization are also the verbs that take the auxiliary verb *essere* as contrasted with *avere*. We hypothesize that *essere* indicates that the subject is not a D-structure subject; note that it appears in the passive, too.

(61)   a. Giovanni è/*ha arrivato.
           Giovanni is/has arrived
       b. Giovanni *è/ha telefonato.
           Giovanni is/has telephoned
       c. Giovanni è/*ha stato arrestato.
           Giovanni is/has been arrested

If we assume strict Uniformity, we would expect that unaccusativity will occur in every language. In some but not all languages there will be particular syntactic constructions that will allow us to find evidence that A-movement occurs in unaccusatives. Such evidence can in fact be found in Japanese. There is an interesting difference between verbs of motion involving a GOAL and verbs of motion that do not. Consider the sentences in (62).[27]

(62)   a. Gakusei-ga   sannin sensei-o   hihanshita.
           student-NOM 3-CL   teacher-ACC criticized
           'Three students criticized the teacher.'
           'The student criticized three teachers.'
       b. Sannin gakusei-ga   sensei-o   hihanshita.
           3-CL   student-NOM teacher-ACC criticized
           'Three students criticized the teacher.'
           'The student criticized three teachers.'
       c. Gakusei-ga   sensi-o   sannin hihanshita.
           student-NOM teacher-ACC 3-CL   criticized
           *'Three students criticized the teacher.'
           'The student criticized three teachers.'
       d. Sensei-ga   gakusei-ni sannin hihansareta.
           teacher-NOM student-by 3-CL   criticized-were
           'Three teachers were criticized by the student.'
           *'The teacher was criticized by three students.'

The word *sannin* is a numeral quantifier (NQ) meaning 'three people'; it contains a classifier selected by the type of nominal being quantified, in this case, humans. When the NQ and the NP c-command one another, the NQ can be construed with the NP.[28] This constraint accounts for

(62*a*), assuming the structure in (63), and assuming that a constituent adjoined to VP c-commands within the IP.[29]

(63) [IP student I [VP 3-CL [VP teacher criticize]]]

In (62*b*) the same c-command relations hold if we assume that the NQ is moved into an adjoined position to the left of the subject NP, so that its trace c-commands the subject and the object. (64) illustrates.

(64)

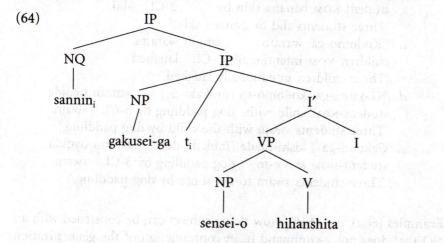

In (62*c*) the NQ is inside of the VP and thus cannot c-command the subject, which explains the fact that it can only be construed with the object. And in (62*d*), the NQ c-commands the trace of the subject, thereby accounting for the interpretation. (65) illustrates.

(65)

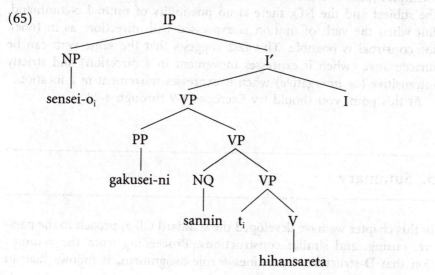

Tsujimura uses the distribution of NQ to probe for the presence of NP-traces. Consider the following.

(66) a. Gakusei-ga   Tokyo-ni sannin tsuita.
    student-NOM Tokyo-at 3-CL   arrived
    'Three students arrived at Tokyo.'

  b. Gakusei-ga   banana-no   kawa-de sannin subetta.
    student-NOM banana-skin by   3-CL   slid
    'Three students slid by banana skin.'

  c. *Kodomo-ga wazato   sannin waratta.
    children-NOM intentionally 3-CL   laughed
    'Three children intentionally laughed.'

  d. *Gakusei-ga kodomo-to (inukaki-de)   sannin oyoida.
    student-NOM child-with dog paddling by 3-CL   swam
    'Three students swam with the child by dog paddling.'

  e. Gakusei-ga   kishi-made (inukaki-de)   sannin oyoida.
    student-NOM shore-to   dog paddling by 3-CL   swam
    'Three students swam to the shore by dog paddling.'

Examples (66a) and (66b) show that a subject can be construed with an NQ that does not c-command it, in contradiction of the generalization that the NQ and the NP must mutually c-command one another. This example is explained if the subject in fact moves from a position internal to the VP to subject position, as in the comparable Italian examples. Examples (66c) and (66d) show that when there is an adverbial between the subject and the NQ, there is no possibility of mutual c-command. But when the verb of motion is expressed with direction, as in (66e), the construal is possible. This fact suggests that the same verb can be unaccusative (when it expresses movement in a direction) and strictly intransitive (or unergative) when it expresses movement in a location.

At this point you should try Exercises 4-9 through 4-11.

5. Summary

In this chapter we have developed the standard GB approach to the passive, raising, and similar constructions. Proceeding from the assumption that D-structure determines θ-role assignment, it follows that an argument that is not in its position with respect to the verb that assigns it a θ-role must undergo movement from that position. Analyses along these lines have been developed for passive, raising, and unaccusatives, among others.

Beginning from the assumption that movement is optional and that landing sites are arbitrary, we are led to certain constraints that produce the more restricted types of movements actually seen. Movement from a θ-position must be to a non-θ-position, a generalization that can be made to follow from the θ-Criterion and the Projection Principle. A-movements are subject to locality constraints, which can be subsumed under the Binding theory if A-movement leaves a trace and that trace is an anaphor.

APPENDIX A: NP MOVEMENT AND QUIRKY CASE

As we have seen, the theory of Case in the GB/PPT framework rests on the following two general propositions:

(A)   Subjects and objects are assigned structural Case at S-structure, regardless of their θ-roles. Subjects are assigned NOMINATIVE Case, while objects are assigned ACCUSATIVE Case.

(B)   All other governed NPs are assigned inherent Case at D-structure, which correlates with their θ-roles.

The theoretical apparatus for (A) involves government and adjacency, while the theoretical apparatus for (B) remains to be specified.

In this appendix we briefly review some empirical phenomena that pose some difficulty for the simple view expressed in (A) and (B). These phenomena fall into two categories, characterized by the fact that in each instance, the Case that appears on an NP is not the one that would be expected given its grammatical role.[30] First the object in some instances is marked with other than ACCUSATIVE Case. For example, some objects in Russian are marked with DATIVE, others with GENITIVE, and still others with INSTRUMENTAL. The direct object in Icelandic may be marked DATIVE or even NOMINATIVE under certain circumstances. Second, the subject in some instances is marked with other than NOMINATIVE Case. For example, some subjects in Russian and Icelandic appear in the DATIVE Case.

We conclude with a discussion of the interaction between NP movement and non-standard or 'quirky' case, showing that the view that NP movement (in the passive, at least) is triggered by a need for an NP to get Case at S-structure may not be completely satisfactory.

A.1. Non-ACCUSATIVE objects

In Russian transitive verbs typically assign ACCUSATIVE Case to their objects.[31] There are several exceptions, however.

(*a*) A negated verb assigns GENITIVE to its direct object when the direct object is in the scope of the negation. For example:

(67) *a.* Ja   ne vižu   knigu.
      I-NOM not see-PRES book-ACC
      'I don't see the book.'
    b. Ja   ne vižu   knigi.
      I-NOM not see-PRES book-GEN
      'I don't see a/any book.'

If the NP is marked with the ACCUSATIVE, it must have a definite interpretation. However, since definiteness is not overtly marked in Russian, a GENITIVE NP may be interpreted as definite.

(68) Ja ne čital   knig.
    I not read-PAST book-PL-GEN
    'I didn't read any books.'
    'I didn't read the books.'

In this case, we say that negation has 'ambiguous scope.' When negation does not take scope over the direct object, the interpretation is one in which there is an existential presupposition object (i.e. 'I don't see the book'); when negation does take scope over the direct object, there is no existential presupposition (i.e. 'I don't see any books' = 'there are no books that I see'). We thus have the following general pattern.

(69) No negation: $\exists x$ I like x
    In the scope of negation: NEG $\exists x$ (I like x)
    Not in the scope of negation: $\exists x$ I (NEG like) x

(*b*) Certain lexical items may assign GENITIVE to their direct object. For example:

(70) *a.* On   ždet   podrugu.
      he-NOM waits-for-PRES friend-ACC
      'He is waiting for (female) friend.'
    b. On ždet   otveta   (na vopros).
      he waits-for-PRES answer-GEN (to question-ACC)
      'He is waiting for an answer (to the question).'

(*c*) Certain lexical items assign INSTRUMENTAL or DATIVE Case to their direct object.

(71)   *a.* On   vredil   ljudjam.
       he-NOM harm-PAST people-DAT
       'He harmed people.'
       b. On   zanimalsja russkim   jazykom.
       he-NOM study-PAST Russian-INSTR language-INSTR
       'He studied Russian.'

A crucial fact about the lexically assigned non-ACCUSATIVE Case is that it cannot be replaced by the GENITIVE in the scope of negation.

(72)   *a.* On   ne   vredil   ljudjam/*ljudej.
       he-NOM NEG harm-PAST people-DAT/*-GEN
       b. On   ne zanimalsja russkim jazykom/*russkovo jazyka.
       he-NOM not study-PAST Russian-INSTR
       language-INSTR/Russian-GEN language-GEN

These facts suggest that GENITIVE Case in the scope of negation should be treated as a structural Case, that is, as an alternative to ACCUSATIVE.[32] In the GB framework of Case theory, this approach raises a number of issues, all of which turn on the assumption that structural Case is assigned under government to the complement of V. It is assumed that the V governs the direct object at D-structure, and assigns a unique θ-role to it. We must somehow produce two S-structure configurations from this single D-structure when there is negation, such that the correlation between the scope interpretation of negation and the marking of Case can be maintained. Suppose that negation fails to take scope over the direct object when it is adjoined to the verb at D-structure, and it does take scope when it is higher than the VP, as illustrated in (73).

(73)   *a.* No scope:

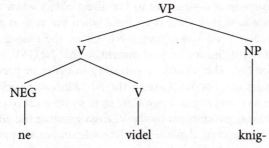

b. Scope:

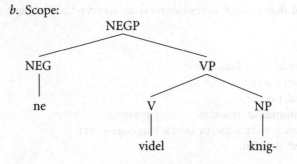

Notice that we have assumed that NEG is a head in (73*b*) so that it will c-command the direct object in its scope.

Here we have two different structures, but in both, the NP *knig-* is the complement of a verb. We could use these two structures to account for the difference in Case assignment, but to do so, we must allow the GENITIVE Case assigned under the scope of negation to pre-empt the ACCUSATIVE structural Case. That is, there must be an explicit ordering, such that the ACCUSATIVE is in some sense a type of 'default' Case assignment; it is the default that is assigned to a governed NP complement of V.

An alternative approach would prevent ACCUSATIVE from being assigned to the direct object in the scope of negation. Suppose that the verb raises to NEG prior to Case assignment, producing the S-structure in (74) from the D-structure in (73*b*).

(74)

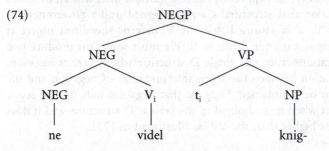

Given the two structures it is again possible to produce a difference in structural Case. ACCUSATIVE is assigned at S-structure to the direct object when the verb directly governs it, while GENITIVE Case is assigned when the verb is adjoined to NEG. In the latter case, V does not govern NP. Given the raising of V to NEG, we could extend our definition of government so that NEG+V_i is in fact the closest governor for NP. This would be necessary in order to prevent the trace of V from assigning ACCUSATIVE Case to the NP. Moreover, since V m-commands NP, it governs it and could assign Case to it, so we must require that the combine NEG+V blocks government by the V. Even granting the possibility of such an analysis it is not clear that the purely configurational approach is correct, in view of sentences like the following.

(75)   On   ne xočet   slušat'   muzyki.
       he-NOM not want-PRES to-listen to-music-GEN

Here, the GENITIVE NP is not an argument of the negated verb (at S-structure).

The other issue that must be considered is why ACCUSATIVE is not assigned to all direct objects. Again, there are two approaches. On the one hand, we could assume that particular verbs lexically specify a Case to assign to their complements. This Case would be assigned prior to structural Case assignment, and would 'pre-empt' structural Case. Once again, structural Case would be the governed default.

But there is also a purely configurational solution that relies on our prior distinction between structural and inherent Case. Suppose that these NPs are not in fact sisters of the verb, but adjuncts to V'. As such, they will not receive structural ACCUSATIVE Case, but inherent Case. Since they are not in a structural Case position, they will not be assigned GENITIVE Case by NEG+V. If this view is correct, we would expect that the verbs that assign DATIVE Case to their objects fall into a particular semantic class, while those that assign INSTRUMENTAL fall into another semantic class. In fact, Neidle (1988) notes that 'the verbs that govern the Genitive tend to be verbs of desire, aim, request or achievement' (p. 31). INSTRUMENTAL is used with certain verbs that express 'authority' (e.g. *upravljat'* 'to govern'), and has a number of more diverse uses as well.[33] Whether such a syntactic/thematic correlation can be maintained in general is a question that requires considerably more analysis than we can undertake here.

A second instance of non-ACCUSATIVE Case assignment to direct objects is found in Icelandic.[34] Some examples are given in (76).

(76)   *a.* Flugfélagið fækkaði   ferðunum   um þriðjung.
           the-airline decreased the-trips-DAT by one-third
           'The airline decreased the number of trips by one-third.'
       b. Skipstjórinn   sökkti skipinu.
           the-captain-NOM sank   the-ship-DAT
           'The captain sank the ship.'

Thus Icelandic raises the same problems with respect to object Case as Russian does. What is even more problematic about Icelandic Case, however, is that in passive and other constructions in which the object θ-role is expressed on the subject, some subjects fail to show NOMINATIVE Case, but instead show the Case of the direct object of the active. We will return to this point in A.3 below.

If the assignment of Cases other than ACCUSATIVE to complements cannot be accounted for in strictly configurational terms, then it appears that the analysis of Case is somewhat more complicated than it originally appeared to be. First, we have inherent Case, which is assigned on the basis of θ-role. Second, we have lexically assigned structural Case, which may or may not be reduced to inherent Case. Third, we have GENITIVE of negation, which is pre-empted by inherent Case and lexically assigned structural Case. Fourth, we have default structural

Case, which is assigned only to governed NPs (perhaps under adjacency). And finally, we have default Case that is assigned to ungoverned NPs.

One way to interpret the picture that has emerged here is that, as before, there are basically two case systems, one for structural case and one for inherent case. However, there is a possibility of overlap between the two systems, such that a structural case position (i.e. an A-position) may be assigned inherent case under some circumstances, and an inherent case position (i.e. a governed position whose governor is not a verb) is assigned structural case under some circumstances. The first situation appears to hold for non-ACCUSATIVE direct objects, while the latter may be what we find in verb-preposition constructions such as *look at* (see Chapter 2, Exercise 2-6). Whether or not this is the correct way to interpret case, we will find that the existence of these apparent overlaps constitutes a difficulty for the role that Abstract Case plays in the GB framework, especially with respect to movement (§ A.3).

A.2. Non-NOMINATIVE subjects

In Russian, predicates expressing obligation and necessity, permission and possibility, and mental and emotional states assign DATIVE Case to their subjects. Some examples are given in (77).

(77)   *a.* Mne nado by čitat' ešče mnogo knig   o   Tolstom.
          I-DAT necessary to-read still more   book.pl-GEN about Tolstoy
          'I really ought to read more books about Tolstoy.'
       b. Vam   ne sleduet tak govorit'.
          you-DAT not should thus to-speak
          'You   should not say such things.'
       c. Mne veselo   bylo sredi vas.
          I-DAT cheerful was among you-GEN
          'I enjoyed myself among you.'
       d. Mne žal' vašu   sestru.
          I-DAT sorry your-ACC sister-ACC
          'I am sorry for your sister.'

To deal with these examples, we must either weaken the view that NOMINATIVE is always assigned to subjects, or analyze these dative subjects as being non-subjects at the point at which they are assigned Case. The latter is clearly preferred from the perspective of Uniformity. The analysis would be one in which the dative subject originates in VP, is assigned inherent DATIVE Case on the basis of its θ-role, and then is moved into subject position while retaining its Case. We pursue some of the theoretical issues surrounding such an analysis in Exercise 4-15.

A.3. NP movement and quirky case

A central tenet of Case theory is that NPs that fail to receive structural Case
either undergo movement to a Case position, or violate the Case Filter. Failure
to receive structural Case may arise either because Case is 'absorbed' by the passive morphology, or because the verb simply fails to assign Case to its direct
object. The phenomenon of Icelandic quirky case constitutes a problem for this
view, as will be shown here.

One aspect of Icelandic quirky case is that a Case other than NOMINATIVE can
be assigned to the subject, and the other is that a Case other than ACCUSATIVE
can be assigned to the object (see (76)). Under the standard view of the passive
construction, when ACCUSATIVE Case is absorbed, the object moves to subject
position and is assigned structural NOMINATIVE Case. This is the general pattern
of the Icelandic passive, in fact, for those verbs that assign ACCUSATIVE.[35]

(78) a. Lögreglan tók Siggu   fasta.
          the-police took Sigga-ACC fast-ACC
          'The police arrested Sigga.'
      b. Sigga   var tekin föst   af lögreglunni.
          Sigga-NOM was taken fast-NOM by the-police
          'Sigga was arrested by the police.'

Crucially, when a verb assigns a quirky case to its object, this case is preserved
in the passive construction.

(79) a. Eg   hjálpaði honum.
          I-NOM helped   him-DAT
          'I helped him.'
      b. Honum var hjápað.
          him-DAT was helped

It can be shown, moreover, that the dative NP in the passive is truly the subject,
and not a topicalized NP adjacent to an empty expletive subject. That is, the
structure is (80a), not (80b).

(80) a.

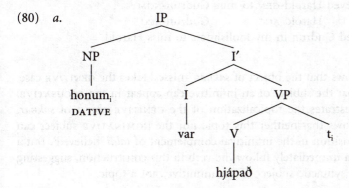

b.

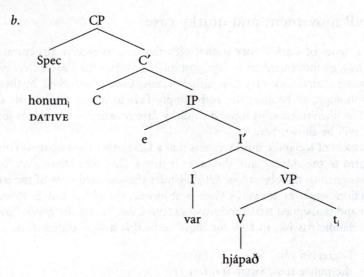

Non-ACCUSATIVE subjects in Icelandic in general show none of the properties of topicalized NPs. For example, only subjects of infinitives are licensed in initial position, as the following examples show.

(81)   *a.* Guðrún   saknar Haraldar.
        Gudrun-NOM misses Harold-GEN
        'Gudrun misses Harold.'
       b. Ég taldi   Guðrúnu   í barnaskap mínum sakna   Haraldar.
        I   believed Gudrun-ACC in foolishness my   to-miss Harold-GEN
        'I believed Gudrun in my foolishness to miss Harold.'
       c. Haraldar   saknar Guðrún.
        Harold-GEN misses Gudrun-NOM
        'Harold, Gudrun misses.'
       d. *Ég taldi   Haraldar   sakna   Guðrún.
        Harald   Guðrúnu
        I   believed Harold-GEN to-miss Gudrun-NOM
        Harold-ACC   Gudrun-ACC
        'I believed Gudrun in my foolishness to miss Harold.'

Example (81*a*) shows that the object of *saknar* 'misses' takes the GENITIVE case. In (81*b*) we see that the subject of an infinitive can appear in the ACCUSATIVE. Example (81*c*) illustrates the topicalization of the GENITIVE object of *saknar*. Example (81*d*) shows that neither this topic nor the NOMINATIVE subject can appear in initial position in the infinitival complement of *taldi* 'believed'. But a DATIVE subject can immediately follow the verb in this construction, suggesting that it is truly the syntactic subject of the infinitive, not a topic.

(82) Ég tel   þeim   hafa   verið hjálpað í prófinu
     I   believe them-DAT to-have been helped in the-exam
     'I believe them to have been helped in the exam.'

To take just one more piece of evidence, in Icelandic a topic is immediately followed by the inflected verb, which is followed by the subject. The verb cannot precede the topic. In a yes-no question, the inflected verb is initial, and is followed by the subject. The following examples show that the dative subject in fact functions like a subject, in active and passive sentences.

(83) *a.* Sigga   hafði aldrei hjálpað Haraldi.
         Sigga-NOM had   never helped Harold-DAT
         'Sigga had never helped Harold.'
     b. Hafði Sigga   aldrei hjálpað Haraldi?
         had   Sigga-NOM never helped Harold-DAT
         'Had Sigga never helped Harold?'
     c. *Hafði Haraldi   Sigga   aldrei hjálpað?
         had   Harold-DAT Sigga-NOM never helped
     d. Haraldi   hafði Sigga   aldrei hjálpað.
         Harold-DAT had   Sigga-NOM never helped
         'Harold, Sigga had never helped Harold.'

In (83a) we have the uninverted order of subject and verb; in (83b) we have the inverted order. When there is a topicalized DATIVE non-subject, the verb cannot be inverted to the left of the topic, as shown in (83c). In fact, the verb must appear to the right of the topic, as in (83d).

Now let us see what happens when the DATIVE is a subject.

(84) *a.* Hefur henni   alltaf þótt   Ólafur   leiðinlegur?
         has   her-DAT always thought Olaf-NOM boring-NOM
         'Has she always found Olaf boring?'
     b. Ólafur   hefur henni   alltaf þótt   leiðinlegur.
         Olaf-NOM has   her-DAT always thought boring-NOM
         'Olaf, she has always found boring.'
     c. *Hefur Ólafur henni alltaf þótt leiðinlegur.

Examples (84a) and (84b) show that the DATIVE subject appears to the right of the inverted verb, just like a NOMINATIVE subject (cf. (83b)). Example (84c) shows that the verb does not appear to the left of the NOMINATIVE non-subject topic *Olafur*, as predicted. In (85) we provide another set of examples that illustrate the same point.

(85) *a.* Var honum aldrei hjápað af foreldrum sínum?
         was he-DAT never helped by parents   his
         'Was he never helped by his parents?'

b. Í prófinu   var honum víst   hjálpað.
in the-exam was he-DAT apparently helped
'In the exam he was apparently helped.'

The importance of quirky case for Case theory is twofold. First, quirky case shows that it must be possible for a verb to assign what we have been calling 'Inherent Case' to A-positions, that is, to subjects and objects. Quirky case is associated with the lexical item, it is assigned at D-structure, and thus it takes precedence over any structural Case. Second, the fact that quirky case is preserved by NP movement means that what triggers NP movement cannot be the failure of an NP to get Case. An alternative view in terms of grammatical relations is that the passive should be analyzed as a mapping of the direct object into the subject position, with the nominative-accusative case marking pattern functioning as a default assignment to the grammatical relations.[36] This view contrasts sharply with that of the standard GB approach, where the NOMINATIVE-ACCUSATIVE case-marking pattern is determined not by the grammatical relations, but by the configuration.

APPENDIX B: PSYCH PREDICATES

A putative case of A-movement concerns what are called psych verbs or psych predicates. These are predicates that express a mental state, as in (86).

(86)   Your analysis ⎰annoyed ⎱ me.
⎰disturbed⎱
⎰pleased ⎱
⎰delighted⎱
⎰disgusted⎱
⎰etc.   ⎱

An interesting fact about these predicates is that they may have subjects that contain anaphors that appear not to be syntactically bound, e.g.

(87)   a. Nasty stories about each other would ⎰annoy   ⎱ the professors.
⎰disturb   ⎱
⎰not please ⎱
⎰disgust   ⎱
⎰surprise   ⎱

b. Stories about herself usually $\begin{Bmatrix} \text{annoy} \\ \text{disturb} \\ \text{delight} \\ \text{disgust} \\ \text{surprise} \end{Bmatrix}$ Mary.

c. Each other's ridiculous claims $\begin{Bmatrix} \text{annoyed} \\ \text{disturbed} \\ \text{pleased} \\ \text{delighted} \\ \text{surprised} \end{Bmatrix}$ the professors.

In each case, the subject c-commands the direct object, but the direct object appears to bind into the subject. Binding depends on c-command, as we have seen (Chapter 3), so these examples constitute something of a paradox. This is especially so because without a psych predicate, the object cannot bind into the subject.

(88)   a. *Nasty stories about each other would definitely convict the professors.
       b. *Stories about herself usually expose Mary to ridicule.[37]
       c. *Each other's ridiculous friends attacked the professors.
       d. *Heavy pictures of each other fell on Susan and John.

But notice that this effect is somewhat mitigated when there is a paraphrase of a psych predicate or a non-psych causative construction.

(89)   a. Nasty stories about each other would definitely make the professors angry (at each other).
       b. Stories about herself usually make Mary feel ridiculous.
       c. Each other's ridiculous friends got the professors to withdraw their publications.
       d. The pictures of himself in the newspaper made John take out insurance.

The fact that causation has a facilitating effect on anaphora raises the possibility that the phenomenon that we are dealing with here is not a purely syntactic one, in the sense that it is determined strictly by the configuration at some level of syntactic representation.[38]

Rather than stipulate a peculiar property of some verbs, we seek a principled account; in the current theory, such an account has to be a syntactic one. If the direct object binds the subject, then it must c-command the subject at some level of syntactic representation. The available level appears to be D-structure, since in S-structure there is no c-command. Moreover, the subject position, into which the NP containing the anaphor moves, must be a non-θ-position, so that the θ-Criterion is not violated. One plausible configuration is the following.

(90)

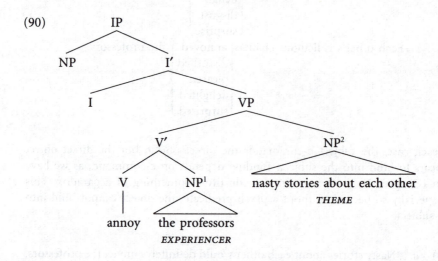

Here, we must assume that NP¹ binds *each other* in NP². This requires an extension of c-command or a reformulation of 'binds' in terms of m-command, which may be independently required because of the binding effect shown in (91).

(91)   I told the professors nasty stories about each other.

Presumably, the structure of the double object construction is that of (90). Moreover, we must assume that the binding of a reflexive can be satisfied at D-structure, which is problematic but not impossible; for discussion see Chapter 8. Of course, the Binding theory may also be satisfied at S-structure, as shown by the following examples.

(92)   *a.* [e] seems to herself [$_{IP}$ Mary$_i$ to like Susan] $\Rightarrow$
        Mary$_i$ seems to herself$_i$ [$_{IP}$ t$_i$ to like Susan]
        b. [e] seems to her [$_{IP}$ Mary$_i$ to like Susan] $\Rightarrow$
        *Mary$_i$ seems to her$_i$ [$_{IP}$ t$_i$ to like Susan]

Here, *herself* and *her* are locally bound by *Mary* only after A-movement has occurred. Finally, we assume that, unlike in the double object construction, NP² fails to get inherent Case, but does get a θ-role. Given this, it will move to the subject position.

If we wish to maintain a strict c-command analysis of binding, then the structure must actually be the following, rather than (90).

(93)

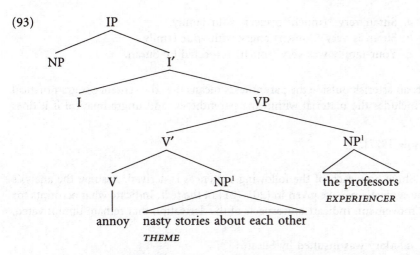

On this analysis, the EXPERIENCER is assigned ACCUSATIVE Case as a consequence of the lexical entry of the verb.[39] Assume that each Case is assigned to at most one argument. Since the NP bearing THEME is in a structural Case position but ACCUSATIVE Case is assigned to the EXPERIENCER, no Case is available for the direct object. Hence the NP bearing THEME must move to the subject position to get Case.[40]

The phenomenon of anaphors in the subjects of psych verbs clearly constitutes a problem for which the strictly syntactic solution is not entirely satisfactory. Application of the Binding theory at D-structure appears to be *ad hoc*. The various movements that are required in this analysis also do not appear to have any motivation other than the need to have the anaphor c-commanded by its antecedent at some level of syntactic representation. An approach that allows anaphors in certain contexts to have antecedents that do not c-command them appears to be a reasonable alternative. See Chapter 8, § 3 for additional discussion.

EXERCISES

4-1. Consider the following data. Explain how this data constitutes evidence that there is a lexical (that is, an adjectival) passive and a syntactic (that is, a verbal) passive.

(1)   John $\left\{\begin{array}{l}\text{acted}\\\text{seemed}\\\text{looked}\end{array}\right\}$ $\left\{\begin{array}{l}\text{happy.}\\\text{annoyed at us.}\\\text{convinced to run.}\\\text{*sleeping.}\end{array}\right\}$

(2)   *a.* Susan very *(much) respects your family.
      b. Susan is very (*much) angry with your family.
      c. Your family was very (much) respected by Susan.

Note: an asterisk outside the parentheses means that the sentence is grammatical if it includes the material within the parentheses, and ungranmatical if it does not.

[Wasow 1977].

4-2. Show how each of the following sentences is derived. Assume the analysis of the syntactic passive given in (20)–(21) of the text. Indicate what accounts for each movement. Indicate any aspects of the derivation that remain unmotivated.

(1)   *a.* Mary was insulted by Susan.
      b. Mary was expected to win the election.
      c. Mary was expected to be arrested.
      d. Mary was certain to be arrested.
      e. Mary is certain to have been believed to have been arrested.
(2)   *a.* Mary seemed angry.
      b. Mary seemed impressed by your performance.
      c. Mary tried to be arrested by the police.

[§ 1.2]

4-3. In the text it is argued that there must be a syntactically derived passive. Nothing rules out the possibility of there being a lexical passive, however. Evidence in favor of the lexical passive would consist of lexical derivational morphology that applied to lexical passives to yield other forms. Consider the rule of *un-* prefixation, illustrated in (1).

(1)   *a.* imaginative, imaginable, interesting, grateful, talented, supportive, oppressive, happy, profitable
      b. unimaginative, unimaginable, uninteresting, ungrateful, untalented, unsupportive, unoppressive, unhappy, unprofitable

Take it as given that *un-* prefixes only to adjectives. (There is another prefix *un-* that affixes to verbs (e.g. *do, undo*) that has a related but different meaning.)

   1. What does the following tell you about the grammatical category of passives? Why?

(2)   *a.* (*un)see, (*un)forgive, (*un)know, (*un)speak, (*un)imagine
      b. unseen, unforgiven, unknown, unspoken, unimagined

2. The following shows that only some adjectives take *un-*. Compare these examples with those in (1*b*). Try to specify exactly what determines whether or not an adjective can take *un-*. Discuss how the forms in (2*b*) satisfy this condition.

(3)   (*un)tall, (*un)red, (*un)busy, (*un)smooth, (*un)round, (*un)shiny,

Cf.

(4)   (un)happy, (un)aware, (un)clean, (un)clear, (un)sure

3. What do the following examples tell you about the conditions under which an adjective can be prefixed with *un-*.

(5)   *a.* the skills were taught (to the children)
        the children were taught (the skills)
       b. untaught skills, untaught children
(6)   *a.* the books were sold (to the customers)
        the customers were sold *(the books)
       b. unsold books, *unsold customers
(7)   *a.* the cereal was fed *(to the baby)
        the baby was fed (the cereal)
       b. *unfed cereal, unfed baby
(8)   *a.* the book was handed *(to the student)
        the student was handed *(the book)
       b. *unhanded book, *unhanded student
(9)   *a.* the book was read (to the students)
       b. the students were read *(the book)

[§ 1.2; Levin and Rappaport 1986]

4-4. Explain how the *θ*-Criterion rules out the possibility that in the syntactic passive the external *θ*-role is assigned to the subject position.
[§ 1.3]

4-5. In the text (§ 2) we suggest that *seem* does not assign Case to the subject of its infinitival complement; consequently, the subject must move to the subject position of *seem* in order to get Case. It might appear that another way to block Case assignment to the subject of the complement of *seem* would be to say that this complement is a CP, not an IP. Evaluate this alternative.
[§ 2]

4-6. Explain the ungrammaticality of the following examples in terms of the ideas developed in this chapter.

(1)   *a.* *Susan was insulted Mary.
      b. *Susan$_i$ was expected us to arrest t$_i$.
      c. *It seems Susan to have arrived early.
      d. *The train$_i$ seems [e]/it to have arrived t$_i$ already.

[§ 3]

4-7. English allows double passives in the case of idioms such as *take advantage of*.

(1)   *a.* We took full advantage of John's generosity.
      b. John's generosity was taken full advantage of.
      c. Full advantage was taken of John's generosity.

How would you go about accounting for this pattern in an account of the passive that relies on the absorption of ACCUSATIVE Case?
[§ 3]

4-8. While NPs must receive Case, CPs do not. How does this assumption explain the following distribution of data?

(1)   *a.* The hosts anticipated that Mary would arrive late.
      b. The hosts anticipated Mary arriving late.
      c. The hosts anticipated Mary's late arrival.
(2)   *a.* It was anticipated (by the hosts) that Mary would arrive late.
      b. *It was anticipated (by the hosts) Mary arriving late.
      c. *It was anticipated (by the hosts) Mary's late arrival.
(3)   *a.* That Mary would arrive late was anticipated by the hosts.
      b. Mary arriving late was anticipated by the hosts.
      c. Mary's late arrival was anticipated by the hosts.

Example (3*a*) constitutes a problem for the view that A-movements are triggered by the Case Filter. Explain why.
[§ 3]

4-9. 1. One test of whether a sequence of phrases is a clausal constituent is whether the subject can be *there*.

(1)   *a.* I expect there to be an explosion.
      b. *I persuaded there to be an explosion.

Explain the difference between these two examples, as shown by the distribution of *there*.

   2. Keeping in mind the answer arrived at in the first part of this exercise, discuss the following grammaticality distribution.

(2)   *a.* I imagined there being an explosion.
       b. There seems to have been an explosion.
       c. There is believed to have been an explosion.
(3)   *a.* Susan is in the next room.
       b. There is a student in the next room.
       c. I imagined Susan in the next room.
       d. *I imagined there a student in the next room.
(4)   *a.* It seems Susan is in the next room.
       b. It seems there is a student in the next room.
       c. Susan seems in the next room.
       d. *There seems a student in the next room.

Can this distribution be predicted, and if so, on what basis?
   3. Compare the behavior of *there* with the behavior of expletive *it*.

(5)   *a.* That you were here is obvious.
       b. It is obvious that you were here.
       c. *I imagined that you were here obvious.
       d. I considered that you were here obvious.
       e. *I imagined it obvious that you were here.
       f. I considered it obvious that you were here.
(6)   *a.* It seems that that you were here is obvious.
       b. It seems it is obvious that you were here.
       c. That you were here seems obvious.
       d. It seems obvious that you were here.

What is the explanation for these facts in terms of the account developed in this chapter?

[§ 4]

4-10. In the text we noted that a sentence like *John bit* cannot mean *John bit himself*, and concluded from this fact that a chain cannot be assigned two θ-roles. On the other hand, a sentence like *John washed* means *John washed himself*, which appears to contradict this conclusion. Evaluate the implications of each of the following strategies for dealing with this problem.

(*a*)   The direct object of *wash* is PRO.
(*b*)   The direct object of *wash* is an empty pronominal, called *pro*.
(*c*)   *Wash* does not take a syntactic direct object, but there is a level of representation (call it Conceptual Structure) in which *wash* takes two arguments and one argument binds the other.

[§ 4]

*4-11. Consider the following facts from German and English.

(1) *German:*
  a. Es wurde getanzt.
     it was   danced
     'There was dancing.'
  b. Es wurde bis spät in die Nacht getrunken.
     it was   till late in the night drunk
     'There was drinking till late in the night.'
(2)   *Es wird diesen   Roman   von vielen Studenten gelesen.
       it is [this-ACC novel-ACC] by many students   read
(3) a. Getanzt wurde.
     'There was dancing.'
  b. *Getanzt es wurde.
(4) *English:*
  a. *[e] was arrested John
  b. *It/there was arrested John.
  c. It was believed [that the conclusion was false].

Provide a characterization of the difference between the German passive and the English passive. In terms of our analysis of the passive in the text, what accounts for the fact that German has impersonal passives (with expletives in subject position) but English does not? Try to avoid a stipulation about the passive construction itself.

[§ 4]

**4-12. The following illustrates the antipassive and the passive in Greenlandic (Woodbury 1977).

(1) a. miirqa-t   paar   -ai
        child-ABS.PL take-care-of -IND.3SG,3PL
        'She takes care of the children.'
  b. miirqu-nik   paar-ši   -vuq
     child-INSTR.PL take-care-of=ANTIP. -IND.3SG
     'She takes care of children.'
(2) a. nakura-p   taku-vaa piniartu-p   qiŋmiq-Ø unatar-aa
        doctor-ERG see-IND hunter-ERG dog-ABS beat-TP.3SG,3SG
        'The doctor saw that the hunter beat the dog.'
  b. nakursap   takuvaa   piniartuq-Ø qiŋmi-mik
     doctor-ERG see-IND.3SG,3SG hunter-ABS dog-INSTR
     unata-i-šuq
     beat-ANTIP.-INTR.3SG
     'The doctor saw that the hunter beat a dog.'

(3) *a.* aŋut-ip   arnaq-∅   taku-vaa
      man-ERG woman-ABS see-IND.3SG,3SG
      'The man saw the woman.'

   b. arnaq-∅   aŋuti-mik   taku-tau-puq
      woman-ABS man-INSTR.SG see-PASS.-IND.3SG
      'The woman was seen by the man.'

[Key: ABS=ABSOLUTIVE, ANTIP.=antipassive, ERG=ERGATIVE, IND=indicative, INTR.=intransitive, 3SG=third person singular, 3PL=third person plural, PASS.=passive, PL=plural.]

Greenlandic is an ergative language, so that the ABS case-mark appears on the subject of the intransitive and the object of the transitive. The subject of the transitive is marked with ERG. INSTR is an oblique case.

In the passive, the θ-role of the subject is suppressed or expressed obliquely (e.g. in a *by*-phrase in English), and the object becomes the subject of an intransitive verb. Since the object of the transitive becomes the subject of an intransitive, it is marked ABS in both cases. In the antipassive, the θ-role of an argument other than the subject is suppressed or expressed obliquely, and the subject becomes the subject of an intransitive verb. Typically, this θ-role is the THEME.

Work out what the treatment of passive and antipassive must be for a language like West Greenlandic that has both. Assume Syntacticization and Uniformity.

4-13. In the text we noted the ungrammaticality of the following sentence.

(1)   *John seems that he is hungry.

However, the following are grammatical.

(2)   *a.* John seems as if he is hungry.
      b. John seems like he is hungry.

In other respects *seem as if* and *seem like* appear to function like *seem that*.

(3)   *a.* It seems that John is hungry.
      b. It seems as if John is hungry.
      c. It seems like John is hungry.
(4)   *a.* *There seemed that there was an explosion.
      b. (?)There seemed like there was an explosion.
      c. (?)There seemed as if there was an explosion.
(5)   *a.* *John seems that Susan is hungry.
      b. *John seems as if Susan is hungry.
      c. *John seems like Susan is hungry.

Discuss the implications of these and related sentences for the Raising analysis of *seem*, on the assumption that there is a single lexical item *seem*.

*4-14. Formulate an account of the sentences in (1)–(5) of Exercise 4-11 that allows us to assume the Raising analysis for *seem*. Take into account as well the following data.

(1)   *a.* Susan$_i$ looks like she$_i$'s hungry.
       b. Susan$_i$ looks like it's been a bad day.
       c. *There looks like Susan$_i$'s hungry.
       d. (?)There looks like there's been an explosion.
(2)   *a.* Susan$_i$ talks as if she$_i$'s tired.
       b. Susan$_i$ talks as if there are potatoes in her mouth.
       c. *There talks as if Susan has potatoes in her mouth.
       d. *There talks as if there's been an explosion.
(3)   *a.* *Susan$_i$ appears like she$_i$'s hungry.
       b. *Susan$_i$ appears as if she$_i$'s hungry.
       c. *Susan$_i$ appears as though she$_i$'s hungry.
       d. It appears as if/as though/*like Susan is hungry.

**4-15. Consider the proposal in Appendix A, § A.2, that a Russian dative subject originates in VP, is assigned inherent DATIVE Case on the basis of its θ-role, and then is moved into subject position while retaining its Case. How would you formulate A-movement under these circumstances? In particular, how would you specify which NP moves into subject position, and what consequences would this analysis have for the analysis of the passive in English?

*4-16. It is suggested in the text (Appendix A, § A.3) that inherent case could be assigned to an A-position. One example is that of Icelandic *sökkti* 'sank' which assigns DATIVE to its direct object in the transitive (cf. (76*b*)). Design an explicit lexical representation for such a verb.

FURTHER READING

....

[Note: The number of asterisks before a reference indicates its level of technical difficulty. You should be able to follow much if not all of what is in those references that lack asterisks.]

The most recent treatment of the passive in GB theory appears to be that of *Baker, Johnson, and Roberts (1989); see also Roberts (1986). The passive has been well studied in generative grammar from a number of other perspectives as well. Postal (1986) is a comprehensive cross-linguistic study of passive constructions. The notion that the grammatical relations are primitive is pursued in the framework of Lexical Functional Grammar (*Bresnan 1982*b*) and Relational Grammar (*Perlmutter and Postal 1983). Similarly, in Head-driven Phrase Structure Grammar (*Pollard and Sag 1994), generalizations regarding the passive are stated directly in terms of the argument structure associated with lexical items and not in terms of the syntactic configurations provided by X′-theory.

The literature in GB theory appears to accept the standard perspective on Raising summarized in this chapter, which is due to Chomsky (1973). For other perspectives, see the papers in *Larson (1991).

For discussion of chain formation, see *Rizzi (1986) and **Chomsky (1993).

It has been proposed that NP movement occurs not only in passives and unaccusatives, but in middle verb constructions, such as *This book reads easily*; see *Hoekstra and Roberts (1993) and *Stroik (1992). For a critique, see *Ackema and Schoorlemmer (1995).

Unaccusativity offers a rich literature. Besides the works cited in the text, see Levin and Rappaport Hovav (1995) and the works cited there.

For additional evidence that supports the conclusion that the dative subjects in Icelandic are true subjects, see Zaenen, Maling, and Thráinsson (1990).

X′-Theory

1. The structure of a phrase

X′-theory is a theory of phrase structure. That is, it is a theory of what constitutes a possible phrase in natural language.

Phrase structure concerns the hierarchical and left-to-right relationships between syntactic categories. For example, in English one type of verb phrase (VP) consists of a verb that precedes its NP complement. Early approaches to phrase structure in generative grammar stipulated both types of relationship for every category of every language. For example, in the grammar of English there was a statement that the verb phrase VP could consist of a V and an NP, where the V precedes the NP. Similarly, in the grammar of Japanese there was a statement that the VP could consist of a V and an NP, where the NP precedes the V. These statements took the form of phrase structure rules (PSRs), as in (1).

(1) *a.* English: VP → V NP
     b. Japanese: VP → NP V

PSRs provide considerable descriptive power, in that they allow for the possibility that for any arbitrary phrasal category XP and categories Y and Z, the rule XP → Y Z describes a possible structure in some natural language. What we actually find over a broad range of cases is considerably more restricted than this: in general, a phrase of type XP contains a head of type X. Moreover, the phrase of type XP contains exactly one head. In this sense, we say that phrases are projections of their heads. They are **endocentric** in the sense that the category of the phrase is the same type as the category of the head. That is, when the head is N, the phrase is NP, when the head is V, the phrase is VP, and so on. By Uniformity, we postulate that *all* phrases are endocentric, across all categories and across all languages. Moreover, we postulate that within a given language, the left-to-right ordering of constituents within categories is uniform (e.g. heads always precede complements). An even stronger assumption, currently under investigation, is that the left-to-right D-structure ordering of constituents is uniform across all categories and across all languages.[1] Such restrictive requirements on hierarchical structure and linear order within phrases produce numerous interesting research problems, as we will see.

Every phrase has a head. Certain heads take complements. Informally, the relationship between a head and its complement is characterized by the fact that they are sisters: each c-commands the other, and they are immediately dominated by the same node.

(2)

Since under certain circumstances the head may also assign Case to its complement, a question arises concerning the proper formal characterization of the head-complement relation. What structural conditions are sufficient to distinguish the complement from all other constituents of the phrase? We pursue this question in § 2.

Consider next the following noun phrase.

(3)   their rejection last week of the agreement

The head of this phrase is *rejection*. The complement is *the agreement*, since it is parallel to the direct object in the verb phrase *reject the agreement*. Uniformity suggests that the same constituent is a complement of a given lexical head across all categories in which the head may be realized.

What, then, are *their* and *last week*? *Their*, while not a complement, is an argument, since it receives a θ-role from *rejection*, in fact the external (subject) θ-role, parallel to *they rejected the agreement*. We call this the specifier of the phrase.

Last week, which is neither complement nor specifier, is an adjunct.

In summary, the head determines the category of the projection, the complement is the sister of the head, the specifier is assigned the external θ-role, and the adjuncts are everything else.

By assumption, these four classes, head, complement, specifier, and adjunct, are exhaustive, in that everything in a phrase falls under one of these classes. If this assumption is correct, questions about general properties of phrases and differences between phrases can now in principle be productively formulated in terms of these classes.

In the earliest versions of X'-theory, the exhaustiveness of the classes just outlined was open to question, because there were elements that did not appear to fall naturally into any of them under any principled characterization of their properties. For example, consider our definition that the specifier bears the external θ-role. What is the class of the determiner *the* in (4)?

(4)   the rejection of the agreement

Since *the* is not an NP, it does not refer, and cannot receive a θ-role. Suppose that it is an adjunct. In English, the adjuncts follow the head, while *the* precedes the head. In fact, it appears that from the perspective of the syntactic organization of the NP, *the* is a specifier just as *their* is, a conclusion that undermines our original characterization of what constitutes a specifier.

Our first pass at a solution to this problem will be simply to stipulate that the class of specifiers includes NP and determiner. We will adopt this view for most of this chapter. However, this is clearly not the optimal solution, and we will explore an alternative in § 3.3.

An important principle of X'-theory, a corollary of Uniformity, is that across syntactic categories, complements, specifiers, and adjuncts bear the same configurational relationship to the head. This principle is suggested by the canonical cases. In English, at least, the complement of a head appears adjacent to it and to the right of it, while the specifier appears to the left. The following examples illustrate.

(5)   a. [$_{V'}$ eat cake]
      b. [$_{N'}$ picture of Einstein]
      c. [$_{V'}$ destroy the city]
      d. [$_{N'}$ destruction of the city]
      e. [$_{A'}$ destructive of the city]
(6)   a. [$_{NP}$ his book]
      b. [$_{AP}$ this tall]
      c. [$_{ADVP}$ this quickly]

The maximal projection is distinguished from the intermediate projections by the fact that the specifier is adjoined at the maximal projection node. Generally, X'-theory proposes that all phrases have the following structure, called the X' schema, ignoring linear order.

(7)

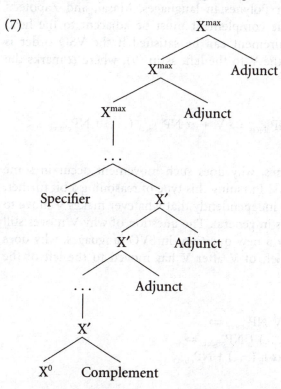

Note that a complement is the sister of X^0, while an adjunct is adjoined to X'. It is an open question whether or not adjuncts can appear at the X^{max} level as well.

In practice, it is assumed that all branching is binary. We will assume uniform binary branching for the discussion that follows, and consider in Appendix A whether there is any empirical content to the question of what types of branching are possible.

As noted, by assumption, the structure in (7) is universal for all categories and across all languages. The consequences of such a strong Uniformity hypothesis are significant. Assuming an independent characterization of specifier and complement, suppose that we find a language in which the specifier intervenes between the head and the complement. Two typical cases are given in (8).

(8)   *a.* V NP$_{subject}$ NP$_{object}$ (VSO order)
      b. N Determiner NP$_{object}$

The situation schematized in (8a) is found in many languages, among them Arabic, Berber, Breton, Welsh and the other Celtic languages, Hebrew, Maori and other Polynesian languages, Masai, and Zapotec.[2] X'-theory requires that the complement must be adjacent to the head at D-structure. This requirement can be satisfied if the VSO order is derived by movement of the V to the left, as in (9), where α marks the landing site of V.

(9) α NP$_{subject}$ (...) V NP$_{object}$ $\Rightarrow$ V + α NP$_{subject}$ (...) t NP$_{object}$

The question then becomes, why does such movement occur in some languages but not in others? Pursuing this type of reasoning a bit further, suppose that we conclude independently that whatever makes V move to α must apply in languages in general. The question of why V moves still remains, but there is now a new question: in SVO languages, why does the subject move to the left of V after V has moved to the left of the subject, as in (10)?

(10) β α NP$_{subject}$ (...) V NP$_{object}$ $\Rightarrow$
β V + α NP$_{subject}$ (...) t NP$_{object}$ $\Rightarrow$
NP$_{subject/i}$ + β V + α t$_i$ (...) t NP$_{object}$

Questions such as these are explored in Chapter 10. The short answer is that constituents move in order to satisfy certain morphological requirements, especially the licensing of inflections such as Case and Tense.

Example (8b) roughly characterizes a situation that occurs in languages such as Basque, Berber, Fulani, Hindi, Loritja, Malay, Songhai, Swahili, Thai, Yoruba, and Zapotec.[3] Again, the optimal analysis under the restrictive X'-theory is one in which the head moves to the left, perhaps adjoining to the determiner.

(11)   Determiner N NP$_{object}$ $\Rightarrow$ N(+)Determiner t$_N$ NP$_{object}$

Having set out the basic structure and logic of X'-theory, let us consider properties of heads, complements, specifiers, and adjuncts in somewhat more detail.

2. Heads and complements

2.1. *Lexical categories*

We have already mentioned the lexical categories: N, V, A, P. Not all languages distinguish these categories fully in both syntax and the lexicon. For example, in Lummi, nouns and verbs are distinguished strictly by morphology; no distinction is made at the lexical level.[4] Compare the Lummi representation in (12) with the English representation in (13), which is taken from Chapter 3.[5]

(12) *a.* čey=lə'=sən[6]
          work=PAST=1s.NOM
          'I worked.'
      b. cəčey=lə'
          DET work=PAST
          'the (one that) worked'
      c. si'em=sə'=sx^w
          chief=FUT=2s.NOM
          'You will be a chief.'
      d. cəsi'em=sə'
          DET chief=FUT
          'the (one that will be a) chief'

(13)   *ENVY:* [_____ NP]
                  |
              THEME

      V: *envy*
      N: *envy*
      A: *envious*

English distinguishes V, N, and A in the lexicon, to the extent that their surface form is not predictable from their syntactic category. In Lummi, on the other hand, there appears to be no basis for a principled lexical distinction between N and V at all. Of course they are distinguished in the syntax, and it is plausible that for some items (e.g. proper names) the verbal form is not realized. One way to approach this situation is to say that what appears in the lexicon is a root (e.g. *čey* 'work'; *si'em* 'chief'). The lexical item acquires a specific syntactic category as it appears in a particular syntactic frame. To list the forms separately in the lexicon would be redundant.

Associated with each lexical category is a maximal projection. The following examples show that with some minor variations, these projections all follow the same pattern in English. The specifier precedes the head, the complement follows the head, and the adjuncts follow the head. Typically the adjuncts follow the complements, also. Where the adjuncts do not follow the complements at S-structure, there must be movement, by the logic of X'-theory, since at D-structure the complement is always closest to the head so that it can receive the complement θ-role.

VP:

(14)   a. called
      b. saw John
      c. saw John last week

(15)   a. believes that John was here
      b. attempted to call

(16)   gave a book to John

NP:

(17)   a. the picture
      b. the picture of John
      c. the picture of John that I found
      d. the picture of John taken last year
      e. John's picture
      f. John's picture of Bill
      g. every picture of Bill that was taken last year

(18)   a. Mary's belief that John was here
      b. Mary's attempt to call

(19)   Mary's gift of a book to John

AP:

(20)   a. angry
      b. very angry
      c. very angry at John

(21)   a. angry that John was here
      b. eager to leave

PP:

(22)   a. (right) [across (the bridge)]
      b. out of the woods
      c. before Mary called

It will be noted that the complement structure is more uniform across categories than the specifier structure. In particular, it seems that while

NP and AP have specifiers, and PP may have a specifier (e.g. *right*), VP does not. Let us now entertain the idea that the specifier of VP is the D-structure subject of the sentence, which moves to a higher specifier position. On this approach, the absence of a specifier of VP in S-structure is an illusion; the specifier position is occupied by the trace of the subject at S-structure. § 3.2 and § 3.3 explore further the principled basis for these apparent differences between categories.

2.2. Functional categories

Continuing to focus on the class of heads, observe that there are many elements in natural language that do not fall into the categories N, V, P, and A. Some examples are given in (23)–(24).

(23) Complementizers
English:
a. I think *that* it is raining.
b. It is difficult *for* us to understand the answer.
c. We wonder *whether* you had a choice in the matter.
d. This is the person *that* I was tell you about.
French:
e. Je crois *que* Mary a   téléphoné.
I think that Mary has telephoned
'I think that Mary telephoned.'
f. Je me suis décidé   à partir.
I refl. am decide-pprt. C to-leave
'I decided to leave.'
Spanish:
g. Creo   *que* ha llamado Mary.
believe-1sg that has call-pprt. Mary
'I believe that Mary called.'
German: *daß* 'that'; *Russian*: *čto* 'that', *Dutch*: *dat* 'that', etc.
(24) Determiners
a. *English*: *the, this, these, NP's, every*, etc.
b. *French*: *ce, cette* 'this', *ces, cettes* 'these', etc.
Russian: *èto, èta* 'this'

We consider the complementizers here and postpone discussion of the status of the determiners until § 3.3.

Consider the categorial status of the *that*-clauses in (23). By X'-theory (assuming Uniformity), they must be maximal projections of some category. Observing the internal structure of the clausal complement, we find that there is one obvious candidate for this category, the complementizer, since V is the head of the VP and thus is not available. Furthermore, it is unlikely that the complementizer itself is a complement or an adjunct, given that it is on a left branch and appears to have no thematic function. It is most likely that the complementizer is a specifier or a head. We will see below that the subject is the specifier of its maximal projection. Given that the entire clause needs to have a head, it is reasonable to postulate that the complementizer is the head of the clause. The structure will then be that of (25), assuming that the specifier position is obligatory and empty if not otherwise filled by lexical material (see § 4 for discussion of this point).

(25)

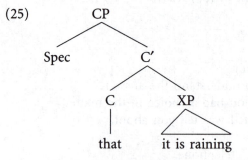

The category C is called a functional category, in contrast with the lexical categories N, A, V, and P. Functional categories do not assign θ-roles in the familiar sense, but they do impose syntactic and semantic restrictions on their complements and their specifiers, just as lexical categories do. Syntactic requirements are satisfied through c(**ategory**)-**selection**, while semantic requirements are satisfied through **s-selection**. S-selection includes θ-role assignment for verbs, e.g. *persuade*.

(26) *persuade* NP [that S]

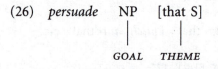

         GOAL   THEME

The next question to consider is the categorial status of the XP *it is raining* in (23*a*). This question brings us to an aspect of syntactic theory of crucial importance, namely, the notion that morphological material, such as verbal inflection, may (and in fact must) have an independent syntactic status. This conclusion is central to Principles and Parameters, and is found in work as early as Chomsky (1955) and Chomsky (1957).

To see the point in the current context, recall that V cannot be the head of XP in (25), because V is the head of VP. The structure of XP must therefore be as follows, order irrelevant.

(27)

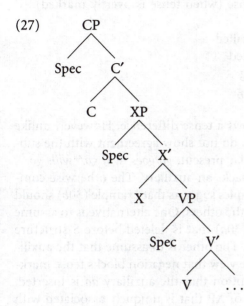

Consider now the following examples.

(28)   *a.* that Mary will call
      b. that Mary will not call
      c. that Mary has called
      d. that Mary has not called
      e. that Mary is calling
      f. that Mary is not calling
(29)   *a.* that Mary has been calling
      b. that Mary will be calling
      c. that Mary will have been calling
(30)   *a.* that Mary called
      b. that Mary did not call
      c. *that Mary not called

The examples in (28) offer a possible head for XP, namely the auxiliary verbs *will* (and other modals, such as *can, must*, etc.), *have*, and *be*. This conclusion immediately becomes problematic, for two reasons. First the auxiliary verbs may appear in sequence, as in (29), which entails that each is the projection of the category that we wish to associate with the full sentence (less the complementizer). But as the following examples show, the leftmost and highest auxiliary has a different status from the others, in that it is the one that bears tense (when tense is overtly marked).

(31)   *a.* that Mary would have called
       b. *that Mary will had called
       c. that Mary will be calling
       d. *that Mary will is calling

The pairing of *will* and *would* shows a tense difference, However, unlike other verbs in English, the modals do not show agreement with the subject NP in the third person singular present: *go/goes, will go/*wills go*.[7]

Second, consider (30*a*), which lacks an auxiliary. The otherwise complete parallelism seen in these examples suggests that example (30*b*) should fall under a uniform analysis with the others. One alternative is to assume that there is an auxiliary verb in (30*a*) that is deleted before S-structure when it immediately precedes a V. The other is to assume that the auxiliary verb is inserted in (30*b*), on the view that negation blocks tense marking of the verb.[8] If we take the option that the auxiliary *do* is inserted, we have a candidate for the head of XP that is uniquely associated with the highest auxiliary, namely Tense. We hypothesize, then, that XP is a projection of Tense, or, more generally, of the verbal inflection, which we have called Infl or I. (32) shows the structure.

(32)

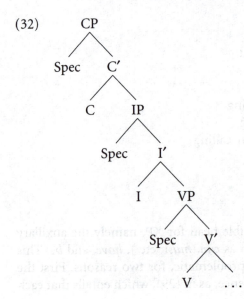

The reason why this conclusion is so important is that it shows that bound morphology, in contrast with a free-standing lexical item, can be the head of a maximal projection in the syntactic representation. This is a welcome result from the perspective of Uniformity, because it allows us to adopt a uniform syntactic analysis of comparable constructions across languages even when the morphological structure of different languages is quite different. Consider, for example, the following Korean sentence.

(33)   Ku-uy apeci-ka   John-i   Mary-lul ttayreyessta-ko
       he-GEN father-NOM John-NOM Mary-ACC hit-that
       sayngkakha.
       think
       'His father thinks that John hit Mary.'

As we see from the translation, *-ko* corresponds to the English *that*; however, *-ko*, unlike *that*, does not occur as a free morpheme that can be separated from the rest of the sentence by adverbs, topics, or parenthetical material.

(34)   *a.* I think that tomorrow I will call Mary.
       b. I think that to Mary I will give this book.
       c. I think that, now that you mention it, I will give the book to
            Mary.

Nevertheless, *-ko* appears outermost in the sequence of verbal morphemes, a fact that follows if we assume that it is a complementizer in more or less the same structure as (32).[9] This assumption is only possible if bound morphemes are syntactically free at D-structure.

A natural generalization of the analysis of English Infl is that all bound inflectional morphology is syntactically independent at D-structure. On one implementation of this view, surface morphological form results from syntactic derivations that consolidate morphemes into complex inflected abstract forms, and subsequent spelling out of these abstract forms as phonologically concrete elements as determined by the lexicon and the phonological rules of the language.[10] To take a simple example, the surface form of the verb *called* is a spelling out of the abstract CALL+PAST, which in turn is formed by syntactic consolidation of PAST and CALL through movement. We will pursue some of the implications of such an approach in Chapter 10, § 2.

At this point you should be able to do Exercise 5-1.

2.3. Complements

It is crucial to the approach developed here that there be a way of unambiguously identifying the complement of a head in terms of the syntactic configuration. That is, the complement must be distinguished from the adjuncts within the same maximal projection. Consider the configuration in (35).

(35)

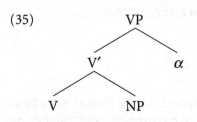

As we have seen, V governs NP and α if government is defined in terms of m-command, but it only governs NP if government is defined in terms of c-command. If government is formulated in terms of c-command, the question arises as to how to assign θ-roles to the adjuncts or to complements that are not sisters of the verb. If government is formulated in terms of m-command, the question arises as to how to restrict structural Case assignment to the complement. The solution to this latter question that was given in Chapter 2 was that the complement is the constituent that is adjacent to and governed by the head.

Alternative formulations are plausible and may in fact be more attractive than the one just sketched out. Suppose, for example, that θ-roles are indeed assigned under government in terms of m-command, but structural Case is assigned under the more restrictive requirement of c-command. We cannot then reduce Case assignment and θ-role assignment to the same notion of government, but this alternative reflects the intuitive difference between the two relations. θ-roles are assigned within the maximal projection of the head, while structural Case is assigned both more narrowly, to subject and object, and somewhat more broadly, to the subject of the infinitive in ECM constructions. In what follows we will adopt this alternative view of θ-role and Case assignment.

3. Specifiers

3.1. The specifier of CP

Here we consider evidence that confirms the X' schema (see (7)) applies to CP. Consider the sentences in (36).

(36)   a. What did you say?
       b. Who will Mary insult?

In these sentences, an NP has moved from object position to initial position in the sentence, and Infl, the head of IP, has moved to the second position. We have already seen that Infl originates in the structure NP-Infl-VP, and we will argue in Chapter 6 that the interrogative NPs originate in non-initial position at D-structure. Given this, we must posit landing sites for the two moved constituents, that is, positions into which they can be inserted that are consistent with the structure-preserving principle (Chapter 2, § 1.2).[11] There must be a phrasal position followed by a head position, which conforms exactly to the structure provided by the X' analysis of CP, as shown in (37).

(37)

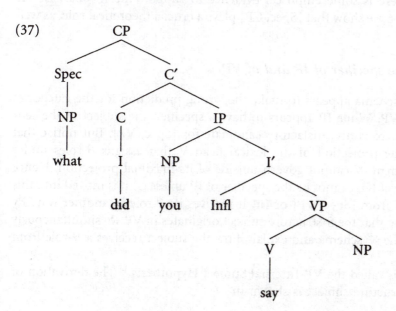

There is no directly comparable evidence for CP structure in embedded clauses, because there is no inversion in standard English embedded questions. However, in Hibernian English such inversion is possible, and there is inversion in standard English with fronted negative focus, or **negative inversion**.[12]

(38)   John said that under no circumstances would he agree to drive
        such a vehicle to work.

We find evidence for the specifier position in embedded questions as in (39).

(39)   I wonder what you will do.

What we do not get in English is a filled [Spec, CP] along with a true overt complementizer such as *that*. On the other hand, we do find such evidence in Middle English and Bavarian German, as shown in the following examples.

(40)   *a.* men shal wel knowe who that I am (M. Eng.)
        b. I woass ned wann dass da Xavea kummt (Bav.)
           I know not when that the Xavea comes

Thus there is some empirical evidence to support the X' analysis.[13] In Chapter 6 we show that [Spec, CP] plays a crucial theoretical role, as well.

3.2. The specifier of IP and of VP

The X' schema appears to make the wrong prediction for the categories IP and VP. While IP appears to have a specifier, the subject of the sentence, there is no satisfactory candidate for [Spec, VP]. But notice that VP is the projection of the lexical head V that assigns θ-roles under government. V cannot govern outside of its maximal projection. Hence the subject NP cannot be the specifier of IP unless (i) it is moved into this position from [Spec, VP] or (ii) it receives its θ-role in another way. By assuming that the S-structure subject originates in VP we simultaneously satisfy the X' schema and explain how the subject receives a θ-role from its head.[14]

This is called the **VP-Internal Subject Hypothesis**.[15] The derivation of the S-structure subject is shown in (41).

(41)

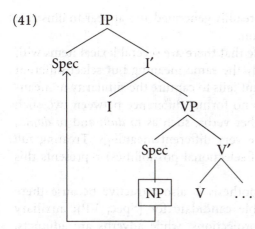

Notice that under this analysis, [Spec, VP] is the sister of V' in the sense that each c-commands the other. This relation allows us to formulate θ-role assignment to the subject under a uniform c-command definition of government, if we assume also that the θ-role assigner for the subject is not V but V'. We raised in Chapter 2 the issue of whether government is defined in terms of m-command or c-command, and considered several possibilities. Among them is that Case is assigned under c-command or through Spec-head agreement, which calls into question whether the m-command definition of government is required for θ-role assignment. Now we can see how to resolve this question.

Evidence that it is in fact V' and not V that assigns the external θ-role is that there are cases in which the complement of the verb contributes to determining the external θ-role. Consider the following examples which illustrate the point.

(42)   a. Mary rolled down the hill.
　　　 b. Mary rolled the book down the hill.
(43)   a. Mary broke the window.
　　　 b. Mary broke her arm.
(44)   a. Mary took a ride.
　　　 b. Mary took a look at Bill.
　　　 c. Mary took a minute to fix the faucet.

In (42), it is impossible to determine the θ-role of *Mary* by just looking at the verb *roll*; the assignment of θ-roles to the rest of the constituents of VP is crucial. The same point is made by the examples in (43) and

(44). Examples like these can be readily generated and appear to illustrate the rule rather than the exception.

It is of course logically possible that there are several lexical items with the form *roll* which have roughly the same meaning but select different complements. But such an account fails to capture the similarity in meaning in a principled way; there is no formal difference between two such verbs *roll* as in (42) and two other verbs, such as *to dam* and *to damn*, which sound the same but have very different meanings. Treating *roll* as a single verb (with a range of selectional possibilities) represents this difference in a natural way.

The VP-Internal Subject Hypothesis is also attractive because there appears to be no other plausible candidate for [Spec, VP]; auxiliary verbs are heads of their own projections, while adverbs are adjuncts. Note in particular that phrasal adverbs cannot precede the V, in general, contrary to what we might expect if they were in specifier position.

(45)   Mary will $\left\{\begin{array}{l}\text{*tomorrow}\\\text{*next week}\\\text{*from home}\\\text{*at home}\\\text{*with pleasure}\\\text{*fast}\end{array}\right\}$ call the bank.

In fact, only *-ly* adverbs and a few others may appear in this preverbal position in VP.

(46)   Mary will $\left\{\begin{array}{l}\text{probably}\\\text{carefully}\\\text{now}\\\text{quickly}\end{array}\right\}$ call the bank.

To investigate why this should be, see Exercise 5-11.

Since the subject in English appears to the left of Infl, there must be movement from the D-structure position to the S-structure position. We hypothesize that this movement occurs because [Spec, VP] is not a Case position, which means that Infl cannot assign Case to this position across the maximal projection VP. (Note the contrast here with ECM, where the V appears to assign Case across IP.) Alternatively, we may hypothesize that while [Spec, VP] is a Case position, an NP in this position must move into [Spec, IP] in English for reasons having to do with something other than Case, e.g. the Extended Projection Principle noted in Chapter 4, § 2. The EPP requires that there be a subject in every clause. On the current alternative, the EPP cannot be reduced to Case theory, of course.

Empirical arguments that NPs originate in [Spec, VP] come from several sources. In English and in French, the distribution of **floated quantifiers** such as those in (47a) can be accounted for if the subject originates within VP, as in (47b).[16]

(47) *a.* The children have all left.
　　　　 Les enfants sont tous partis.
　　 b. [$_{IP}$ [the children]$_i$ have [$_{VP}$ [t$_i$ all] left]]
　　　　 [$_{IP}$ [les enfants]$_i$ sont [$_{VP}$ [t$_i$ tous] partis]]

Yiddish has a VP-internal subject not only at D-structure, but at S-structure.[17] Yiddish displays the **verb second (V2)** property typical of the Germanic languages, where the inflected verb immediately follows a single topicalized constituent.

(48) *a.* Dos bukh shik ikh avek.
　　　　 the book send I　 away
　　 b. Ikh vel avekshikn dos bukh.
　　　　 I　 will send away the book

Crucially, topicalization in an embedded clause also produces the V2 effect; the order is C-XP$_{Topic}$-V-NP- . . .

(49) *a.* Avrom gloybt az Max shikt avek dos bukh.
　　　　 Avrom believes that Max sends away the book
　　 b. Ir zolt visn zayn az vayn ken men makhn fun troybn
　　　　 you should know　 that wine can one make　 from grapes
　　　　 oykh.
　　　　 also

The inflected V obviously cannot move into the position occupied by C in these examples. It appears, then that the topic undergoes movement into [Spec, IP], while V adjoins to Infl in order to receive its inflection. The structure is given in (50).

(50)

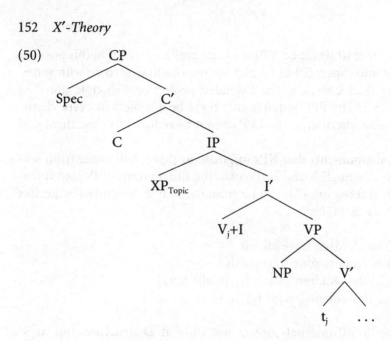

This analysis supports the VP-Internal Subject Hypothesis for Yiddish.

But now notice that if the NP is not moved from [Spec, VP], it must receive Case without undergoing movement. If this analysis is correct, it lends support to the view discussed earlier in connection with English that the VP-internal subject moves to [Spec, IP] for reasons other than Case.

Let us summarize the main points thus far. We assume that the subject originates as [Spec, VP] and raises to [Spec, IP] to satisfy the Case Filter, although other explanations for the raising must be explored. Government is defined in terms of c-command. A specifier is assigned Case under Spec-head agreement, while a complement is assigned Case under government. θ-roles are assigned under government as well, where the θ-role is assigned by the sister, not directly by the head.

3.3. The specifier of NP

Let us turn now to the determiner, exemplified by English *the*. We assumed in § 1 that the determiner is a specifier. But by the assumptions of X'-theory, *the* must be the head of a maximal projection. Let us call this projection DP. If DP can be the specifier of NP, and if a possessive NP can be the specifier of NP, then we have a non-uniform analysis, illustrated in (51).

(51)

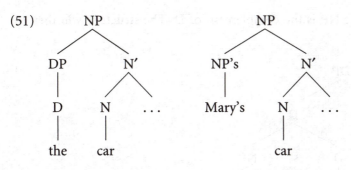

Under this analysis the possible specifiers of NP are of (at least) two different syntactic categories, and while one, the possessive NP, is an argument and receives a θ-role, the other, DP, is not. Moreover, DP under this analysis appears never to have a specifier or a complement of its own.

One way to impose greater uniformity on the analysis is to take the possessive marker to be the head of DP, so that the structure of *Mary's car* will be that of (52).

(52)

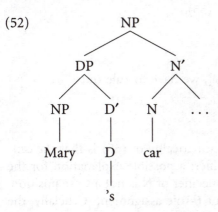

But now we have a situation in which some specifiers are DP, while other specifiers are NP. For example, the subject of a sentence does not appear to be a DP, but is simply an NP.

(53) *a.* Mary(*'s) owns a car.
     b. *The left.

To achieve further uniformity in the analysis under the X' framework, let us suppose rather that D is in fact the head of a maximal projection, but also that the NP is the complement of D. The structure will then be that of (54).[18]

(54)

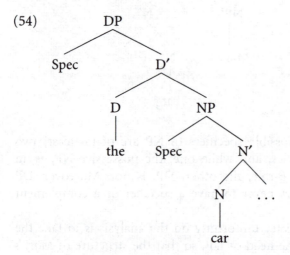

Where does the possessive NP go in this structure? If we assume that it is [Spec, DP], we have to rule out (55).

(55)   *Mary's the car

But if we assume that it is [Spec, NP], we have to rule out (56).

(56)   *the Mary's car

A possible explanation for the ungrammaticality of (55) is that *the* cannot assign GENITIVE Case to its specifier; a possible explanation for the ungrammaticality of (56) is that the specifier of N is not a Case position. But let us consider not only Case, but θ-role assignment. Crucially, the specifier of DP is outside of the NP, while the specifier of NP is inside of the NP. If we wish to account for the assignment of θ-role under government by a head, we must choose the option in which the possessive NP originates as the specifier of NP. So the D-structure is actually (57).

(57)

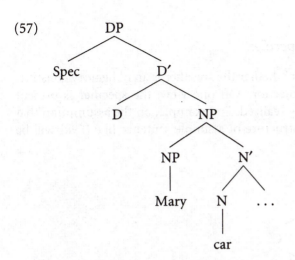

It is now an open question how *Mary* gets Case. One plausible option is that D, which governs *Mary*, assigns GENITIVE Case into the NP complement. Not all instances of D assign Case, as noted above; in fact, no overt determiner can precede a Case-marked possessive.

(58) $\left\{\begin{array}{l}\text{*the}\\ \text{*a}\\ \text{*every}\\ \text{*my}\\ \text{*this}\\ \text{*all}\\ \text{*some}\\ \text{*which}\end{array}\right\}$ Mary's car

An alternative possibility is that *Mary* cannot receive Case in the [Spec, NP] position but must move to [Spec, DP]. Case would then be assigned under the Spec-head agreement configuration by the empty head D, but not by the overt determiners. (Spec-head agreement was introduced in Chapter 2; it is one basic mechanism, and perhaps the only mechanism, through which constituents are licensed in particular positions.) Such an analysis is most compatible with the VP-Internal Subject analysis developed in § 3.2, which also assumes that the subject raises to get Case in the Spec position of a functional head. From the perspective of Uniformity, therefore, this analysis is to be preferred, and it is the one that we will take to be correct. From this point, also, we will notate noun phrases as 'DP', but we will continue to describe them in the text as 'noun phrases' or 'NP' where no confusion arises.

3.4. Obligatoriness of specifier

In this section we consider whether the specifier is an obligatory constituent of every maximal projection. On one view, the specifier is present whether or not it is overtly realized. For example, on the assumption that every clause is a CP, the structure of a simple sentence like (59*a*) will be (59*b*).

(59) *a.* Mary will call.
     b.

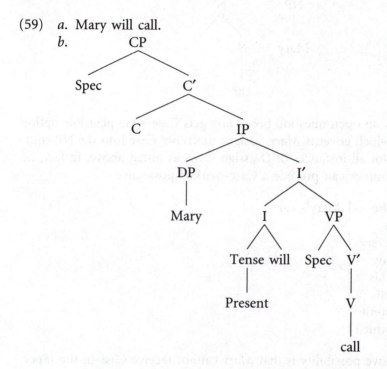

On an alternative view, a projection has a specifier position only if something exists to fill this position.[19] On this view, specifier is similar to complement, since when a verb lacks a complement there is little evidence that there is an empty DP in complement position.[20] Pursuing the analogy with complements, we observe that a constituent may appear in complement position only if it satisfies the selectional requirements of the head. It is natural to adopt the same view for specifiers. What remains to be worked out is precisely what is meant by 'satisfies the selectional requirements of the head.'

If a phrase lacks a specifier, then the question arises as to what the category of the phrase actually is. In the system that we have outlined, there are two possible structures.

(60) *a.*

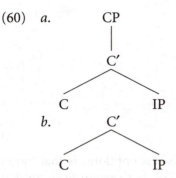

In (60*a*) we have a non-branching CP, while in (60*b*) the maximal projection is C′ as opposed to CP. There appear to be no syntactic generalizations that adhere to the CP/C′ distinction.[21] In effect, when C′ is maximal, as in (60*b*), it counts as C^{max}. Consider the following formal characterization of *projection*.[22]

(61)   *Project α*: a word of syntactic category X is dominated by an uninterrupted sequence of X nodes.

(62)   *Projection Chain of X* $=_{def}$ an uninterrupted sequence of projections of X.

(63) *a. Maximal Projection*: $X = X^{max}$ iff $\forall Y$ which dominate X, Category(Y) $\neq$ Category(X).[23]

   b. Minimal Projection: $X = X^0$ iff X immediately dominates a word.

On this view, a head has grammatical features, called ϕ-**features**. ϕ-features are those that must be satisfied through agreement in the course of a derivation, e.g. person, number. Other grammatical features, such as Case, Tense, and so on, are assigned through various mechanisms of agreement and adjunction in the course of a derivation. Maximization of the uniformity of feature assignment can be achieved by reducing all of these mechanisms to Spec-head agreement: if a constituent β has a feature F, this feature must be 'satisfied' through agreement, either at S-structure or at some abstract level of representation.[24]

Some languages appear to lack overt D and C entirely. In the terms just summarized, we might say that these functional categories are always 'inert' for agreement, so that a constituent in 'specifier position' would never be licensed. It is in fact the case that in a language such as Japanese there are no overt lexical determiners comparable to English *the*, and possessive DPs and even demonstratives function syntactically like adjuncts.

(64)   *a.* John-ga   hon-o   yonda.
          John-NOM book-ACC read-PAST
          'John read the book.'
       b. John-no ko-no   hon.
          John-NO this-NO book
          'this book of John's'
          (Fukui 1986)

One conclusion, within the framework of X' assumptions, is that 'noun phrases' in languages such as Japanese are DP, but vacuously so, in that D is always empty, and similarly for C. This is the maximally uniform analysis, in that it assumes that every language has and expresses the full set of functional categories at all levels of syntactic representation. A weaker alternative is that the functional categories D and C simply do not exist in Japanese, in violation of the strong uniformity assumption regarding the inventory of categories across languages. In contrast it has been suggested that Japanese has the functional category I(nfl) but I(nfl) has weaker agreement features in Japanese than does I in English.[25] This will produce the result that [Spec, IP] in Japanese, while it exists, is never filled. The relative strength of agreement features is a matter of parametric variation between languages. By assuming that a feature is strong in one language and weak in another, it is possible to maintain uniformity in the inventory of features. Syntactic differences follow if only the strong features must be satisfied at S-structure. The weak features, while present in some abstract sense, have no S-structure effects. See § 5 below and Chapter 10, § 3 for elaboration.

At this point you should be able to do Exercises 5-2 through 5-9.

4. Adjuncts

Everything that is not a head, complement, or specifier in a projection is an adjunct. Adjuncts are not assigned θ-roles by the head, that is, they are not 'classified' by the head, so to speak. Some examples are shown in (65).

(65)   *a.* house *in the woods*
       b. *old* refrigerator
       c. leave *because he was frightened*

    d. run *slowly*
    e. live *in the woods*
    f. book *that I bought*
    g. taller *than Mary (is)*
    h. very tall

Because 'adjunct' includes whatever does not fall into the other three classes, it is not surprising to find that there is no homogeneous characterization of the term. For example, some adjuncts express thematic roles, such as LOCATION (*in the woods* in (65a) and (65e)), while others do not.

As we will see in the next two chapters, the status of adjuncts becomes particularly important in the theory of A'-movement. In particular, the question arises as to the precise relationship between (i) the fact that a phrase expresses a θ-role with respect to a head, (ii) the fact that a phrase is an obligatory complement of a head, or non-sister of the head that is nevertheless c-selected by the head, and (iii) the fact that a phrase is governed by a head under c-command.

Sometimes the θ-role expressed by the adjunct (assuming that it is an adjunct) is required by the verb; e.g.

(66) *a.* Mary put the clock on the shelf.
    b. *Mary put the clock.
    c. *Mary put on the shelf.

This obligatoriness suggests that perhaps the PP is not an adjunct but an argument, but since it is not a sister of the verb, it cannot be a complement in the strict syntactic sense. In order to accommodate this situation we could change our requirement that all branching is binary (see § 1), redefine sister, redefine complement, or redefine government. Notice that there are some verbs that obligatorily select adverbs or measure phrases.

(67) *a.* Bill worded the letter very carefully.
    b. Bill worded the letter with the precise intention of insulting Mary.
    c. Bill worded the letter so as to avoid any connection with the scandal.
    d. *Bill worded the letter.
    e. *Carefully, Bill worded the letter.
    f. *Bill carefully worded the letter.
(68) *a.* Mary weighs 300 pounds.
    b. Mary weighs exactly what a champion should.

    c. Mary weighs too much.

    d. *Mary (really) weighs.

We will assume that 'obligatory' is not equivalent to 'complement,' and that the syntactic selection of arguments by heads is not equivalent to government. This allows for the possibility that adjuncts can be c-selected or s-selected by a head while allowing government to be defined in terms of c-command, as we have proposed.

5. Government and parameters

Next we turn to the question of constituent order. Under the view that Case and θ-role are assigned under government, we have one prime source for word order variation: government. Suppose, for example, that government is directional, in that in any given language, a head either governs to the left or to the right. If a head governs to the right, then its complement(s) will appear to the right of it, barring movement. Similarly for leftward government. Using this distinction, we can account for the fact that in English the direct object follows the verb, but in Japanese the direct object precedes the verb.

(69) *a.* John-ga   hon-o   yonda.
         John-NOM book-ACC read-Past
    b. John read the book.

More generally, if adjuncts are governed directionally, they will all appear on the same side of the verb as does the complement. So in English, everything in VP appears to the right of V, while in Japanese, everything appears to the left. English is V-initial, while Japanese is V-final. This is the classic case of parametric variation; the parameter that determines directionality of government is called the **Head Parameter**.[26]

    The other logical candidate for explaining variation in word order is movement. As the discussion in the preceding sections suggests, parametric variation in word order may be due not to the value of a parameter that stipulates the direction of government in a given language, but to a parameter that does not explicitly mention directionality but that entails a particular surface order. Suppose, for instance, that Case is an agreement feature. Let us call the head that assigns this feature Agr. Let us assume the basic structure in (70).[27]

(70)

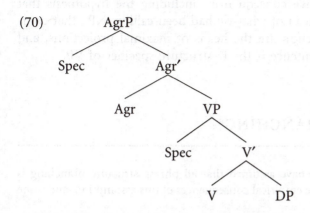

Now, if the feature of Case is strong in one language, DP must move to [Spec, AgrP] in order to agree with Agr on the Case feature. In doing so it crosses over the verb, producing the order O-V. On the other hand, if the feature of Case is weak, DP does not move to [Spec, AgrP] at S-structure; hence the order is V-O. Thus, the parametric variation in word order is reduced to an independent parameter of the strength of the Case feature.

Whether all parametric variation can be accounted for in this way is still an open question. One problem concerns the fact that in some languages, the verb must follow all constituents of VP, including those that are not assigned Case by V. If we assume that all of the VP constituents (except perhaps the subject) originate in D-structure to the right of V, we have to assume a substantial number of heads and features whose primary function is to force the movement of these non-Cased constituents to the left before S-structure. There is no question that such an analysis can be constructed, but whether there is independent evidence for all of the heads and features is a different matter. We pursue this question further in Chapter 10.

6. Summary

In this chapter we surveyed X'-theory, the theory of possible phrases. On a restricted and uniform view of phrase structure, every phrase has exactly one head; everything is a head, a complement, a specifier, or an adjunct. Holding closely to such a view has a number of interesting and at times provocative consequences, including the hypothesis that the determiner is the head of what we had been calling 'NP', that complementizers and inflection are the heads of maximal projections, and that the subject of a sentence is the D-structure specifier of VP.

APPENDIX A: BRANCHING

Throughout this text we have assumed that all phrase structure branching is binary. Let us consider the empirical consequences of this assumption, and some alternatives.

Consider a situation in which there are three constituents in a phrase, as in (71).

(71) $[_\alpha$ A B C]

If both binary and multiple branching are possible options, there will be three possible ways to group the constituents of α, as shown in (72).

(72)   *a.* $[_\alpha$ A B C] (flat multiple branching)
       b. $[_\alpha$ [A B] C] (binary branching)
       c. $[_\alpha$ A [B C]] (binary branching)

Suppose that α has four constituents.

(73)   *a.* $[_\alpha$ A B C D] (flat multiple branching)
       b. $[_\alpha$ A [B C D]] (multiple branching)
       c. $[_\alpha$ A [B C] D] (multiple branching)
       d. $[_\alpha$ [A B C] D] (multiple branching)
       e. $[_\alpha$ A [B [C D]]] (binary branching)
       f. $[_\alpha$ [A B] [C D]] (binary branching)
       g. $[_\alpha$ [[A B] C] D] (binary branching)
       h. $[_\alpha$ [A [B C]] D] (binary branching)
       i. $[_\alpha$ A [[B C] D]] (binary branching)

As the number of constituents of α grows, the number of possible groupings grows rapidly. From the point of view of the language learner, the number of possible hypotheses consistent with evidence from the target language should be minimal, and ideally only one. By eliminating multiple branching, we can reduce the number of hypotheses substantially. But by the same token, by eliminating binary branching we can also reduce the number of hypotheses substantially.

The only assumption about branching that produces exactly one hypothesis given that the constituents of the phrase can be independently identified as such is flat multiple branching, where there is no internal structure.

Suppose that we impose the additional constraints on possible hypotheses to the effect that the head must be most deeply embedded in the phrase (i.e. it is c-commanded by everything in the phrase) and it must be either in initial or in final position. Suppose that the head is *H*. For the case of three and four constituents we now have the following possibilities.

(74) *a.* [$_\alpha$ H B C] (flat multiple branching)
   b. [$_\alpha$ [H B] C] (binary branching)
(75) *a.* [$_\alpha$ H B C D] (flat multiple branching)
   b. [$_\alpha$ [H B C] D] (multiple branching)
   c. [$_\alpha$ [[H B] C] D] (binary branching)

By imposing these head constraints, we reduce the number of binary branching hypotheses to one. On the basis of these considerations we can conclude that there are in fact two assumptions about branching that will yield a unique structure for any set of constituents that form a phrase: flat multiple branching, and binary branching with most deeply embedded, peripheral head.

Consider now the empirical issues. The classical tests for constituency in VP appear to suggest that the structure of VP involves strictly binary branching. For example, *do so* and VP Topicalization can affect part of the VP, as shown in (76) and (77).

(76) *a.* Bill read the book in the library, and Mary did so (in the museum).
   b. Bill fixed the faucet with a screwdriver in fifteen minutes with great difficulty, and Mary did so (with a hammer)(in twenty minutes) (with no problem at all).
(77) *a.* They said that Bill would read the book somewhere, and read the book he did in the library.
   b. They said that Bill would read the book in the library, and read the book in the library he did.

What these tests show is that parts of the VP may be moved or replaced by a pro-form, leaving behind the rest of the VP. Since the parts left behind may or may not be affected, depending on the context, it appears that they, too, are part of the VP. Assuming Syntacticization, the possibility of applying such tests to parts of VPs suggests that the parts are in themselves constituents, which is consistent with a binary branching structure along the lines of (78).

(78) [$_{VP}$ [$_{VP}$ [$_{VP}$ fix the faucet] with a screwdriver] in fifteen minutes] . . .

But it is well-known that the standard tests for VP constituency fail in certain cases. Consider the following examples.

(79)   a. *Bill gave a present to me, and Mary did so to my brother.
       b. They said that Bill would give a present to someone, and give a
          present he did, to me.[28]
(80)   a. *Bill put some money on the table, and Mary did so on the shelf.
       b. They said that Bill would put some money somewhere, and put
          some money he did, on the table.
(81)   a. *Bill gave Mary a book, and Susan did so a magazine.
       b. ?They said that Bill would give Mary something, and give Mary he
          did a magazine.
(82)   a. *Bill drank the coffee hot, and Mary did so cold.
       b. They said that Bill would drink the coffee somehow, and drink the
          coffee he did, hot.

The *do so* test and the VP Topicalization test give conflicting results. In fact, the *do so* test suggests that there is a multiple branching structure in VPs headed by *put* and *give*, while VP Topicalization suggests that there is a binary branching structure. Our assumption that there is only one type of branching rules out the possibility that there could be two types of branching in a language, let alone two types of branching for selected lexical items.[29]

Let us suppose for the sake of argument that the structure of VP is as in (78), that is, binary branching. The failure of the *do so* test to apply in these examples cannot depend on the constituent structure. Examination of the cases shows that there are two conditions under which *do so* is ungrammatical: (i) where the material left behind is obligatorily subcategorized,[30] and (ii) where the material left behind is predicated of something that has been replaced by *do so*. In the case of *put* and *give*, for example, all arguments are obligatory.

(83)   a. *Bill gave the book.
       b. *Bill gave Mary.
(84)   a. *Bill put the book.
       b. *Bill put on the table.

In the case of *drink the coffee hot*, *hot* is predicated of *coffee*.

We can even imagine reducing the condition (i) to condition (ii), if we adopt the following analysis of the double object construction.[31] Suppose that the direct object is predicated of the indirect object, producing a type of possessor relation. That is, in *give Mary the book*, *the book* is predicated of *Mary*, implying that Mary has the book. For the case of *put*, it is possible to envision a predication relation between the direct object and the location: in *put the book on the table*, the table is the location of the book.

If this line of reasoning is on the right track, then the *do so* test tells us nothing about the internal structure of the VP. It is entirely possible to envision an interpretation of *do so* that covers any portion of an antecedent VP that does not break the predication links. *Do so* reveals the syntactic structure only if the distribution of *do so* is a syntactic phenomenon, rather than one that is properly formulated in terms of semantic representation.

Consider now the evidence of VP Topicalization. On the face of it the evidence seems to point to binary branching. But note that for some speakers, at least, it is possible to topicalize the V alone, leaving behind the entire rest of the VP. The following examples require marked contrastive stress.

(85) *a.* They said that Bill would give something to someone, and give he did a PRESENT to ME.
   b. They said that Bill would put something somewhere, and put he did some MONEY on the TABLE.

There are at least three ways to view these cases. First, it is possible that the verb alone simply moves to the left. Such an analysis is ruled out in most current theories because it would involve the adjunction of a head (that is, the V) to a maximal projection (that is, to IP or CP). Second, it is possible that the entire VP moves to the left and then everything in the VP moves to the right. An illustration is given in (86).

(86)

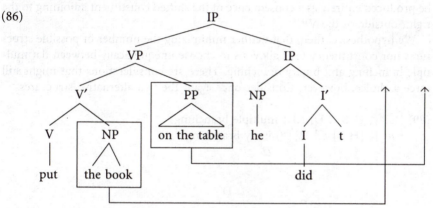

The third possibility is that these constituents move out of the VP before the VP moves to the left, as in (87).

(87)

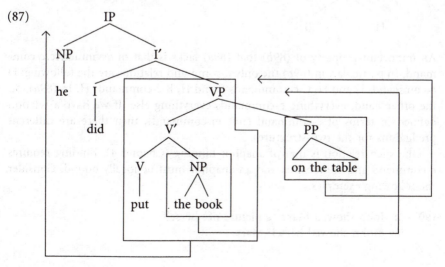

The plausibility of one of these latter two derivations is suggested by the fact that English independently has a rightward movement construction in VP, called Heavy Shift. It is typified by the examples in (88).

(88)   *a.* I gave t to Bill [the books that I bought]
     b. I gave t t yesterday [to Bill] [the books that I bought]
     c. I gave t t yesterday [the books that I bought] [to Bill]

However, if Heavy Shift is responsible for the VP Topicalization facts when the V alone is moved, it can also account for the other examples that we have been considering. That is, if Heavy Shift produces a binary branching structure as a consequence of the extraction of constituents from VP and adjunction to a higher position in the sentence, we cannot use VP Topicalization as evidence about the internal structure of the VP. In effect, there is a branching structure, but it can be produced entirely as a consequence of the shifted constituent adjoining to the right, outside of the VP.

We hypothesize, then, that neither minimizing the number of possible structures nor constituency tests allow us to choose unequivocally between flat multiple branching and binary branching. There are considerations that might still force a choice, however. Consider once again the two alternative structures.

(89)   *a.* [$_\alpha$ H B C D] (flat multiple branching)
     b. [$_\alpha$ [H B] C] D]] (binary branching)

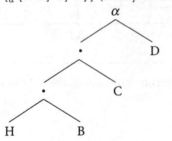

An important property of (89*b*) that (89*a*) lacks is that of **asymmetric c-command**. In particular, in (89*b*) the only c-command relations are the following: D c-commands C and H, C c-commands B and H, B c-commands H. In (89*a*), on the other hand, everything c-commands everything else. If we have a relation defined in terms of c-command (not m-command), then there are different predictions for the two structures.

One such relation is that of anaphor binding (Chapter 4). Binding requires c-command and coindexing, and an anaphor must be locally bound. Consider the following examples.

(90)   *a.* John showed Mary (a picture of) herself.
     b. *John showed herself Mary.

(91) *a.* John put Mary next to a picture of herself.
      b. John told Mary about some nasty stories about herself.

The examples in (90) suggest that the direct object does not c-command the indirect object to the left of it. If the VP has a flat structure, c-command (or at least binding) must be reformulated so as to make reference to the left-to-right order of the constituents, given that there can be no binding from the right to the left.[32] By the principle of Primacy of Configuration (see Chapter 1), mention of left-to-right order is to be avoided in this theory in favor of hierarchical structure. Thus it appears that (89*b*) is the correct structure.

But here we also have a problem, because the constituents to the left do not c-command the constituents to the right, even though they appear to bind them. If we allow binding to be determined by m-command within the VP, then we will have to restrict binding so that it will not apply from right to left. On the basis of considerations such as these, it has in fact been proposed that the structure of the VP is quite different from either of the structures in (89), i.e. that it has the structure in (92).

(92) $[_\alpha \Delta B [_\alpha \Delta C [_\alpha H D]]]$

Here, c-command corresponds to the left-to-right order. Since the head H ends up in a left peripheral position at S-structure, it must move up successively through the empty heads marked Δ. We will explore in greater detail the motivations for this analysis and some of the consequences in Chapter 10, § 3.

APPENDIX B: THE STATUS OF GRAMMATICAL RELATIONS

In the development of GB theory, a fundamental methodological principle has been that configurational relations are fundamental, while notions such as Subject and Object are secondary; they are defined in terms of the configuration. For example, Chomsky (1965) defines Subject as the [NP, S] and Object as [NP, VP], where the notation [X, Y] abbreviates 'X immediately dominated by Y.' Any generalizations that appear to involve Subject or Object can be formulated in terms of these configurations; the implicit claim is that the configurational approach will offer greater generality and empirical adequacy.

In contrast to this position there have been a number of proposals to account for certain grammatical phenomena in terms of grammatical relations directly, and not in terms of configuration. Some such accounts define a relation of relative prominence between arguments in terms of a relational hierarchy stated in terms of grammatical relations, rather than in terms of the configurational hierarchy formulated in terms of c-command in GB theory. For example, Relational Grammar states a construction such as Passive in terms of the 'promotion' of the direct object to subject.[33] In LFG[34] and in HPSG[35] the grammatical relations are ordered with respect to one another according to the following hierarchy, which plays a role in various rules and principles.

(93)   SUBJ > DO > IO > . . .

B.1. HPSG binding theory

There are a number of phenomena discussed in this book that appear to be sensitive to some type of hierarchical relationships. In general, the relationship that is crucial is binding, which is c-command with coindexing. The empirical question that arises in connection with such phenomena is whether the binding relation is most effectively formulated in terms of c-command. The one phenomenon that we have already considered is Binding theory: an anaphor must be locally bound, a pronoun cannot be locally bound, and an R-expression cannot be bound (Chapter 3).[36]

Evidence that c-command does not determine binding with respect to the Binding theory, for example, is offered in the HPSG framework.[37] Suppose that we define a relation of o-command (as contrasted with c-command), such that an argument higher on the hierarchy o-commands arguments lower on the hierarchy within the same clause. The relevant definitions are the following:[38]

(94)   Y locally o-commands Z just in case Y is higher on the obliqueness hierarchy than Z.
(95)   Y o-commands Z just in case Y locally o-commands X dominating Z.
(96)   Y (locally) o-binds Z just in case Y and Z are coindexed and Y (locally) o-binds Z. If Z is not (locally) o-bound, then it is said to be (locally) o-free.
(97)   Principle A: A locally o-commanded anaphor must be locally o-bound.
       Principle B: A personal pronoun must be locally o-free.
       Principle C: A non-pronoun must be o-free.

Facts of the sort given in (98) are claimed to be evidence that o-command, and not c-command of the GB Binding theory, is the proper hierarchical relation.

(98)   *a.* The children$_i$ thought that [[each other$_i$'s] pictures] were on sale.
       b. The children$_i$ thought that [pictures of [each other$_i$/themselves$_i$]] were on sale.

Since the anaphors in these cases are not locally o-commanded, there is no requirement that they be locally o-bound. This treatment thus avoids the complications involving the i-within-i Condition, SUBJECT, and defining the governing category associated with the Binding theory (see Chapter 3).

It might be suggested that anaphors in *picture* NPs are in general not subject to any Binding theory conditions stated for local anaphora. Rather, they are long distance anaphors that in English happen to have the same form as the local anaphors, as suggested in Chapter 8. By removing such anaphors from the domain of Binding theory, the GB account can be significantly simplified; the type of anaphora illustrated in (98) does not present a problem.

Such a response is not available in connection with the sentences in (99).[39]

(99)   a. Mary talked to John about Susan.
       b. Mary talked to John$_i$ about himself$_i$.
       c. Mary$_j$ talked to John about herself$_j$.
(100) a. Mary talked about Susan to John.
       b. *Mary talked about John$_i$ to himself$_i$.
       c. Mary$_j$ talked about herself$_j$ to John.

What we see here is that the *to* and the *about* phrases can appear in either order in the VP. However, it is impossible for the antecedent of an anaphor to be in the *about* phrase while the anaphor itself is in the *to* phrase (see (100a)). This unexpected ungrammaticality follows directly from o-command, on the plausible assumption that the indirect object is higher on the obliqueness hierarchy than is the adjunct *about* phrase.[40]

Notice, moreover, that c-command appears to be doubly inadequate here. First of all, whatever the c-command relations are, it is questionable whether *John* c-commands *himself* in (99b) but not in (100b). Furthermore, given the branching structure of the PP, it is not clear that in any of these cases that the antecedent c-commands (and therefore binds in the GB sense) the anaphor. These and other difficulties can of course be addressed by assuming (and justifying) different syntactic structures in which the c-command relations hold as intended (see Chapter 10, § 5).

In summary, the HPSG approach argues that while binding theory is syntactic, the syntactic primitives that are necessary to account for binding are grammatical relations, not configuration.

B.2. LFG

The independent existence of grammatical relations is also a fundamental assumption of Lexical-Functional Grammar (LFG) (Bresnan 1982a). In this framework, the description of a sentence involves three interrelated representations: a(rgument)-structure, c(onfigurational)-structure, and f(unctional)-structure. A-structure is essentially a representation of the θ-role assignments in a sentence, c-structure is the phrase structure, and f-structure is a representation of the grammatical relations. There are mappings between these levels that define the class of possible sentences in a language.

The most problematic level, from the GB perspective, is f-structure. What evidence is there that f-structure is independently required? Again, the case for the independence of grammatical relations must involve syntactic generalizations that cannot be adequately expressed strictly in terms of θ-roles or in terms of configuration. Bresnan (1994) makes just such a case.

Bresnan considers certain inversion phenomena in English and in Chicheŵa, a Bantu language of East-Central Africa. Both languages have a construction, called **locative inversion**, in which the subject follows the verb and a locative or directional expression appears in preverbal position.

(101)   *English*:
   a. A lamp was in the corner.
   b. In the corner was a lamp.
   c. John went into the room.
   d. Into the room went John.

(102)   *Chicheŵa*:[41]
   a. Ku mu-dzi ku-li   chi-tsîme.
      17 3-village 17.SUBJ-be 7-well
      'In the village is a well.'
   b. Ku mu-dzi ku na-bwér-á   a-lęndo
      17 3-village 17.SUBJ-REC.PST-come-FV 2-visitor
      'To the village came a visitor.'

The examples from Chicheŵa are particularly interesting because they show that the verb agrees with the fronted adverb, not with the postposed subject. The agreement is shown by the appearance of the same noun class marker on the NP and on the verb. When the subject appears in canonical preverbal position, the verb agrees with it.

(103)   Chi-tsîme chi-li   ku mu-dzi.
        7-well   7.SUBJ-be 17 3-village
        'The well is in the village.'

Given that the fronted locative has a noun class marker and participates in agreement, it is reasonable to suppose that in Chicheŵa, at least, the locatives are NPs (as Bresnan suggests). In contrast, in English the verb agrees with the postverbal subject.

(104)   a. In the room was/*were a man.
        b. In the room *was/were women.

Bresnan argues that this difference in the agreement patterns in the two languages is evidence for a c-structure difference between them in the case of the locative inversion construction. In Chicheŵa, the NP is in the configurational 'subject' position. In English, the PP is in the configurational topic position. However, in all other respects the two constructions are identical, and in particular, the fronted constituent in both languages behaves like a subject in a number of respects. For example, the PP appears to undergo Raising in English (Chapter 4, § 2). The following examples are Bresnan's.

(105)   *a.* Over my window seems ___ to have crawled an entire army of ants.
      b. In these villages are likely ___ to be found the best examples of this cuisine.
(106)   *a.* An entire army of ants seems ___ to have crawled over my window.
      b. The best examples of this cuisine are likely to be found in these villages.

And extraction of the PP produces *that-t* violations (cf. Chapter 6, § 4.3).

(107)   *a.* It's in these villages that we all believe ___ can be found the best examples of this cuisine.
      b. *It's in these villages that we all believe that ___ can be found the best examples of this cuisine.
(108)   *a.* It's this cuisine that we all believe ___ can be found in these villages.
      b. *It's this cuisine that we all believe that ___ can be found in these villages.

At this point, it might appear that we have evidence that the preposed PP in English is an NP, and should therefore be in [Spec, IP]. But, Bresnan argues, the PP is not a configurational subject, only a functional subject. There are a number of pieces of evidence to support this claim. One is the failure of the verb to agree with the preposed PP. Another is that Subject Aux Inversion does not occur with locative inversion.

(109)   *a.* *Did on the wall hang a Mexican serape?
      b. *Was among the ruins found a skeleton?

But PPs that are truly subjects allow SAI—

(110)   Is under the bed a good place to hide?

—and agreement with the verb (Levine 1989).

(111)   Under the bed and in the fireplace are not the best places to leave your toys.

Furthermore, locative inversion cannot occur in infinitives.

(112)   *I expect on this wall to be hung a portrait of our founder.

   Bresnan's claim is, then, that the subjecthood of the PP in the English is a mixed phenomenon. It has the grammatical function Subject, but is not in the configurational subject position. In order to accommodate this dissociation, there must be two representations, one for each type of subject. These two representations are f-structure and c-structure in the LFG framework.

   Clearly, the argument for the independence of f-structure is the evidence that the preposed PP in English cannot be in [Spec, IP]. In order for this claim to go through, it must be shown that there are no plausible accounts of the failure of SAI with locative inversion and the non-occurrence of locative inversion in an infinitival complement in terms of the [Spec, IP] analysis.

EXERCISES

5-1. Identify the lexical and functional heads in the following sentences.

(1)   a. England will go head-to-head with Brazil in the final match.
      b. The idea that I would do such a thing is absurd.
      c. Mary's suggestion that we should quit was well-received.

[§ 2.1–§ 2.2]

5-2. Identify the specifiers, complements, and adjuncts in each of the following phrases. Justify your answers.

(1)   a. the reason for our discomfort
      b. ten feet tall
      c. John loves Mary deeply.
      d. far over the limit
      e. This is fun!

[§ 1–§ 3]

5-3. A persistent problem that arises in a maximally uniform X'-theory is that there are significant apparent non-uniformities. Consider, for example, the NPs in (1).

(1) a. Mary has Bill's books
     b. Mary has a book of Bill's

Superficially, at least, it appears that the specifier of the NP in (1*b*) is to the right instead of to the left of the head.

1. Is it appropriate to say that in general the English specifier can appear either to the left or to the right of the head? Why (not)?

2. Formulate at least two plausible analyses for (1*b*) that maintain the generalization that the specifier is to the left of the head.

[§ 3]

5-4. Consider the selection of English prepositions in complex constructions, e.g.

(1) a. angry at/with/*from/*by etc.
     b. look at/*with/*from/*by etc.
     c. happy *at/with/*from/*by etc.
     d. watch *at/*with/*from/*by etc.

These examples show that verbs and adjectives in English select prepositional phrase complements headed by some prepositions, but not by others; the choice depends on the verb or adjective. Is this c-selection, that is, simply a formal matter, s-selection, that is, determined by semantic interpretation, or neither? Explain your answer.

[§ 1–§ 3]

*5-5. In the text we distinguished c-selection, which is syntactic, and s-selection, which is semantic. Conceivably c-selection is determined entirely by s-selection. However, there are certain cases of c-selection that do not appear to be semantically predictable.[42]

(1) a. I asked what time it was.
     b. I wondered what time it was.
(2) a. I asked the time.
     b. *I wondered the time.

1. Discuss the proposal that c-selection may be reducible to s-selection. Specifically, what other explanations in terms of the theory developed thus far can be found for the counterexample to the ungrammaticality of (2*b*)? That is, what devices can you think of that would plausibly rule out this example, in lieu of simply stating that *wonder* does not select an NP complement?

2. Consider your answer to 1 in light of sentences such as the following.

(3) a. What I was wondering was whether you had called.
     b. *What I was wondering was the time.
(4) a. Something that I've been wondering for a long time is whether you
        plan to run for President again.
     b. *Something that I've been wondering for a long time is your date of
        birth.

What are the selectional properties of *wonder*?

[§ 1–§ 3]

*5-6. Discuss the implications of the following for the analysis of noun phrases.

(1) a. *Italian*:
        il   mio cappello
        the my hat
     b. *Greek*:
        to spiti   mou
        the house my

Specifically, what do these constructions suggest about the status of possessive
pronouns? What do they suggest about the status of possessive noun phrases
such as *Mary's*?

[§ 1–§ 3]

*5-7. In this exercise you are asked to consider the formal role of an adjectival
modifier of NP. Adjectives in English precede the N, just as determiners do,
which raises the question of whether they are heads or adjuncts. There is some
evidence that the adjective is the head of a prenominal adjective phrase, since it
can take what might be thought of as a specifier.

(1) a [[(very) old] car

On the other hand, prenominal adjectives cannot have adjuncts adjoined to
them, which suggests that they are heads.

(2) an $\left\{ \begin{matrix} \left\{ \begin{matrix} \text{old} \\ \text{*older than Mary} \end{matrix} \right\} \text{car} \\ \left\{ \begin{matrix} \text{angry} \\ \text{*angrier than Mary} \end{matrix} \right\} \text{driver} \end{matrix} \right\}$

If the adjective is a head, then by the logic that we have been using, it is the
complement of another head, yielding structures like (3).

(3)

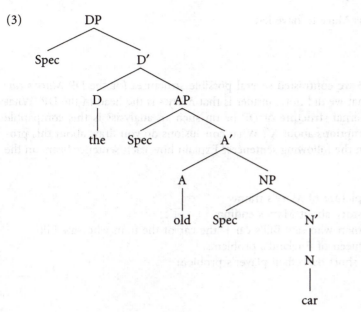

1. If this is the correct structure, what is the status of the examples in (4)?

(4)   a. *the angry at Mary
      b. *every tall

2. What are the implications of the following?

(5)   a. the young and the restless
      b. You take the high road and I'll take the low.
(6)   a. We recruit large young halfbacks.
      b. This halfback is large.
      c. This halfback is young.
      d. *This halfback is large young.
      e. We only recruit the young.
      f. ?We only recruit the large.
      g. *We only recruit the large young.

[§ 1–§ 3]

*5-8. In the text (§ 3.2) we discuss the possibility that a subject DP gets its Case in [Spec, VP] and moves to [Spec, IP] to satisfy the Extended Projection Principle, not to get Case. If this view is correct, what are its implications for the account of Raising proposed in Chapter 4? How does the raised subject get Case, and where does it move to? What are the implications of this approach for the analysis of ungrammatical examples such as (1)?

(1)   *It seems Mary to have left

[§ 3.2]

*5-9. In § 3.3 we contrasted several possible structures for the DP *Mary's car*. One option that we did not consider is that *Mary's* is the head of the DP. What would the internal structure of DP be on such an analysis? Is this compatible with our assumptions about X′? What conclusions do you draw about this proposal based on the following sentences? Explain how each sentence bears on the proposal.

(1)   *a.* *the picture of Mary's frame
 b. *the story about Mary's ending
 c. *the man who saw Bill's car [=the car of the man who saw Bill]
 d. the Queen of England's problems
 e. every short basketball player's problem

[§ 3.3]

*5-10. In the text it was suggested that intransitive verbs lack a complement. This suggestion seems natural in view of the fact that such verbs take only one argument, but the following examples suggest that some intransitive verbs, at least, can actually take complements.

(1)   *a.* Genghis died a horrible death.
 b. John sang a horrible song.
 c. Susan slept the sleep of the innocent.
 d. Bill smiled a wicked smile.

How would you handle examples such as these within the framework of Case and θ-role assignment outlined in this book?

**5-11. In the text it was noted that in English, only certain adverbs can precede the verb. Is there any generalization that accounts best for which adverbs can appear in this position? Some illustrative examples are the following.

(1)   Mary will ⎰ *tomorrow ⎱ call the bank.
            ⎪ *next week ⎪
            ⎪ *from home ⎪
            ⎨ *at home ⎬
            ⎪ *with pleasure ⎪
            ⎪ *fast ⎪
            ⎪ *at once ⎪
            ⎩ *right away ⎭

(2) Mary will $\left\{\begin{array}{l}\text{probably}\\\text{carefully}\\\text{now}\\\text{quickly}\\\text{then}\\\text{soon}\\\text{never}\\\text{later}\end{array}\right\}$ call the bank.

**5-12. Consider the requirement that all branching be binary branching. Binary branching is consistent with sentences like the following, which illustrates ellipsis.

(3) Mary saw the movie in Chicago, and Bill did in LA [i.e. saw the movie].

On the other hand, binary branching seems to make the wrong predictions when the adjunct is obligatory.

(4) *Mary put the orange juice in the refrigerator, and Bill did in the freezer [i.e. *put the orange juice].

Then again, the following test suggests that there is binary branching generally.

(5) a. They said that Mary would see the movie somewhere, and [see the movie] she did in Chicago.
     b. They said that Mary would put the orange juice somewhere, and [put the orange juice] she did in the refrigerator.

The following data suggest that the obligatoriness of the adjunct is not what determines the possibility of treating a subpart of the VP as a unit.

(6) a. Bill hammered the chicken cutlets (flat)
     b. ... and Mary did (*flat) too
     c. What Bill did (*flat) was hammer the chicken cutlets

Formulate a hypothesis that accounts for the grammaticality distributions noted here, and test it against your own examples.

FURTHER READING

....

[Note: The number of asterisks before a reference indicates its level of technical difficulty. You should be able to follow what is in those references that lack asterisks, and much of what is in those works with asterisks will be accessible to you as well.]

For references on phrase structure, see the Further Reading section at the end of Chapter 2.

There is an extensive literature on argument structure and how it maps onto phrase structure. For important general perspectives, see Bresnan (1982a; 1994), and Jackendoff (1983; 1990). A particularly far-reaching proposal on the nature of argument structure and its formal representation is made by *Grimshaw (1990). Some representative works on the properties of particular argument structure types are: Carrier and Randall (1992), Jackendoff (1992), Keyser and Roeper (1984; 1992), Levin and Rappaport (1986; 1988).

The VP-Internal Subject Hypothesis is supported by evidence from a range of languages. Woolford (1991) argues that in Niuean and Chamorro, the subject is either internal to V' or in [Spec, VP]. In Breton the subject may be in [Spec, VP]. She argues that in Jacaltec, which is an ergative language, the subject originates as a sister of V. Evidence from English coordination is presented by McNally (1992) and Burton and Grimshaw (1992). Similarly, *Kitagawa (1986) and *Kuroda (1988) argue that Japanese has a VP-internal subject, using theoretical considerations that go beyond the scope of this text. Raposo and Uriagereka (1990) propose that certain NPs originating in VP receive NOMINATIVE Case from Infl without raising into [Spec, IP]. See Contreras (1991) for arguments that the subject in Spanish originates in VP-final position. Diesing (1992) argues that allowing for a VP-internal subject provides a correct syntactic account of the distinction between the subject NP in *Some firemen are available* (meaning 'there are some firemen available' and *Some fireman are tall* (meaning 'there are some tall firemen', and not '*there are some firemen tall').

Pesetsky (1982a) argues that the difference between *wonder* and *ask* noted in the text is not that of subcategorization, but of Case. *Wonder* does not assign ACCUSATIVE Case to its complement, while *ask* does. For arguments against Pesetsky's analysis, see Rothstein (1992).

The phenomenon of locative inversion has been studied from a number of perspectives; see for example *Bresnan (1994), *Coopmans (1987), *Levine (1989), *Hoekstra and Mulder (1990), and *Rochemont and Culicover (1990).

A′-Movement

In Chapter 4 we examined the properties of A-movement. The most characteristic property of A-movement is that it forms a chain that is assigned Case at one position and a θ-role at another position. For instance, in the passive, the θ-role is assigned to the D-structure position of the subject while Case is assigned to [Spec, IP].

(1) John$_i$ was arrested t$_i$
    NOMINATIVE   *THEME*

In contrast, there are movements with the property that both Case and θ-role are assigned to the D-structure position of the moved constituent. For example, consider the *wh*-question in (2).

(2) Who(m)$_i$ did you see t$_i$?

We will show that *who(m)$_i$* is the D-structure direct object of *see*, and receives ACCUSATIVE Case in this position as well. (The overt case marking of *whom* suggests that this is so, in fact.) We therefore analyze the landing site of this movement as a non-argument or A′-position, that is, one that cannot receive structural Case. Movement to such a position is called **A′-movement**.[1]

1. *Wh*-Movement

We will begin our examination of A′-movement with *wh*-Movement, which is the most salient example. In a language like English, *wh*-Movement occurs in *wh*-questions, relative clauses, and a number of other constructions. It is typified by the positioning of a phrase containing a *wh*. Some examples involving *wh*-questions are given in (3). We will discuss examples of relative clauses and other constructions involving *wh*-Movement later in this chapter.

(3) a. *What* will you do?
     b. *Who* will you visit?
     c. *Which book* will you read?
     d. *Whose book* will you read?
     e. *To whom* did you give the book?
     f. *Who* did you give the book to?

The target of *wh*-Movement is a *wh*-phrase. In English, the preposition may be stranded (as in (3f)) or **pied piped**, as in (3e).[2] The term 'Pied Piping' refers to the situation in which some material is carried along as the consequence of the movement of a particular element.

The analysis suggested by the theory that we have developed thus far is that the *wh*-phrase in these sentences is fronted into [Spec, CP] from the position in which it is assigned Case. At S-structure there is a trace that is coindexed with the fronted *wh*-phrase; the two form an A'-chain. More generally, an A'-chain exists when a trace is coindexed with an element in A' position.

As in the case of A-movement, the moved *wh*-phrase at S-structure (e.g. in the examples in (3)) is not in a position in which it can be assigned θ-role and Case directly by the appropriate governor. In order to maintain uniformity, we must suppose that the clause-initial phrase is linked to the D-structure position. The Projection Principle requires that there be a trace; the θ-Criterion requires that the landing site be a non-θ-position.

Let us consider some evidence that shows that what the theory entails is in fact correct. Consider the phenomenon of number agreement, illustrated in (4).

(4) a. John arrests/*arrest Susan and Mary.
     b. Susan and Mary *is/are arrested by John.

In the passive (4b), the conjoined DP *Susan and Mary* must move into subject position before number agreement is assigned or checked. This tells us that agreement occurs at or after S-structure. Now consider (5).

(5) a. Which person do you think ____ was/*were {at the party?
                                                  {arrested by John?}

b. Which people do you think[___ *was/were {at the party?
                                              {arrested by John?}

[handwritten margin note at top: S complement]

These examples show that the verb of the complement agrees with the fronted *wh*-phrase in number. But at S-structure, the *wh*-phrase is no longer in [Spec, IP]. Since number agreement occurs at or after S-structure, it must be the case that there is a formal link between the S-structure position of the *wh*-phrase and the position from which it was moved. This link is captured by the chain consisting of the fronted *wh*-phrase and its trace.

[handwritten margin note: so trace has # to agree in & that is passed on to fronted wh via chain]

The same conclusion can be arrived at through a consideration of a variety of phenomena, all of which show that the fronted *wh*-phrase is linked through a chain to a canonical D-structure position. We leave discussion of these phenomena as an exercise (see Exercise 6-1).

The Projection Principle entails that *wh*-Movement of a non-subject argument must leave a trace. The Extended Projection Principle requires that movement of a subject will always leave a trace. But these principles do not in themselves require traces for all adjuncts, since many adjuncts, for example those expressing TIME or INSTRUMENT, are in general neither c-selected or s-selected by the verb, e.g.

(6)   John read the book (at breakfast)(with a magnifying glass).

It follows either that movement of unselected adjuncts does not leave a trace, or that these principles are not sufficiently strong. To induce traces everywhere, we would have to assume a general principle to that effect, i.e.

(7)   **Trace Principle:** All movements leave traces.

We will assume here that principle (7) holds. It has become a standard assumption in Principles and Parameters theory, even though it does not follow from the Projection Principle. Principle (7) does appear to follow from the more general requirement that S-structure must contain sufficient information to fully interpret a sentence. Understanding this requirement to mean that S-structure must permit every moved constituent to be identified with its D-structure location, ubiquity of traces follows straightforwardly. This requirement and (7) appear to express virtually the same stipulation.[3]

2. Targets

Let us look more closely at what the target is in *wh*-Movement.

(3) a. *What* will you do?
     b. *Who* will you visit?
     c. *Which book* will you read?
     d. *Whose book* will you read?
     e. *To whom* did you give the book?
     f. *Who* did you give the book to?
(8) a. *When* will you leave?
     b. *How* will you fix the faucet?
     c. *Why* did you leave?
     d. *In which book* did you find the answer?
     e. *In whose book* did you find the answer?
     f. *How big* is the pig?

In *wh*-questions, a *wh*-phrase is a *wh*-word (*who*), a phrase with *wh* in the specifier position (*which book*), or a PP with a *wh*-phrase complement (*to whom, in whose book*).

Relative clauses have similar but somewhat different targets.

(9) a. the person *who* you will visit
     b. the books *which/*what/*which books* you will read
     c. the person *whose book* you will read
     d. the place *where* you live
     e. *the way *how* you will fix the faucet
     f. the reason *why* you left
     g. the person *to whom* you will give the money
     h. the person *who* you will give the money to
     i. the book *in which* you found the answer
     j. the person *in whose book* you found the answer

In addition, a relative clause need not have a *wh*-form in initial position.

(10) a. the person *that* you will visit
     b. the person *that* will visit you
     c. the place *that* you live

   d. the reason that you left
   e. ??the person that you will give the money
   f. *the book that you found the answer
   g. *the person in that's book you found the answer
   h. *the person to that you gave the book

That cannot be a possessive (see (10*b*)) or the complement of a preposition (see (10*h*)). *That* is not a possible interrogative, either, as seen in (11).

(11)   *That will you visit?

We will assume that relative *that* is a complementizer, like its non-relative counterpart in clausal complements. For discussion of the syntax of *that*-relatives, see § 6.2.

   In English, Pied Piping is marginally freer in relative clauses than in questions, because in relative clauses the relative pronoun need not be in the specifier position of the target phrase.

(12)   *a.* This is the box, *in the corner of which* was found the money.
     b. This box, *in the corner of which* I put the money, is now worthless.
     c. This is the box, *sitting in the corner of which* was found the money.
     d. This is John, *silly pictures of whom* I saw on the post office wall.

Such a construction is not possible in German, raising questions about how fronting in the relative clause is licensed across languages.[4] Note also that these relatives are appositive; the Pied Piping illustrated here does not occur in non-restrictive relatives. See Exercise 6-10 for further exploration of this issue.

   The differences between *wh*-questions and relative clauses suggest that, in spite of the morphological similarities in English, they involve fundamentally different targets. This conclusion is consistent with what we find in other languages, where *wh*-questions and relative clauses are morphologically quite unrelated, e.g.

(13)   *German:*
     a. das Regal in das   er die Bücher gelegt hat
        the shelf in which he the books placed has
        'the shelf into which he placed the books'

   b. In welcher Regal hat er die Bücher gelegt?
        in which shelf has he the books   placed
        'On which shelf has he placed the books?'
(14) *a.* ein Mann, den   Hans eingeladen hat
         a   man, who-acc John invited   has
         'a man, who John invited'
     b. Wen   hat Hans eingeladen?
         who-acc has John invited
         'Who has John invited?'

What does appear to be common to the two constructions, though, is that both involve movement. We will see in § 4 that such movement is subject to the same locality constraints in both constructions.

3. Landing sites

In **short movement**, the *wh*-phrase moves to the initial position of the CP that contains its D-structure position. We have postulated that this position is [Spec, CP].

(15) $[_{CP}$ what$_i$ will$_j$ $[_{IP}$ you t$_j$ do t$_i$]]

In languages such as English, a *wh*-phrase may move out of its clause.

(16) $[_{CP}$ what$_i$ will$_j$ $[_{IP}$ John t$_j$ claim $[_{CP}$ (t$_j$) that $[_{IP}$ you did t$_i$]]]]

We will review arguments that in such a construction there is an intermediate trace in the complementizer position of the lower clause.
    There are also instances of **long movement**, in which a *wh*-phrase moves out of its clause in a single step. Some examples from English are given in (17).

(17) *a.* Which professor did you go to MIT [in order to work with t]?
     b. This is the cake that John left the party [without even trying t]?
     c. John is the only person that I didn't know [whether or not to believe t].

In each of these cases, there is no landing site in the lower clause, so that the movement must be directly to the higher clause.

In general, the X'-theoretic considerations that led us to conclude that short movement involves movement to [Spec, CP] lead us to the same conclusion in the case of successive movement and long movement.

Let us consider where the landing site must be with respect to the D-structure position of the target. The following examples show that the *wh*-phrase cannot move down from a higher clause to a lower clause. In (18) the *wh*-phrase moves from the subject position in the higher clause to the complementizer in the lower clause, while in (19) the *wh*-phrase moves from object position in the higher clause.

(18)   who$_i$ wonders [$_{CP}$ e [$_{IP}$ John got sick]] $\Rightarrow$
       *t$_i$ wonders [$_{CP}$ who$_i$ [$_{IP}$ John got sick]]
(19)   I asked who$_i$ [$_{CP}$ e [$_{IP}$ John got sick]] $\Rightarrow$
       *I asked t$_i$ [$_{CP}$ who$_i$ [$_{IP}$ John got sick]]

In these ungrammatical derivations, *who$_i$* does not c-command its trace; apparently, the trace must be bound in order for there to be a proper chain. The same requirement was implicit in our analysis of A-movement in Chapter 4. We can easily build c-command into our definition of chain.[5]

(20)   A chain is an ordered set of nodes $\langle \alpha_1, \ldots, \alpha_i, \ldots, \alpha_n \rangle$ such that
       (i)   all the nodes are coindexed and
       (ii) for every pair $\langle \alpha_i, \alpha_{i+1} \rangle$, α_i c-commands α_{i+1}.

This c-command requirement is a stipulation that might follow from some deeper principle. In other syntactic frameworks the c-command requirement is not a stipulation, but it is not clear how to eliminate it in the Principles and Parameters approach. In work leading up to GB theory it was hypothesized that the c-command requirement follows from the Binding theory, on the assumption that *wh*-trace is an anaphor and must be locally bound.[6] More recent work has shown that *wh*-trace is an R-expression. From this it follows that Binding theory must be a theory of A-binding, since otherwise Condition C would always rule out *wh*-Movement, as illustrated in (21).

(21)   *a.* *He$_i$ saw Bill$_i$. (violates Condition C)
       b. He$_i$ saw himself$_i$. (satisfies Condition A)

    c. *Who$_i$ did he$_i$ see t$_i$.
    d. Who$_i$ saw himself$_i$.

Example (21*a*) violates Condition C because the R-expression *Bill$_i$* is bound (by *he$_i$*). Example (21*b*) is grammatical since the anaphor *himself* is bound within its governing category, by *he$_i$*. Example (21*c*) is ungrammatical under the coindexing interpretation; it cannot have the interpretation of (21*d*). It follows that t_i cannot be an anaphor, which is licensed by Condition A in this position. On the other hand, the ungrammaticality of (21*c*) follows directly if t_i is an R-expression.[7]

    The requirement that the trace be bound may follow from a general theory of 'identification' of dependent elements, since without an antecedent it is impossible to determine what the trace expresses; see § 5.

    The *wh*-phrase moves to an empty specifier position. By the structure-preserving principle,[8] if a position is filled, nothing else can land there. The structure-preserving principle is a version of the requirement that syntactic structures must satisfy X'-theory at all levels of representation.

(22)   *a.* John wondered for whom Susan bought which book.
       b. *John wondered for whom which book Susan bought.
(23)   *a.* John wondered which book Susan bought for whom.
       b. John wondered for whom Susan bought which book.
       c. *Which book$_i$ did John wonder for whom$_j$ Susan bought t$_i$ t$_j$?
       d. *For whom$_j$ did John wonder which book Susan bought t$_i$ t$_j$?

    But there are theoretical and empirical complications that have to be dealt with. First, the theory as we have formulated it does not rule out the possibility of adjunction to a position to the left of a clause-initial *wh*-phrase. Examples such as the following suggest that this adjunction occurs in English.

(24)   *a.* To John, which books did you give?
       b. On the table, how many books did you put?
       c. Tomorrow, where do you plan to go?
       etc.

These fronted expressions are topicalized; we will discuss **topicalization** further in § 6.1. What is important to note here is that while non-*wh*-phrases may be topicalized to the left of a *wh*-phrase, a *wh*-phrase may not be topicalized (or otherwise moved) to the left of a fronted *wh*-phrase in English.

(25)   *a.* *To whom which books did you give?
         (cf. Which books did you give to whom?)

b. *Where how many books did you put?
(cf. How many books did you put where?)
c. *When where do you plan to go?
(cf. Where do you plan to go when?)

We must rule out such multiple *wh*-Movement in cases where there is no landing site for more than one *wh*-phrase. This can be done if we require that *wh*-Movement be structure-preserving, but we must also block non-structure-preserving adjunction of a *wh*-phrase.

These facts suggest that we must not only provide a landing site for a fronted *wh*-phrase, but some licensing conditions under which a moved *wh*-phrase may appear at S-structure only in [Spec, CP]. Such licensing conditions are not unfamiliar to us; they were introduced in Chapter 5, § 3.2 in connection with Spec-head agreement. In this case, what would license the fronted *wh*-phrase in [Spec, CP] is an agreement relationship with the complementizer that is the head of *wh*-questions. Let us notate this head as C[+wh] (the head of an interrogative clause), and let us continue to assume that the *wh*-phrase is also marked with the feature [+wh]. The head of a declarative clause would be C[−wh]. A well-formed *wh*-question in English will have the following S-structure configuration.

(26)

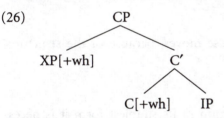

Adjunction of a second XP[+wh] to CP will result in the failure of the second one to be licensed, on the assumption that C[+wh] agrees with a unique specifier.

(27)

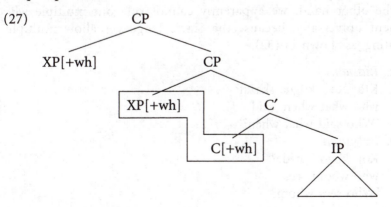

Along similar lines, there cannot be two subject noun phrases in English because only one of them will agree with the inflectional head of IP, and the other one will not be licensed. By X'-theory there can be only one C[+wh] in a clause, just as there can be only one Infl.

Not only does the *wh*-phrase move to the specifier position of C[+wh], but if the head of CP is C[+wh], some *wh*-phrase in the sentence *must* move to this position.

(28)   *a.* Who did you see?
       b. *Did you see who?

On the face of it, these observations display an attractive symmetry, expressed as the *wh*-Criterion.[9] The following is an idealized version.

(29)   *Wh*-Criterion:
       (*a*) C[+wh] must have a [+wh] phrase as its specifier.
       (*b*) A [+wh] phrase must be the specifier of C[+wh].

But this symmetry is difficult to maintain because of the fact that a sentence can contain more than one *wh*-phrase. In such a case it is sufficient that *one* such *wh*-phrase move to the specifier position—

(30)   What did you put where?

—and of course only one *wh*-phrase moves, because of the structure-preserving principle.

(31)   *Where what did you put?

In order to maintain the *wh*-Criterion in its simplest form it is necessary that all *wh*-phrases that do not move at S-structure move at some other level of (syntactic) representation. We will discuss in Chapter 8 such a level of representation, called **Logical Form**, or **LF**.

On the other hand, we apparently cannot rule out multiple *wh*-Movement universally, because the Slavic languages allow multiple *wh*-fronting, as shown in (32).

(32)   *a. Russian*:
           Kto čto   kogda skazal?
           who what when   said
           'Who said what when?'
       b. Bulgarian:
           Koj kogo vižda?
           who whom sees
           'Who sees whom?'

c. *Serbo-Croatian*:
   Ko   koga   vidi?
   who whom   sees
   'Who sees whom?'
d. *Czech*:
   Kdo koho   videl?
   who whom   saw
   'Who saw whom?'
e. *Polish*:
   Kto co   robił?
   who what   did
   'Who did what?'
   (Rudin 1988)

There is evidence that there are in fact two structures for multiple *wh*-fronting. In some languages (e.g. Bulgarian), all of the *wh*-phrases are adjoined at [Spec, CP]. In effect, each *wh*-phrase adjoins to the one to the left of it, producing a left-branching structure of the form [[[XP] XP] ...].[10] In this case, the fronted *wh*-phrases are a single constituent. In other languages (e.g. Serbo-Croatian, Polish, and Czech), the leftmost *wh*-phrase is in [Spec, CP], and the ones to the right of it are adjoined to IP.[11] (33) illustrates.

(33)   a. *Bulgarian*: [$_{CP}$ [$_{Spec}$ [koj] kogo] C[+wh] [$_{IP}$ vižda]]

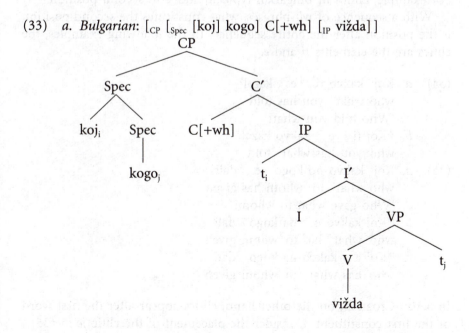

b. *Serbo-Croatian:* [$_{CP}$ [$_{Spec}$ ko] C[+wh] [$_{IP}$ koga [$_{IP}$ vidi]]]

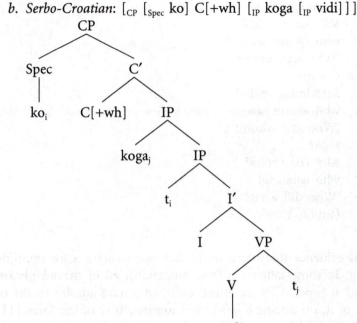

Evidence that the set of *wh*-phrases is a single constituent in Bulgarian consists of examples in which the entire sequence must function as a unit. For example, clitics in Bulgarian typically move to second position.[12]

With a sequence of *wh*-phrases, what constitutes the second position is the position after the entire sequence. In the following examples, the clitics are the elements *ti* and *e*.

(34) a. Koj kakvo ti   e   kazal?
          who what you has told
          'Who told you what?'
      b. *Koj ti   e   kakvo kazal?
          who you has what told
(35) a. Koj kakvo no kogo e   dal?
          who what to whom has given
          'Who gave what to whom?'
      b. *Koj kakvo e   na kogo dal?
          who what has to whom given
      c. *Koj e   kakvo na kogo   dal?
          who has what to whom given

In Serbo-Croatian, on the other hand, clitics appear after the first word or the first constituent. Consider the placement of the clitic *je* in (36).

(36)   a. Njegova prijateljica je profesor književnosti.
       his   friend-FEM is professor of literature
       b. Njegova je prijateljica profesor književnosti.
       his   is friend-FEM professor of literature

What we see in sentences with multiple fronted *wh* is that only the position after the first *wh*-phrase counts as second position, not the position after the entire sequence. In the following examples, *mu*, *li*, and *je* are clitics and *mu je* and *li je* are clitic clusters.

(37)   a. Ko mu je šta   dao?
          who him has what given
          'Who gave him what?'
       b. *Ko šta   mu je dao?
          who what him has given
(38)   a. Ko li je što   kome   dao?
          who Q has what to-whom given
          'Who has given what to whom?'
       b. *Ko što   li je kome   dao?
          who what Q has to-whom given
       c. *Ko što   kome   li je dao?
          who what to-whom Q has given

Rudin offers a range of evidence that supports the structural difference between the two groups of languages.

While in general the evidence appears to be strong that in Bulgarian the *wh*-phrases form a constituent, the claim that in Serbo-Croatian the *wh*-phrases adjoin to IP is somewhat more controversial. It is often claimed that *wh*-phrases that do not move in S-structure are adjoined to IP at LF, that is, at the level at which the scope of logical operators is represented.[13] On the other hand, in the *Barriers* framework (Chomsky 1986*b*) nothing can adjoin to IP, for theory-internal reasons. If we further stipulate that a phrasal movement must be to a specifier position that is licensed by Spec-head agreement, then adjunction to IP appears to be ruled out as a special case, as noted earlier. We might speculate that each adjoined noun phrase counts as a specifier of I, and that each is licensed by a single feature of I. This would be a departure from the standard conception of X' structure, in which there is one specifier for each head.

The phenomenon of multiple *wh*-fronting thus remains as an open problem for the analysis of A'-movement sketched out in this section. A further problem is to explain why some languages allow multiple *wh*-fronting, while others, like English, do not. The fact that the two types of multiple *wh*-fronting discussed above occur within a closely related group of languages suggests that there is some property that is common to both types, a property lacking in languages without multiple *wh*-fronting. What this property might be is not clear if we consider the particular analyses proposed by Rudin. While both analyses yield multiple *wh*-fronting, the structural descriptions are very different in the two types. We leave this problem as an important and unsolved question in the analysis of *wh*-Movement.

At this point you should be able to do Exercises 6-1 through 6-4.

4. Constraints on A'-movement

We turn in this section to the analysis of constraints on A'-movement. Examples such as the following suggest that long movement of *wh* in a language like English is unbounded.

(39) Who$_i$ do you think that Susan said that John thinks . . . that Lee saw t$_i$?

If so, the most natural and simplest way to understand *wh*-Movement is that it moves a *wh*-phrase to any [Spec, CP] that (i) c-commands its original position and (ii) permits Spec-head agreement on the feature [+wh] as outlined earlier.

It turns out that *wh*-Movement is not completely unbounded, in that there are circumstances under which extraction of a *wh*-phrase produces an ungrammatical sentence. The presumption is that the basis for this ungrammaticality is a syntactic one.

4.1. Ross's constraints

Because of their role in categorizing a number of important problems in syntactic theory, the constraints proposed by Ross (1967) have a special status in the study of constraints on A'-movement. Ross observed that extraction was blocked out of a number of configurations with particular properties. Subsequent research has attempted to uncover general properties of the configurations that block extraction, with considerable but not complete success. A brief survey of the phenomena noted by Ross will identify the core cases and shed some light on the current state of affairs.

The most significant of Ross's constraints for present purposes are the following. We have paraphrased them into more current terminology.

(40)   *The Complex NP Constraint:* No element contained in a sentence
         dominated by an NP may be extracted from that NP. That is,

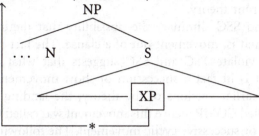

(41)   *The Left Branch Condition:* The specifier of NP or AP cannot be
         extracted from NP or AP, e.g.

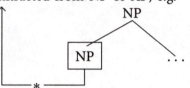

(42)   *Sentential Subject Constraint:* No element can be extracted from
         a CP that is a subject.

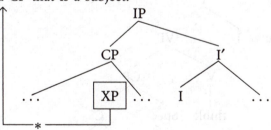

4.2. The *Conditions framework*

The *Conditions* framework sought to extend and revise the constraints.[14] We have already discussed two of the constraints in this framework, the Tensed S Condition (TSC) and the Specified Subject Condition (SSC), in Chapter 3. As originally formulated, these locality conditions blocked extraction out of complements. However, it is clear that extraction out of complements is quite possible in English.

(43)   *a.* Who$_i$ do you think [$_{CP}$ [e] [$_{IP}$ t$_i$ saw John]]?
       b. Who$_i$ do you think [$_{CP}$ [e] [$_{IP}$ John saw t$_i$]]?
       c. Who$_i$ do you expect [$_{CP}$ [e] [$_{IP}$ John to see t$_i$]]?

The problem is how to maintain these constraints while accounting correctly for *wh*-Movement out of a sentential complement. The solution to this problem gives rise to a cluster of theoretical mechanisms that have persisted into the current theory.

In essence, TSC and SSC eliminate the possibility that there can be 'long' A-movement, that is, movement out of a clause. The fact that *wh*-Movement does not violate TSC and SSC suggests that what appears to be long movement is in fact a succession of short movements from clause to clause. On earlier versions of the theory, the landing site for *wh*-Movement was called COMP, hence this movement was called **COMP-to-COMP** movement or successive cyclic movement. The following illustrates, using our current CP structure.

(44)

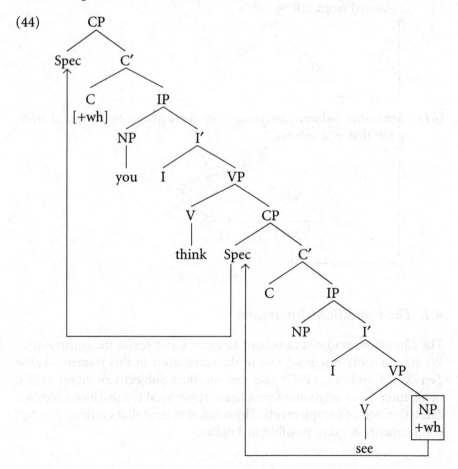

By definition, movement from the Spec position of CP to the Spec position of another CP does not count as extraction from a Tensed S. Neither, for that matter, does movement from IP into the S. Neither, for that matter, does movement from IP into the immediate Spec position. And this latter movement does not count as extraction out of the domain of a subject, so the SSC does not apply.

The central intuition here is that the specifier acts as an 'escape hatch' for *wh* extraction. The specifier is at the same time part of CP and part of IP in the relevant respects. Thus, a constituent of a sentence may escape from the sentence into the specifier position, which is both in the sentence and outside of it. Once outside, the constituent can continue to move to higher positions.

An important component of this analysis is that, after moving to the [Spec, CP] position, a constituent cannot then move to an argument position in the higher clause. Violation of the prohibition would make possible 'long' A-movement, since an argument could move into [Spec, CP] and then into an argument position, as in (45).

(45) [e] was believed $[_{CP} [_{Spec}$] that $[_{IP}$ John$_i$ was here]] $\Rightarrow$
      [e] was believed $[_{CP} [_{Spec}$ John$_i$] that $[_{IP}$ t$_i$ was here]] $\Rightarrow$
      *John$_i$ was believed $[_{CP} [_{Spec}$ t$_i'$] that $[_{IP}$ t$_i$ was here]]

Allowing A'-to-A movement would subvert the locality restrictions imposed by the TSC and the SSC. The following principle is therefore necessary in this framework, and in any framework that allows for an escape hatch.

(46) There can be no A'-to-A movement.

Principle (46) is not without problems, however. For one thing, it does appear to be a stipulation, and we would like to be able to derive it from some more general principle. Moreover, it is not entirely clear how to define 'A'-position' and 'A-position.' If θ-roles are assigned within VP, for example, [Spec, IP] is not a θ-position, yet it appears to be an A-position from the perspective of subsequent movement. On the other hand, [Spec, CP] is not a θ-position, but does appear to be an A'-position. A'-positions might be just those that are licensed for 'operators', but this step raises the additional question of what counts as an operator and what does not. We leave the question open here, recognizing that it is a complex yet fundamental one for this theory.[15]

Next we consider the Subjacency Condition, which captures the impossibility of extraction from complex NPs and from sentential subjects under a single condition. The intuition is that extraction from a relative clause requires the *wh*-phrase to cross too great a number of maximal projections, which we will call **bounding nodes**, e.g.

(47)   *What$_i$ will [$_{IP}$ you hire [$_{NP}$ a man [$_{CP}$ who$_j$ [$_{IP}$ t$_j$ can fix t$_i$]]]]?

Because the specifier position of the lower CP is filled, extraction must cross the lower IP, the lower CP, the NP, and the higher IP. But when we look at an appositive, we see that the specifier position is not filled, yet extraction is blocked.

(48)   *What$_i$ did [$_{IP}$ you hear [$_{NP}$ the report [$_{CP}$ that [$_{IP}$ John said t$_i$]]]]?

The common feature of the two extractions is that both involve crossing of NP and IP. Let us suppose that these are the bounding nodes. This will also account for the fact that it is in general ungrammatical to extract from an embedded *wh*-question.

(49)   *a.* *what$_i$ did [$_{IP}$ you wonder [$_{CP}$ to whom$_j$ [$_{IP}$ John gave t$_i$ t$_j$]]]
       b. *to whom$_j$ did [$_{IP}$ you wonder [$_{CP}$ what$_i$ [$_{IP}$ John gave t$_i$ t$_j$]]]

Embedded *wh*-questions that block extraction are called **wh-islands**.[16]
  These data suggest the following preliminary hypothesis.

(50)   **Subjacency:** Movement cannot cross more than one bounding node, where the bounding nodes are IP and NP.

It is striking that this constraint does not rule out extraction from complements on the analysis that we have just developed. The reason is that what appears to be long movement is actually a succession of short movements from specifier position to specifier position, as in (44). None of these movements violates Subjacency. We can also see that successive cyclic movement is not possible in the examples illustrating the Complex NP Constraint. Consider (51).

(51)   [$_{CP}$ C[+wh] [$_{IP}$ you will hire [$_{NP}$ a man [$_{CP}$ who$_j$ [$_{IP}$ t$_j$ can fix what$_i$]]]]]

Extraction of *what$_i$* involves movement across the lower IP and the NP. Movement across the lower IP is forced by the fact that the specifier position of the lower CP is filled by the relative pronoun.

This last observation raises several questions. First, is there independent evidence that when the subject of a relative clause is relativized, the subject actually moves to [Spec, CP]? A similar question can be raised for *wh*-questions, e.g.

(52)   *a.* a man [$_{CP}$ who saw John]
       b. Who saw John?
       c. I wonder who saw John.

Crucially, if the *wh*-subject does not move into [Spec, CP], the [Spec, CP] is vacant, which allows in principle for an escape hatch. The question of the landing site for subject *wh* is explored further in Exercise 6-11.

Second, Subjacency does not account for the fact that extraction from a subject is blocked. Consider the examples in (53).

(53)   *a.* [$_{CP}$ who$_i$ would [$_{IP}$ [$_{CP}$ t$'_i$ that John saw t$_i$] surprise Susan]]

       b. *[$_{CP}$ who$_i$ would [$_{IP}$ [$_{NP}$ a funny picture of t$_i$] surprise Susan]]

In (53*a*) extraction may pass through the specifier of the lower CP, producing no Subjacency violation.[17] In (53*b*) extraction should produce a violation on a strict interpretation of Subjacency, but we have already seen that extraction from such NPs in object position is grammatical; plausibly, whatever permits such extractions could also permit extraction in (53*b*). The problem of why extraction from subject NPs is impossible while extraction from object NPs is allowed thus constitutes a problem for this version of Subjacency. The *Conditions* framework therefore requires a separate Subject condition that blocks extraction from subjects. This extra condition and the problem with Subjacency are both eliminated in the *Barriers* framework (Chapter 7).

4.3. The *that-trace* effect

Consider now the following sentences.

(54)   *a.* Who$_i$ do you think [$_{CP}$ that [$_{IP}$ you will see t$_i$]]?
       b. Who$_i$ do you think [$_{CP}$ [$_{IP}$ you will see t$_i$]]?
(55)   *a.* *Who$_i$ do you think [$_{CP}$ that [$_{IP}$ t$_i$ will see you]]?
       b. Who$_i$ do you think [$_{CP}$ [$_{IP}$ t$_i$ will see you]]?

A stipulative approach is to rule out (55a) with the ***that-t* Filter**, which says that the sequence *that-t* is ungrammatical.[18] More generally, we appear to have a ban against the sequence complementizer-trace in English.[19]

(56) a. I would prefer you to leave first.
      b. Who would you prefer t to leave first?
      c. I would prefer for you to leave first.
      d. *Who would you prefer for t to leave first?
(57) a. I wonder whether/if you want to leave now.
      b. *Who do you wonder whether/if t_i wants to leave now?[20]

A stipulative approach that simply bans certain sequences is unattractive from the point of view of explanation. The preferred alternative is that the ungrammaticality of the *that-t* effect is the reflex of some grammatical principle or set of principles that disallow traces in this particular configuration.

Prior to the *Barriers* framework of Chomsky (1986b) it was generally assumed that the structure of a sentence was that in (58).

(58)

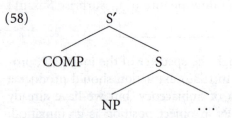

On this analysis, COMP is the escape hatch for successive cyclic extraction. If COMP is empty, the *wh*-phrase may substitute into it, but if COMP is occupied by *that*, the *wh*-phrase must adjoin to it.

(59) a. who$_i$ do you think [$_{S'}$ [$_{COMP}$ t_i' that] you will see t_i]
      b. who$_i$ do you think [$_{S'}$ [$_{COMP}$ t_i'] you will see t_i]
(60) ✗ a. who$_i$ do you think [$_{S'}$ [$_{COMP}$ t_i' that] t_i will see you]
      b. who$_i$ do you think [$_{S'}$ [$_{COMP}$ t_i'] t_i will see you]

What is crucial in this analysis is the configuration in the COMP.

(61)

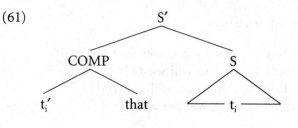

(62)

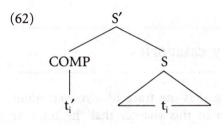

Notice that in (61), t_i' does not c-command t_i. In (62) it does c-command t_i, if we assume that c-command is sensitive to the first branching node above the c-commander.

(63) α c-commands β iff the first branching node that dominates α dominates β.

It follows on this analysis that the trace in subject position does not have a local antecedent, that is, an antecedent in S', if *that* is present. If *that* is absent, the trace in COMP is the local antecedent for the trace in subject position. A series of theoretical proposals leading to what is now known as the **Empty Category Principle** (ECP) has sought to explain the *that-t* effect in principled terms. A common thread of these proposals is that the trace in subject position is not 'properly' governed, in some sense, when there is an overt complementizer.[21] The subject trace is not **lexically governed** by a lexical head, since the subject is not a complement, and it is not **antecedent governed** by a local c-commanding antecedent. Notice that when we make the shift from the structure in (61) to the structure that conforms to X'-theory, the intermediate trace c-commands the trace in subject position regardless of whether the complementizer is empty or *that*.

(64)

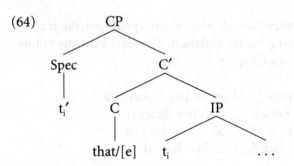

This point proves to be problematic; we take it up again at length in Chapter 7, in our discussion of the *Barriers* framework.

At this point you should be able to do Exercises 6-5 through 6-8.

5. *Wh*-trace and other empty categories

In Chapter 5 we considered evidence that the trace of a moved noun phrase is an anaphor. We have seen in this chapter that the trace of *wh*-trace is not an anaphor. The following examples suggest that it is an R-expression.

(65) a. *He$_i$ likes John$_j$.
      b. *Who$_i$ does he$_i$ like t$_i$?
(66) a. *John$_i$ likes John$_j$.
      b. *Who$_i$ does John$_i$ like t$_i$?
(67) a. *She$_i$ thinks that I like John$_j$.
      b. *Who$_i$ does she$_i$ think that I like t$_i$?
(68) a. *John$_i$ thinks that I like John$_j$.
      b. *Who$_i$ does John$_i$ think that I like t$_i$?

The *a*-examples here illustrate Condition C of the Binding theory. The R-expression is c-commanded by a noun phrase with which it is coindexed. On the standard analysis the *b*-examples appear to show the same type of violation, but in these examples, the interrogative is not c-commanded by the coindexed noun phrase. These sentences are ungrammatical in the sense that we cannot intend for the interrogative and the noun phrase or pronoun to range over the same individuals, in contrast to (69).

(69) Who$_i$ thinks that he$_i$ likes John?

Either Condition C applies before *wh*-Movement applies, or the trace of *wh* is involved in the Binding theory violation. Consider now the following examples, repeated from Chapter 5.

(70) a. [e] seems to herself [$_{IP}$ Mary$_i$ to like Susan] $\Rightarrow$
          Mary$_i$ seems to herself$_i$ [$_{IP}$ t$_i$ to like Susan]
      b. [e] seems to her [$_{IP}$ Mary$_i$ to like Susan] $\Rightarrow$
          *Mary$_i$ seems to her$_i$ [$_{IP}$ t$_i$ to like Susan]

Herself and *her* are locally bound by *Mary* only after A-movement has occurred. Thus, Conditions A and B of the Binding theory must apply at

S-structure, after NP movement. If we conclude from this that Condition C also must apply at S-structure, it follows that the *wh*-trace is an R-expression, since at S-structure the pronoun c-commands the trace of the *wh*-phrase, not the *wh*-phrase itself.

The notion that an empty category can be an R-expression is consistent with the view that the trace of a noun phrase is an anaphor. Recall the analysis in Chapter 3 of NP types in terms of the features [anaphoric] and [pronominal]. If we view the noun phrases as being both overt and empty, then the existence of the empty R-expression helps to fill in one of the remaining gaps.

(71)   Overt noun phrases

	[+a]	[−a]
[+p]		pronoun
[−p]	anaphor	R-expression

(72)   Empty noun phrases

	[+a]	[−a]
[+p]	PRO	
[−p]	NP trace	*wh* trace

We can explain the [+a, +p] gap in (71) by observing that this type of noun phrase cannot be governed, and hence cannot be assigned Case. An overt noun phrase must have Case, so an overt noun phrase cannot have these feature values. On the other hand, the gap in (72) corresponds to the empty pronoun. There is substantial evidence that the empty pronoun does exist. Consider the following Spanish examples.

(73)   *Spanish:*
    a. Llamó.
        call-PAST.3SG
        'He/she called.'

    b. Compró   el libro.
        buy-PAST.3SG the book
        'He/she bought the book.'
    c. Hay   muchas problemas.
        there-are many   problems
        'There are many problems.'
    d. Es muy interesante que llamó.
        it-is very interesting that call-PAST.3SG
        'It is very interesting that he/she called.'

These examples illustrate the fact that where English has a referring pronoun (as in (73*a*) and (73*b*)), a language such as Spanish will have no overt noun phrase at all. Similarly, where English has an **expletive**, such as *there* in (73*c*) or (73*d*), Spanish lacks an overt form.

    Even though there is no overt subject in (73*a*) and (73*b*), the corresponding θ-roles are assigned. There is an AGENT in both sentences, the CALLER in the first and the BUYER in the second. By Uniformity, there must be a noun phrase at a level of syntactic representation to which these θ-roles are assigned. We therefore assume that in these two sentences there is an empty pronominal subject. This pronoun is called *pro* ('little pro').

6. Other A'-movement constructions

6.1. Overt movements

The general picture that emerges from our consideration of *wh*-Movement is that it obeys (at least) the following constraints.

(74) *a.* Subjacency
     b. ECP
     c. Subject condition

It turns out that there are several constructions that show the same properties.

(75) *Topicalization*
    a. *John$_i$, I never liked the people who believed t$_i$.
    b. *John$_i$, I was wondering who liked t$_i$.
    c. John$_i$, I believe (*that) t$_i$ just left.
    d. *John$_i$, that Susan saw t$_i$ surprised me.
    e. *John$_i$, an expensive picture of t$_i$ would surprise me.

(76) *Relativization*
    a. *John is the person who$_i$ I never liked the people who
        believed t$_i$.
    b. *John is the person who$_i$ I was wondering who liked t$_i$.
    c. John is the person who$_i$ I believe (*that) t$_i$ just left.
    d. *John is the person who$_i$ that Susan saw t$_i$ surprised me.
    e. *John is the person who$_i$ an expensive picture of t$_i$ would
        surprise me.

In the *a*-examples, we see violations of the Complex NP Constraint, now subsumed under Subjacency. In the *b*-examples, we see *wh*-island violations, also subsumed under Subjacency. The *c*-examples show ECP violations, and the *d*- and *e*-examples illustrate violations of the Subject condition, again subsumed under Subjacency. A straightforward analysis is one in which the topic and the relative pronoun move into [Spec, CP], on a par with the interrogative pronoun.[22]

6.2. Empty operator movement

The pattern seen in (74) is also found in constructions where it is not as obvious what is moving.

(77) *that-relatives*
    a. *John is the person that I never liked the people who
        believed t$_i$.
    b. *John is the person that I was wondering who liked t$_i$.
    c. John is the person that I believe (*that) t$_i$ just left.
    d. *John is the person that that Susan saw t$_i$ surprised me.
    e. *John is the person that an expensive picture of t$_i$ would
        surprise me.

(78)   *Infinitival relatives*
   a. John is the person to like t_i.
   b. *John is the person to like the people who believe t_i.
   c. John is the person to believe (*that) t_i just left.
   d. *John is the person for [that Susan saw t_i] to surprise me.
   e. *John is the person for an expensive picture of t_i to surprise me.

(79)   *Comparatives*
   a. John runs faster than Susan does.
   b. *John runs faster than I like the people who do t_i.
   c. *John runs faster than that Susan does t_i surprised me.
   d. *John runs faster than Susan doing t_i would surprise me.

(80)   *Purpose clauses*
   a. John bought this book to read t_i.
   b. *John bought this book to give to someone who would read t_i.
   c. *John bought this book to show who would read t_i.
   d. *John bought this book to show (that) t_i was not difficult.
   e. *John bought this book to show that [that I had read t_i] was unlikely.
   f. *John bought this book to show that the author of t_i is a genius.

While there are other problems affecting the grammaticality of some of these examples, the pattern seen for *wh*-Movement appears to hold here too. For example, (80*b*) is a Complex NP Constraint violation, (80*c*) a *wh*-island violation, (80*d*) an ECP violation, (80*e*) and (80*f*) Subject Condition violations. The same pattern appears in the *b–f* examples of (77)–(79) that appears in the *a–e* examples of (75)–(76), where there appears to be actual movement.

The problem is, if there is a trace in these examples, as we have indicated, what is it a trace of? By Uniformity, if traces are created by movement, then there must be movement here. Since what is moved is not visible, it must be that there are invisible elements that can undergo movement to [Spec, CP] in much the same way that overt operators such as interrogative and relative pronouns can. That is, there are not only empty noun phrases such as *pro*, PRO, NP trace, and *wh*-trace, but **empty operators** as well, in parallel with the overt operators. These are also called **null operators**. We notate the empty operator as OP. On this view, the analysis of a sentence like (80*a*) is (81).

(81)

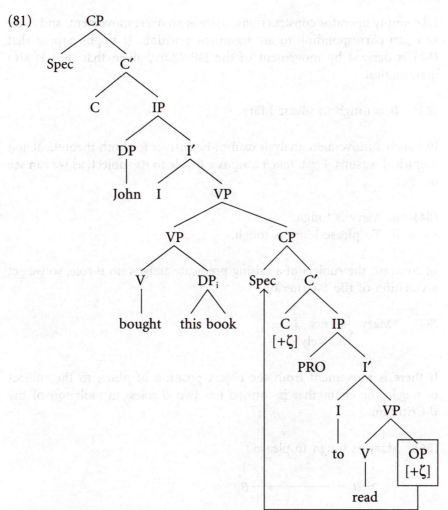

We assume that the empty operator bears some feature [+ζ] that triggers its movement to [Spec, CP].

6.3. Tough *Movement*

The construction called *tough* Movement, exemplified in (82), displays some of the properties of empty operator constructions.

(82)   Mary$_i$ is tough to please t$_i$.

Like empty operator constructions, there is no overt movement, and there is a gap corresponding to an argument position. It might appear that (82) is derived by movement of the DP *Mary*, given that (83) is also grammatical.

(83)   It is tough to please Mary.

But such a movement analysis cannot be correct for both theoretical and empirical reasons. First, *tough* assigns a θ-role to its subject, as we can see in (84).

(84)   *a.* Mary is tough.
     b. To please Mary is tough.

In contrast, the subject of a raising predicate assigns no θ-role, so we get a violation of the θ-Criterion.

(85)   *Mary $\begin{cases} \text{seems} \\ \text{is likely} \end{cases}$.

If there is movement from the object position of *please* to the subject of *tough*, the chain that is formed has two θ-roles, in violation of the θ-Criterion.

(86)   Mary$_i$ is tough to please t$_i$

$$\underset{\theta_1 \underline{\hspace{3cm}} \theta_2}{}$$

    We could avoid this problem by positing that *tough* optionally assigns a θ-role to its subject, and that the movement occurs just when there is no θ-role assigned to the subject. But then we would expect that *tough* would behave like a Raising predicate, such as *likely*. Compare the following.

(87)   *a.* It is likely that John will win.
    b. *It is likely for John to win.
    c. *It is likely John to win.
    d. John is likely t to win.
(88)   *a.* It is tough that John will win.
    b. It is tough for John to win.

    c. *It is tough John to win.
    d. *John is tough t to win.

As an adjective, *tough* does not assign Case. If *for* is absent, *John* will not get Case, and so should move into the subject position of *tough*. But this does not occur, as shown in (88*d*).

    The empirical reason against this type of movement is that there are well-formed sentences that have the same properties as (82) but have no corresponding sentence of the form in (83). Consider the following.

(89) *a.* Mary$_i$ is a tough person to please t$_i$.
     b. *It is a tough person to please Mary.
(90) *a.* This house$_i$ is a devil to take care of t$_i$.
     b. *It is a devil to take care of this house.
(91) *a.* That I know all the answers would be a very tough
       proposition for me to argue for.
     b. *It would be a very tough proposition for me to argue (for)
       that I know all the answers.

    On the basis of these considerations it seems plausible that *tough* Movement might have an empty operator analysis.[23] This proposal is motivated by the similarity between *tough* Movement and other constructions that leave a trace. Notice, however, that while movement of an empty operator in the case of a relative produces precisely the distributional pattern of overt operator movement in relatives and in questions, the pattern produced in the case of *tough* Movement is somewhat different.

(92) *a.* I asked who$_i$ you believe you saw t$_i$.
     b. This is the person who$_i$ I believe you saw t$_i$.
     c. This is the person OP$_i$ I believe you saw t$_i$.
     d. Mary is tough to believe you saw t$_i$?
(93) *a.* I asked who$_i$ you believe that you saw t$_i$.
     b. This is the person who$_i$ I believe that you saw t$_i$.
     c. This is the person OP$_i$ I believe that you saw t$_i$.
     d. ?Mary is tough to believe that you saw t$_i$?
(94) *a.* I asked who$_i$ you believe t$_i$ saw you.
     b. This is the person who$_i$ I believe t$_i$ saw you.
     c. This is the person OP$_i$ I believe t$_i$ saw you.
     d. ??Mary is tough to believe t$_i$ saw you.

(95)   *a.* *I asked who_i you believe that t_i saw you.
       b. *This is the person who_i I believe that t_i saw you.
       c. *This is the person OP_i I believe that t_i saw you.
       d. *Mary is tough to believe that t_i saw you.

Like the overt operator and empty operator constructions, *tough* Movement is grammatical when the gap is not a subject and there is no complementizer in the complement clause. When the gap is a subject and
there is a complementizer, we get a *that-t* effect uniformly. But when the
gap is a non-subject and there is a complementizer, or when the gap is
a subject and there is no complementizer, the *tough* Movement construction degrades in grammaticality, while the movement constructions do
not. These facts therefore raise the possibility that there is another way
to create chains than by movement, and that there are subtle differences
between the conditions under which movement may occur in complex
syntactic configurations and the conditions under which chains can be
created in those configurations. We take up this idea again in Chapter 7,
Appendix A in our discussion of weak and strong islands.

6.4. Rightward movement

We note here several constructions of English that appear to show that
rightward movement is possible. Unlike in the case of leftward movement, it is not clear what type of Spec-head agreement could license such
movement, since there is no independent argument for functional heads
to the right in English. To the extent that these constructions illustrate
actual rightward movement, they raise questions about the generality of
the requirement that all movements are licensed by agreement with a
functional head.

6.4.1. Extraposition

We have already seen instances of extraposition, as in (96).

(96)   *a.* [That John was here] is obvious.
       b. It is obvious [that John was here].

There are a number of arguments against the view that the CP in (96*b*)
is moved out of subject position to the right. First, the complementizer

can sometimes be omitted in the extraposed CP, which appears to be possible only when the CP is the complement of a lexical head.

(97)   *a.* *[(that) John was here] is obvious
       b. It is obvious [(that) John was here].
       c. I believe [(that) John was here].
       d. I believe very strongly [*(that) John was here].

If extraposition involved movement, we would expect the moved constituent to be adjoined in a position where it c-commands its trace, for example, IP. But then it would not be governed within VP. It is also known that extraction from adjuncts is ungrammatical,[24] but extraction from extraposed constituents is not problematic.

(98)   Where is it obvious [that John was sitting t]?

Second, there are instances of the extraposed pattern that occur at D-structure.

(99)   [e] is believed [$_{CP}$ that John was here]

Believed takes a sentential complement, but does not assign Case to it. When the complement is CP, the absence of structural Case is not a problem. Example (99) therefore produces the extraposition pattern directly, as in (100).

(100)   It is believed that John was here?

On the basis of considerations such as these, it appears that there is no rightward movement in the extraposition construction. Nevertheless, the relationship between the extraposed constituent and the expletive subject is a local one.[25] Consider the following.

(101)   *a.* [That [that John is here]$_i$ is obvious]$_j$ is surprising.
        b. [That it$_i$ is obvious [that John is here]$_i$]$_j$ is surprising.
        c. It$_j$ is surprising [that it$_i$ is obvious [that John is here]$_i$]$_j$.
        d. *[That it$_i$ is obvious]$_j$ is surprising [that John is here]$_i$.

In the ungrammatical example in (101*d*), the extraposed clause must be linked to an expletive within the subject, as illustrated in (102).

(102)

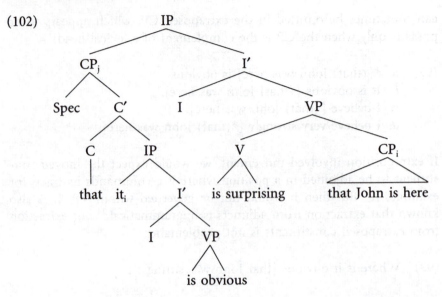

Here, *it*$_i$ does not c-command CP$_i$ and vice versa; hence the two do not form a chain. The requirement that there be a chain, which derives from the requirement that a θ-role be assigned to the extraposed CP, effectively produces the locality effect over a range of cases. For other cases, where the expletive c-commands the clause but not locally, other principles block a non-local chain. For example, consider (103).

(103)   *It$_i$ is obvious [that you think [that John called]$_i$]$_j$.

If there is a chain formed between *it*$_i$ and CP$_j$, the THEME θ-role is assigned to this CP, and no θ-role is assigned to the inclusive CP$_j$. Clearly this violates the θ-Criterion.

  In summary, there is a good argument against rightward movement in the extraposition construction.

6.4.2. *Heavy Shift*

Another candidate for rightward movement is Heavy Shift, illustrated in (104).[26]

(104)   *a.* I gave [a book about linguistics] to John.
         b. I gave to John [a book about linguistics].
(105)   *a.* I gave [a book] to John.
         b. ?I gave to John a book.
         c. I gave to John, a book, and I gave to Susan, a magazine.

As the contrast between (105*b*) and (105*c*) shows, a condition on Heavy Shift is that the DP in rightward position must be construed as a focus.[27] That is, this DP must be understood as being in contrast, or as an answer to a question (such as 'What did you give to John?'). Such a focus interpretation is facilitated by 'heaviness' of the DP, or by contrast.

The syntactic issue concerning Heavy Shift is whether the heavy DP moves to the right in this construction, leaving behind a trace in its D-structure position. If so, the derived structure is that of (106).

(106)

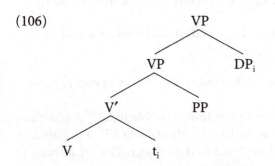

On this analysis, DP$_i$ and the trace form a chain, which accounts for the fact that DP$_i$ is assigned ACCUSATIVE Case and the object θ-role even though it is not adjacent to the verb in S-structure. Another piece of evidence is that Heavy Shift produces the **parasitic gap** phenomenon, which is usually associated with A′-movement (see § 7).[28]

(107)   *a.* Which reports$_i$ did you file t$_i$ without reading e$_i$.
    b. I filed t$_i$ without reading e$_i$ [all of the reports on my desk]$_i$.

Thus it is plausible to view Heavy Shift as rightward movement. But we will see in Chapter 10 that what appears to be rightward movement may in fact be analyzed as leftward movement. In effect, it is possible that what appears to the right is stranded by movement of everything else to the left. We will also discuss whether the directionality of movement actually has any empirical implications, or whether the availability of alternative ways of producing essentially the same configuration shows that the only empirically relevant property of 'movement' is the antecedent-trace relation, not how it is derived in a given structure.

6.4.3. *Extraposition from DP*

The last putative rightward movement construction that we will consider is extraposition from DP. The examples in (108) illustrate.

(108)   *a.* Several people walked in *who we had known from our days in college.*

    b. A number of interesting books are now available *about constraints on extraction.*

In sentences such as these, the italicized expression modifies the antecedent DP as though it was a constituent of the DP. A plausible interpretation of this relationship is that the italicized expression has undergone movement to the right, producing a structure such as that in (109).

(109) $[_{IP}[_{IP}[_{DP}$ several people $t_i]$ I $[_{VP}$ walked in$]]$ [who we had known ... $]_i]$

That is, the extraposed phrase is adjoined to the lowest maximal projection that dominates the DP.

A movement analysis of this construction is problematic.[29] A constituent extraposed from subject can in fact be adjoined to VP, a position in which it does not c-command the trace in the subject. This adjunction is shown by the fact that VP Ellipsis can include the extraposed constituent.

(110)   Several men walked in who we had known while we were in college, and then several women did.

Furthermore, *wh*-Movement cannot extract a constituent from a subject, as we have seen (the Subject Condition). If the subject is an island to extraction, it is not clear why extraposition from a subject should be possible.

The extraposed constituent is thus base-generated as an adjunct to IP or VP, and is interpreted as a 'complement' of its antecedent according to the following principle.

(111) β is a potential complement of α only if α and β are in a government relation.

Government is defined in terms of local c-command, where there is no barrier between α and β. Within the domain of a single IP, the subject governs IP- and VP-adjuncts on the plausible view that none of the maximal projections constitutes such a barrier; moreover, a VP-adjunct locally governs the direct object, allowing for the proper interpretation of an object-extraposed constituent as well. The structure in (112) illustrates, where SX stands for a subject-extraposed clause and OX stands for an object-extraposed clause.

(112)

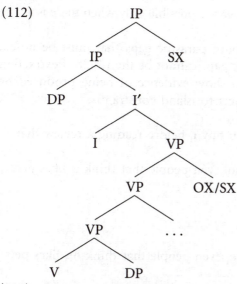

(113) I met several people last night at the party *who we had known while we were in college.*

7. Parasitic gaps

We conclude this chapter with a discussion of parasitic gaps, illustrated by the following examples. The gaps apparently produced by extraction are indicated by t_i, while the parasitic gaps are indicated by e_i. (While some of these sentences may not be perfect, many speakers judge them to be more grammatical than the corresponding island violations in (115).)

(114) a. Which book$_i$ did you lose t_i before reading e_i?
       b. John is a person who$_i$ even people that like e_i insult t_i.
       c. Who$_i$ does the fact that John dislikes e_i disturb t_i?
       d. Who$_i$ do good friends of e_i gossip about t_i?

The parasitic gaps are in positions from which there cannot be extractions.

(115) a. *Which book$_i$ did you lose your watch before reading t_i?
       b. *John is a person who$_i$ even people that like t_i insult me.
       c. *Who$_i$ does the fact that John dislikes e_i disturb you?
       d. *Who$_i$ do good friends of e_i gossip about you?

In fact, it appears that a parasitic gap is possible only when there is a true gap.[30]

There are three other facts about parasitic gaps that must be noted. First of all, although the parasitic gaps cannot be the result of extraction of the overt *wh*-phrase, they do show evidence of being produced by movement, in that they are subject to island constraints.[31]

(116)   *a.* *Which book$_i$ did you buy t$_i$ before reading a review that criticized e$_i$?

      b. *John is a person who$_i$ even people that think e$_i$ likes pets insult t$_i$.

cf.

      c. ?John is a person who$_i$ even people that think he$_i$ likes pets insult t$_i$.

(117)   *a.* *Which book$_i$ did you buy t$_i$ before claiming that e$_i$ should never have been published?

cf.

      b. Which book$_i$ did you buy t$_i$ before claiming that it$_i$ should never have been published?

Second of all, the true gap cannot c-command the parasitic gap.

(118)   *a.* Who$_i$ did you insult t$_i$ when you tried to praise e$_i$?

      b. *Who$_i$ t$_i$ insulted you when you tried to praise e$_i$?

cf.

      c. Who$_i$ t$_i$ insulted you when you tried to praise her$_i$?

Finally, the fronted *wh* must c-command the parasitic gap.

(119)   I asked who$_i$ you had insulted t$_i$ without allowing yourself/ *myself to apologize to e$_i$.

The *without* clause must be attached to the clause of which *you* is the subject when it contains *yourself,* and to the clause of which *I* is the subject when it contains *myself.* Notice that the latter is ungrammatical.

When this phrase is adjoined to the higher clause, it is not c-commanded by who_i in the lower clause.

It is clearly desirable to derive the possibility of the parasitic gap construction from general properties of grammars that do not specifically mention parasitic gaps. One approach that would achieve this result is one in which an empty category is interpreted as a bound variable when it is c-commanded by an operator such as a *wh*-phrase.[32] On such a theory, a parasitic gap would automatically receive this interpretation when the *wh*-phrase moves to a c-commanding position.

Consider in this light the evidence that parasitic gaps show Subjacency effects. There are two possible interpretations for these data. On the one hand, it is possible that parasitic gaps are produced by movement. On the other hand, it is possible that Subjacency applies not only to chains produced by movement, but to chains formed at S-structure through a process of binding empty categories to c-commanding operators.

Let us consider these two alternatives, beginning with the movement analysis. A likely candidate for the moved constituent is the empty operator OP. Let us test this hypothesis on (118*a*).

(120)   you insult who_i when you tried to praise OP_j

One problem is to figure out where the empty operator goes. It must move to [Spec, CP], adjoin higher than CP, or adjoin to IP. Suppose that the empty operator moves to [Spec, CP], as in (121).

(121)   you insult who_i [$_{PP}$ when [$_{CP}$ Spec you tried to praise OP_j]]

It is not apparent that this analysis can be extended to the cases in which the parasitic gap appears in a relative clause, as in (122).

(122)   *a.* John is a $person_i$ who_i [even $people_j$ who_j like e_i] insult t_i
         b. a $person_i$ [$_{CP}$ Spec even $people_j$ [$_{CP}$ Spec who_j t_j like OP_i] insult who_i]

Here, who_i moves to the higher [Spec, CP], and who_j moves to the lower [Spec, CP]. Therefore there is no [Spec, CP] into which OP_i can move. One solution to this problem is that the relative empty operator coindexed with *people* in subject position remains in subject position at S-structure, and moves to the Spec position at LF.[33]

A similar problem is raised by (123).

(123)   Who$_i$ would you never introduce t$_i$ to sworn enemies of e$_i$?

In this case, again, it is not clear where the empty operator could move to. Again, we could stipulate that the empty operator adjoins to the DP *enemies of e$_i$* but such adjunction is excluded in the *Barriers* framework. It is possible that the operator adjoins to the PP *of e$_i$*. In general the question of the landing site of the empty operator appears to require some *ad hoc* stipulations. We leave this issue aside here, recognizing that it poses a difficulty for the operator movement analysis of parasitic gaps.

In the case of (123) we have an additional problem because there is some indication from considerations of binding that the direct object c-commands the indirect object. Consider the following examples.

(124)   *a.* I introduced every student$_i$ to her$_i$ teacher.
        b. I introduced everyone$_i$/Mary$_i$ to herself$_i$.
        c. I introduced the students$_i$ to each other$_i$.

By assumption, in order to be interpreted as a bound variable a pronominal must be c-commanded by its antecedent (see Chapter 3). But if the direct object in (124) c-commands the *to*-phrase, it does in (123), too. Then this example appears to violate the requirement that the true gap not c-command the parasitic gap. It is reasonable to conclude, therefore, that in (124) the direct object does not c-command the *to*-phrase at S-structure, although it may c-command it at some other level of representation for the purposes of binding.

Let us now consider the conditions under which a moved empty operator gives rise to a legitimate parasitic gap construction. Consider **chain composition**, whereby the *wh*-Movement chain and the empty operator chain form a single composed chain.[34] The notion of chain composition recalls our definition of chain in (20).

(125)   If C = ($\alpha_1, \ldots, \alpha_n$) is the chain of the real gap, and C′=
        ($\beta_1, \ldots, \beta_m$) is the chain of the parasitic gap, then the
        'composed chain'
             (C, C′) = ($\alpha_1, \ldots, \alpha_n, \beta_1, \ldots, \beta_m$)
        is the chain associated with the parasitic gap constructions and
        yields its interpretation. (Chomsky 1986*b*)

The composed chain, like any chain, must have one θ-role, which explains why the trace of the *wh*-phrase cannot c-command the empty operator in the parasitic gap chain. Of course, since parasitic gap sentences are well formed, it must be that only the strict c-commanding composite chains produce θ-Criterion violations. That is, the composed chain in (126) is well formed.

(126)

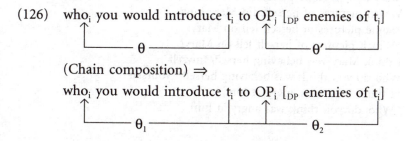

(Chain composition) ⇒

The major problem with the chain composition analysis is that the existence of parasitic gaps does not follow automatically as a consequence of the interaction of various components of the grammar. It is necessary to stipulate a special operation of chain composition to account for the possibility of parasitic gaps on this approach.

An alternative possibility is that there is a chain formed between the fronted *wh*-phrase and the parasitic gap, with no intervening empty operator. Under chain formation, the parasitic gap becomes identified with the higher chain in the sense that it is bound by the head of the higher chain, which is the intended result. Because this proposal crucially assumes the definition of 'barrier' to account for the fact that a parasitic gap can appear in a position from which extraction is impossible, we postpone discussion of this alternative until Chapter 7.

EXERCISES

6-1. In the text we showed how in English, subject-verb agreement constitutes evidence for *wh*-trace, given that subject-verb agreement holds at S-structure. Indicate which of the following data allow similar arguments for *wh*-trace, and develop the argument as appropriate.

(1)   *a.* Susan took considerable advantage of Mary
      b. *I was thinking about (considerable) advantage.
      c. How much advantage did Susan take of Mary?
(2)   *a.* Mary worded the letter carefully.
      b. *Mary worded the letter.
      c. How did Mary word the letter?

(3)   a. Who(m) did Mary see?
    b. Who(m) did you believe to have seen Mary?
    c. Who(*m) did you believe had seen Mary?
(4)   a. Mary bought some pictures of herself.
    b. Which pictures of herself did Mary buy?
    c. *Some pictures of herself fell on Mary?
    d. *Which pictures of herself fell on Mary?
(5)   a. I think Mary was behaving herself/*myself
    b. Who do you think was behaving herself/*yourself
    c. *I think John$_i$ was angry at him$_i$
    d. *Who$_i$ do you think was angry at him$_i$

[§ 1]

6-2. Using labelled brackets and indexed traces, show the derivation of each of the following sentences. If there are ambiguities, provide as many derivations as there are D-structures.

(1)   a. Who will Susan call?
    b. Who did you say Susan will call?
    c. Who did you say that Susan will call?
(2)   a. Why will Susan call?
    b. Why did you say Susan will call?
    c. Why did you say that Susan will call?
(3)   What do you think is happening?

[§ 1–§ 3]

6-3. One of the longest-standing puzzles of English syntax concerns the following data.

(1)   a. I was wondering what PRO to do
    b. *Mary$_i$ is the person who PRO to see
(2)   a. *I was wondering what you to do
    b. *Mary$_i$ is the person who you to see
(3)   a. *I was wondering what for you do to
    b. *Mary$_i$ is the person who for you to see
(4)   a. I was wondering what you will do
    b. Mary$_i$ is the person who you should see
(5)   a. *I was wondering PRO to do
    b. Mary$_i$ is the person PRO to see

Describe the puzzle and show why it is a puzzle.

[§ 3]

*6-4. Consider the following French examples.

(1) *Je croyais Jean être arrivé.
I believed John to-be arrived
'I believed John to have arrived.'
(2) Je croyais avoir fait une erreur.
I believed to-have made a mistake
'I believed myself to have made a mistake.'
(3) Je croyais Jean intelligent.
I believed John intelligent
'I believed John intelligent.'

What do these examples suggest about complement structure and Case assignment in French? Does the following example pose a problem for your answer? Why?

(4) le garçon que je croyais être arrivé
the boy that I believed to-be arrived
'the boy that I believe to have arrived'

[§ 3]

6-5. Explain the ungrammaticality of each of the following sentences in terms of the theory outlined in this chapter.

(1) *a.* *What$_i$ did you wonder who$_j$ t$_j$ said t$_i$?
b. *Who$_i$ would a movie about t$_i$ appeal to you?
c. *Where$_i$ did the fact that Susan put the ice cream t$_i$ make you angry?
d. *What$_i$ did you read a book that explained t$_i$?
e. *Why$_i$ did you wonder who$_j$ t$_j$ left t$_i$?
f. *How$_i$ is Susan the right person [to fix the faucet t$_i$]?
g. *Who$_i$ did you wonder whether t$_i$ called?
h. *Who$_i$ did the fact that Susan insulted t$_i$ surprise you?

[§ 4]

*6-6. In an English multiple *wh*-question, if the subject is a *wh*-phrase it must precede the other *wh*-phrases in S-structure.

(1) *a.* Who gave what to whom?
b. ??What did who give to whom?
c. ??Who did who give what to?
d. ??To whom did who give what?

This constraint, referred to in the literature as the **superiority constraint**, does not appear to apply to non-subjects.

(2) *a.* What did you give to whom?
     b. Who did you give what to?
     c. To whom did you give what?

Matters become more complex when we consider multiple *wh*-questions that span more than one clause, such as the following. (The judgements may differ among native speakers.)

(3) *a.* Who told you (that) you should read what?
     b. ??What did who tell you (*that) you should read?
(4) *a.* ?Who did you tell that the class should read what?
     b. ??What did you tell who that the class should read?
(5) *a.* Who did you tell (that) what was irrelevant?
         [not a multiple *wh*-question without *that*, but an embedded question]
     b. ??What did you tell who (*that) was bothering you?

Try to formulate a formal statement of the superiority condition in configurational terms.

[§ 4]

*6-7. Consider the following sentence.

(1)   *What$_i$ did you wonder to whom$_j$ John gave t$_i$ t$_j$?

It turns out that there is in fact a possible derivation of this sentence. Indicate what this derivation is, and state at least two different constraints that would block it.

[§ 4]

*6-8. Some verbs, such as *think*, take complements without *that*. In this case it is possible to extract the subject, since there is no *that-t* effect.

(1) *a.* I don't think anybody likes Susan.
     b. the one who I don't think anybody likes t
     c. the one who I don't think t likes anybody

Similarly for *claim*, *know*, *believe*, *imagine*, etc. However, there are some contexts in which the complementizer is optional, but the subject cannot be extracted.

(2) *a.* It's not obvious/clear/possible/likely you talked to the owner.
     b. The only person who it's not obvious/clear/possible/likely you talked to t was the owner.
     c. *The only person who it's not obvious/clear/possible/likely t talked to the owner is you.

State in descriptive terms what the difference is between the contexts that allow subject extraction and those that do not. To what grammatical property can you attribute the difference? The following data may prove relevant.

(3) *a.* What did you think/believe/claim/imagine?
    b. *What is it obvious/clear/possible/likely?
(4) *a.* I ??think/believe/claim/imagine John to have arrived.
    b. *It is obvious/clear/possible/likely John to have arrived.

[§ 4]

6-9. Consider the following data from Italian.

(1) il   ragazzo che   è ovvio   che le   piaccia
    the boy   that (it) is obvious that to-her pleases
    'the boy that it is obvious pleases her'
(2) Chi pensi   che sia partito?
    who you-think that has left
    'Who do you think has left?'
(3) Si   ammirano   troppo.
    themselves they-admire too-much
    'They admire themselves too much.'

Contrast the Italian pattern with the English pattern. How can you account for the difference? The following data provide a hint.

(4) Hanno telefonato molti amici.
    have   telephoned many friends
    'Many friends have telephoned.'
(5) Sono arrivati molti amici.
    have arrived many friends
    'Many friends have arrived.'
(6) Ne   sono arrivati molti.
    of-them have arrived many
    'Many of them have arrived.'

[§ 4]

**6-10. Compare the following data (from Webelhuth 1989).

(1) *a.* the President, a picture of whom hung on the wall, ...
    b. *German:* *der Präsident, ein Bild vom dem an der Wand hing, ...
    c. *Dutch:* *de president, een foto van wie aan de muur hing, ...
    d. *Swedish:* *presidenten, en bild appositive vem hängde på väggen, ...
    e. *Danish:* *præsidenten, et billede af hvem hænger paa væggen, ...
    f. *Norwegian:* *presidenten, et bilde av hvem hang paa veggen, ...

It is apparent that English is the only one of the Germanic languages that allows Pied Piping of a DP that contains a relative pronoun. Webelhuth therefore proposes that the English-type relative Pied Piping requires a special mechanism in the grammar of English. Taking into account the following examples, what form would this mechanism take?

(2) a. We entered the room, sitting in the corner of which was a picture of our President.
    b. Sitting in the corner of the room was a picture of our President.

(3) a. ??This is my theory of relative clauses, proud of which I would never pretend to be.
    b. ??Proud of my theory of relative clauses I would never pretend to be.

(4) a. On my desk I have a pile of papers, in order to file which I have to set aside an entire afternoon.
    b. In order to file these papers I have to set aside an entire afternoon.

(5) a. *On my desk I have a pile of papers, [filed which] I never have.
    b. *Filed this pile of papers, I never have.
    c. They said that I never have filed this pile of papers, and filed this pile of papers, I never have.

(6) a. It's raining, which bothers me.
    b. It's raining, which you know.
    c. It's raining, about which you are aware.

[§ 6]

6-11. In the text the possibility is raised that *wh*-subjects do not undergo short movement to [Spec, CP], as in the following.

(1) a. Who left?
    b. the person who left

The issue is a complex one, and it is difficult to find clear-cut empirical evidence to argue one way or the other. Assess the implications of the following pieces of data with respect to this issue.

(2) a. *Who did leave? (compare with (1b))
    b. Who did you say t left?

(3) a. Not a single person did they see.
    b. Not a single person saw them.
    c. *Not a single person did see them.

(4) a. They saw someone, but I forget who they saw.
    b. They saw someone, but I forget who.
    c. Someone saw them, but I forget who saw them.
    d. Someone saw them, but I forget who.

**6-12. Consider the following data from Spanish.

(1) *a.* Compré un/el libro.
I-bought a/the book
'I bought a/the book.'
   b. Lo compré.
it I-bought
'I bought it.'
   c. *Compré
I-bought
'I bought (it).'
(2) *a.* Compraste café?
you-bought coffee
'Did you buy coffee?'
   b. Sí, compré.
yes, I-bought
'Yes, I bought (some).'

Let us call the omission of the direct object in (2*b*) object drop. Discuss the pattern shown by the following cases of object drop, and suggest an analysis that will account for it.

(3) *a.* Juan traerá   cerveza a la fiesta?
Juan will-bring beer   to the party
'Will Juan bring beer to the party?'
   b. Su novia   me   dijo que traería.
his girlfriend to-me said that he-would-bring
'His girlfriend told me that he would bring (some).'
   c. *Existe el   rumor de que traerá
it-exists the rumor of that he-will-bring
'There exists the rumor that he will bring (some).'
(4) *a.* Quien trajo   cerveza a la fiesta?
who   brought beer   to the party
'Who brought beer to the party?'
   b. *No conozco al   muchacho que trajo.
no I-know   the boy   that he-brought
'I don't know the boy that brought (some).'
(5) *a.* Pepe necesita gafas?'
Pepe needs   glasses
'Does Pepe need glasses?'
   b. *Que necesita es obvio
that   he-needs is obvious
'That he needs (them) is obvious.'

   c. *Que necesite es extraño.
     that he-may-need is strange
     'That he may need them is strange.'

   d. Es obvio que necesita
     it-is obvious that he-needs
     'It is obvious that he needs (them).'

   e. Es extraño que necesite.
     it-is strange that he-may-need
     'It is strange that he may need them.'

(6) *a.* Encontraron entradas para la película?
     you-found tickets for the movie
     'Did you find tickets for the movie?'

   b. Sí, encontramos.
     yes, we-found
     'Yes, we found (some).'

   c. *Sí, pudimos entrar al cine porque encontramos.
     yes, we-could go-into the cinema because we-found
     'Yes, we were able to go into the cinema because we found (some).'

[Campos 1986]

**6-13. The following are data from the Flemish dialect spoken in the region
between Knokke-Heist and Bruges in West Flanders.

(1) *a.* ... den vent *da* Pol t getrokken   heet
     the man that Pol t made-a-picture-of has
     'the man that Pol has made a picture of'

   b. *... den vent *die* Pol t getrokken   heet
     the   man who Pol t made-a-picture-of has
     'the man who Pol has made a picture of'

(2) *a.* ... den vent *da* t gekommen is
     the man that t come is
     'the man that has come'

   b. ... den vent *die* t gekommen is
     the man who t come is
     'the man who has come'

(3) *a.* ... den vent da Pol peinst *da* Marie t getrooken   heet
     the man that Pol thinks that Marie t made-a-picture-of has
     'the man that Pol thinks that Marie has made a picture of'

   b. *... den vent da Pol peinst *die* Marie t getrooken   heet
     the   man that Pol thinks who Marie t made-a-picture-of has
     'the man that Pol thinks who Marie has made a picture of'

(4) *a.* ... den vent da Pol peinst *da* t gekommen is
     the man that Pol thinks that t come is
     'the man that Pol thinks that has come'

b. . . . den vent da   Pol peinst *die*   t gekommen is
   the   man that Pol thinks who t come   is
   'the man that Pol thinks who has come'

(5) a. Wien peinst Pol da   t Valère gezien heet
       who thinks Pol that t Valère seen   has
       'Who does Pol think has seen Valère?'

   b. Ik weten niet wien da   Pol t gezien heet
      I know not who that Pol t seen   has
      'I don't know who Pol has seen.'

   c. *Ik weten niet wien Pol t gezien heet
      I   know not who Pol t seen   has
      'I don't know who Pol has seen.'

Contrast the pattern of extraction from *that*-complements in English and in West Flemish. To what extent is it possible to extend the ECP analysis of the English *that-t* effect to the West Flemish cases?
[Bennis and Haegeman 1984]

**6-14. One of Ross's constraints not discussed in the text is the Coordinate Structure Constraint:

(1) Coordinate Structure Constraint (CSC): In a coordinate structure, no conjunct may be moved, nor may any element contained in a conjunct be moved out of that conjunct. (Ross 1974: 181)

The first part of this constraint blocks sentences such as (2), while the second blocks sentences such as (3).

(2) You drink beer and what ⇒ *What do you drink beer and t?
(3) You drink beer and eat what ⇒ *What do you drink beer and eat t?

Ross (1967) and subsequently Schmerling (1975), Goldsmith (1985), and Lakoff (1986) noted that the CSC admits of exceptions. For example,

(4) How many hot dogs$_i$ can you eat t$_i$ and not get sick?
(5) Who$_i$ did John sit around all day and gossip about t$_i$?

In (4) there appears to be extraction from the left conjunct only, while in (5) there appears to be extraction from the right conjunct only.

In order to answer the following questions you will have to construct your own examples in English, or convert this problem into a comparable one in a language other than English (assuming that the same generalizations hold).

1. What, if anything, is the difference in interpretation between the *and* that blocks extraction (as in (3)) and the *and* that allows extraction (as in (4) and (5))? Be as precise as you can, and justify your claims.

2. Are there differences between (4), where it is possible to extract from the left conjunct, and (5), where it is possible to extract from the right conjunct? Be as precise as you can, and give evidence to support your claims.

FURTHER READING

....

[Note: An asterisk before a reference indicates that it presupposes some material that we cover in future chapters. You should be able to follow what is in those references that lack asterisks, and much of what is in those works with asterisks will be accessible to you as well.]

There are various definitions of proper government in the literature in addition to that summarized in the text, just as there are various versions of government. Among the most widely cited are Aoun and Sportiche (1983) and *Rizzi (1990) (which we discuss in Chapter 7). *Davis (1987) explores some of the empirical consequences of various definitions of government and the relationship between government and proper government. She argues that proper government cannot be formulated in terms of government.

*Aoun (1986) argues that the constraints on the antecedent-trace relation can be formulated entirely in terms of Binding theory, suitably extended and generalized. For a critique, see *Lasnik and Uriagereka (1988).

The question of the landing site in topicalization has been widely studied in recent years. See among others: Authier (1992), Baltin (1982), *Lasnik and Saito (1992), and *Rochemont (1989). Works on the syntax of topicalization and its relationship to focus constructions include *Drubig (1992), *Haider (1990), and the papers in *Kiss (to appear). The proper landing site for *wh* in various languages is discussed by Deprez (1991), Goodall (1991), and Grosu (1975), among others.

A phenomenon that is superficially related to topicalization, that of **scrambling**, has spawned an extensive literature as well. (Scrambling is the apparently free reordering of constituents of a phrase.) On the question of whether scrambling is a type of A'-movement or an A-movement, see Bayer and Kornfilt (1991), Fanselow (1990), *Mahajan (1990), and *Webelhuth (1989). Other works on aspects of scrambling include: Den Besten and Webelhuth (1990), *Haegeman (1992), *Takahashi (1993), and the papers in *Grewendorf and Sternefeld (1990). *Müller and Sternefeld (1993) offer a comprehensive approach to the syntactic differences between *wh*-Movement, topicalization, and scrambling.

For a general discussion of empty operators, see *Browning (1987). This work investigates relative clauses and parasitic gaps, among other constructions.

Research on parasitic gaps was initiated with the publication of Engdahl (1983); see also Taraldsen (1981). Important proposals for the analysis of parasitic gaps can be found in Bennis and Hoekstra (1984), *Cinque (1990), Contreras (1984),

Kayne (1983), Longobardi (1985), *Manzini (1994), Pollard and Sag (1994), and *Postal (1994). Perhaps the most convincing analysis is due to *Frampton (1990).

The syntactic properties of relative clauses in a number of languages are surveyed by Smits (1989). A classic study of free relatives can be found in Bresnan and Grimshaw (1978); see also Larson (1987). Emonds (1979) is concerned with appositive relatives, which we have not discussed. See Safir (1986) for an approach to relative clauses in GB terms.

*May (1985) proposes that the direct object quantifier phrase adjoins to VP at LF, and Culicover (1992) provides additional evidence for this proposal.

Barriers

1. The goal of *Barriers*

In Chapter 6 we determined that movements are subject to constraints. In particular, we saw that certain configurations created **extraction islands**, that is, syntactic domains, extraction from which produces ungrammaticality. Ross's constraints, and later, the constraints of the *Conditions* framework, provided characterizations of these configurations, but failed to provide a deeper explanatory account of why just those configurations constitute extraction islands. Moreover, the various constraints are rather heterogeneous, in that it does not appear possible to reduce them to one or two simpler formulations. The *Barriers* framework seeks to remedy these deficiencies.

The goal of the *Barriers* framework is to unify the components of the theory that deal with government and with bounding. As we have seen, government is central to Case theory and the Binding theory. It is clear that the assignment of Case is a relatively restricted phenomenon, in that a governor is constrained to assign Case 'locally', in some sense to be made precise. On the other hand, the theory of movement is constrained by principles such as Subjacency and the ECP, so that movement too is local in some sense. In the *Barriers* framework, Chomsky sought to develop a single notion of **barrier** in terms of which government and movement would be constrained in terms of the same conception of locality. In this chapter we will outline this approach, focusing on the core ideas, then consider some problems with it, and then some proposals to rectify these problems.

The basic approach is as follows. Consider the relationship between a governor α and what it c-commands. The most general conception of government is one in which α governs everything in its c-command domain that is not separated from α by a barrier. The definition of barrier would of course be independent of government. A schematic representation of the relationship between government and barriers is given in (1). Assume for the sake of illustration that YP is a barrier.

(1)

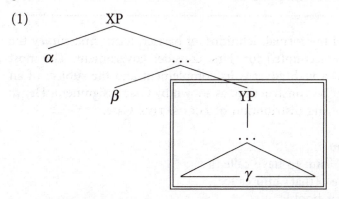

Here, α governs β, and it c-commands YP and everything that YP dominates. However, because YP is a barrier, α cannot govern γ or anything else that YP dominates, although α does govern YP itself.

Consider now movement. The bounding nodes of the *Conditions* framework are examples of **absolute barriers** to extraction, in that they contribute to the creation of islands independently of the syntactic context. While absolute barriers are given up in the *Barriers* framework, they do illustrate the notion of barrier with respect to movement: a movement barrier (or a combination of movement barriers) blocks movement. A schematic representation is given in (2), where again, YP is a barrier.

(2)

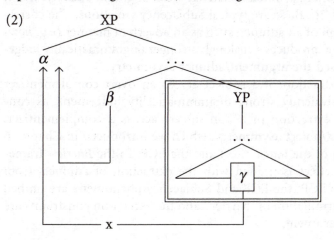

In this case, β can move to α, because there is no intervening barrier. However, YP is a barrier, so extraction across YP to α is blocked.

2. What barriers should do

Before developing the formal definition of barrier, let us first survey the phenomena to be accounted for. First consider government. The most salient fact is that a verb governs its complement and the subject of an infinitive in the ECM construction, as shown by Case assignment. Hence we have the following distribution of ACCUSATIVE Case.

(3)   *a.* I saw him.
      b. I believe [him to have called].
      c. *I believe [(that) him called].
(4)   *a.* I read [his book].
      b. *I read [him book].

Example (4*b*) shows that the verb cannot assign Case to the Specifier position of the DP.

For movement, the *Barriers* framework seeks to unify a range of locality constraints such as the Complex NP Constraint, the Subject Condition, Subjacency, and so on under a single formulation. (See Chapter 6, § 4 for discussion of these constraints.) The data reveal two major asymmetries. First, the extraction of an argument (more specifially, an object) from an island domain produces relatively weak ungrammaticality, which we notate here as '??'; these are typical Subjacency violations. The corresponding extraction of an adjunct, such as an adverb of manner (e.g. *how*) or reason (e.g. *why*) produces a strikingly stronger ungrammaticality judgement. This is called the **argument/adjunct asymmetry**.

Second, the extraction of a subject across an overt complementizer produces an equivalently strong ungrammaticality judgement, as contrasted with the extraction of a non-subject across a complementizer. This is the **subject/object asymmetry**, which we introduced in Chapter 6 in our discussion of the *that-t* effect and the ECP. In the *Barriers* framework, the *that-t* effect is unified with the extraction of adjuncts from islands under the ECP, the ECP and Subjacency phenomena are unified in terms of the formulation of 'barrier,' and the extraction constraints are unified with government.

In order to highlight the argument/adjunct asymmetry we use examples with *word the letter*, which obligatorily selects a manner adverbial.

(5) John worded the letter *(carefully)?

Because of this selection restriction, it is possible to eliminate potential ambiguity when the adverb crosses from the domain of one verb into the domain of another, as in (6a). In this case, as contrasted with (6b), the adverb must be understood as modifying the embedded VP.

(6) *a.* How carefully do you think that John worded the letter?
    b. How carefully did you say that John cooked the spaghetti?

The following examples show that extraction of the direct object produces a 'weak' Subjacency violation.

(7) *a.* ??Which letter$_i$ did you meet [a man who worded t$_i$ carefully]?
    b. ??Which letter$_i$ did [that you worded t$_i$ carefully] impress John?
    c. ??Which letter$_i$ did John call you [after she worded t$_i$ carefully]?
(8) *a.* ??This is the letter which$_i$ I met [a man who worded t$_i$ carefully].
    b. ??This is the letter which$_i$ [that you worded t$_i$ carefully] impressed John.
    c. ??This is the letter which$_i$ John called you [after he worded t$_i$ carefully].

Violations of the sort illustrated in (7c) and (8c) are called CED violations, after the **Condition on Extraction Domains**.[1] As we will see, CED is subsumed under Subjacency. The relatively greater ungrammaticality of the examples in (7) compared with those in (8) may be due to the semantic peculiarity of questioning a constituent of a (presupposed) subordinate clause.

Parallel to these cases are adjunct extractions from the same configurations, which in general produce a stronger ungrammaticality judgement than the comparable extractions of arguments.

(9) *a.* *How carefully$_i$ did you meet the man [that worded the letter t$_i$]?
    b. *How carefully$_i$ did [that you worded the letter t$_i$] impress John?

    c. *How carefully$_i$ did John call you [after he worded the
        letter t_i]?

A similar pattern is produced by *why*. In each case the adjunct is to be
understood as questioning the reason for writing the letter.

(10)   *a.* *Why$_i$ did you meet the man [that wrote the letter t_i]?
      b. *Why$_i$ did [that you wrote the letter t_i] bother John?
      c. *Why$_i$ did John call you [after he wrote the letter t_i]?

    The same argument/adjunct asymmetry also appears very clearly in
extraction from embedded *wh*-questions, so-called *wh*-islands.

(11)   you wonder [I wrote which letter how carefully]
      a. you wonder how carefully I wrote which letter
      b. you wonder which letter I wrote how carefully
(12)   *a.* ??Which letter$_i$ did you wonder [how carefully$_j$ I wrote t_i t_j]?
      b. *How carefully$_j$ did you wonder [which letter$_i$ I wrote t_i t_j]?

    We turn next to the subject/object asymmetry. As we saw in our dis-
cussion of ECP and the *that-t* effect in Chapter 6, extraction of an object
across the *that* complementizer is relatively unproblematic in English,
while extraction of a subject produces severe ungrammaticality.[2]

(13)   *a.* Which letter$_i$ did you say [that you wrote t_i]?
      b. *Who$_i$ did you say [that t_i wrote that letter]?

The same asymmetry appears in configurations where extraction of the
object is somewhat ungrammatical, such as the cases in (7) and (12a).

(14)   you met a man [that said what$_i$]

        ??what$_i$ did you meet a man [that said t_i]
(15)   you read a book [that who$_i$ wrote]

        *who$_i$ did you read a book [that t_i wrote]

Here, extraction of the subject produces complete ungrammaticality,
while extraction of the object is admittedly ungrammatical but far more
acceptable. Cases illustrating the same pattern for the Subject Condition,
CED, and *wh*-questions are given in (16).

(16) a. *Who_i did [that t_i worded the letter carefully] impress John?
      b. *Who_i did John get angry [after t_i called to complain]?
      c. *Who_i do you wonder [what_j t_i said t_j]?

Finally, there is a subject/object asymmetry with respect to extraction, in that extraction from an object is in general fully grammatical, while extraction from a subject produces violations that fall under the rubric of the Subject Condition.

3. What makes a barrier?

In the *Barriers* framework, certain maximal projections are barriers in virtue of the syntactic configurations in which they appear. The key idea that defines this framework is that a barrier arises when a maximal projection is not assigned a θ-role by a head. This captures the CED, that is, the generalization that adjuncts are islands for extraction, while complements are not, as exemplified in (17).

(17) a. ??Who_i did you visit John because you liked t_i?
      b. Who_i did you tell John that you liked t_i?

Under the unification in terms of barriers, the same notion of barrier must be involved in defining extraction islands and in blocking government into a maximal projection. So, other things being equal, if a constituent of a maximal projection XP in the configuration in (18) cannot be governed by an external head for some reason, that XP is not only a barrier to government, but it must be a barrier to extraction. We will mark the barrier by putting a double box around it.

(18)

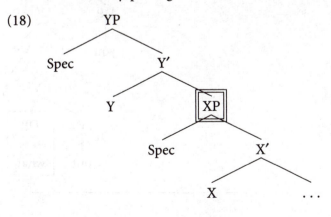

If XP is a barrier, Y cannot govern [Spec, XP] in this configuration. We will see that this strict equivalence of government barriers and extraction barriers is somewhat too strong, but the general thrust of the unification will be preserved.

It should be noted that the idea that a barrier blocks government extends not only to lexical government as it is revealed through Case assignment, but to antecedent government (see Chapter 6, § 4.4). This point will be crucial in the formulation of the ECP in terms of barriers.

Now let us see exactly how to define the barriers in terms of the configuration. Consider first the phenomenon of *wh*-islands. The configuration is illustrated by (19).

(19) *a.* *what does John wonder where you put?

  b.

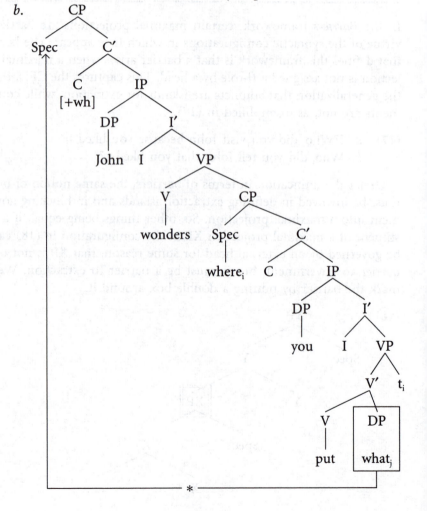

In order to move into the higher Spec, *what*$_j$ must cross several maximal projections, including IP and CP. In general, crossing IP is not problematic, as seen in the derivation of a simple question.

(20)

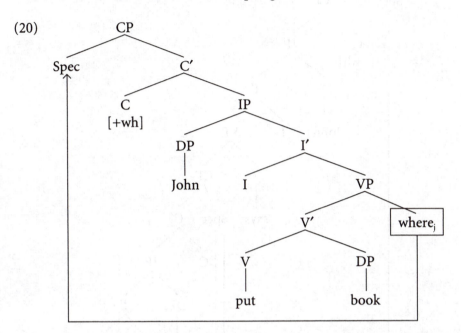

Furthermore, we know that IP is not a barrier to government, because V can govern across IP in ECM constructions. Therefore, in (19) CP must be a barrier to extraction.

It appears thus far that the barrierhood of CP will be sufficient to produce a Subjacency violation. As a first hypothesis, we will associate Subjacency violations with crossing a single barrier. We will see shortly that this simple formulation of Subjacency will not work.

Note that CP is not always a barrier to extraction. For example, extraction from CP is possible in successive cyclic movement, as in (21).

(21)

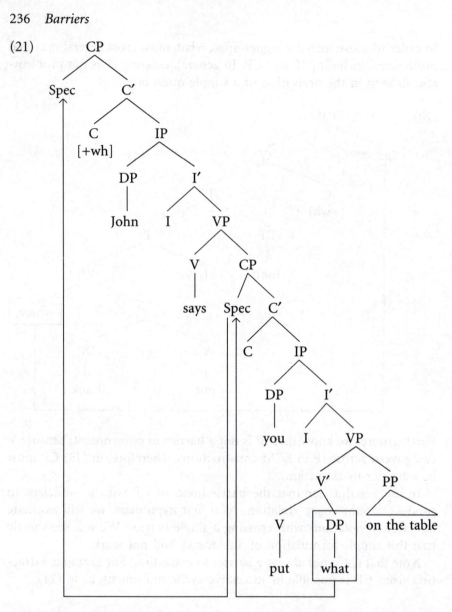

The evidence thus suggests that there is a barrier to extraction only when extracting from IP across both the IP and the CP. IP itself is not a barrier in this configuration, and CP itself is not inherently a barrier. In effect, CP **inherits barrierhood** with respect to *what* when the DP crosses both IP and CP in a configuration such as (19).

In addition, as we noted earlier, an adjunct is a barrier. Consequently, a relative clause is a barrier to extraction, as is an adverbial, as illustrated in (22).

(22)

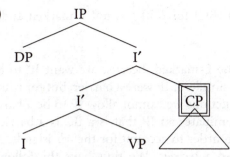

In the *Barriers* framework, the goal of unifying the notion of 'barrier for movement' and 'barrier for government' requires a change in the definition of government. In order to explain how the *Barriers* framework works, we will reformulate government here, but we will not assume it in later chapters.

The notion of government that we have developed thus far is a relation that is determined by configuration alone. A constituent β is assigned a θ-role by a head α if α governs β and if α is a θ-assigner. It is possible, of course, that α governs β but does not assign a θ-role to γ; such a situation arises when β is not a complement but an adjunct. The intuition about the relationship between θ-role assignment and barriers is that if there is a barrier between α and β, then α cannot govern β and therefore cannot assign a θ-role to β.

The *Barriers* framework seeks to define government in terms of barriers. It would thus be circular to say that β is a barrier when β is not governed. The notion θ-**government** is therefore introduced in the *Barriers* framework as the relation that holds when a head assigns a θ-role to its sister. Crucially, this relation does not depend on government as we have understood it thus far.

(23) α θ-governs β iff α and β are sisters and α assigns a θ-role to β.

On this view, (θ)-government is defined in terms of θ-role assignment, and is not an essential condition for θ-role assignment. This definition is therefore a departure from our approach to government in earlier chapters, where θ-assignment depends on government.

A head α **L-marks** β if α is lexical and θ-governs β. An adjunct is therefore not L-marked. IP and VP are not L-marked, since while C and I head govern IP and VP respectively (and may even assign 'θ-roles' to them in some extended sense of the term 'θ-role') C and I are not lexical. We can define **blocking category** in terms of L-marking.

(24)   γ is a blocking category (BC) for β iff γ is not L-marked and γ
       dominates β.

It is crucial here that IP not be L-marked, because we want IP to be a
blocking category. It would be simpler if IP were a barrier, but for reasons
of government in ECM constructions we cannot allow IP to be a barrier.
But a CP that immediately dominates an IP that is a BC is a barrier, a
consequence that we require in order to account for the *wh*-islands. And
an adjunct that is a BC is also a barrier. We thus have the following
definitions.

(25)   α is a barrier for β iff
       (i)   α is a blocking category for β and α is not IP or
       (ii) α immediately dominates γ, a blocking category for β.

Here, 'immediately dominates' is taken to mean 'is the lowest maximal
projection that dominates'.

Looking back at the *wh*-island configuration, we see that IP is a BC,
which makes CP a barrier for extraction from IP across CP. Crucially,
the CP is a complement, so that it is L-marked; hence it must acquire its
barrierhood through inheritance, if the unification of *wh*-islands with
other island phenomena in terms of barriers is to be accomplished. Similarly, in the relative clause configuration, CP is both a BC and a barrier,
which makes NP a barrier by inheritance even though it is L-marked by
V. (We switch here from NP to DP in order to maintain consistency
with the original formulations.)

(26)

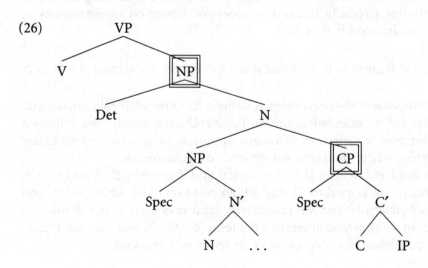

Using this approach, we are able to resolve a problem that arose in connection with the *Conditions* account of Subjacency, discussed in Chapter 6. Recall that we found that it is possible to extract from NP, as in (27).

(27) Who$_i$ did [$_{IP}$ you remember [$_{NP}$ a picture of t$_i$]]?

However, it is impossible to extract from the relative clause in DP.

(28) *a.* *Who$_i$ did [$_{IP}$ you meet [$_{NP}$ a person [$_{CP}$ [$_{Spec}$ t$_i'$] that saw t$_i$]]]?
     b.

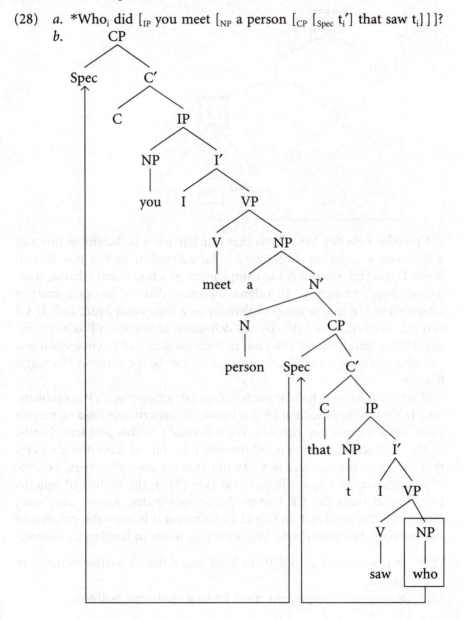

In the relative clause configuration, the NP inherits barrierhood from the CP, which is a BC and a barrier. Extraction from a relative clause therefore crosses two barriers, even if it is possible to use the [Spec, CP] escape hatch. Extraction from an adverbial adjunct also crosses two barriers, since the adjunct is one barrier and the IP that dominates it is the second barrier.

(29)

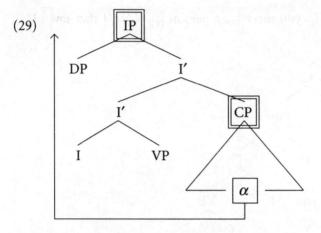

Consider now the hypothesis that one barrier is sufficient to produce a Subjacency violation. L-marking is formulated in such a way that IP is not L-marked, since it is the complement of a functional (that is, non-lexical) head, namely C. It follows therefore that VP is not L-marked either, since VP is also the complement of a functional head, Infl. If VP is not L-marked, it is a BC. By the definition of barrier, VP is a barrier. Since extraction from VP does not in itself produce Subjacency violations (cf. *what did you* [$_{VP}$ *say t$_i$*]), Subjacency cannot be the product of a single barrier.

If we allow barriers to be inherited, then extraction from VP is problematic. If VP is a barrier, then IP is a barrier by inheritance, and extraction from VP will cross two barriers. We will return to this problem shortly.

The Subjacency violations illustrated thus far all have the property that the extraction crosses not one but two (or more) barriers, because of inheritance. In the *wh*-island case (see (21)), the higher IP inherits barrierhood from the CP barrier that it dominates. As we have seen, Complex NP Constraint and CED violations also involve the crossing of two barriers. We thus define Subjacency in terms of barriers as follows.[3]

(30) α is subjacent to β if there is no more than 1 barrier between α and β.

(31) Subjacency: movement must be to a subjacent position.

Strikingly, this formulation of Subjacency now accounts for the subject/object asymmetry associated with the Subject Condition of the *Conditions* framework. Consider the following configuration.

(32)

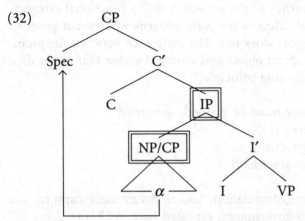

The subject of the sentence is not L-marked, since it is not the sister of a θ-assigner. Hence it is a BC. Since it is not IP, it is also a barrier. The IP that dominates the subject is then a barrier, by inheritance. Hence extraction from a subject crosses two barriers, in violation of Subjacency. In contrast, short extraction from an object does not violate Subjacency, since the object is L-marked and no barriers are crossed.

4. ECP violations

Consider now the argument/adjunct asymmetry. Extraction of an adjunct from an island is a stronger violation than is extraction of an argument. In the *Barriers* framework, this asymmetry is attributed to the fact that an adjunct is not L-marked, while an argument is. This difference between arguments and adjuncts recalls the ECP briefly introduced in Chapter 6 in connection with the *that-t* effect. We noted the following pair of sentences, and suggested that there might be a principled explanation for their differences in grammaticality.

(33) *a.* Who$_i$ do you believe [$_{IP}$ t$_i$ left]?
      b. *Who$_i$ do you believe [$_{CP}$ that [$_{IP}$ t$_i$ left]]?

Notice that extraction over *that* is not problematic when a non-subject is extracted, as in (34).

(34)   Who$_i$ do you believe [$_{CP}$ that [$_{IP}$ I saw t$_i$]]?

We have seen that the governor of the direct object is the verb, a lexical category, while the governor of the subject is Infl, a functional category. Let us say that a lexical category **properly governs** whatever it governs, while a functional category does not. The difference between the grammatical extraction of a direct object and a subject across *that* might then be explained by the following principle.[4]

(35)   An empty category must be properly governed.
(36) α properly governs β iff
    (i) α lexically governs β or
    (ii) α antecedent governs β.

In terms of the *Barriers* formulation, lexical government captures the same relation as does θ-government, repeated here in (37).

(37) α θ-governs β iff α and β are sisters and α assigns a θ-role to β.

Replacing 'lexically' by 'θ' in (36), we get the following.

(38) α properly governs β iff
    (i) α θ-governs β or
    (ii) α antecedent governs β.

Now, in order to apply proper government to extraction of an adjunct from an island, it must be the case that the trace of the adjunct is neither θ-governed nor antecedent governed. The key to blocking antecedent government under this unified approach is to define antecedent government in terms of barriers. But as we have already seen, government is blocked by a barrier. Therefore, if an adjunct crosses a single barrier, its trace is not antecedent governed. By the definition of θ-government, the trace of an adjunct is never θ-governed. Hence extraction of an adjunct from an island always produces an ECP violation.

In contrast, extraction of an argument from an island produces a Subjacency violation. While the trace of the argument is not antecedent governed (because of the barrier), it is by definition θ-governed. There is one important exception to this general statement, which is that subjects are not θ-governed. Hence we would expect that the extraction of a subject would produce an ECP violation in those contexts where the trace is not antecedent governed. We turn to such cases in the next section.

5. Minimality barriers and the ECP

In § 4 we saw how the ECP blocks extraction of a subject across a complementizer in English. The crucial part of the configuration is given in (39).

(39)

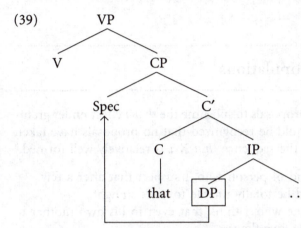

For the ECP to rule out this extraction, it must be that the trace of the DP is not antecedent governed. But under our definition of barriers, IP cannot be a barrier to government, hence it cannot be a barrier to antecedent government. Therefore, in order to unify the *that-t* effect with other ECP violations, we must say that C′ in this configuration is a barrier.[5] The barrierhood of C′ does not follow from L-marking, but from a different relation, called minimality.

This conception of barrier is one that we have already touched on: a closer governor blocks government by a more distant governor. Consider (40).

(40) They saw [$_{DP}$ Susan's [$_{N'}$ picture of John]]

The GENITIVE Case is assigned to *Susan* in the DP by government within the DP. We want the governor that assigns this Case to take precedence over the governor *saw*.

More generally, γ constitutes a minimality barrier to government by α in the configuration

(41) ...α...[$_\gamma$...δ...β...]

where γ is a projection of δ.

In order to apply this notion to the *that-t* effect, we assume that when C is overt, it is a governor. Its immediate projection is a barrier, if we allow non-maximal projections to be barriers as well as maximal projections. Granting this, t_i is blocked from being antecedent governed by an antecedent in [Spec, CP], and thus there is an ECP violation. By stipulation, the empty C is not a governor, and extraction of the subject is then possible.

6. Problems and stipulations

While we are surveying proposals to subsume the *that-t* effect under grammatical principles, it should be recognized that no proposals have taken account of the fact that the sequence *that-X-t* is relatively well formed.[6]

(42)   a. John is the kind of person who$_i$ I suspect that after a few drinks t_i would be totally unable to walk straight.
   b. John is someone who$_i$ I think that even to his own mother t_i would refuse to give flowers.
   c. Mary met the man that Susan said that *(for all intents and purposes) t was the mayor of the city.
   d. This is the tree that I said that *(just yesterday) t had resisted my shovel.
   e. Susan is the person who$_i$ I said that under no circumstances t_i would run for President.

Culicover (1993) suggests that no strictly grammatical account, such as the ECP, can be extended to accommodate cases such as these.

The account of the *that-t* effect in terms of minimality barriers, while it achieves the desired unification of the *that-t* effect with other ECP violations, does involve a number of stipulations. Rizzi (1990) calls into question this view of minimality and offers an alternative account of the *that-t* effect; we discuss his proposals in § 7.

Earlier we encountered another stipulation, that when IP is a blocking category it is not a barrier. And there is still one other stipulation that must be taken into account which concerns the status of VP, noted in § 3. Note that just as IP is a blocking category, so is VP, because I is not a lexical governor. Therefore VP can be a barrier. But if VP is a barrier and IP is a barrier by inheritance, any extraction from VP will have to cross two barriers.

(43)

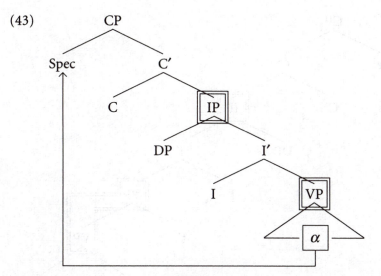

However, short extraction from VP does not in general produce ungrammaticality. A solution is to allow a maximal projection to adjoin to another maximal projection, creating a new node, as in (44).[7]

(44)

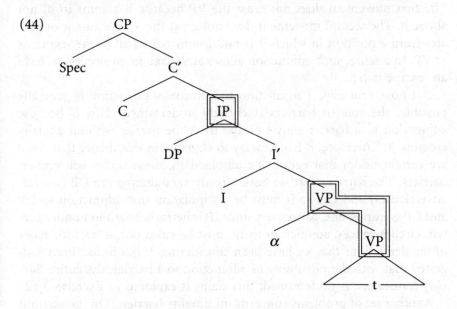

The new node that is created is assumed not to constitute an independent projection, but is part of the projection that was adjoined to. As the structure in (44) shows, the barrier VP is represented as consisting of two **segments**, neither of which in itself is a barrier.[8]

(45)

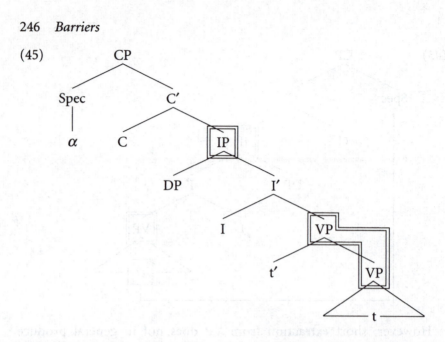

Intuitively, the adjunction of α to VP does not cross the barrier VP, nor does the movement of α from its intermediate position to [Spec, CP]. The first movement does not cross the VP because it adjoins to it, not above it. The second movement does not cross the VP because it originates from a position in which it is not dominated by all of the segments of VP. In a sense, such adjunction allows any maximal projection to have an 'escape hatch.'

But now, crucially, if adjunction to a maximal projection is generally possible, the role of barriers is entirely undermined. This is because adjunction to a barrier allows escape from the barrier without actually crossing it. Therefore, it is necessary to stipulate in this theory that there are certain nodes that cannot be adjoined to; these nodes will remain barriers. The barriers that we have already encountered are DP (for relative clauses) and CP, so it must be a stipulation that adjunction to DP and CP is impossible. Moreover, since IP inherits barrierhood under certain circumstances, adjunction to IP must be ruled out at least for types of the derivations that we have been considering. It has in fact been suggested that with the possibility of adjunction to a barrier, the entire *Barriers* framework is undermined; this claim is explored in Exercise 7-12.

Another set of problems concerns **minimality barriers**. On the account outlined, a governor (such as C^0) blocks antecedent government as well as head government into its projection. This is how the complementizer blocks antecedent government of the subject trace by the constituent in [Spec, CP], in (39), elaborated below as (46).

(46)

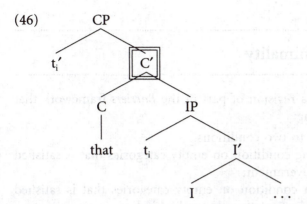

Notice that it is crucial that the barrier be the immediate projection of C^0 and not simply the maximal projection. The potential antecedent governor must be *outside* of the barrier.

This view of minimality barriers raises several problems, quite independent of its stipulative qualities.[9]

1. V' would be a barrier to extraction of direct objects. But direct objects are easily extracted from V'. (This problem may be eliminated by adjunction to VP, since only one barrier is crossed.)
2. I' should be a barrier to extraction from VP. Again, such extraction is not problematic.
3. When C^0 is *that* it does not block extraction of adjuncts from IP. If C' is a barrier, these extractions should be ECP violations. (47) illustrates.

(47)

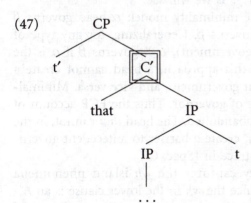

These problems can be handled by various additional stipulations, of course. However, the overall picture is one that suggests a reanalysis and reformulation; we discuss one such approach in § 7.

....

7. Relativized Minimality

....

Rizzi (1990) proposes a revision of part of the *Barriers* framework that consists of the following:

The ECP is reduced to two conditions.

(i) a formal licensing condition on empty categories that is satisfied through head government;

(ii) an identification condition on empty categories that is satisfied either by antecedent government or by binding.

Some of the islands that are accounted for by Subjacency under the *Barriers* account are accounted for in terms of a relativized minimality condition, not the rigid minimality condition of Chomsky (1986*b*). Hence this framework lacks the full unification of all extraction islands in terms of barriers.

7.1. *Minimality barriers*

Rizzi's strategy is the following. Rather than say that minimality produces a type of barrier, suppose that minimality is a phenomenon quite distinct from the type of barrier associated with the failure of L-marking. This approach moves away from the idea that the same definition of barrier can work for ECP and Subjacency, as we will see.

The approach is based on the minimality model: α head governs β if α is the minimal head that governs β. Generalizing, for any type of government X (e.g. antecedent government), α X-governs β if α is the minimal X that governs β. On this approach, a head cannot create a minimality barrier for antecedent government, and vice versa. Minimality is defined relative to the type of governor. Thus the ECP account of the *Barriers* framework must be abandoned. The head *that* cannot, in the Relativized Minimality approach, create a barrier to antecedent government by an extracted DP or its trace in [Spec, CP].

This approach to minimality captures the *wh*-island phenomena without appeal to Subjacency, since the *wh* in the lower clause is an A'-antecedent that blocks antecedent government from a more distant A' governor, e.g.

(48)   *a.* *Who$_i$ did you wonder [$_{CP}$ what$_j$ t$_i$ saw t$_j$]?
       b. *Where$_i$ did you wonder [$_{CP}$ what$_j$ John put t$_j$ t$_i$]?

Other evidence that does not follow from the **rigid minimality** account of *Barriers* includes the fact that in French, *combien* 'how many' cannot be extracted from a DP across *beaucoup* 'much'. *Beaucoup* blocks antecedent government of the trace of *combien*.

(49) *a.* Combien   de livres a-t-il   consulté t?
            how-many of books has-he consulted t
      b. Combien$_i$ a-t-il consulté [t$_i$ de livres]?
(50) *a.* Il a   consulté [beaucoup de livres].
            he has consulted many   of books
      b. Il a beaucoup$_i$ consulté [t$_i$ de livres].
(51)   Il a   beaucoup consulté ces   livres.
            he has much   consulted these books

Beaucoup in VP adverbial position is a potential A′-antecedent (assuming that it is also the specifier of VP). Hence it intervenes between *combien* and its trace.

(52) *a.* [Combien de livres] a-t-il   beaucoup consultés t?
            how-many of books has-he much   consulted t
      b. *Combien$_i$ a-t-il   beaucoup consulté [t$_i$ de livres]?
            how-many has-he much   consulted t of books

Similarly,

(53) *a.* Comment$_i$ a-t-il   résolu   [beaucoup de problèmes] t$_i$?
            how   has-he resolved many   of problems   t
      b. *Comment$_i$ a-t-il beaucoup$_j$ [résolu [t$_j$ de problèmes] t$_i$]?

In (53*b*) the presence of the adverbial *beaucoup$_j$* blocks antecedent government by *comment$_i$* of its trace *ti*.

Along similar lines, negation appears to act as an A′-specifier, blocking extraction of adjuncts to an A′-position; these are 'inner islands'.[10]

(54) *a.* *Bill is here, as$_i$ they don't know t$_i$.
      b. ?It is [in this way]$_i$ [that John didn't fix the car t$_i$].
      c. *It is [in this way]$_i$ [that I don't think [that John fixed the car t$_i$]].
      d. Il n'a   [pas [résolu [beaucoup de problèmes]]].
            he NE-has NEG resolved many   of problems
            'He has not [resolved many problems].'
            'He has resolved few problems.'

   e. Il n'a   [pas [beaucoup$_i$ résolu   [t$_i$ de problèmes]]].
      he NE-has NEG many/much resolved t of problems
      'He has not [resolved many problems].'
      '*He has resolved not many problems.'

7.2. *Licensing and identification*

Rizzi's account of minimality renders the *Barriers* version of the ECP unworkable. The *Barriers* version is a **disjunctive ECP**, in that proper government consists of either antecedent government or θ-government. In general, we should be suspicious of such disjunctive definitions, since they suggest that we have not captured a true generalization. In contrast, Rizzi's approach is one of **conjunctive ECP**. On conjunctive ECP, some type of relation to an antecedent and some type of head government must hold. Failure of either will cause a violation. Thus, the *that-t* effect could in principle be due not to a failure of antecedent government, as on the disjunctive approach, but to a failure of head government.

   Suppose that the following is a general requirement of non-pronominal empty categories.

(55)   A non-pronominal empty category must be properly head
       governed.

'Properly head governed' cannot mean 'lexically governed,' because of (56)–(57) (assuming that Infl is not a lexical governor, of course).

(56)   I asked John to go home, and [go home] I [Infl] think [t′
        that [he did t]].
(57)   *a.* I wonder whether John [Infl] won the race.
       b. *John, I wonder whether t [Infl] won the race.
       c. ?... and win the race I wonder whether he [Infl] did t

Infl 'properly head governs' *t*, the trace of VP. Note that Infl c-commands the VP, but not the subject. We can therefore say that Infl properly head governs the VP but not the subject, making c-command a condition for proper head government. That is, while Infl may well 'head govern' the subject in the sentence that it assigns NOMINATIVE Case to the subject, there is a narrower notion of *proper* head government in terms of c-command that is relevant to licensing the subject trace. Head government must also be formulated so that *that* does not properly head govern the subject. These two observations form the basis for the Relativized Minimality account of the *that-t* effect.

The Relativized Minimality approach has two components: Formal Licensing, in effect the ECP, and **Identification**. Head government is Formal Licensing; antecedent government or some type of θ-government is Identification.[11] Formal Licensing is configurational well-formedness; it has to do with where a particular empty category is allowed to appear in a syntactic configuration. Identification provides the empty category with content; it provides the meaning and reference associated with the θ-role assigned to the position occupied by the empty category.

Let us think of antecedent government as simply c-command without the intervention of barriers. We also assume that adjuncts lack referential indices. The intuition that Rizzi suggests is that only constituents that have a θ-role are 'referential'. Referential expressions have indices, and hence can be bound, under the standard definition of binding that requires coindexing. Given this assumption, antecedent government is the only way in which an adjunct trace can be identified. The adjunct does not have a referential index, its trace does not have an index, and therefore the trace cannot be bound. On the other hand, the trace of an argument has an index, and thus may be identified through binding, which is not a local relation. With these assumptions, we have the following formulations.

(58) ECP: A non-pronominal empty category must be properly head governed (Formal Licensing).

(59) Identification: an empty category must be antecedent governed or bound.

Let us see how this applies to some problematic examples.

(60) *Who$_i$ do you think [t$_i'$ that [t$_i$ left]]?

Here, t is antecedent governed by t' but not properly head governed, since by assumption *that* is not a proper head governor. What then of (61)?

(61) who$_i$ do you think [$_{CP}$ t$_i'$ C [$_{IP}$ t$_i$ left]]

In this case, we must assume that empty C *is* a proper head governor. Rizzi proposes to relate this fact to Spec-head agreement, in the following way. Suppose that only the empty complementizer agrees with its specifier. The structure of (61) will then be (62).

(62)   who$_i$ do you think [$_{CP}$ t$'_i$ C$_i$ [$_{IP}$ t$_i$ left]]

Notice that C$_i$ agrees now not only with its specifier, but with the subject trace. Rizzi proposes that this allows the complementizer to function as a proper head governor of the subject trace. Since t$'_i$ also antecedent governs the subject trace, the ECP is satisfied, and the trace is properly identified.

Consider next the following examples; assume that *whether* is in [Spec, CP] and that the head of the embedded CP is C[+wh].

(63)   *John$_i$, I wonder whether t$_i$ won the race.

Here, t$_i$ is not head governed by C[+wh]. Hence this example violates ECP.

(64)   ? . . . and [win the race] I wonder [whether he did t]

Here, Infl head governs *t*, so ECP is satisfied. But *t* is not antecedent governed, so there is a failure of Identification. (We assume that *whether* blocks an intermediate trace in [Spec, CP].) Next, consider the following.

(65)   I asked John to go home, and [go home] I think [t$'$ that [he did t]].^{12}

Here, Infl head governs *t* and *t$'$* antecedent governs *t*, so there is no violation.

(66)   How do you think [t$'$ that [Bill solved the problem t]]?

Here, *t* is antecedent governed by *t$'$* and properly head governed by V.

There are additional complications of the Relativized Minimality theory, but the general direction is shown by the examples that we have considered. Adjuncts to VP must be head governed from outside of VP, i.e. by Infl or other functional categories; they are not head governed by V. Certain long movements are not required to pass through [Spec, CP], since the Identification requirement mentioned above can be satisfied not only by antecedent government, but by (possibly long distance) binding. Only DPs can be bound; we thus predict that only DPs will allow long distance extraction from configurations where antecedent government will not hold. Consider, for example, the following.[13]

(67) a. I went to Harvard in order to work with Professor Jones.
      b. Who$_i$ did you go to Harvard in order to work with t$_i$.
      c. *[With whom]$_i$ did you go to Harvard in order to work t$_i$.
(68) a. I went to my desk in order to word the letter carefully.
      b. Which letter$_i$ did you go to your desk in order to word t$_i$ carefully.
      c. *How carefully did you go to your desk in order to word the letter t.

The purpose clauses are adjuncts. The tree in (69) illustrates the structure of (67c).

(69)

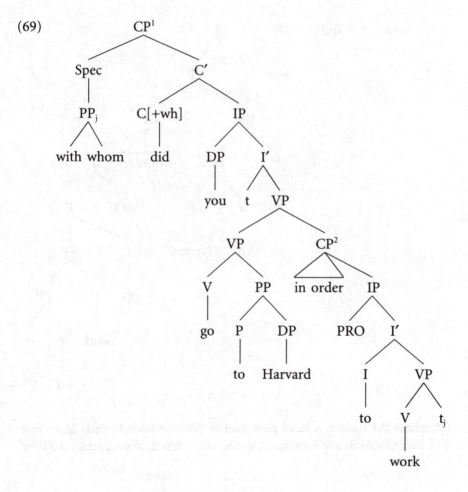

CP^2 is an adjunct, and hence a barrier, since it is not assigned a θ-role by the verb *go*. Antecedent government cannot apply across this adjunct barrier.[14] Nevertheless, it is possible to extract a DP across this barrier (cf. (67*b*)), because the trace t_i is bound by the DP, in spite of the barrier, as illustrated in (70).[15] (Such barriers do not constrain binding, only antecedent government.)

(70)

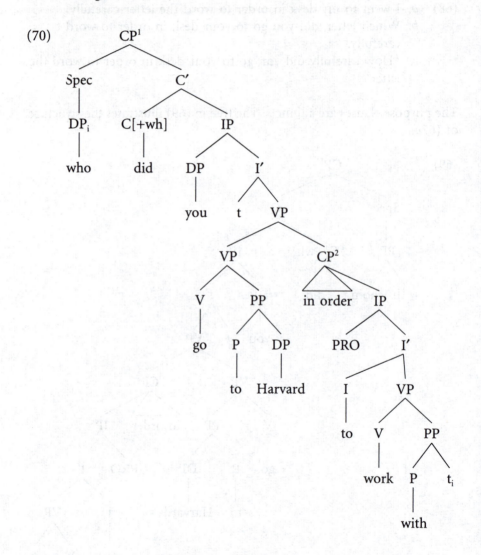

Of course the trace t_i is head governed in (70), so both Formal Licensing and Identification are satisfied. On the other hand, if we extract a PP or an adverbial across the barrier, its trace must be antecedent governed in order to be identified, since it lacks a referential index and cannot be bound. The barrier blocks antecedent government, regardless of whether or not the verb is a proper head governor. So we get a violation in (67c) and (68b), but not in (67b) and (68a).

Finally, the formal definition of 'antecedent govern' is not entirely straightforward. Rizzi points out that without some restriction on the formation of chains, there is no guarantee that for $<\alpha, \beta>$ such that α c-commands β, α will count as a genuine antecedent governor for β. Rizzi therefore adds the requirement that α and β must be non-distinct, that is, they cannot differ in any features. The definition of antecedent government is then the following.

(71) α antecedent governs β if and only if
    (i) α and β are non-distinct;
    (ii) α c-commands β;
    (iii) no barrier intervenes;
    (iv) Relativized Minimality is respected.

Crucially, only the trace of α will share all of α's features. Thus, antecedent government will hold only between α and its trace, even when α does not bind its trace (because of the lack of indices).

8. Move α

Here we summarize briefly the proposal of Lasnik and Saito (1992) to resolve some of the problems in the *Barriers* framework. With respect to the question of overt movement, Lasnik and Saito ask the following questions:

(72) *a.* what counts as a barrier?
     b. what kinds of government are there?

The *Barriers* framework is simplified by defining Subjacency in terms of a single barrier, by eliminating the notion of blocking category and associated special stipulations about IP, by removing the assumption that VP is a barrier, and by eliminating minimality barriers.

There is a persistent pattern to be found in the extraction phenomena, which we summarize here in (73).

(73)   *a.* extraction from *wh*-islands
   • arguments: ??
   • adjuncts: *
   b. extraction from adjuncts
   • arguments: ??
   • adjuncts: *
   c. extraction from subject
   • arguments: ??
   • adjuncts: *
   d. extraction from complex NP islands
   • arguments: ??
   • adjuncts: *

The reader can verify that these claims are correct (Exercise 7-4).

The generalization that emerges from these observations is that an ECP violation occurs when an adjunct is extracted from a Subjacency island (except in the case of the *that-t* effect). Lasnik and Saito therefore propose that antecedent government is a form of local binding that is subject to Subjacency. That is, α antecedent governs β if and only if α binds β and α and β are subjacent. Extraction of arguments from islands will produce configurations in which the traces are not antecedent governed. The failure of antecedent government is responsible for the '??' judgements seen in (73), which we may call 'Subjacency violations.' The arguments are lexically governed, however, and so no ECP violation occurs.

On the other hand, adjunct traces not subjacent to their antecedents are neither lexically governed nor antecedent governed. The failure of both types of government is a strong ECP violation, and is responsible for the '*' judgements in (73).

On this approach, it is possible to eliminate the barrierhood of VP; hence adjunction to maximal projections may occur freely, in contrast to the *Barriers* approach. Eliminating the notion of blocking category permits the following definitions for barrier and Subjacency.

(74) γ is a barrier for β if
   a. γ is a maximal projection

b. γ is not L-marked, and

c. γ dominates β.

(75) β is subjacent to α if for every γ, γ a barrier for β, the maximal projection immediately dominating γ dominates α.

(Lasnik and Saito 1992: 87)

Lasnik and Saito (1992: 184) stipulate that VP is never a barrier in virtue of the fact that θ-marking, and hence the possibility of non-L-marking, is irrelevant for VP.

On the definition of Subjacency in (75), movement can cross one barrier. Consider (76).

(76)

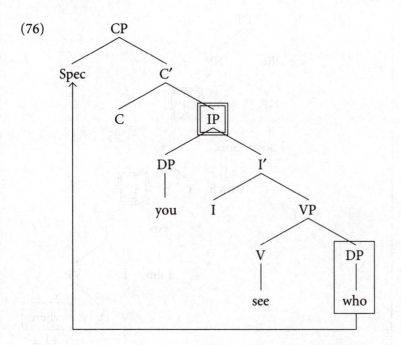

IP is not L-marked by C, and thus it is a barrier. This is clearly an improvement over the stipulation in *Barriers* that IP can be a BC but not a barrier. *Who* crosses this barrier, but its landing site is dominated by CP, which is the maximal projection that immediately dominates the barrier IP. Hence we have antecedent government of the trace by the moved DP.

On this definition of barriers, it is impossible for a constituent to adjoin to the barrier and thereby escape from it. Consider the case of extraction from relative clauses.

(77)

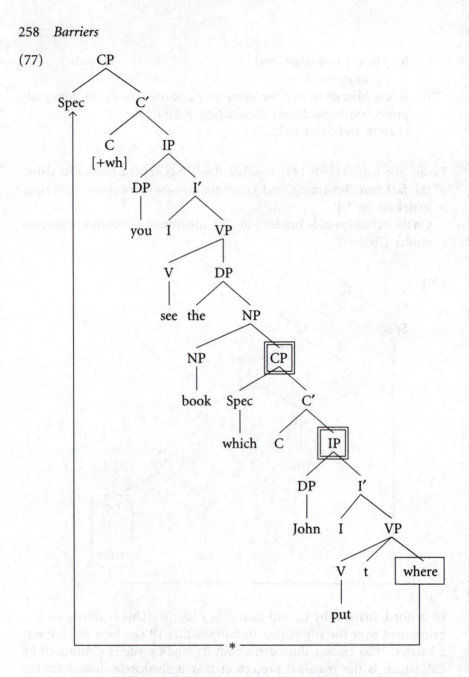

In this example, IP is a barrier because it is not L-marked by C, and CP is a barrier as well. In order not to violate Subjacency, *where* would have to move first into the domain of CP, but [Spec, CP] is filled. But suppose that *where* adjoins to IP. Assume that the node created by adjunction is a separate maximal projection, rather than merely a segment of the original node. In this case, adjunction to IP creates a new IP that is a barrier, so that extraction to the higher [Spec, CP] will still cross two barriers. In (78) we provide the relevant portion of the structure.

(78)

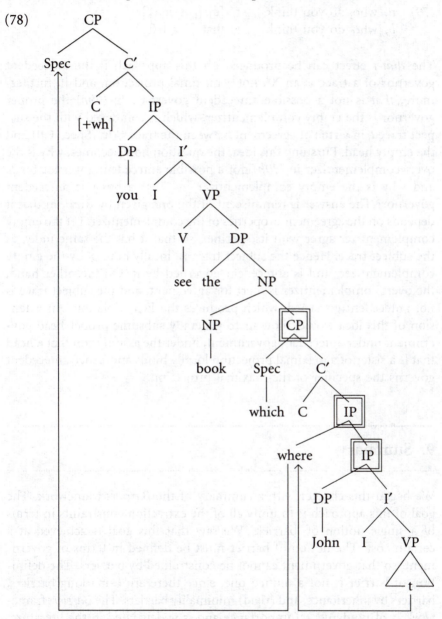

The *that-t* effect is due to an ECP violation on this approach. The subject trace is not properly governed if it is not antecedent governed.

Note that the trace in [Spec, CP] c-commands the subject trace, and there is no intervening barrier.

(79)   *a.* who$_i$ do you think [$_{CP}$ t$_i'$ [e] [$_{IP}$ t$_i$ left]]
        b. who$_i$ do you think [$_{CP}$ t$_i'$ that [$_{IP}$ t$_i$ left]]

The *that-t* effect can be produced on this approach if the antecedent governor of a trace is an X^0, not a maximal projection, and if, furthermore, *that* is not a possible antecedent governor. In (79*a*) the proper governor is the empty complementizer, which is coindexed with the suspect trace t_i in virtue of agreement between the trace t_i' in [Spec, CP] and the empty head. Pursuing this idea, the question now becomes, why is the overt complementizer in (79*b*) not a possible antecedent governor for t_i, and why is the empty complementizer in (79*a*) a possible antecedent governor? The answer is reminiscent of the one given by Rizzi, in that it depends on the agreement properties of the complementizer. Let the empty complementizer agree with its specifier, so that it has the same index as the subject trace. Hence the subject trace is 'locally bound' by the empty complementizer, and is antecedent governed by it. On the other hand, the overt complementizer is inert for agreement, and the subject trace is not antecedent governed, which produces the ECP violation. An extension of this idea would allow us to generally subsume proper head government under antecedent government, under the assumption that a head that is a sister of a maximal projection locally binds and hence antecedent governs the specifier of the maximal projection.

9. Summary

We began this chapter with a summary of the *Barriers* framework. The goal of this approach is to unify all of the extraction constraints in terms of a single notion of 'barrier.' We saw that this goal is achieved at a certain cost. The notion of barrier must be defined in terms of government, so that government cannot be constrained by barriers. The definition of barrier is not a unified one, since there are L-marking barriers, barriers by inheritance, and (rigid) minimality barriers. The *Barriers* framework is of fundamental importance and is widely cited in the literature; much current work presupposes familiarity with the general approach, in particular movement through successive adjunction and the creation of intermediate traces in a chain. The specific formulations of barrier and BC, however, have been supplanted by later proposals.

The Relativized Minimality approach of Rizzi (1990) avoids some of the problems of the *Barriers* framework by dissociating *wh*-island phenomena from other Subjacency phenomena, and by accounting for *that-t* effects not in terms of a failure of antecedent government due to minimality but in terms of a failure of head government. Relativized Minimality is widely assumed as the account of *wh*-islands. The account of the *that-t* effect relies heavily on the technical device of coindexing and the assumption that head government occurs when the empty complementizer is coindexed with the subject trace. The remainder of the ECP account in this approach relies heavily on a notion of referentiality that is as yet not completely understood.

In many respects the Move α approach of Lasnik and Saito (1992) is the most satisfactory within the general context of *Barriers*-type accounts, that is, formal syntactic characterizations of extraction constraints. This approach succeeds in simplifying the definition of barrier and nicely relates Subjacency to the ECP by incorporating the definition of Subjacency into the definition of antecedent government. In order to extend this approach to *that-t* effects it is necessary to formulate antecedent government in such a way that a head is the antecedent governor for a trace. This is an unnatural step that suggests that *that-t* effects are not to be subsumed under a general approach to barriers, a possibility that was already raised in Chapter 6, § 4.3.

Our characterization of this line of research is the following. There is a cluster of constructions that produce Subjacency violations when arguments are extracted from them: complex NPs, subjects, and adjuncts. Extraction of adjuncts from the same configurations produces stronger, 'ECP' violations, as observed by Lasnik and Saito (1992). *Wh*-islands fall under a Relativized Minimality constraint that enforces the binding of a trace by a more local binder of the same type. And *that-t* effects are due to something else entirely, the nature of which is at present not entirely clear.

10. Parasitic gaps

Having developed the *Barriers* framework and explored some possible modifications, we are now in a position to return to the analysis of parasitic gaps introduced in Chapter 6. The analysis of parasitic gaps that we discussed there was one in which the parasitic gap is produced by the movement of an empty operator that creates a chain; this chain is then composed with the chain of the main operator to produce a composed chain in which the parasitic gap is bound by the main operator.

The main conceptual problem with the chain composition approach is that parasitic gaps do not occur as a direct consequence of independently required aspects of the grammar; it is necessary to stipulate a special chain composition relation in order to license the parasitic gaps. What would be preferable is an analysis in which the sub-chain that contains the parasitic gap becomes licensed as a consequence of the structure of the chain containing the true gap.[16]

The key to this proposal is that movement necessarily involves adjunction to all intermediate maximal projections. Each adjunction leaves a trace. We indicate the structure

(80)   [IP t_i [IP

as

(81)   [IP:i

and so on. The derivation of *what did you read* will then be as in (82).

(82)   [CP what$_i$ did [IP:i you [VP:i read t_i]]]

Here there is an intermediate trace of *what$_i$* adjoined to IP and another adjoined to VP.

What is crucial in this proposal is that extraction from a direct object permits adjunction to intermediate maximal projections, while extraction from an adjunct or a subject does not permit such adjunction above the adjunct or subject. This restriction is formulated in terms of the Head Government Condition on Adjunction (HGCA), as follows. Here, the direction of canonical government is the direction in which a verb governs its direct object.[17]

(83)   HGCA: A *wh*-element can only be adjoined to a maximal
        projection XP from a position that is canonically governed by
        the head of XP.
        (Frampton 1990)

If we extract from a subject, as in (84), the HGCA blocks adjunction to the IP.

(84)

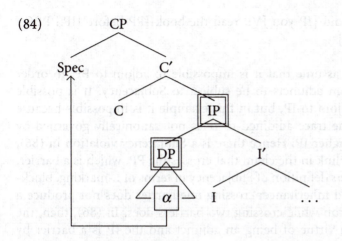

The head of IP is I, which does not canonically govern the subject position. DP is a barrier because it is not L-marked, and IP inherits barrierhood. Therefore extraction from subject is a Subjacency violation. On the other hand, extraction from a direct object allows adjunction to all of the maximal projections above it, since the direct object is canonically governed.

(85)

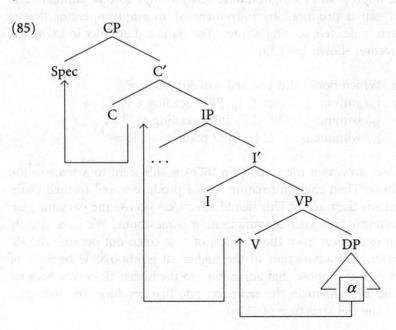

In comparison, the derivation of a Subjacency violation will have the form in (86).

(86)   [CP what$_i$ did [IP you [VP read the book][PP before [IP:i PRO filing t$_i$]]]]

It is necessary to assume that it is impossible to adjoin to PP, in order for extraction from adjuncts to be subject to Subjacency. It is possible in principle to adjoin to IP, but in this example it is impossible because of the HGCA. The trace adjoined to IP is not canonically governed by the head of the higher IP. Hence there is a Subjacency violation in (86), because there is a link in the chain that crosses the PP, which is a barrier. Assume the *Barriers* definition of Subjacency in terms of L-marking, blocking categories, and inheritance; crossing one barrier does not produce a Subjacency violation while crossing two barriers does. In (86), then, the PP is a barrier in virtue of being an adjunct and the IP is a barrier by inheritance.

Finally we come to parasitic gaps themselves. Crucially, chain formation is distinct from movement. Movement produces the traces that make up a chain, but chain formation is an operation that links traces together into a chain. It is thus conceivable that traces produced by two separate movements could be formed into a single chain if they bear the appropriate configurational relationships to one another. The parasitic gap is produced by movement of an empty operator that is subsequently deleted, leaving a trace. The italicized adjunct in (87a) has the derivation shown in (87b).

(87)   a. Which books did you sell *without reading*?
       b. [PP without [CP Spec C [IP PRO reading OP$_i$]]] ⇒
          [PP without [CP OP$_i$ C [IP PRO reading t$_i$]]] ⇒
          [PP without [CP t$_i'$ C [IP PRO reading t$_i$]]] ⇒

Suppose, now, that the trace t_i' in (87b) is subjacent to a trace in the main clause. Then chain formation would produce a well-formed chain that contains the trace t_i. This would effectively license the parasitic gap. The question is, can such a configuration come about? We have already seen that extraction from the position of t_i' is ruled out because the PP is a barrier, and adjunction to the higher IP is impossible because of the HGCA. But suppose that adjunction to the higher IP occurs because of another movement in the sentence, one that produces the true gap. Consider the full structure of (87a).

(88)

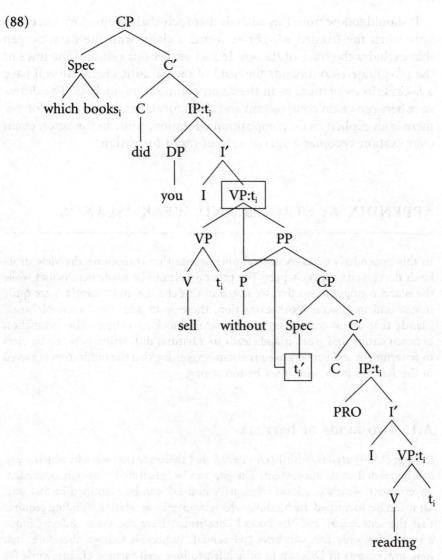

The crucial link is shown in the tree. While PP is a barrier, it is the only barrier between the linked traces. Therefore, chain formation can link *which books* with the trace in the object position of *reading* without producing a Subjacency violation. Crucially, this chain is not produced by movement of *which books* from this position, since, as we have seen, such movement does result in a Subjacency violation.

Which books also must head the chain containing the true gap. It follows then that in a parasitic gap construction, there are two overlapping chains that share a single head.

It should follow from this analysis that such chain formation is licensed only when the fronted *wh*-phrase forms a chain with the parasitic gap that excludes the trace of the *wh*. In fact we get this result: if the trace of the *wh*-phrase c-commands the head of the parasitic chain, we will have a θ-Criterion violation, as in the chain composition analysis. The difference between chain composition and chain formation is that in the former there is an explicit chain composition operation, while in the latter, chain composition becomes a special case of chain formation.

APPENDIX A: STRONG AND WEAK ISLANDS

In this appendix we survey several phenomena that complicate the view of islands developed in this chapter. The general point to be made here is that while the island configurations that we noted in this chapter and Chapter 6 are quite robust and in general block extraction, there is an additional class of 'weak' islands that allow certain extractions while blocking others. The distinction between strong and weak islands leads to a natural distinction between barriers to government and barriers to movement, suggesting that the unification achieved in the *Barriers* framework may be too strong.

A.1. Two kinds of barriers

Cinque (1990) argues, with Rizzi (1990), that there are two ways in which a gap can be related to its antecedent. The gap can be 'identified' through antecedent government, which is a local relation. A non-DP can be identified in this way. Or it can be 'identified' by binding, which is not a local relation. Binding requires that the antecedent and the bound constituent have the same index; Cinque assumes that only DPs can have (referential) indices. It follows, therefore, that long movements of DPs can in principle produce well-formed chains; while for movements of non-DPs, only local movements are possible.

Cinque proposes that the two types of identification are subject to different types of barriers, which produce different types of islands. Antecedent government is sensitive to the presence of both strong and weak barriers. Binding is sensitive to the presence of strong barriers only. From this it follows that there can be long movement of a DP from a context that will not allow the movement of a non-DP; this is because a weak island will block antecedent government but not binding.

Here are some examples. A strong island corresponds to the familiar Subjacency islands: CNPC, CED, and the Subject Condition.

(89) *a.* *How carefully$_i$ did you read a letter that was worded t$_i$?
     b. *How carefully$_i$ did you call Mary after wording the letter t$_i$?
     c. *How carefully$_i$ would [to word the letter t$_i$] be impossible?
(90) *a.* ??Which letter$_i$ did you meet a man who worded t$_i$ carefully?
     b. ??Which letter$_i$ did you call Mary after wording t$_i$ carefully?
     c. ??Which letter$_i$ would [to word t$_i$ carefully] be impossible?

A weak island is a *wh*-island, an inner island (see § 7.1), a factive island, or an extraposition island.

(91) *a.* *How carefully$_i$ were you wondering which letter to word t$_i$?
     b. *How carefully$_i$ didn't you word the letter t$_i$?
     c. *How carefully$_i$ did you regret that you had worded the letter t$_i$?
     d. *How carefully$_i$ was it time to word the letter t$_i$?
(92) *a.* Which letter$_i$ were you wondering how carefully to word t$_i$?
     b. Which letter$_i$ didn't you word t$_i$ carefully?
     c. Which letter$_i$ did you regret that you had worded t$_i$ carefully?
     d. Which letter$_i$ was it time to word t$_i$ carefully?

In (89)–(90) we see the influence of the strong barrier. It renders extraction of an adjunct entirely ungrammatical, and the extraction of an argument slightly less so. In (91)–(92), on the other hand, the weak barrier is claimed by Cinque to have the same impact on the extraction of an adjunct, but has little if any impact on the extraction of the argument.[18] Thus the pattern is the following:

(93)

Barrier	Argument extraction	Adjunct extraction
Strong	Subjacency violation	ECP violation
Weak	No violation	ECP violation

Noting the similarity between strong islands and Subjacency islands, it makes sense to link the definition of strong island to the absence of L-marking. Looking at the examples of weak islands, we hypothesize that extraction takes place in these cases out of a maximal projection that is not a complement of a θ-assigner, although the maximal projection is assigned a θ-role. Let us consider the individual cases.

Example (92*a*) shows extraction from a *wh*-island. Assuming Rizzi's account of Relativized Minimality, the *wh*-island should not be a barrier for long extraction of a referential DP; however, antecedent government of the trace of an adjunct should be blocked, as it is in (91*a*). A similar account fits the negative island case in (91*b*)/(92*b*). For the factives in (91*c*)/(92*c*), Cinque proposes an account reminiscent of that offered by Stowell (1981): the complement is assigned a θ-role by the verb but is not a sister of the verb. A similar account can be developed for the extraposition cases in (91d)/(92d).

It can be seen that Cinque's account rests on a distinction between the assignment of θ-roles *per se*, and the direct assignment of a θ-role to a complement, what we have understood as L-marking. Cinque calls this 'direct selection'. Moreover, the fact that a subject is a strong island (see (89)–(90)) suggests that the direction in which a θ-role is assigned is also relevant. Finally, complements of verbs and adjectives are L-marked, but not complements of nouns, as shown by the fact that an N-complement appears to be a strong island.

(94) *a.* ??Which letter did you express the notion that you would word t carefully?

   b. *How carefully did you express the notion that you would word the letter t?

These observations lead to the following definitions.

(95)   The direction in which Case and θ-role are assigned to the complement is the canonical government direction.

(96)   A maximal projection that is not θ-marked by a [+V] category in the canonical direction is a barrier for binding (weak barrier).

(97)   A maximal projection that is not L-marked by a [+V] category is a barrier for government (strong barrier).

Cinque notes, furthermore, that IP and VP must be included in this account, since they are maximal projections. While they are not assigned θ-roles in the strict sense, they are (c-)selected, by C and I respectively. C and I could be taken to be [+V] in some extended sense, since they are functional categories that extend the projection of V.[19] With these two modifications we arrive at what is essentially Cinque's proposal.[20]

(98)   A maximal projection that is not selected by a [+V] category in the canonical direction is a barrier for binding.

(99)   A maximal projection that is not directly selected by a [+V] category is a barrier for government.

A.2. Clitic left dislocation

Consider now the following data from Italian illustrating clitic left dislocation (CLLD).[21]

(100) *a.* [$_{PP}$ Al mare], ci siamo   già   stati.
             to the seaside. there-(we)-have already been

b. [$_{AP}$ Bella], non lo è   mai stata.
   beautiful   not-it-(she) ever was

c. [$_{VP}$ Messo da parte], non lo è   mai stato.
   get out of the way   not-it-(he) ever was

d. [$_{CP}$ Che bevi],   lo dicono tutti.
   that you drink, it says   everybody

Cinque shows that this construction allows a constituent of any category to appear in 'left-dislocated' position; moreover, there can be more than one such phrase in a single sentence.

(101)   Di vestiti, a me, Gianni, in quel negozio,   non mi ce ne ha
        clothes   to me Gianni in that shop (he) not-to-me-there-of-them
        mai comprati.
        ever has bought

This construction resembles the English (and Italian) Left Dislocation (LD) construction, in which a constituent is left-dislocated and there is a resumptive pronoun. But this latter construction allows only DP to be left-dislocated, and in the Italian case, the resumptive in the CLLD construction cannot be a full pronoun but must be a clitic.

(102)   *a.* John, I really don't trust him.
        b. *To John, I really don't want to give this money to him.

(103)   *a.* Quella città, non sono   mai stato là.
           that   town, not-(I)-have ever been there
        b. *In quella città, non sono mai stato là.
        c. In quella città, non ci   sono mai stato.
           in that   town not-there-(I) have ever been

A crucial difference between LD and CLLD in Italian is that only CLLD is subject to locality constraints.

(104)   *a.* *[$_{PP}$ A Carlo], ti parlerò   solo del   [$_{DP}$ le persone [$_{CP}$
               to Carlo I will talk to you only about the people
            che gli   piacciono]].
            that to him appeal

        b. *Se [$_{AP}$ ricco], credi   che [$_{IP}$ [$_{CP}$ esserlo stato] non
            if   rich   you think that to have been it does not help him
            gli giovi], t$_i$ sbagli.
            him   you are wrong

        c. *[$_{PP}$ A voi], Mario corre più   di [$_{CP}$ quanto non vi   sembri].
               to you Mario runs more than   not it to you seems

(105)   *a.* John, I know very few people who like *(him).
　　b. Mary, I know why you like ?(her).
　　c. John, the fact that you like *(him) is surprising.
　　d. Mary, many of *(her) friends speak Italian.
　　　　etc.

On the basis of this difference it might appear that CLLD is derived by a type of *wh*-Movement, while the clitic is a resumptive element that bears the relationship to the moved constituent that trace bears to a moved *wh*-phrase. Cinque rules out this possibility on the grounds that CLLD does not behave like *wh*-Movement in other respects. For example, CLLD does not license parasitic gaps, while true *wh*-Movement does.

(106)   *a.* What$_i$ did you eat t$_i$ without liking e$_i$?
　　b. *Gianni$_i$, l'ho　　cercato　　per mesi t$_i$, senza　trovare e$_i$.
　　　　Gianni　him-have (I)-looked-for for months without to-find

Moreover, and significantly, if CLLD were a special case of *wh*-Movement we would expect it to behave just like *wh*-Movement in all configurations in which Subjacency is in effect. While CLLD does show certain locality effects, as we have seen, it is somewhat less constrained than *wh*-Movement, as the following illustrate.

(107)   *a.* Loro, il　libro, credo　che a　Carlo sia　sicuro　che no glielo
　　　　them the book I-think that to Carlo it is certain that　to-him-it
　　　　daranno　　mai.
　　　　they-will-give never
　　b. Anna, a cui$_i$　'non ricordo　　[$_{CP}$ quando [$_{IP}$ hanno dato
　　　　Anna　to whom I don't remember when　　they gave
　　　　il premio t$_i$]], . . .
　　　　the prize
　　c. *?Gianni, a cui$_i$　　non so　　[$_{CP}$ quando si saprà
　　　　Gianni　to whom I don't know　when　one will know
　　　　[$_{IP}$ cosa　daranno t$_i$]], . . .
　　　　what they will give

Cinque points out that it is possible to extract over a single *wh*-operator in Italian (see (107*b*)), but not over two such operators (see (107*c*)). If *wh*-movement is involved in CLLD, there would be two such operators in (107*a*), but the sentence is grammatical. Therefore, Cinque argues, CLLD does not involve *wh*-Movement. Moreover, while *wh*-Movement out of sentential complements is possible (through 'COMP-to-COMP' movement), CLLD is not possible in such contexts.

(108) *a.* Per quale ragione$_i$ ha   detto che se ne andrà t$_i$?
        for what reason he-has said that SE NE will-leave
     b. *Per questa ragione$_i$ ha   detto che se ne andrà t$_i$?
        for this   reason he-has said that SE NE will-leave

The possibility of *wh*-Movement through the intermediate COMP position allows the derivation of (108*a*), while (108*b*) is blocked by Subjacency.

But now, if CLLD is not movement then there must be mechanism for forming chains that does not involve movement; such a mechanism applies over S-structure representations. Movement is another way in which a chain can be formed, of course. Crucially, both types of chain formation must be subject to locality effects such as Subjacency, which is associated with strong barriers. Cinque concludes that in the case of CLLD we have the appearance of leftward movement, but no actual movement. CLLD obeys strong islands but, unlike topicalization, does not involve *wh*-Movement. Obeying strong islands is a property not exclusively of *wh*-Movement, but also of binding chains, which arise either via movement or base generation. CLLD enters only into binding chains because it cannot be derived through successive cyclic *wh*-Movement. Therefore CLLD must be base-generated.

Summing up, on Cinque's account there are two types of identification of empty categories (following Rizzi), two types of barriers, and two ways of creating chains. Empty categories are identified through either antecedent government or binding. Weak barriers are barriers for antecedent government but not for binding. Chains may be created through movement or base-generated.

EXERCISES

7-1. For each of the following sentences, indicate what the BCs and the barriers are in terms of the *Barriers* framework, why they have this status, which if any constraints are violated, and why.

(1) *a.* *what$_i$ did you read the book$_j$ that t$_j$ proved t$_i$
    b. *who$_i$ did you believe John claimed that t$_i$ had won
    c. *to whom$_i$ did you speak to John [before giving the book t$_i$]
    d. *who$_i$ would pictures of t$_i$ disturb you
    e. *who$_i$ did you read the book$_j$ that t$_i$ wrote t$_j$
    f. *how$_i$ did you wonder [whether I had fixed the car t$_i$]
    g. *how$_i$ did John wonder [who$_j$ t$_j$ wanted [to fix the car t$_i$]]
    h. *who$_i$ would [the fact that the police arrested t$_i$] amaze you
    i. *who$_i$ did you wonder [whether t$_i$ had fixed the car with a screwdriver]

*7-2. 1. Consider the following examples from the perspective of the *Barriers* theory.

(1)   *a.* We discussed Mary's kissing the frog prince.
      b. *Who$_i$ did you discuss [$_\alpha$ Mary's kissing t$_i$].

To what would you attribute the ungrammaticality of (1*b*)? What must the category α be in order for your explanation to work? Why?
   2. Now consider the following examples.

(2)   Who did you resent [$_\alpha$ PRO kissing e].
(3)   Who did you resent [$_\alpha$ Mary kissing e].

What must the category α be in these cases. Why?
   3. What do your answers to 1 and 2 suggest about the analysis of gerunds? [Battistella 1983]
   4. Discuss the status of the following examples in light of your answer to 3.

(4)   *a.* It was nice [PRO seeing you].
          It was nice [that I could see you].
      b. *It was nice [my seeing you].
          *It was nice [the concert].

*7-3. In the text we noted that the use of minimality barriers in the *Barriers* framework raises certain questions:

(i)   V′ should be a barrier to extraction of direct objects, but it is not.
(ii) I′ should be a barrier to extraction from VP, but it is not.
(iii) When C⁰ is *that* it does not block extraction of adjuncts from IP.

Discuss how would you modify the *Barriers* framework to meet these objections.

7-4. Demonstrate that extraction of an adjunct from the following islands produces ECP violations, while extraction of an argument produces weaker Subjacency violations: tensed relative clauses, infinitival relative clauses, DP subjects, sentential subjects, *wh*-islands, appositives to DPs, clausal adjuncts, and infinitival purpose clauses. For instance, the following examples show the result of extracting an argument *what* and an adjunct *how* or *why* from a *wh* island.

(1)   *a.* ?What$_i$ did you wonder where$_j$ we put t$_i$ t$_j$?
      b. *How$_i$ did you wonder what$_j$ we fixed t$_j$ t$_i$?
      c. *Why$_i$ did you wonder where$_j$ we went t$_j$ t$_i$?

If you are a native speaker of a language other than English, provide comparative data where appropriate.

7-5. Consider the following sentence.

(1) *how did John announce [$_{DP}$ a plan [$_{CP}$ t′ [$_{IP}$ PRO to fix the car t]]]

CP is not a barrier, since it is a complement of the noun and hence L-marked. How would this sentence be treated in the *Barriers* framework, the Relativized Minimality framework, and the framework of Lasnik and Saito (1992)?

7-6. The ECP approach to the *that-t* effect has to deal with the fact that the configuration that is ungrammatical in cases of extraction from subject position seems to be more or less the same as the one that is grammatical in cases of relativization of subjects. Compare the following.

(1) *a.* *who$_i$ do you think [$_{CP}$ t′$_i$ that [$_{IP}$ t$_i$ left]]
     b. John is the person [$_{CP}$ OP$_i$ that [$_{IP}$ t$_i$ left]]
     c. John is the person [$_{CP}$ REL [$_{IP}$ t$_i$ left]]

In the *Barriers* framework, following a suggestion by Pesetsky (1982*b*), we could say that the operator and the complementizer in the relative clause merge into a single constituent that is coindexed with the subject trace. In the Relativized Minimality framework, we could say that the relative complementizer (but not the complementizer of the *that*-complement) contains Agr (Rizzi 1990). Show how these two solutions would solve the problem.

*7-7. Show how we might use the ECP to account for the following distribution of data (taken from Chapter 6).

(1) *a.* *[(that) John was here] is obvious.
     b. I believe [(that) John was here].
     c. I believe very strongly [*(that) John was here].

[Stowell 1981]

*7-8. Following up on your answer to Exercise 7-7, what conclusions can you draw from the following data?

(1) *a.* It is obvious [(that) John was here].
     b. It is obvious to me [(that) John was here].
     c. It is obvious to me from your remarks [(that) John was here].

*7-9. Consider the following sentences.

(1) *a.* John$_i$ is a person who I don't really like his$_i$ paintings very much.
     b. John$_i$ is a person who everyone who knows him$_i$ is a government employee.

    c. John$_i$ is a person who the fact that I don't like him$_i$ very much
       shouldn't play a great role in my decision making.

    d. John$_i$ is a person who I call the police every time I see him$_i$ in the
       street.

These sentences illustrate the fact that in non-standard English, it is possible to
get around potential island violations by putting a resumptive pronoun in the
position where a trace would go. Now consider the following examples.

(2)   *a.* John is a person (that) I don't really like.
    b. John is a person (that) everyone knows.
    c. John is a person (that) I call every time I see the police.

(3)   *a.* John$_i$ is a person *(that) I don't really like his$_i$ paintings very much.
    b. John$_i$ is a person *(that) everyone who knows him$_i$ is a government
       employee.
    c. John$_i$ is a person *(that) the fact that I don't like him$_i$ very much
       shouldn't play a great role in my decision making.
    d. John$_i$ is a person *(that) I call the police every time I see him$_i$ in the
       street.

Describe the pattern that you find in these examples and explain why it constitutes a puzzle.

*7-10. Aoun *et al.* (1987) claim that *that* blocks extraction of an adjunct from
a complement. What predictions does this claim make about the grammaticality
and possible interpretation(s) of the following sentences? Verify whether or not
these predictions are correct. If this claim were correct, what implications would
it have for the *Barriers* framework?

(1)   *a.* How carefully did you say John worded the letter?
    b. How carefully did you say that John worded the letter?

(2)   *a.* How carefully do you believe John worded the letter?
    b. How carefully do you believe that John worded the letter?

[Aoun *et al.* 1987].

7-11. The following appear to be typical CED violations.

(1)   *a.* ??Who did you go home without Mary talking to?
    b. ??Who did you go home before Mary talked to?

Show that if we allow adjunction to barriers, there exists a derivation in which
there exists at most one barrier between any two adjacent traces. Why does this
result pose a problem for the *Barriers* framework?

[Johnson 1985]

*7-12. In Italian, a pronominal direct or indirect object of a tensed verb normally appears as a clitic adjoined to the left of the verb.

(1) Gianni gli   presenterà   Maria.
     Gianni to-him will-introduce Maria
     'Gianni will introduce Maria to him.'

A non-pronominal argument appears in an argument position in the VP.

(2) a. Gianni presenterà   Maria a   Francesco.
        Gianni will-introduce Maria to Francesco.
        'Gianni will introduce Maria to Francesco.'
     b. *Gianni presenterà Maria (a) gli.

In the standard analysis of argument clitics in generative grammar, due to Kayne (1975), the pronominal argument moves from its canonical position to the position that it appears in in S-structure. For present purposes, we will assume that the clitic adjoins to the verb, that the movement is an A-movement, and that after adjunction the clitic c-commands its trace.

   A pronominal direct or indirect object of a verb in the infinitive normally appears as a clitic adjoined to the right of the verb.

(3) Giovanni sperava di legger*lo*.
     Giovanni hoped   of to-read-it
     'Giovanni hoped to read it.'
(4) Piero deciderà di parlar*ti*   di parapsicologia.
     Piero will-decide of to-speak-to-you of parapsychology
     'Piero will decide to speak to you about parapsychology.'

Crucially, in cases such as these the clitic cannot appear as a clitic adjoined to the left of the tensed main verb.

(5) a. Credo   che Gianni *la* presenterà   a Francesco
        I-believe that Gianni her will-introduce to Francesco.
        'I believe that Gianni will introduce her to Francesco.'
     b. *La credo che Gianni presenterà a Francesco
(6) a. Sentivo Mario parlar*le*   di parapsicologia
        I-heard M.   to-speak-to-her of parapsicologia
        'I heard Mario speak to her about parapsychology.'
     b. *Le sentivo Mario parlar di parapsicologia
(7) a. Piero affermava di conoscer*la*   molto bene
        Piero stated   of to-know-her very   well
        'Piero stated he knew her very well.'
     b. *Piero *la* affermava di conoscere molto bene

(8)   *a.* Angela pareva aver*lo*   riacompagnato a casa
        Angela seemed to-have-him taken   home
        'Angela seemed to have taken him home.'
      b. *?Angela *lo* pareva aver riacompagnato a casa

But there are some verbs for which this restriction does not hold, and the clitic may be adjoined either to the infinitive or to the higher verb.

(9)   *a.* Mario vuole/sa   riserver*lo* da solo
        Mario wants/can to-solve-it of alone
        'Mario wants to/can solve it by himself.'
      b. Mario *lo* vuole/sa risolvere da solo
(10) *a.* Gianni continua a raccontar*gli* stupide storie
        Gianni continues to tell-to-him stupid stories
        'Gianni is continuing to tell him stupid stories.'
      b. Gianni *gli* continua a raccontare stupide storie

Some other verbs that allow adjunction of the clitic are *dovere* 'have to', *potere* 'be able to', *cominciare a* 'begin to', *finire* 'finish', *stare per* 'be going to', *venire a* 'come to', *andare a* 'go to', *tornare a* 'come back to'.

   1. What does the ungrammaticality of the examples (5*b*)–(8*b*) tell you about the structure of infinitival complementation in these examples? Explain your answer.
   2. What does the grammaticality of the examples (9*b*)–(10*b*) tell you about the structure of infinitival complementation in these examples? Discuss the advantages and disadvantages (if any) of various ways of guaranteeing that such a structure will be present just in the case of those verbs that allow adjunction of the clitic from the complement.
[Rizzi 1978; Burzio 1983]

*7-13. Consider the following examples from French.

(1)   *a.* le livre que Jean croit   que Marie aime
        the book that Jean believes that Marie likes
        'the book that Jean believes that Marie likes'
      b. le livre que Jean croit   qu'aime Marie
        the book that Jean believes that likes Marie (subj.)
        'the book that Jean believes that Marie likes'
(2)   *a.* le livre que Jean regrette que Marie aime
        the book that Jean regrets that Marie likes
        'the book that Jean regrets that Marie likes'
      b. *le livre que Jean regrette qu'aime Marie
        the book that Jean regrets that likes Marie (subj.)
        'the book that Jean regrets that Marie likes'

(3)   *a.* Qui crois-tu   qui aime ce livre?
          who believe-you who likes this book
          'Who do you believe likes this book?'
     b. *Qui regrette/comprends/oublies-tu qui aime ce livre?
          who regret/understand/forget-you who likes this book
          'Who do you regret/understand/forget likes this book?'
(4)   *a.* Who do you believe likes this book?
     b. *Who do you regret/understand/forget (that) t likes this book?

The order verb-subject shown in (1*b*) (that is, *aime Marie* instead of *Marie aime*) is called Stylistic Inversion. We can see that Stylistic Inversion can occur in an embedded clause just in case it is possible to extract a subject *wh*-phrase from such a clause. The verbs that do not permit subject extraction are 'factives'; those that do are called 'bridge' verbs. These classes appear to be more or less the same in French and English. A major difference between English and French is that French does not allow deletion of the complementizer; when the subject is extracted the complementizer appears as *qui* instead of *que* (as in (3*a*)).

Given these observations, what is the generalization that ties together (2*b*) and (3*b*)? Can you think of a way to express this generalization in a simple way using the principles of the *Barriers* framework?

[Adams 1985]

FURTHER READING

....

The *Barriers* framework has given rise to numerous specific analyses, as well as proposals to refine in one way or another the definitions of barrier, antecedent government, head government, proper government, and related notions. Among these are Aoun *et al.* (1987), and Rochemont and Culicover (1990). Lasnik and Uriagereka (1988) provides a summary of many of the main ideas and issues.

Manzini (1992; 1994) offers a radical reformulation of the locality conditions of the *Barriers* framework without making reference to notions such as *barrier* and *L-marking*.

Baker (1988) applies the *Barriers* theory to the analysis of a wide range of languages, with striking results for the theory of morphosyntax. Application of the *Barriers* theory to the syntax of the Germanic languages, particularly scrambling phenomena, can be found in Grewendorf and Sternefeld (1990). Müller and Sternefeld (1993) extends and modifies the *Barriers* framework to account for the interaction of scrambling, topicalization, and *wh*-Movement in a variety of languages, including English, German, Dutch, Russian, and Japanese. Rochemont (1989) proposes an application of Subjacency in terms of barriers to account for topic islands. Watanabe (1992) proposes a way of applying constraints such as Subjacency in a language where there appears to be no overt movement.

Browning (1989) provides evidence to support the position of the *Barriers* framework that the ECP is not reducible to the CED, in contrast with an alternative approach to island constraints in terms of connectedness. For the latter, see Kayne (1983), Longobardi (1985), and May (1985). An interesting work within the same general framework is Koster (1987).

Chung (1994), using evidence from *wh*-Movement in Chamorro, argues that the Cinque/Rizzi distinction between short and long movement is correct, and that long movement is possible only where 'referentiality' holds of the extracted constituent.

LF Representations

In this chapter we consider some of the motivations for and uses of the level of syntactic representation called Logical Form, or LF. Intuitively, LF is the level at which the logical properties of a sentence are represented. By Syntacticization, LF is a syntactic level, subject to the principles that govern syntactic representations.

Crucially, movements at LF contribute to the interpretation of the sentence, but not to the form of the sentence. Thus their existence can only be inferred from judgements about the meaning of sentences, and from theoretical considerations. So, while it is a relatively straightforward matter to stipulate that logical properties have a syntactic representation, it is another thing entirely to show that they *must* be accounted for in the syntactic component of the grammar.

1. Quantifier Raising

1.1. *The syntactic representation of scope*

The logical properties of interest are those of scope. A quantifier is said to take scope over another element if the latter is dependent on the quantifier. The following illustrates.

(1)   *a.* Someone knows every human language.
      b. ∃x, x a person, ∀y, y a human language, x knows y
      c. ∀y, y a human language, ∃x, x a person, x knows y

Sentence (1*a*) is ambiguous. It can mean either that there is someone who knows all of the human languages, as shown in (1*b*), or that for each language there is at least one person that knows it, as shown in (1*c*). In the logical representations, the quantifier to the left is said to have wide scope and the quantifier to the right is said to have narrow scope.[1]

A syntactic representation of scope would be one in which the scope of a quantifier correlates with its position in the syntactic configuration. The natural relation to use would be c-command, since if α c-commands β it is higher than β in the syntactic representation. At S-structure, *someone* in (1*a*) c-commands *every human language*, so the S-structure would be sufficient to provide a syntactic account of the scope in the interpretation given in (1*b*). But since there is only one S-structure for the sentence, there is no way to represent the interpretation given in (1*c*) at S-structure in terms of c-command.

The syntactic solution to this problem is to posit the existence of a level of syntactic representation in addition to D-structure and S-structure at which the appropriate c-command relations hold. Call this level Logical Form or LF. It is generally assumed that LF is derived from S-structure by the application of Move α.

Since LF is a level of syntactic representation, we expect the usual constraints and principles to hold. In particular, we expect among other things that:

(2) *a.* Move α leaves a trace (because of the Projection Principle).
  b. Move α can only move a constituent to a position in which it c-commands its trace.
  c. Move α moves a constituent to a legitimate landing site.
  d. ECP holds.
  e. Subjacency holds.

While there is some evidence to support the prediction that ECP holds, there is evidence that Subjacency does not hold for LF movements, as we will see.

Application of Move α to a quantifier phrase (QP) is called **Quantifier Raising**, or QR.[2] The application of QR to (1*a*) produces the following two structures, depending on which QP is adjoined higher.

(3) *a.* [$_{IP}$ someone$_i$ [$_{IP}$ every human language$_j$ [$_{IP}$ t$_i$ knows t$_j$]]]
  b. [$_{IP}$ every human language$_j$ [$_{IP}$ someone$_i$ [$_{IP}$ t$_i$ knows t$_j$]]]

There is a straightforward procedure for translating from the syntactic representations in (3) into the logical representations in (1*b*) and (1*c*) (see Exercise 8-2).

There are numerous issues here that need to be addressed. For example, we are assuming that QR adjoins the QP to IP. Since LF is a syntactic representation, it must be possible in general to adjoin one constituent to another, and it must be possible in particular to adjoin something to IP. We discuss in § 1.2 whether such adjunctions should be allowed. To consider another example, in order for one quantifier phrase to take scope over the other(s) by c-command, only one needs to move. However, there are arguments that all of the quantifiers move at LF, which we take up in § 1.3.

1.2. *The landing site of QR*

Consider the landing site of QR. To this point we have looked at movements to specifier position that are licensed by feature agreement, e.g. *wh*-Movement. There does not appear to be any reason to view QR as a type of *wh*-Movement; rather, QR can adjoin QP to IP.[3] This issue recalls the discussion of *wh*-Movement in Slavic in Chapter 6, where we saw that in some languages (e.g. Bulgarian), all of the *wh*-phrases are clustered in [Spec, CP], while in others (e.g. Polish and Serbo-Croatian), one *wh*-phrase moves to [Spec, CP] while the others adjoin to IP. Thus we have evidence that adjunction to IP must be freely available, and in the absence of any licensing in [Spec, CP], all movements for scope will be adjunctions to IP.[4] Furthermore, topicalization in English, as illustrated in (4), appears to be adjunction to IP, as illustrated in (4).[5]

(4)   I think [$_{CP}$ that [$_{IP}$ [$_{DP}$ bananas like these]$_i$ [$_{IP}$ you should never buy t$_i$]]].

Because the landing site of the topicalized phrase is to the right of the complementizer, adjunction to IP is the most natural analysis.[6]

1.3. *ECP at LF*

Let us look now at evidence that the ECP applies at LF. Consider the following examples.[7]

(5)   *French*:
    a. Je n'ai   vu   personne.
       I NE-have seen no one
      'I have seen no one.'

    b. Personne ne sera   arrêté.
       no one   NE be-FUT arrested
       'No one will be arrested.'

These examples show that *personne* 'no one' may appear in subject or object position; *ne*, a negative marker, must appear in the sentence as well. The following examples show that the negative marker may be in the higher clause with certain verbs, but not when *personne* is a subject.

(6)   *a.* J'ai   exigé   que personne ne soit arrêté.
        I-have demanded that no one   NE be arrested
        'I demanded that no one be arrested.'
    b. Je n'ai   exigé   qu'ils   arrêtent personne.
        I NE-have demanded that-they arrest   no one
        'I didn't demand that they arrest anyone.'
    c. *Je n'ai   exigé   que personne soit arrêté.
        I   NE-have demanded that no one be arrested
        'I didn't demand that anyone be arrested.'

    Suppose that there is a requirement that *personne* appear in the same clause as *ne*. This requirement is satisfied in the simple sentences at S-structure, but it can only be satisfied in (6*a*) and (6*b*) if it undergoes some type of raising into the higher clause. This raising clearly does not apply at S-structure, since *personne* appears in the lower clause at S-structure. It is reasonable to hypothesize that this raising takes place at LF.

    Now notice that this hypothesis yields just the right analysis for (6*c*), if we assume that ECP applies at LF as well as at S-structure. The result of applying QR to (6*c*) yields the following configuration.

(7)   [$_{IP}$ personne$_i$ [$_{IP}$ je ne ai exigé [$_{CP}$ que [$_{IP}$ t$_i$ soit arrêté]]]]

The configuration *que t$_i$* in French turns out to be identical to the English *that-t* configuration that originally motivated the ECP.

    Pursuing a similar strategy for English, we would predict that the sentences in (8) are not ambiguous, while those in (9) and (10) are. While in all cases the second QP is in a lower clause, only in the first group of sentences is it the subject of a tensed sentence and adjacent to *that*.

(8)   *a.* Someone believes that every human language is related to
        Indo-European.
    b. Someone expects that every runner will win the race.

(9) *a.* Someone believes every human language to be related to Indo-European.
   b. Someone expects every runner to win the race.
(10) *a.* Someone believes that it is important to study every human language.
   b. Someone believes it to be important to study every human language.
   c. Someone expects that the race will be won by every runner.
   d. Someone expects the race to be won by every runner.

To the extent that clear judgements are possible, the predictions are only weakly supported in the case of English. The sentences in (9) and (10) appear to be ambiguous to the same extent that those in (8) are. For some speakers, the sentences in (8) are not ambiguous, but those in (9) and (10) are not, either. For such speakers, (9*b*) does not mean 'For every runner x, someone expects x to win the race,' and (10*d*) cannot mean, 'for every runner x, someone expects the race to be won by x.' We cannot account for the absence of these readings in terms of the ECP, so the ECP may not be relevant to (8), either. For other speakers, all of these sentences are ambiguous, and for these judgements, the ECP is not relevant, either.[8]

We return to the question of whether the ECP applies at LF in our discussion of LF *wh*-Movement in § 3. At this point you should be able to do Exercise 8-1.

2. Antecedent-contained deletion

The phenomenon of VP ellipsis provides an interesting argument for the existence of LF as an independent level of syntactic representation. This phenomenon is illustrated by the following sentences.

(11) *a.* Everyone wanted to leave, but Susan didn't.
   b. John has already seen the movie, but Bill hasn't.

In classical transformational grammar, such sentences were derived by a deletion transformation, called VP Ellipsis, which deleted the material in the second conjunct under 'identity' with the material in the first conjunct, as in (12).

(12)   John has already [seen the movie], but Bill hasn't [seen the movie] ⇒
       John has already [seen the movie], but Bill hasn't [∅].

Some care has to be taken with the notion of 'identity,' in light of sentences such as the following.

(13)   *a.* John plans to see the movie, and Bill already has [seen the movie].
       b. John loves his children, but Bill doesn't [love his children].

Example (13*a*) shows that ellipsis can occur when the two VPs are not morphologically identical. That is, the morphologically unmarked *see the movie* is identical to the past participial *seen the movie* for the purposes of ellipsis.[9] Example (13*b*), which is ambiguous, shows that the notion of identity in question does not include referential identity. One reading of (13*b*) is (14*a*), where referential identity holds, and one reading is (14*b*), where it does not.

(14)   *a.* John$_i$ loves his$_i$ children, but Bill$_j$ doesn't love John$_i$'s children.
       b. John$_i$ loves his$_i$ children, but Bill$_j$ doesn't love his$_j$ (that is, Bill's) children.

The second type of identity is called **sloppy identity**.

An alternative, non-transformational approach to ellipsis is one in which an empty VP is assigned an interpretation with respect to some overt VP in the sentence.[10] The question of identity arises here, too, but reversed. We must determine what aspects of the antecedent VP are relevant to the interpretation and what aspects are irrelevant. Again, it appears that morphological and referential differences can be ignored.

While the transformational approach to ellipsis is clearly syntactic, the interpretative approach is less clearly so. On one view, the representation of the empty VP is the meaning of the antecedent VP at some appropriate level of semantic representation. A syntactic analog of this approach is to say that the full, antecedent VP is **reconstructed** into the position occupied by the empty VP at some level of syntactic representation, i.e. LF.[11]

Leaving open the question of whether there are empirical differences between these two interpretative approaches to ellipsis, let us consider a phenomenon that shows crucially that the antecedent of the empty VP cannot be an overt S-structure VP. The following illustrates **antecedent-contained deletion**.[12]

(15)   John read everything that you did.

The question here is, what is the antecedent of the empty VP following *did*? Consider the structure in (16).

(16)

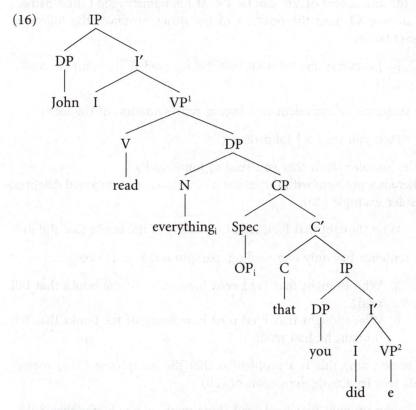

Notice that there is no VP in the sentence that can be the antecedent for VP². VP¹ is definitely not a possible candidate, because VP¹ actually dominates and therefore contains VP². If the antecedent of VP² contains VP², what is the antecedent of this second VP²? It can be seen that there is no final resolution of this regress problem assuming the structure in (16).[13] So VP² cannot have an antecedent. But, since VP² in fact does have an antecedent (the sentence is quite easily understood), the structure on which the antecedent of VP² is determined cannot be (16), i.e. at S-structure.

Moreover, the empty VP² cannot be dominated by VP¹ in the representation in terms of which its antecedent is determined. In some sense, VP² must be 'moved out from under VP¹' in order for it to be able to have an antecedent.

Since the expression containing VP² is a quantifier phrase (i.e. *everything that you read*), a natural way of moving VP² is to apply QR to this QP. The result will be (17).

(17) [IP [DP everything OP that you did [VP e]²] [IP John [VP read t]¹]]

Now the antecedent of VP² can be VP¹ at LF, namely *read t*. Reconstruction of one VP into the position of the other produces the following representation.

(18) [IP [DP everything OP that you did [VP read t]²][IP John [VP read t]¹]]

This structure is equivalent to a logical representation of the form

(19) {∀x: you read x | John read x}

that is, 'for all x such that you read x, John read x.'

There is a problem with this analysis of antecedent-contained deletion. Consider example (20).[14]

(20) Who thought that Fred read how many of the books that Bill did?

This sentence has only one reading, paraphrasable as (21*a*).

(21) *a.* Who thought that Fred read how many of the books that Bill read?
      b. Who thought that Fred read how many of the books that Bill thought he had read?

The reason why this is a problem is that the paraphrase (21*b*) corresponds to a legitimate derivation of (20).

(22) who thought that Fred read [how many of the books that Bill did [e]] ⇒
      [how many of the books$_j$ that Bill did [e$_j$]]$_i$ [who [VP thought that Fred read t$_i$]$_j$]

Here, the empty VP *e$_j$* is coindexed with the overt VP *thought that Fred read t$_i$*. Substituting the overt VP for the empty VP produces a representation that is equivalent to (21*b*).

(23) [how many of the books$_j$ that Bill [VP thought that Fred read]$_j$]$_i$ [who [VP thought that Fred read t$_i$]$_j$]

In contrast, overt *wh*-Movement produces the ambiguity.

(24) How many of the books that Bill did did you think that Fred read.

Observing these facts, we note that there is another type of LF movement that gets VP² out from under VP³ which avoids the problem.[15] On this account, Case is assigned to a DP in [Spec, AgrOP], overtly in some languages, but at LF in English. That is, in order to satisfy the Case Filter (or its equivalent), the DP must undergo LF movement to [Spec, AgrOP]. In this theory, the DP must move to the lowest AgrO that c-commands it, for reasons of economy.[16] (25) illustrates.

(25)

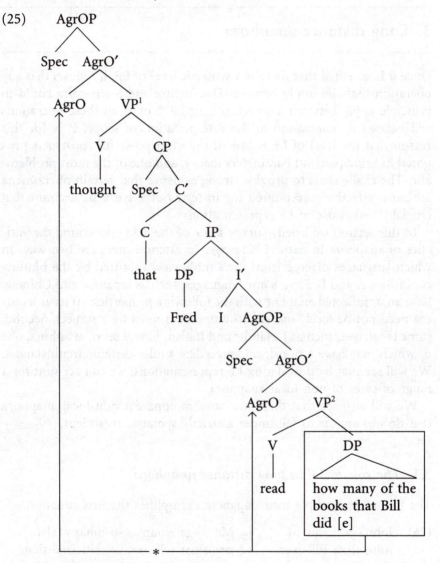

Crucially, the DP cannot move to the [Spec, AgrOP] in the clause containing *thought*. So the only VP that does not dominate the empty VP is VP², which must be the antecedent.

Antecedent-contained deletion thus constitutes an argument for LF movement based on the demonstration that the S-structure representation is not capable of accounting for certain cases of VP ellipsis.

3. Long distance anaphora

Once it is accepted that there is a syntactic level of LF, it follows that any operation that can apply between D-structure and S-structure could in principle apply between S-structure and LF. Not all of these operations will necessarily contribute to the interpretation of scope. It is for this reason that the level of LF is one of the most powerful constructs proposed in Principles and Parameters theory, and one of the most problematic. The challenge is to provide strong evidence that certain phenomena are most effectively accounted for in terms of a syntactic account that crucially makes use of LF representations.

In this section we briefly survey some of the data concerning the varieties of anaphora in natural language. In essence, there are two ways in which languages diverge from the simple view captured by the binding conditions A and B. First, some languages, such as Japanese and Chinese, have an uninflected anaphor with the following properties: (i) its antecedent need not be local, and (ii) its antecedent must be a subject. Second, some languages, such as Icelandic and Italian, have a set of anaphors, one of which may have a non-local antecedent under certain circumstances. We will see that by postulating LF representations, we can account for a range of cases of non-local anaphora.

We will also see that there are cases of apparent non-local anaphora that do not appear to fall under a strictly syntactic treatment.

3.1. The role of LF in long distance anaphora

The following example from Japanese exemplifies the first situation.

(26)   John$_i$-ga   Bill$_j$-ni   [$_{CP}$ [$_{IP}$ Mary$_k$-ga zibun$_{i/*j/k}$-o hihansita]-to]
        John-NOM Bill-DAT   Mary-NOM self-ACC   criticized that
        itta
        said
        'John said to Bill that Mary criticized self.'
        (Aikawa 1993)

(27) John$_i$-ga   Bill$_j$-ni   zibun$_{i/*j}$-o syookaisita
John-NOM Bill-DAT self-ACC   introduced
'John introduced himself/*herself to Mary.'

The behavior of anaphora in Japanese highlights several points, including obligatory subject orientation and the possibility of a long distance antecedent. It is natural to ask why Japanese and English should differ on both points. As we have seen, English typically has only local anaphora (disregarding for the moment the matter of anaphors in DPs). And as the following examples illustrate, the antecedent of a reflexive in English need not be a subject.

(28)   *a.* John talked to Susan$_i$ about herself$_i$.
       b. John saved Susan$_i$ from herself$_i$.

An explanation for subject-orientation has been sought in terms of Agr. Agr agrees with the subject of the sentence, as an instance of Spec-head agreement. If the reference of the anaphor in Japanese is somehow tied to the agreement of Agr, then subject-orientation will follow. Two possibilities have been proposed: that the anaphor undergoes movement at LF to Agr, and that the anaphor is bound to Agr at LF. (29) illustrates the first type of proposal, and (30) the second.

(29)   [$_{IP}$ DP$_i$ Agr$_i$ [$_{VP}$ ... DP[anaphor] ...]] $\Rightarrow$
       [$_{IP}$ DP$_i$ Agr$_i$+DP[anaphor] [$_{VP}$ ... t ...]]
(30)   [$_{IP}$ DP$_i$ Agr$_i$ [$_{VP}$ ... DP[anaphor] ...]] $\Rightarrow$
       [$_{IP}$ DP$_i$ Agr$_i$ [$_{VP}$ ... DP[anaphor]$_i$ ...]]

On the first approach, the anaphor must be an X^0 category, since it adjoins to a head, namely Agr. It is assumed that the reflexive moves because it lacks certain grammatical features, such as person and number, that it must acquire in order to be properly interpreted. An anaphor can have a long distance antecedent just in case it can move from one Agr to another at LF, as in (31).

(31)   John$_i$-ga Bill$_j$-ni [$_{CP}$ [$_{IP}$ Mary$_k$-ga zibun$_i$-o hihansita Agr$_1$]-to] itta
       Agr$_2$ $\Rightarrow$
       John$_i$-ga Bill$_j$-ni [$_{CP}$ [$_{IP}$ Mary$_k$-ga t$_i$-o hihansita zibun$_i$+Agr$_1$]-to]
       itta Agr$_2$ $\Rightarrow$
       John$_i$-ga Bill$_j$-ni [$_{CP}$ [$_{IP}$ Mary$_k$-ga t$_i$-o hihansita t$_i'$+Agr$_1$]-to] itta
       zibun$_i$+Agr$_2$

In this example, *zibun*$_i$ originates in the object position of the lower clause, adjoins to Agr$_1$ in the lower clause, and then adjoins to Agr$_2$ in the higher clause. Since this movement occurs at LF, there should not be any Subjacency violations (see § 4). The following examples bear out this prediction.

(32) *a.* John$_i$-ga   watasi$_j$ minna-ni   Bill$_k$-ga   zibun$_{i/j/k}$-o
     John-NOM I-(NOM) everyone-DAT Bill-NOM zibun-ACC
     hihansita koto-o   hanasita to   ommotte-iru
     criticized the-fact-that-ACC told   that think
     'John thinks that I told everyone the fact that Bill criticized zibun.'
     (Aikawa 1993)

   b. [sono kodomo]$_i$-wa [zibun$_i$-ga   kawaigatte-ita] inu-ga
     the   child-TOP   [[zibun-NOM was-fond-of] dog]-NOM
     sinde-simatta
     died
     'Speaking of the child, the dog that he himself was fond of died.'
     (Kuno 1973)

   c. Taroo$_i$-ga   zibun$_{i,j}$ no kodom-o sinsatu-si-ta isya$_j$-o
     Taro-NOM self$_{ij}$'s   child-ACC examined   doctor-ACC
     sonkei-si-ta
     respected
     'Taro$_i$ respected the doctor$_j$ who examined self's$_{i,j}$ child.'
     (Inoue 1976)

   d. John-wa,   [zibun-o nikunde iru] onna-to   kekkonsita
     John-TOP, [self-ACC hating is]   woman-with married
     'John$_i$ married a woman who hated zibun$_i$.'

There appear to be no ECP violations, either, as shown by the grammaticality of (33).

(33) John-ga   zibun-o tensai da to   omotte-iru
     John-NOM self-NOM genius be that think
     'John thinks that zibun is a genius.'

On an analysis in which the anaphor is bound by Agr, many of the same facts follow. In this case, the anaphor receives the relevant features in virtue of being in a chain with Agr. Long distance anaphora then requires that a sequence of Agrs form a chain with the anaphor, as illustrated in (34).

(34)

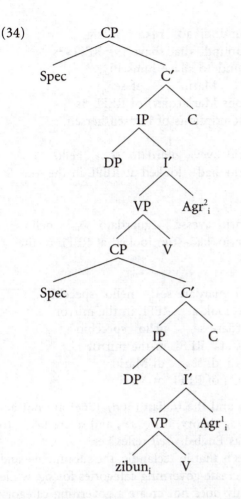

The question of which of these approaches is to be preferred is a complex one that we do not pursue here.

The second divergence from the simple Binding theory is exemplified by the following examples from Icelandic and Italian. 'Ind' denotes indicative mood, 'subj' denotes subjunctive, and 'inf' denotes infinitive.

(35) *Icelandic:*[17]

    a. Jón$_i$ segir   að María$_j$ elskar   sig$_{j/*i}$
        John say-PRES-IND that Mary love-PRES-IND REFL-3SG
        'John says that Mary loves herself/*himself.'

    b. Jón$_i$ segir   að María$_j$ elski   sig$_{j/i}$
        John say-PRES-IND that Mary love-PRES-SUBJ REFL-3SG
        'John says that Mary loves herself/him(self).'

c. Jón$_i$ skipaði   Gudmundi$_j$ að raka   sig$_{j/i}$
John order-PAST Gudmund that shave-INF REFL-3s
'John$_i$ ordered Gudmund$_j$ to shave himself$_{i/j}$.'

d. Jón$_i$ heyrði lysingu   Mariu$_i$ af sér$_{i/j}$
John heard descriptions Maria(GEN) of REFL-3s
'John heard Maria's descriptions of himself/herself.'

(36)   *Italian:*[18]

a. Alice$_j$ sapeva che Mario$_i$ aveva guardato sè$_{i/*j}$ nello
Alice knew   that Mario had   looked-at REFL in the
specchio
mirror

b. Alice$_j$ pensava che Mario$_i$ avesse   guardato sè$_{i/*j}$ nello
Alice thought that Mario had-SUBJ looked-at REFL in-the
specchio
mirror

c. Alice$_j$ disse a Mario$_i$ di guardare sè$_{i/*j}$ nello specchio
Alice told Mario   to look-at   REFL in the mirror

d. Alice$_j$ vide Mario$_i$ guardare sè$_{i/j}$ nello specchio
Alice saw Mario look-at   REFL in-the mirror

e. Alice$_j$ guardò   i ritratti di sè$_{i/j}$ di Mario$_i$
Alice looked-at portraits of REFL of Mario

The Icelandic cases (35b)–(35d) and the Italian (36d)–(36e) are not accounted for by the simple binding theory, if *sig, ser,* and *sé* are taken to
be anaphors in the same sense as English *-self* reflexives.

What we see in these examples is that in Icelandic, the subjunctive and
the infinitive apparently do not create governing categories for *sig,* while
in Italian the infinitive apparently does not create a governing category
for *sé.* We might suppose, given these data, that there is a slightly different Binding theory for Icelandic and another slightly different one for
Italian; this would be an instance of parametric variation. But Icelandic
hvor ödrum 'each other' can never have a long distance antecedent, nor
can Italian *se stesso.*[19]

(37)   *Icelandic:*

a. *Ðeir telja   að   ég hati hvor ödrum
they   believe that I   hate each other

b. *Ðeir skipuðu mér að raka   hvor ödrum
they   ordered me to shave each other

(38)   *Italian:*

a. Mario$_j$ disse che Gianni$_i$ amava se stesso$_{i/*j}$
Mario said that Gianni loved himself

b. Mario_j ordinò a Gianni_i di amare se stesso_{i/*j}
   Mario ordered Gianni to love   himself

c. Mario_j vide Gianni_i colpire se stesso_{i/*j}
   Mario saw Gianni to-hit himself

d. Mario_j vide fotografie di se stesso_{i/*j} di Gianni_i
   Mario saw pictures of himself   of Gianni
   'Mario saw Gianni's pictures of himself.'

In fact, paradoxically, the standard Binding theory does hold for Icelandic and Italian, but not for the particular lexical items *sig*, *ser*, and *sé*.

3.2. Varieties of long distance anaphora

In addition to long distance anaphora, we can also find cases in which the antecedent of the anaphor is not present in the sentence at all. The following sentences from English and Japanese illustrate this phenomenon of **discourse anaphora**.

(39) *English*:
   a. As for myself, the party ended quite early.
   b. As for yourself, young man, there will be no free lunch this week.

   Japanese:
   c. A: Dareka-ga   John-no kawari-ni kita-n-desu ka?
        someone-NOM John-GEN in-place-of come   Q?
        'Did someone come in place of John?'
      B: Iie, zibun-ga   kita-n-desu
        No, zibun-NOM came
        'No, I came.'
   (Aikawa 1993)

In the Japanese case, *zibun* must be a subject in order to have a discourse antecedent.

Putting the matter in its simplest terms and ignoring many of the finer points, it appears that there are two and perhaps three types of anaphora, each of which is subject to different types of conditions. The distinction is overtly marked in some languages, such as Icelandic and Italian, while in languages such as English the same forms are used for all types of anaphora.

The type of anaphora discussed last is sometimes called logophoric. It is characterized by the fact that the antecedent of the anaphor depends in part on the perspective expressed by the sentence; this antecedent may be in discourse or it may be in the sentence itself. For example, it appears that (40) is analogous to (39a) in interpretation, but not in the syntactic location of the antecedent.

(40)   Mary admitted that, as for herself, the party was over.

Roughly speaking, the situation appears to be that the antecedent of the anaphor is the individual who is aware of the proposition expressed by the sentence. Since speaker and hearer are always aware in this way, in virtue of being participants in the discourse, they are always available as potential antecedents of the logophoric anaphor. But such awareness can also be imputed to a third person, as in (40). Notice that when the perspective shifts in this way, it is difficult to understand the speaker or the hearer as being the antecedent.

(41)   *Mary admitted that, as for myself/yourself, the party was over.

But when the third person cannot be aware of the proposition, as in (42), the perspective remains that of the speaker and hearer.[20]

(42)   Mary was unaware that, as for myself/yourself, the party was over.

Setting aside logophoric anaphora for a moment, there appear to be two other types of anaphora, at least descriptively. One is local anaphora, in which the antecedent of an anaphor is 'local' in the sense that it is within the 'same sentence'; ECM of course complicates this intuition somewhat.

(43)   a. I gave myself a present.
       b. I cut myself.
       c. I expect myself to win.

The second is long distance anaphora, in which the antecedent of an anaphor is an argument external to the clause that contains the anaphor, as we have seen.

A straightforward approach to this diversity of anaphora would be to stipulate at the level of linguistic theory that there are two types of anaphors, those that are local and those that are not. Let us call the first type SELF, and the second SE (alluding to the behavior of the Italian *se*). In Dutch, there are in fact two forms, *zich* and *zichzelf*. Both can be used for local anaphora, but *zich* has a more restricted distribution and may also be used for long distance anaphora.

(44) *a.* Jan$_i$ liet   mij voor $\begin{Bmatrix} \text{*zichzelf}_i \\ \text{zich}_i \end{Bmatrix}$ werken.

　　　 Jan made me for   him   to-work
　　　 'Jan made me work for him.'

　　 b. Jan$_i$ droogde $\begin{Bmatrix} \text{zich}_i \\ \text{zichzelf}_i \end{Bmatrix}$ af.

　　　 Jan dried   himself

　　 c. Jan schaamde $\begin{Bmatrix} \text{zich}_i \\ \text{*zichzelf}_i \end{Bmatrix}$.

　　　 Jan ashamed himself
　　　 'Jan was ashamed.'

　　 d. Max$_i$ haat $\begin{Bmatrix} \text{zichzelf}_i \\ \text{zich}_i \end{Bmatrix}$.

　　　 Max hates himself
　　　 (Everaert 1991)

It appears from data such as this that *zichzelf* is an instance of SELF, which requires a local antecedent, while *zich* is an instance of SE.[21]

What we find across languages is that there are differences in the conditions under which SE can have an antecedent. In the Italian examples in (36), for example, it can be seen that the subject is 'accessible' to the long distance anaphor *se* when it is the subject of a verb of perception. In Icelandic, the subject of a higher clause is 'accessible' to the long distance anaphor *sig* when it is in some sense 'responsible' for the truth of a complement proposition, as expressed by the use of the subjunctive.

Now let us reconsider logophoric anaphora. The role of 'accessibility' of an antecedent on the basis of 'awareness' or 'responsibility' is very reminiscent of the role of perspective in discourse anaphora. It is plausible, therefore, to take the logophoric interpretation to be a special case of non-local anaphora, where there is no antecedent within the sentence. The pattern that emerges is then the following.

(45)

	SELF (local)	SE (long distance)
has local antecedent	grammatical (local anaphora)	grammatical (local binding)
has long distance antecedent	ungrammatical	grammatical, subject to accessibility conditions (long distance anaphora)
has no syntactic antecedent	ungrammatical	grammatical, subject to accessibility conditions (discourse anaphora)

Although it summarizes the main type of anaphora, this picture fails to provide a straightforward account of the difference between English -*self* and Japanese *zibun*. Because there is no overt differentiation between SELF and SE in either of these two languages, we might expect that in both of them the anaphors would have all of the properties of both SELF and SE. While this is true for Japanese, it is not true for English. In English, long distance anaphora is possible when the anaphor is in a *picture*-NP, as shown in (46), and appears to be ruled out otherwise.

(46)   *a.* John says that Mary loves herself/*himself.
       b. John thinks that this picture of himself is fabulous.
       c. *John thinks that we own a fabulous picture of himself.

But we will show below that cases such as (46*c*) can be considerably improved under certain conditions.

It also appears that English -*self* cannot have an antecedent that is more distant than a potential intervening antecedent. Compare this pattern with that of the Icelandic *sig*, illustrated in (47), repeated from (35).

(47)   *a.* Jón$_i$ segir   að María$_j$ elski   sig$_{j/i}$.
          John say-PRES-IND that Mary love-PRES-SUBJ REFL-3SG
          'John says that Mary loves herself/him(self).'
       b. Jón$_i$ heyrði lysingu   Mariu$_i$ af sér$_{i/j}$.
          John heard descriptions Maria-GEN of REFL-3s
          'John heard Maria's descriptions of himself/herself.'

But it can be argued that the restriction on English is a consequence of perspective, since the following examples appear to allow for an 'extra-distant' interpretation of the anaphor.

(48) a. John$_i$ says that Mary was unaware that, as for himself$_i$, the party was over.

  b. John$_i$ says that Mary was unaware that there were pictures of himself$_i$ on the post office wall.

Another difference between long distance *-self* in English and long distance anaphors in other languages is that *-self* does not require a subject antecedent. Cf.

(49) a. Mary told Bill$_i$ that there was a picture of himself$_i$ on the wall of the post office.

  b. *Japanese*:
  John$_i$-ga Bill$_j$-ni [Mary$_k$-ga zibun$_{i/*j/k}$-o hihansita to]
  John-NOM Bill-DAT [Mary-NOM zibun-ACC criticized that]
  itta.
  said
  'John said to Bill that Mary criticized self.'
  (Aikawa 1993)

Let us suppose that the subject orientation of Japanese *zibun* is due to the fact that it must form a chain with some Agr in order to receive agreement features, as discussed above. We would therefore predict that in all languages, uninflected anaphors would display a similar subject orientation in long distance anaphora. Reuland and Koster (1991) provide comparative data that appears by and large to support this prediction. The table in (50) summarizes the data for uninflected anaphors from their survey of long distance anaphors.

(50)

Language	Long distance anaphor	Subject orientation?
Icelandic	*sig/sin*	yes
Norwegian	*seg/sin*	yes
Dutch	*zich*	yes
Polish	*siebie*	yes
Czech	*se/sebe*	yes
Latin	*se*	unclear
Italian	*se*	unclear
Finnish	*itse*	yes
Chinese	*ziji*	yes

To conclude this discussion of long distance anaphora, consider the following question: why can't the English reflexive in argument position have a long distance antecedent? To put the question another way, why can't English -*self* function as a SE anaphor in argument position? Once again, we can make the argument that long distance anaphora is not ruled out, but simply very difficult because of other factors. Consider the following examples.

(51) a. Mary$_i$ says that it would be very difficult for herself$_i$ to accept your theory of anaphora.
   b. Mary$_i$ says that it was incumbent upon herself$_i$ not to abandon the car after the breakdown.
   c. Mary$_i$ says that there was only herself$_i$ to blame, and no one else.

(52) a. *?Mary$_i$ says that you would find it very difficult for herself$_i$ to accept your theory of anaphora.
   b. ?Mary$_i$ says that you argued that it was incumbent upon herself$_i$ not to abandon the car after the breakdown.
   c. ?Mary$_i$ says that you should blame only herself$_i$ and no one else.

What these examples suggest is that there is a possibility of long distance anaphora even from an argument position in English just in case the minimal predicate that contains the anaphor expresses the point of view of the antecedent. In (51) the predicates *difficult for herself . . .*, *incumbent upon herself . . .*, etc. express Mary's judgement because of the absence of an intervening subject DP; in (52) these predicates express the judgement of *you*.

What this discussion shows is that it may be possible to construct a general theory of anaphora that preserves a simple version of Condition A for the cases of local anaphora. Such a theory would have the following form.

(53)   SELF must have a local antecedent.

The issue then becomes one of explaining why (53) holds; one possibility[22] is that SELF imposes a 'reflexivity' requirement on the verb, such that two of its arguments must be coindexed. Since the arguments of a verb are necessarily local with respect to one another, the locality requirement expressed in (53) follows directly. If we exempt the subject argument as being an argument through which the reflexivity of a verb is marked, then we can directly derive the fact that in English, reflexives cannot appear in the subject position of a tensed sentence, e.g.

(54) *Mary thinks that herself will win

4. *Wh*-Movement in LF

We have raised in this chapter the possibility that there exists an abstract syntactic level of representation LF at which Move α applies quite generally. By Uniformity, we would expect that this level of representation is exactly like S-structure, in the sense that whatever can happen in the mapping from D-structure to S-structure can happen in the mapping from S-structure to LF. The only difference between S-structure and LF, on this view, is that we can see the effects of rules that apply between D-structure and S-structure on the **phonetic form** (PF) of the sentence.

Suppose that we allow for the possibility that there are certain conditions that may be satisfied at LF or that can only be satisfied at LF. If the condition is not satisfied in S-structure but is satisfied in LF, we can account for the fact that a sentence that would otherwise be ungrammatical is in fact grammatical. To take a simple example, suppose that the complementizer C[+wh] must license a constituent with the feature [+wh] in [Spec, CP] through Spec-head agreement. (In such a case we say that C 'discharges' the feature.) If this condition can be satisfied only at S-structure, then we would predict, falsely, that there are no languages that lack *wh*-Movement.[23] Consider the following sentences from Chinese.[24]

(55) Ni xihuan shei?
     you like   who
(56) Zhangsan wen wo [shei mai-le shu].
     Zhangsan ask me who bought books
     'Zhangsan asked me who bought books.'
(57) Zhangsan xiangxin [shei mai-le shu].
     Zhangsan believe   who bought books
     'Who does Zhangsan believe bought books?'
(58) Zhangsan wen wo [ni maile   shenme]
     Zhangsan ask me you bought what
     'Zhangsan asked me what you bought.'

(59) Zhangsan renwei [ni maile   shenme]
      Zhangsan think   you bought what
      'What does Zhangsan think you bought?'
(60) Zhangsan zhidao [shei mai-le shu].
      Zhangsan know   who bought books
      a. 'Who does Zhangsan know bought books?'
      b. 'Zhangsan knows who bought books.'

Observe the contrast between the position of the *wh*-phrase in Chinese and English. In Chinese, the *wh*-phrase does not move (it is a **wh-in-situ** language) while in English the *wh*-phrase moves to the initial position in its clause; it is in [Spec, CP].

Although the *wh*-phrases are *in situ* in Chinese, these questions are interpreted just like the corresponding English question, in which the *wh*-phrases undergo movement at S-structure. In (56) and (58) the *wh*-phrase takes scope over the complement, which is interpreted as an embedded question. In (57) and (59) the *wh*-phrase takes scope over the entire sentence, which is interpreted as a main question. Both possibilities are available for (60).

We continue to assume that at S-structure, the scope of *wh* is a direct reflex of the syntactic structure. Thus, the sentences (56) and (57) must have different structures, and there must be two structures associated with (60). In particular, in Chinese there must be a syntactic structure for a sentence like (55) with the property that the *wh*-phrase is in [Spec, CP]. Since there is no basis for assuming that there are two different S-structure configurations allowed for these examples, our recourse is to posit that there are two LF configurations. Where *wh* takes wide scope, as in (57) and (60*a*), the *wh*-phrase is moved to the specifier of the highest CP at LF; where *wh* takes narrow scope, it is moved to the specifier of the lower CP.

In English, on the other hand, *wh*-Movement applies in the mapping from D-structure to S-structure. A *wh*-phrase is in [Spec, CP] at S-structure and hence at LF. The two languages differ at S-structure, but at LF they are identical with respect to the position of the *wh*-phrase. That is, the LF of the Chinese (55) is more or less as follows.

(61) shei$_i$ ni xihuan e$_i$
      who$_i$ you like   t$_i$

In fact, English also shows LF movement of *wh* in cases of multiple *wh*. Consider the following.[25]

(62) Who remembers where we bought which book?

This sentence is ambiguous. The ambiguity can be expressed in term of the scope of the *wh*-phrases. On one reading, *which book* has narrow scope. In this case the question is, Who remembers what the place/book pairs are? That is,

(63) For which person x, x remembers for which place y and for which book z, we bought z at y.

A possible answer to this question is 'John remembers where we bought which book.'

On the other reading, *which book* has wide scope. In this case, the question is, For which person/book pairs does the person remember where we bought the book? That is,

(64) For which person x and for which book z, x remembers for which place y, we bought z at y.

A possible answer to this question is 'John remembers where we bought *Barriers* and Bill remembers where we bought *Aspects of the Theory of Syntax*.'

It is clear, once again, that S-structure is not sufficient to account configurationally for the scope of the *wh*-phrases, since there is only one S-structure and at least two scope interpretations. In English as in Chinese it must be the case that *wh*-Movement occurs at S-structure; the difference between the two is that *wh*-Movement can occur at S-structure in English, but not in Chinese.

The idea that *wh*-Movement at LF obeys ECP is exactly what we would expect under a syntactic account of scope. Along the same lines, we would expect that *wh*-Movement obeys Subjacency. In fact, there are certain examples that suggest that *wh*-Movement in Chinese behaves like overt *wh*-Movement in English, in that it obeys Subjacency.[26]

(65) *[$_S$ [$_{DP}$ [$_{S'}$ tou-le sheme de] neige ren]   bei dai-le]
            stole what   DE that   person by caught
     '*What was [the man that stole t] caught.'
(66) *[$_S$ [$_{DP}$ [$_{S'}$ ni weisheme mei mai de] neiben she]   hen hao]
            you why   not buy DE that   book very good
     '*Why is [the book that you did not buy t] very good.'

(67)   *[$_S$ [$_{S'}$ Zhangsan tao-le shei] zhen kexi]
         Zhangsan marry who real pity
   '*Who is [that Zhangsan married t] a real pity.'
(68)   *[$_S$ [$_{S'}$ Zhangsan tao-le shei], ni   zhidao-le
         Zhangsan marry who you know
   '*who do you know that Zhangsan married t.'

In (67) the *wh*-phrase appears in a sentential subject, while in the other cases, it appears in a relative clause. Extraction from such configurations is blocked by Subjacency. The fact that the *wh*-phrase cannot take sentential scope in these cases suggests that Subjacency is operative here.

But there are cases that are unexpectedly grammatical.

(69)   *[$_S$ [$_{DP}$ [$_{S'}$ shei yao mai de] shu] zui gui
                who want buy DE book most expensive
   '*who are books [that t wants to buy] most expensive.'
(70)   [$_S$ ni xiang kan [$_{DP}$ [$_{S'}$ ta shemeshihou pai de] dianying]]
         you want see   he when   film DE movie
   'When do you want to see movies [that he filmed t].'
(71)   [$_S$ ni xihuan [$_{DP}$ [$_{S'}$ wo piping she de] wenzhang]]
         you like   I criticize who DE article
   '*Who do you like articles in which I criticize t.'

One possibility is that in fact LF extraction is not subject to Subjacency, which explains the grammaticality of (70) and (71).[27] The ungrammatical examples would then be due to other factors, such as the specificity of the determiner *neige* 'that'.

Nevertheless, there are exceptions to the generalization that *wh*-Movement at LF does not obey Subjacency. In particular, *weisheme* 'why' and *zeme* 'how' appear to obey Subjacency, in that they cannot be extracted from *wh*-islands.

(72)   Ni   xiang-zhidao [shei weisheme da-le Zhangsan]?
       you wonder   who why   beat Zhangsan
   'For which person x, you wonder why x beat Zhangsan.'
       Not: 'For which reason y, you wonder who beat Zhangsan for y.'
(73)   Ni   xiang-zhidao [shei zeme pian-le Zhangsan]?
       you wonder   who how cheated Zhangsan
   'For which person x, you wonder how x cheated Zhangsan.'
       Not: 'For which way y, you wonder who cheated Zhangsan in y.'

Similar facts hold for English overt extraction of adjuncts.

(74) a. ?*What$_i$ did you wonder why$_j$ I bought t$_i$ t$_j$?
     b. *Why$_j$ did you wonder what$_i$ I bought t$_i$ t$_j$?
(75) a. *When$_j$ did you wonder what$_i$ I bought t$_i$ t$_j$?
     b. *Where$_j$ did you wonder who$_i$ I met t$_i$ t$_j$?
     c. *How$_j$ did you wonder who$_i$ I pleased t$_i$ t$_j$?

The obvious solution to this apparent paradox is that extraction of adjuncts from islands produces not Subjacency violations, but ECP violations. In order for this explanation to hold, it must be the case that ECP applies not only at S-structure, as in English, but at LF, for languages like Chinese that lack overt *wh*-Movement as well as for English multiple *wh*-questions (see Exercise 8-4). This is precisely what we would expect if LF is a level of syntactic representation that is subject to the same constraints as any other level of syntactic representation. From this perspective, the proposal that Subjacency does not apply at LF becomes problematic, and calls for additional research.

5. Superiority

Example (76) illustrates a construction for which an explanation in terms of the application of ECP at LF has been proposed.

(76) a. I don't remember who$_i$ said what$_j$.
     I don't remember who$_i$ thinks that I said what$_j$.
     (cf. Who$_i$ thinks that I said 'boo'?)
    b. *I don't remember what$_i$ who$_i$ said.
     *I don't remember what$_i$ who$_i$ thinks I said.
     (cf. I don't remember what$_i$ you think I said.)

The ungrammaticality noted in (76b) is called a superiority effect after the Superiority condition of the *Conditions* framework, stated as follows.

(77) No rule can involve X, Y in the structure
     ...X...[$_\alpha$...Z...- WYV...]...
     where the rule applies ambiguously to Z and Y and Z is superior to Y.

(78) α is **superior** to β if every maximal projection dominating α dominates β but not conversely.[28]

As formulated, the Superiority condition is quite independent of all of the other constraints in the *Conditions* framework. We can derive the superiority effect from the ECP if the ECP applies at LF.[29] Suppose that *wh-in-situ* adjoins to [Spec, CP] at LF; the resulting structures are given in (79).

(79)   a. $[_{CP} [_{Spec} [_{Spec} \text{who}_i] \text{what}_j] [_{IP} t_i \text{ say } t_j]]$
     b. $[_{CP} [_{Spec} [_{Spec} \text{what}_j] \text{who}_i] [_{IP} t_i \text{ say } t_j]]$

The adjunction structure is the same as the S-structure proposed for multiple *wh*-fronting in Bulgarian, as we discussed in Chapter 6. Application of *wh*-Movement at LF for English *wh-in-situ* requires no special stipulation, since we have already shown that such LF movement occurs in languages that lack overt movement.

Suppose that the index of the head of the complex specifier is transmitted to the maximal specifier. In (79a) this index is i, while in (79b) it is j. We now have the follow LF structures.

(80)   a. $[_{CP} [_{Spec} [_{Spec} \text{who}_i] \text{what}_j]_i [_{IP} t_i \text{ say } t_j]]$
     b. $[_{CP} [_{Spec} [_{Spec} \text{what}_j] \text{who}_i]_j [_{IP} t_i \text{ say } t_j]]$

The difference between these two structures is the following. In (80a) the trace in subject position is coindexed with, c-commanded by, and hence antecedent governed by the specifier. Thus it satisfies the ECP. The object trace is not coindexed with an antecedent that c-commands it, but since it is lexically governed by the verb, it too satisfies the ECP. In (80b), on the other hand, the subject trace is neither lexically governed nor antecedent governed. Hence the superiority effect in (33) is due to an ECP violation at LF.

Similar ECP effects are predicted when the *wh-in-situ* in a multiple *wh*-question is an adjunct. In such a case, the index of the specifier is that of the moved *wh*, so the adjunct is not antecedent governed. (81) illustrates.

(81)   a.   ?I don't remember who$_i$ left why$_j$.
        $[_{CP} [_{Spec} [_{Spec} \text{who}_i] \text{why}_j]_i [_{IP} t_i \text{ left } t_j]]$
     b.   ??I don't remember what$_i$ you did why$_j$.
        $[_{CP} [_{Spec} [_{Spec} \text{what}_i] \text{why}_j]_i [_{IP} \text{you did } t_i t_j]]$

In this case judgements vary, and it is not clear that the examples are as strongly unacceptable as those involving superiority. Nevertheless, these examples are clearly less grammatical than those in which the adjunct is in [Spec, CP] and the argument moves at LF, a prediction that follows from the ECP analysis.

(82)   I don't remember why you did what.

It is also possible to alleviate the superiority effect itself, by replacing the simple *wh*-words with *wh*-phrases containing *which*.[30]

(83)   *a.* Which books did which people read?
       b. Which books did which people say that you read?

It is entirely possible, then, that the superiority effect is due to some other factor, or to a formulation of the ECP that distinguishes the cases in (83) from those in (76*b*). However, Pesetsky (1987) suggests that the apparent counterexamples are due to the fact that *wh*-phrases can get scope in two ways, by movement (which produces superiority effects), and by 'unselective binding' by a external operator Q. The representation of the well-formed (83*a*), for example, would be (84).

(84) Q_{ij} [which people$_i$ read which books$_j$]

Even though the phrase *which books* undergoes movement, the scope of *which books* and *which people* is determined by the Q-operator, not by movement (at LF). Therefore the configuration that produces the superiority effect does not arise, and there is no ECP violation.[31]

Of course, there must be a distinction between those *wh*-phrases that are subject to LF movement and those that are subject to the Q-operator. Suppose that the former are true quantifiers and must undergo movement at LF, while the latter are not true quantifiers. Rather, they are D-linked, a term that is intended to suggest that they receive reference (or more accurately, delimit the range of possible answers) in part, at least, through a linking to discourse. There is no precise characterization of what makes an expression D-linked; however the notion of D-linking is often appealed to in the literature when a particular example appears not to be sensitive to some constraint on *wh*-questions.

Recall the proposal in § 2 that Subjacency does not apply at LF. On the current approach, LF movement is subject to Subjacency and the difference between D-linked and non-D-linked *wh*-phrases constitute evidence for the existence of LF. The non-D-linked phrases appear to obey movement constraints such as Subjacency and the ECP, while the D-linked phrases do not. The evidence involves languages with no overt *wh*-Movement, where phrases that cannot have a D-linked interpretation cannot appear within islands. For example, in Japanese *ittai* adjoined to a *wh*-phrase functions like *the hell* in English.

(85)　Mary-wa [John-ga ittai　nani-o　yonda to] itta-no?
　　　Mary-Top John-NOM the-hell what-ACC read　that said-Q
　　　'What the hell did Mary say that John read?'

In English, *the hell* cannot be D-linked.

(86)　*a.* *Who read what the hell?
　　　b. Who the hell read what?

And in Japanese, *ittai* cannot appear within a Subjacency island.

(87)　*a.* *Mary-wa John-ni　ittai　nani-o　ageta hito-ni
　　　　　Mary-Top John-DAT the-hell what-ACC give　man-DAT
　　　　　atta-no?
　　　　　met-Q
　　　　　'*What the hell, did Mary meet the man that gave t, to John?'
　　　b. *Mary-wa John-ga　ittai　nani-o　yomu mae-ni
　　　　　Mary-Top John-NOM the-hell what-ACC read　before
　　　　　dekaketa-no?
　　　　　left-Q
　　　　　'*What the hell did Mary leave before John read t₁?'

On the other hand, when the simple *wh*-phrase appears, the Subjacency violation does not occur.

(88)　*a.* Mary-wa John-ni nani-o ageta hito-ni atta-no?
　　　b. Mary-wa John-ga nani-o yomu mae-ni dekaketa-no?

These *wh*-phrases are D-linked and hence do not have to move at LF.

6. γ-marking

We conclude with a somewhat surprising application of the notion of LF. Consider the example in (89).

(89) [$_{CP}$ Why$_i$ did [$_{IP}$ you leave t$_i$]]?

Why is an adjunct, and as such is not θ-governed. It is not even lexically governed, if lexical government involves θ-role assignment. So, on the assumption that its trace must be properly governed, *why* must be antecedent governed. Thus extraction of *why* from IP satisfies the (disjunctive) ECP.

But what if there is extraction of an adjunct from VP?

(90) I wonder [$_{CP}$ how$_i$ [$_{IP}$ John will [$_{VP}$ fix it t$_i$]]].

Here *fix* is a lexical governor and thus VP should be a barrier to government by a more distant governor. So *fix* should block antecedent government of t$_i$ by *how*, which is the wrong result. It is for this reason that Relativized Minimality holds that a head should only block government by a more distant head (see Chapter 7, § 7). Otherwise it is necessary to find a way for the adjunct *how$_i$* to govern into VP even though VP is a barrier or to say that VP is not a barrier at all (see Chapter 7, § 8). Thus, Relativized Minimality cannot employ the *Barriers* device of allowing the overt complementizer to project a (minimality) barrier to antecedent government.

Notice also that while extraction of subjects is blocked by the presence of the complementizer *that*, extraction of adjuncts is not. *That* makes C′ a barrier to extraction under the *Barriers* analysis, so the following sentence should be ungrammatical.

(91) [$_{CP}$ How$_i$ do you think [$_{CP}$ t$_i'$ [$_{C'}$ that [$_{IP}$ I will fix it t$_i$]]]]?

The problem here is, if *that* creates a barrier for the subject, it should create a barrier for a non-subject adjunct. On the Relativized Minimality account, this is not a problem, because it is posited that there is a head distinct from *that* (some component of Infl) that head governs the trace of the adjunct. Antecedent government of t$_i$ by t$_i'$ satisfies the Identification requirement. This derivation is a problem for the *Barriers* approach, however.

A different solution is proposed by Lasnik and Saito (1984; 1992).

They observe that when *that* is absent, there is no barrier to antecedent government. Therefore, they propose that at LF, *that* can delete, and whether or not the trace of an adjunct is properly governed is checked only at this level. The crucial property of LF here is that deletion and movement at LF do not affect the phonetic form of the sentence. We can see how this works in (92).

(92)   S-structure after *wh*-movement:
[$_{CP}$ how$_i$ do you think [$_{CP}$ t$_i'$ [$_{C'}$ that [$_{IP}$ I will fix it t$_i$]]]]
LF after deletion of *that*:
[$_{CP}$ how$_i$ do you think [$_{CP}$ t$_i'$ [$_{C'}$ [e] [$_{IP}$ I will fix it t$_i$]]]]
Apply ECP to the adjunct trace at LF: No violation.

Now, if the deletion of *that* freely occurs at LF, why can it not occur in those cases where the trace is a subject? We can see that such deletion would yield a configuration in which the subject trace was properly governed (at LF), since after *that*-deletion we would have the configuration in (93).

(93)   LF after deletion of *that*:
[$_{CP}$ who$_i$ do you think [$_{CP}$ t$_i'$ [$_{C'}$ [e] [$_{IP}$ t$_i$ left]]]]

This result is clearly unwelcome, since we want the sentence with the sequence *that-t* at S-structure to violate the ECP at S-structure and at LF. But notice that there is a major difference between the cases where LF deletion of *that* gives the right result and those in which it gives the wrong result. The right result occurs when the trace is an adjunct, and the wrong result occurs when it is an argument. Let us suppose, say Lasnik and Saito, that the ECP applies to arguments at S-structure, but does not apply to adjuncts until LF. Mark an argument [$+\gamma$] or [$-\gamma$] depending on whether it is properly governed at S-structure. Then, at LF, mark adjuncts in the same way, after *that*-deletion. If a trace is marked [$-\gamma$], the sentence is ruled ungrammatical. The derivations in (94) illustrate.

(94)   *a.* [$_{CP}$ who$_i$ do you think [$_{CP}$ t$_i'$ [$_{C'}$ that [$_{IP}$ t$_i$ left]]]] $\Rightarrow$
[$_{CP}$ who$_i$ do you think [$_{CP}$ t$_i'$ [$_{C'}$ that [$_{IP}$ t$_i$ left]]]] $\Rightarrow$
$-\gamma$
[$_{CP}$ who$_i$ do you think [$_{CP}$ t$_i'$[$_{C'}$ [e] [$_{IP}$ t$_i$ left]]]]
$-\gamma$
b. [$_{CP}$ how$_i$ do you think [$_{CP}$ t$_i'$ [$_{C'}$ that [$_{IP}$ I will fix it t$_i$]]]] $\Rightarrow$
[$_{CP}$ how$_i$ do you think [$_{CP}$ t$_i'$ [$_{C'}$ [e] [$_{IP}$ I will fix it t$_i$]]]] $\Rightarrow$
[$_{CP}$ how$_i$ do you think [$_{CP}$ t$_i'$ [$_{C'}$ [e] [$_{IP}$ I will fix it t$_i$]]]]
$+\gamma$

The device of marking arguments with [γ] at S-structure and adjuncts with [γ] at LF has the desired affect of explaining why subjects are sensitive to the presence of *that*, while adjuncts are not. On balance, however, this is not a particularly satisfying explanation, since this difference with respect to *that* is simply shifted to another arena, that of γ-marking. None the less, the analysis is important, since it illustrates the methodological principle of the Principles and Parameters approach that a sentence may be grammatical in virtue of satisfying certain conditions at LF.

7. Summary

In this chapter we have considered a number of applications of LF. LF was originally motivated as a level of representation at which scope differences could be distinguished. By Syntacticization, LF is assumed in GB theory to be a level of syntactic representation. From this it follows that everything that we find in the mapping between D-structure and S-structure should be found in the mapping between S-structure and LF.

There is evidence that ECP applies at LF, but that Subjacency does not; this is problematic for the view that LF is a level of syntactic representation. The discussion of D-linking raised the possibility that Subjacency does hold at LF, appearances to the contrary notwithstanding.

Once LF is assumed to exist, it follows that there can be LF movements that do not have consequences for scope. We considered two cases. One is the movement of anaphors, which accounts for the subject orientation of long distance anaphora as well as a number of other properties. The other is the movement of direct objects to [Spec, AgrO], which accounts for the phenomenon of antecedent-contained deletion. We also considered the proposal that γ-marking at LF can account for the *that-t* effect.

EXERCISES

8-1. We have seen that there is a scope ambiguity in English when there are two quantifiers in the same sentence. Explain why the following sentence is not ambiguous.

(1) Every father$_i$ loves some of his$_i$ children.

[§ 1]

**8-2. According to our theory, quantifier scope is determined by QR at LF, and ECP but not Subjacency constrains LF movement. To test this theory, make up appropriate sentences in a language in which scope ambiguity is possible (your native language if possible), and then test whether the predicted interpretations are possible. [Hint: the sentences should test whether a quantifier phrase can move from a (i) subject, (ii) object, (iii) adjunct position over a Subjacency barrier.] Summarize your conclusions.

[§ 1]

8-3. Using labelled bracketings, give the LF representations for the following sentences. Be sure to indicate traces where appropriate. If there is an ambiguity, give all the representations.

(1) *a.* Who bought how many bananas?
     b. Everyone loves someone.
     c. Who do you think did what?
     d. Who remembers where we put what?

[§ 4]

*8-4. Discuss whether Subjacency applies to LF *wh*-Movement in English *wh*-questions. In order to do this exercise you will need to formulate examples that are similar to the Chinese examples cited in the text, and elicit grammaticality judgements from native speakers. What do you conclude, and why?

[§ 4]

**8-5. The following sentences are ambiguous. On one reading they are completely contradictory, and on the other they make perfect sense.

(1) *a.* Mary thinks that John$_i$ is taller than he$_i$ is.
     b. John thinks that Mary$_i$ can run faster than she$_i$ can.
     c. Mary thinks that John$_i$ is a nicer person than he$_i$ is.

The contradictory reading of (1*a*), for example, is that Mary thinks 'John is taller than he is', while the coherent reading is that the height that Mary believes that John has is greater than the height that he actually has.

 Show that there is no plausible S-structure account of the ambiguity, that is, that there is only one plausible S-structure for these sentences. Then outline how the ambiguity can be accounted for in a theory involving LF movement. Try to be precise about what is moving, and where it is moving to.

Here are some further data that may be of help. Note that the following are not ambiguous; they only have the contradictory reading.

(2)   a. Mary whispered that John$_i$ is taller than he$_i$ is.
   b. The fact that Mary$_i$ can run faster than she$_i$ can really disturbs me.
   c. John regretted the fact that Mary$_i$ was taller than she$_i$ was.

The following sentences are of marginal grammaticality.

(3)   a. ??Who did Mary whisper that John saw?
   b. ??Who does the fact that Mary saw really disturb you?
   c. ??Who did John regret the fact that Mary saw?

[Postal 1974]

*8-6. May (1985) claimed that a scope ambiguity does not arise when a *wh*-phrase is moved over a quantifier at LF.

(1)   a. Who is married to every student in the class?
   b. Who is every student in the class married to?

In the first case, there is only one reading, which is a contradictory one, on the assumption that only one person can be married to each student. Hence the logical form is something like (2).

(2)   for which x, x a person, for all y, y a student in the class, x is married to y.

On the other hand, (1*b*) is ambiguous. It has the contradictory reading that every student in the class is married to the same person, and the sensible reading that each person in the class is married to someone.

(3)   a. for which x, x a person, for all y, y a student in the class, y is married to x
   b. for all y, y a student in the class, for which x, x a person, y is married to x.

Compare these observations with the superiority effect. Are there any generalizations, and if so, how can they be accounted for?

8-7. Using the following data from Finnish, state the binding conditions for the Finnish anaphors *toisiansa* 'each other' and *itse*.

(1)   a. He$_i$ rakastavat toisiansa$_i$.
      they love   each other-POSS
      'They love each other.'

    b. Kysyin   ystäviltä toisistaan$_i$.
       asked-1.SG friends each other-POSS
       'I asked the friends about each other.'

    c. Ystävät$_i$ näkavät [$_{IP}$ toistensa$_i$ tiskaavan].
       friends saw   each other-GEN wash-up-PTC-GEN
       'The friends saw each other wash the dishes.'

    d. Ystävät$_i$ näkavät [$_{IP}$ tyttöjen$_j$ katsovan   toisiaan$_{*i/j}$].
       friends saw   girls-GEN   watch-PTC-GEN each other-POSS
       'The friends saw the girls watch each other.'

(2) *a.* Pekka$_i$ näki Matin$_j$ katsovan   itseään$_{i/j}$.
       Pekka saw Matti-GEN watch-PTC-GEN self-POSS
       'Pekka saw Matti watch himself.'

    b. Pekka$_i$ näki että Matti$_j$ katsoi   itseään$_{*i/j}$.
       Pekka saw that Matti-GEN watched self-POSS
       'Pekka saw that Matti watched himself.'

    c. *Puhuin   Pekalle$_i$ itsestään$_i$
       spoke-1.SG Pekka self-POSS
       'I spoke to Pekka about himself.'

(3)   Pekka$_i$ lauloi Matin$_j$ puolustaessa   itseään$_{*i/j}$.
       Pekka sang Matti-GEN defend-INF-INESS self-POSS
       'Pekka sang while Matti defended himself.'

[Steenbergen 1991]

8-8. Explain whether the following sentences illustrate long distance anaphora, logophoric anaphora, or neither.

(1) *a.* John$_i$ was walking innocently down the street when a heavy picture of himself$_i$ came crashing to the pavement.

    b. The steps that Mary$_i$ has taken over the past few months will guarantee that if it's ever claimed that there are pictures of herself$_i$ for sale in the flea market, it will be possible to successfully bring suit for libel.

    c. Bill$_i$ suggested that it was not going to be easy for Susan and himself$_i$ to break the world's record given the poor equipment that had been made available.

    d. Nasty stories about herself$_i$ make Mary$_i$ feel like hiring a lawyer.

*8-9. Assume that the ECP account of the superiority effect is correct. Given this, what is the evidence that in LF quantifiers adjoin to IP in LF while *wh*-phrases adjoin to [Spec, CP] in LF?

*8-10. Consider a dialect of English in which the following judgements hold.

(1) *a.* Who$_i$ expects who$_i$ to win?

    b. Who$_i$ expects you to do what$_i$?

(2) *a.* Who$_i$ expects who$_i$ will win?
      b. *Who$_i$ expects that who$_i$ will win?
      c. Who$_i$ expects who$_i$ will win?
(3) *a.* Who remembers why we bought what?
      b. Who remembers how we bought what?
      c. *Who remembers what we bought why?
      d. *Who remembers what we bought how?

Explain this pattern of judgements in terms of the theory outlined in this chapter.

**8-11. For some language other than English determine the grammaticality judgements for examples parallel to those in Exercise 8.10 and draw the appropriate conclusions regarding whether there is evidence in this language to support the analysis of LF *wh*-Movement in this chapter.

FURTHER READING

The proper way of dealing with *wh*-questions in languages that lack overt *wh*-Movement has been a major research theme for many years. Aoun and Li (1993) argue that in some cases, there is no LF movement of *wh-in-situ* in English and Chinese. Rather, there is 'a Qu-operator that is raised to the appropriate Spec of Comp position by S-structure,' which produces the proper scope relations. Rizzi (1991) proposes an account of the fact that in French, *wh*-Movement is obligatory when it has non-main clause scope, but optional otherwise. Saito and Hoji (1983) is an important paper on the status of various types of movements in Japanese and the structure of LF. Takahashi (1993) argues that Japanese actually has overt *wh*-Movement, in the form of long distance scrambling of *wh*. Watanabe (1993) argues that there is actually overt *wh*-Movement in languages that appear to lack it; what moves at S-structure is an abstract *wh*-morpheme.

Superiority has not been a major focus of the literature. Rivero (1980) notes that there is a superiority effect in Spanish when the subject precedes the verb, but not when it follows the verb.

Antecedent-contained deletion was first noted by Bouton (1970), and an analysis in terms of logical form is given by Sag (1976). May (1985) proposed the QR analysis summarized in the text. Many of Baltin's (1987) criticisms of May's proposal are countered by Larson and May (1990). Fiengo and May (1994) is an extensive development of the syntactic approach to ellipsis through reconstruction at LF.

Chomsky (1986*a*: 175), Pica (1987), and Reinhart and Reuland (1991; 1993) have suggested that an anaphor undergoes movement at LF to Agr; others have proposed that there is a binding relation between Agr and the anaphor (Everaert 1986a, Johnson 1984, Progovac 1992, Aikawa 1993, Bondre 1993).

In addition to a theory of local anaphora, we also require a theory of long distance anaphora, and a theory of logophoricity. See the papers in Koster and Reuland (1991), especially Hellan (1991) and Reinhart and Reuland (1991), and Sells (1987) for additional empirical details from a variety of languages as well as discussion of a range of important theoretical alternatives. Hendrick (1988) is a study of anaphora in Celtic.

Pesetsky (1987) proposes to derive psych verb constructions through *tough* Movement (Chapter 6), thereby unifying the treatment of cases like *These pictures of himself$_j$ annoy John$_j$* and *[These pictures of himself$_j$]$_i$ are tough for John$_j$ to appreciate t_i*. For some other approaches to the phenomenon of reflexives in subjects, see also Giorgi (1984), Jackendoff (1972), and Pollard and Sag (1992).

Cole, Hermon, and Sung (1990) argue that the differences in the behavior of long distance reflexives in English and Chinese can be accounted for in much the same terms that are used to account for the fact that English has overt *wh*-Movement and Chinese does not; the difference is attributed to Infl; it is claimed to be lexical in Chinese but not in English, with different government properties as a result, since only lexical items can be L-markers in the sense of the *Barriers* framework. Hestvik (1992) extends the proposal by Pica (1987) and others that reflexives move at LF to pronouns. On this approach the Binding theory applies at LF. Hestvik suggests that pronouns in English move to [Spec, VP] while pronouns in Norwegian adjoin to Infl, thereby accounting for a number of differences between English and Norwegian with respect to the distribution of bound pronouns and reflexives.

The Japanese anaphor *zibun*, and the related *zibun-zisin*, have been extensively studied; see for example Kuno (1973), a number of papers in Shibatani (1976), and more recently Katada (1991).

Binding and Logical Form

1. Crossover

In this section we consider what the proper level for the representation of binding is. In previous discussions, we assumed that binding is computed at S-structure, and there were some hints that it might also be necessary to satisfy the binding conditions at D-structure. Here we consider the possible role of LF. The binding conditions from Chapter 3 are given in (1).

(1) Binding conditions
  a. An anaphor must be bound within its governing category.
  b. A pronominal must be free within its governing category.
  c. An R-expression must be free.

   After considering a number of paradoxes and disjunctive conditions, we will conclude that a unified account of binding at S-structure can be maintained if we view a trace as a partial copy of a moved constituent. In particular, the trace does not contain copies of adjuncts of the moved constituent, just the argument structure of the constituent. Taking this view, we may allow the binding conditions to apply at S-structure, while bound pronouns translate freely as variables at LF.

1.1. Strong crossover

There are phenomena that suggest that a moved constituent behaves as though it is in the position of its trace with respect to binding. There are other phenomena that suggest that a moved constituent does not behave as though it is in the position of its trace with respect to binding.

Consider first the following example of **strong crossover**.

(2) *a.* *He₍ᵢ₎ thinks that Mary likes Bill₍ⱼ₎.
     b. *Who₍ᵢ₎ does he₍ᵢ₎ think that Mary likes t₍ᵢ₎?

The phenomenon illustrated here is 'crossover' because the bound noun phrase *who* crosses over the binding pronoun. Condition C rules out (2a); it seems reasonable that the same principle should rule out (2b), since its logical structure is something like 'name the X₍ᵢ₎ such that he₍ᵢ₎ likes X₍ᵢ₎.' There are at least three possibilities for how Condition C can rule out (2b).

(3) Condition C applies at D-structure. If a sentence violates Condition C at D-structure, then the sentence is ungrammatical regardless of what happens at S-structure.
(4) Condition C applies to the trace of *wh* at S-structure.
(5) Condition C applies in the same way to the chain <who₍ᵢ₎, t₍ᵢ₎> as it does to an unmoved DP at S-structure.

If (3) were correct, then example (2b) would be ungrammatical because *he₍ᵢ₎* c-commands *who₍ᵢ₎*.

(6)

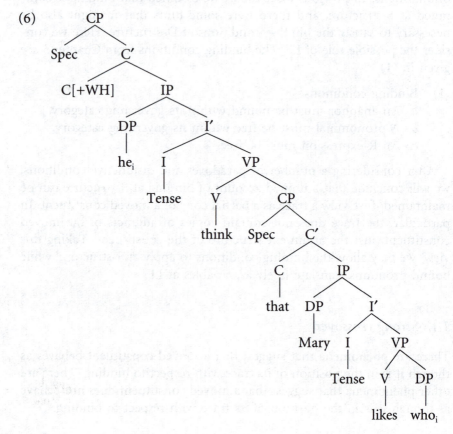

This possibility appears to be ruled out by the following sentences.

(7) a. *He$_i$ thinks that Mary likes the person who gave Bill$_i$ a book.
   b. [Which person who gave Bill$_i$ a book]$_j$ does he$_i$ think that Mary likes t$_j$?

If Condition C applies at D-structure, it will rule out (7b). If movement does not apply, this sentence will be wrongly marked ungrammatical. But it appears that movement may then apply and suspend the violation. Hence (7b) will be wrongly marked ungrammatical. So we can rule out the first option: Principle C does not apply strictly at D-structure.[1]

Consider the second option. Suppose that the trace of *wh* is an R-expression. Then Principle C rules out (2b) directly. But what about (7b)? There is no Condition C violation in this case, because *he$_i$* and *t$_j$* are not in a binding relation (they are not coindexed). So the second option seems favored.

But now, consider the following.

(8) a. *She$_i$ thinks that Bill likes Mary$_i$'s mother.
   b. *[Whose$_i$ mother]$_j$ does she$_i$ think that Bill likes t$_j$?

There is apparently no Condition C violation in (8b), because of the fact that the pronoun does not c-command an R-expression with the same index, hence does not bind an R-expression. On the other hand, (8b) should be a Condition C violation just like (8a) is. This seems to rule out the second option, as well, and suggests that Condition C applies at D-structure, which we have already ruled out.

If (5) were correct, then (2b) would be ungrammatical in virtue of the fact that *he$_i$* c-commands the trace of *who$_i$* at S-structure; we must assume on this approach that if α c-commands the trace of β, then it c-commands the chain of which β is a part.

(9)

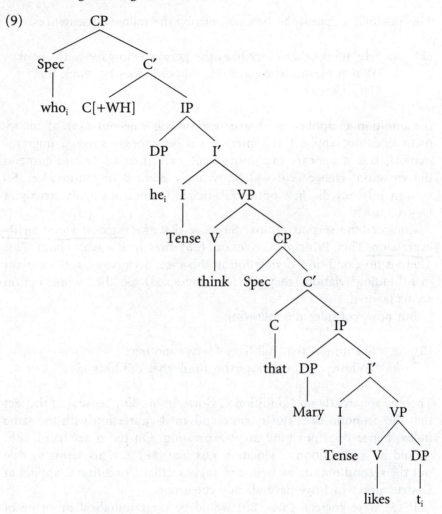

We will postpone discussion of this third option for a little while.

Let us consider the possibility that Condition C applies not at S-structure but at LF. Are the LF representations significantly different? First we look at the ungrammatical example (7a). What is its logical form? To answer this we must first determine what the logical form of a *wh*-question is in general. Consider (10) and (11).

(10)   *a.* Who saw Mary?
       b. for which x, x a person, x saw Mary
(11)   *a.* Who did Mary see t?
       b. for which x, x a person, Mary saw x

It was originally proposed by Chomsky (1977) that there was a simple algorithm for translating sentences such as (11*a*) into LFs such as (11*b*): translate the *wh*-phrase into a logical expression containing a variable binder, and translate the trace into the variable.

(12) who → for which x, x a person
　　　which dog → for which x, x a dog
　　　where → for which x, x a place
　　　etc.

(13) Mary see t → Mary see x
　　　etc.

Such an algorithm produces the correct interpretation for simple cases such as those in (10) and (15*c*).

One obvious problem with this proposal concerns what to do with sentences like (14).

(14) Whose friends did Mary insult t?

The algorithm just described does not work, since the phrase that moves and leaves a trace behind is *whose friends*, while the *wh*-phrase that binds a variable in the logical paraphrase of this sentence is *who*. There are two ways to repair it. One is to apply the algorithm recursively, first taking the entire DP to be a *wh*-phrase, and then just the specifier, i.e.

(15) *a.* whose friends → for which y, y whose friends → for which
　　　　x, x a person, for which y, y x's friends
　　　b. Mary insult t → Mary insult y
　　　c. for which x, x a person, for which y, y x's friends, Mary
　　　　insult y

But (15*c*) is not what the sentence means, exactly. What it means is given in (16).

(16) for which x, x a person, Mary insulted x's friends

But this representation cannot be derived directly from (14) using Chomsky's algorithm.

One solution that has been proposed is one of 'reconstruction,' in which the fronted *wh*-phrase is moved to the position of its trace (hence 'reconstructed'), and the *wh*-operator is moved to sentence-initial position at LF to indicate its scope in LF. This may be the rule QR (Quantifier Raising) seen in Chapter 8.

(17)   whose friends [Mary insult t] $\rightarrow_{LF}$
Mary insult whose friends $\rightarrow$
whose$_x$ [Mary insult x's friends]
whose$_x$ $\equiv$ for which x, x a person

Now consider what happens when we throw pronouns into the mix.

(18)   Who$_i$ said that Mary saw him$_i$?

In this sentence *him$_i$* is bound by *who$_i$*. Therefore, whatever variable, say
x, that we associate with *who* must also be associated with *him$_i$*. That is,
the representation that we want to derive is something like (19).

(19)   for which x, x a person, x said that Mary saw x

The question is, how do we derive this result automatically? Notice that
we must distinguish between the sentence in (18) and that in (20).

(20)   *a.* *Who$_i$ did he$_i$ say that Mary saw t$_i$?
        b. for which x, x a person, x says that Mary saw x

In other words, when we translate the trace of the *wh* into the variable *x*
and the bound pronoun into the variable *x*, we still need to distinguish
them at LF. If Condition C applies at LF, there must be some formal
distinction at that level between the pronoun and the variable *x*. If *x* corresponds to an R-expression, as in (20*b*), it cannot be bound by *he*. But
there is no formal distinction of this sort between (19) and (20*b*). This
suggests that even at LF the pronouns are distinguished from the variables
that correspond to traces, or that binding is determined at S-structure.
    Now consider (21), taken from (7).

(21)   [Which person who gave Bill$_i$ a book]$_j$ does he$_i$ think that Mary
        likes t$_j$?
(22)   for which x$_j$, x$_j$ a person who gave Bill$_i$ a book, he$_i$ thinks that
        Mary likes x$_j$

Again, this seems to work well with Condition C applying at LF. There
is no violation, as required. But now consider the ungrammatical example in (23).

(23) *Whose$_i$ mother$_j$ does she$_i$ think that Bill likes t$_j$?
(24) for which x$_i$, x$_i$ a person, she$_i$ thinks that Bill likes x$_i$'s mother

Strikingly, there is a Condition C violation in the representation in (24), which correctly predicts the ungrammaticality of the sentence.

What is the difference between (21) and (23)? As can be seen from the logical representations, in the case of (21)/(22), the DP *Bill$_i$* that is coindexed with the pronoun is not moved into a position where it can be c-commanded by the pronoun *he$_i$*, so there is no Condition C violation. In the case of (23)/(24) the DP x$_i$ is c-commanded by the pronoun *she$_i$*, which produces the Condition C violation.

Notice what we have done here to get this result. We have created a logical form by putting an operator 'for which x' at the beginning of the sentence, followed by a 'restriction' (e.g. 'x a person,' 'x a person who gave Bill a book,' etc.) followed by a 'nuclear scope' containing the variable (*he thinks that Mary likes x*).[2] The operator 'for which x' applies only to arguments, not to specifiers, so that we do not get, for example,

(25) for which x$_i$, he$_i$ thinks that Mary likes x$_i$ person who gave Bill a book

In effect, the operator is a *wh*-determiner, and the restriction is the associated head and its modifiers. The fronted *wh*-phrase is moved to the position of its trace ('reconstructed'), and the *wh* operator is moved to sentence-initial position to indicate its scope in LF.

The sentences that do not show the Condition C effects are instances of **anti-reconstruction**. One way to generate the logical forms is to return the fronted phrase to its trace position and then move the *wh*-operator to a position in which it takes scope. What is crucial in getting the distinction that we have observed is that the entire NP, that is, the head and its modifiers (the restriction), must take scope as well. (This is by no means the standard view.)

What is shown here is that if the pronouns and the variables are distinguished at LF, if the modifiers of a DP are included in the restriction and not the nuclear scope, and if Condition C applies to such representations as are derived by the algorithm that we have described, we can account for the reconstruction/anti-reconstruction facts straightforwardly.[3] This is not an optimal solution, and we will consider alternatives as we look at additional data.

Consider the possibility that Condition C applies in some way to the chain at S-structure, not simply to the trace. What is the difference between the chains in the grammatical example involving *the person who Bill saw* and the ungrammatical one involving *whose mother*?

(26) $[_{DP} \ldots [_{CP} \ldots \alpha_i \ldots]]_j \ [\ldots \text{s/he}_i \ldots \text{t}_j \ldots]$
(27) $*[_{DP} \ \alpha_i\text{'s} \ldots]_j \ [\ldots \text{s/he}_i \ldots \text{t}_j \ldots]$

One possibility is to formulate the difference in terms of the configuration of the respective chains.[4]

(28) α binds β iff
   (i) α and β are coindexed and
   (ii) α c-commands β or
   (iii) α c-commands γ where γ is the trace of some δ and β is in an argument of δ (not in an adjunct).

But while this generalization may (or may not) be correct in all cases, it does not yet appear to constitute an explanation of what is going on.

1.2. Reconstruction and binding

We are now entertaining two alternatives. One is that Condition C applies at LF after reconstruction and QR, and the second is that it applies in some way to the chain at S-structure. If Condition C applies after reconstruction, what about Conditions A and B? If the Binding theory is unitary in some sense, all of the conditions should apply at the same level. First we provide additional evidence that Condition C applies at LF.[5]

(29)   a.   *She$_i$ likes Mary$_i$.
   b.   *Mary$_i$, she$_i$ likes t$_i$.

This sentence shows that either the trace is subject to Condition C, or there is some type of reconstruction so that (29*b*) is represented as (29*a*).

(30)   a.   Mary$_i$ likes herself$_i$.
   b.   Herself$_i$, Mary$_i$ likes t$_i$.

If t$_i$ is an R-expression that is coindexed with *Mary$_i$*, then (30*b*) should be ungrammatical, on the assumption that Condition C applies at S-structure. Thus Condition C must apply at D-structure or at LF. Since we have already ruled out the first, the second must be correct. If we do not apply the Binding theory to chains at S-structure, Condition C must apply at LF as before, with some reconstruction of the topic *herself* into the position of the trace.

Consider next Condition A.

(31)   *a.* Mary$_i$ found some pictures of herself$_i$.
        b. [Which pictures of herself$_i$]$_j$ did Mary$_i$ find t$_j$?

Let us do reconstruction, with subsequent raising of the quantifier by QR.

(32)   for which x$_j$, x$_j$ pictures of herself$_i$, Mary$_i$ saw x$_j$

This will obviously not suffice, because *herself$_i$* is not bound within its governing category in this representation. In fact, it is not bound at all. But of course, *herself$_i$* is bound at the previous stage of reconstruction, before the *wh*-phrase is extracted.

(33)   Mary$_i$ saw [which pictures of herself$_i$]$_j$

This fact suggests that our particular mechanical approach to reconstruction, in which a fronted phrase is moved down to the position of its trace and then the interrogative is moved up into initial position at LF, may not be quite correct. Crucial to Condition A is that it applies to the D-structure representation or to something very similar to it.

What about the possibility that Condition A applies at D-structure? This cannot be correct, because of examples like the following.

(34)   Mary$_i$ appears to herself$_i$ [t$_i$ to be a good candidate for President].

Here, *herself$_i$* is bound within its GC only after Move α.[6] Summing to this point, it appears that Condition C must apply at LF, and there is contradictory evidence that suggests that Condition A must apply at D-structure and that it must not. Let us consider the alternative analysis, in which the binding conditions apply to chains at S-structure. Because of the fact that there can be no binding of a reflexive into an adjunct, the complex (28) can be simplified as follows.

(35) α binds β iff
        (i) α and β are coindexed and
        (ii) α c-commands β or the trace of a constituent that contains β.

It can be seen that this formulation will apply correctly at S-structure to examples such as (30*b*) and (31*b*).

But now we appear to have a split. Condition A applies to the chain at S-structure while Condition C applies at LF. What about Condition B? The relevant example is the following.

(36)   *a.* *Mary$_i$ likes him$_i$.
         b. *Him$_i$, Mary likes t$_i$.

In (36*b*), *him$_i$* should count as being bound within its governing category. Any of the three alternatives, D-structure, S-structure, or LF with reconstruction, will yield this result. Our discussion of Raising rules out the possibility of D-structure (see Chapter 4), so we conclude that Condition B applies either to the chain at S-structure or to LF after reconstruction.

Finally, consider the following.

(37)   It was himself$_{i,j}$ that John$_i$ said that Bill$_j$ had insulted t$_{i,j}$.

Only the *j* reading should be correct, because of the following.

(38)   John$_i$ said that Bill$_j$ had insulted himself$_{*i,j}$

But both readings are possible, as (37) illustrates.

These examples suggest that there is a stage in the reconstruction, or an interpretation of the chain, in which the intermediate trace that is linked to the focus constituent serves as the 'reconstruction site,' so to speak.[7] That is, there is an intermediate reconstruction of the form in (39).

(39)   . . . Mary$_i$ said [himself$_i$] that Bill$_j$ had insulted t$_i$

This result can be achieved in terms of S-structure or LF using our definition in (35), if the intermediate trace counts as 'the trace of a constituent that contains β.'

Summarizing to this point, it appears that Condition C applies at LF after reconstruction, Condition B may apply at S-structure or LF, while Condition A can apply at neither S-structure nor LF. We resolve this situation in the next section.

1.3. Problems with LF movement and reconstruction

Consider now the following example.

(40)   *He$_i$ thinks that Mary likes everyone$_i$.

This is a Condition C violation. QR at LF yields

(41)   for all x_i, x_i a person, he_i thinks that Mary likes x_i

which is also a Condition C violation. So we may continue to assume that Condition C applies at LF. Now, what about

(42)   *He_i thinks that Mary likes everyone that $Bill_i$ meets.
(43)   for all x_i, x_i a person that $Bill_i$ meets, he_i thinks that Mary likes x_i

This sentence should be grammatical, if *Bill*$_i$ is part of the restriction, and if Condition C applies after QR. Compare with

(44)   Everyone that $Bill_i$ meets, he_i thinks that Mary likes.

which is grammatical.

If we compare these examples with those involving *wh*-Movement, we see clearly what the problem is. In the case of QR, it appears that Condition C applies before QR, to what is essentially the S-structure representation. In the case of *wh*-Movement, it appears that Condition C applies after reconstruction and subsequent raising of the *wh*-phrase at LF, with the relative clause containing the problematic DP in tow.

Logical representations such as those in (43) are not syntactic representations, although it is possible that they correspond exactly to syntactic representations at, say, LF.[8] A variant of such an approach has been proposed for strong crossover. Condition C would hold directly at S-structure and/or LF. On the face of it, such an analysis would appear to be impossible, because the R-expression that is bound by the c-commanding pronoun is moved in these cases. But there is another possibility: the R-expression in the case of (20a), for example, is not really moved.[9] Rather, it is copied into [Spec, CP].

(45) he_i said that Mary saw who_i $\Rightarrow$
       who_i he_i said that Mary saw who_i

In this representation, *he*$_i$ clearly c-commands the lower copy of *who*$_i$. The obvious problem with this proposal is that actual *wh*-questions in English do not appear to have copies of the *wh*-phrase in their original position.

(46)   *a.* Who_i did you say that Mary saw?
       b. *Who_i did you say that Mary saw who_i?

The obvious way around this problem is to assume that the copy is there, but that it is not phonetically visible. Hence the S-structure and LF of (46a) are (47), where the material that is struck out is syntactically present but phonetically null.

(47)   who$_i$ did you say that Mary saw ~~who$_i$~~

In the case of strong crossover, the *wh-in-situ* will produce the Condition C violation.

(48)   who$_i$ did he$_i$ say that Mary saw ~~who$_i$~~

When *wh*-Movement applies, the trace of the *wh*-constituent is a phonetically empty copy of the argument structure of the fronted constituent.

With this device we have another way of looking at the interaction between *wh*-Movement and Condition C that does not produce the paradox that Condition C applies both before QR and after reconstruction and subsequent raising of the *wh*-phrase. Let us suppose that reconstruction *per se* does not exist. The alternative is that the fronted constituent is linked to its trace. What is linked to the trace participates in Condition C, and we have seen empirical evidence that adjuncts in a fronted constituent do not behave as if they are in the original position with respect to Condition C. So, rather than link the entire fronted constituent to its trace, we link only the argument structure of the fronted constituent to its trace.[10] The effect of this step is to exempt adjuncts from acting as though they are reconstructed with respect to Condition C.

To accomplish this result on the copy approach, we leave behind just a copy of the head and its arguments.

(49)   D-structure: he$_i$ thinks that Mary likes [which person who gave
                    Bill$_i$ a book]$_j$
       S-structure: [which person who gave Bill$_i$ a book]$_j$ he$_i$ thinks
                    Mary likes [~~which person~~]$_j$

There is no Condition C violation in this case. In contrast, if we put a quantifier phrase into this same structure, the adjunct is c-commanded by the subject at S-structure.

(50)   D-structure: he$_i$ think that Mary likes [every person who gave
                    Bill$_i$ a book]$_j$
       S-structure: he$_i$ think that Mary likes [every person who gave
                    Bill$_i$ a book]$_j$

Hence the sentence with the *wh*-phrase is grammatical, while that with the quantifier phrase is not.

Now consider the following.

(51) D-structure: she$_i$ think that Bill likes [whose$_i$ mother]$_j$
      S-structure: [whose$_i$ mother$_j$] does she$_i$ think that Bill likes
      [~~whose$_i$ mother~~]$_j$

Here, *whose$_i$* is part of the argument structure of *whose mother* and hence appears in the trace at S-structure. Condition C applies, since *she$_i$* c-commands *whose$_i$*. Similarly, Condition C can apply at S-structure to rule out the following example, on the assumption that *Mary$_i$* is part of the argument structure of the direct object.

(52) D-structure: she$_i$ bought [which picture of Mary$_i$]$_j$
      S-structure: [which picture of Mary$_i$] she$_i$ bought [~~which
      picture of Mary$_i$~~]

This analysis has several advantages. The first is that it eliminates the paradox, since now we have a way of distinguishing between the S-structures of *wh*-Movement and of sentences that contain quantifiers. In all cases, Condition C can apply at S-structure. As a consequence, the application of QR at LF has no impact on the binding relations. Second, it is now possible to return to the earlier definition of binding, one that does not explicitly mention traces. That is, in place of (35) above we can have the following.

(53) α binds β iff
      (i) α and β are coindexed and
      (ii) α c-commands β.

This definition is clearly preferable to the disjunctive definition in (35).

Third, we can now unify the Binding theory so that all of its conditions apply at S-structure. With our revised view of traces, there is no longer any argument for Condition C applying at LF while the other conditions apply at S-structure.

Fourth, we can generalize the analysis to handle the cases that suggested that Condition A applies to LF, e.g. (30), repeated here.

(30) *a.* Mary$_i$ likes herself$_i$.
      b. Herself$_i$, Mary$_i$ likes t$_i$.

The S-structure of (30*b*) contains a copy of the topicalized DP, as in (54).

(54)   Herself$_j$, Mary$_i$ likes ~~herself$_j$~~.

It is this copy that satisfies Condition A.

   To summarize, by introducing the idea that a trace is a copy of the head and arguments of a moved phrase, we allow all of the binding conditions to apply to S-structure representations.

1.4. *Lebeaux's proposal*

A related approach to reconstruction/anti-reconstruction was proposed by Lebeaux (1988) and has proven useful in the Minimalist Program (Chapter 10, § 3). In this proposal, arguments and adjuncts are introduced into a phrase marker at different points in its derivation. The construction of a phrase marker involves introduction of pieces of the phrase marker intermixed with movements of pieces of the phrase marker from one position to another.[11] Both types of operation are viewed as 'transformations.' The key to the current proposal is that adjuncts can be inserted prior to movement or after movement, while arguments must be introduced prior to movement. By assumption, the Binding theory applies at all levels.

   The consequences of this approach can be seen in the following examples.

(55)   *a.*   [Which pictures that Mary$_i$ painted]$_j$ does she$_i$ like t$_j$ the most?
       b.   *[Which pictures of Mary$_i$]$_j$ does she$_i$ like t$_j$ the most?

In the first example, the DP *Mary$_i$* is contained in an adjunct. So we begin with the structure

(56)   she$_i$ likes which pictures$_j$ the most

and move *which pictures.*

(57)   which pictures$_j$ she$_i$ likes t$_j$ the most

Now we insert the adjunct, which has been independently constructed.

(58)   which pictures$_j$ *that Mary$_i$ painted* she$_i$ likes t$_j$ the most

Notice that *she$_i$* at no point c-commands *Mary$_j$*, and hence there is no possibility of a Condition C violation.

In the second example, *Mary$_i$* is an argument of *picture*. Hence it must be inserted prior to movement.

(59) she$_i$ likes [which pictures of Mary$_i$]$_j$ the most

At this point the Binding theory applies, and there is a Condition C violation. The violation is not eliminated after movement, and so the example in (55*b*) is ungrammatical.

1.5. Summary

We have discussed the interactions between binding and LF. After considering a number of paradoxes and disjunctive conditions, we concluded that a unified account of binding at S-structure can be maintained if we view a trace as a partial copy of a moved constituent. In particular, the trace does not contain copies of adjuncts of the moved constituent, just the argument structure of the constituent. Taking this view, we may allow the binding conditions to apply at S-structure, while bound pronouns translate freely as variables at LF.

2. Weak crossover and QR

Consider the following examples, which illustrate the phenomenon of **weak crossover**.

(60) *a.* The person that he$_i$ likes insulted John$_i$.
      b. His$_i$ mother likes John$_i$.
(61) *a.* *Who$_i$ did the person that he$_i$ likes insult t$_i$?
      b. *Who$_i$ does his$_i$ mother like t$_i$?

The direct translation into an LF yields unproblematic representations.

(62) *a.* for which x$_i$, x$_i$ a person, [the person that he$_i$ likes]$_j$ insult x$_i$
      b. for which x$_i$, x$_i$ a person, [his$_i$ mother]$_j$ likes x$_i$

Notice that there is no c-command relation between the pronoun and the trace, so there is no possibility of a Condition C violation. One way to make these into Condition C violations is to copy the index up from inside the DP to the DP itself, and then have the copied index yield a 'weak' violation.[12]

(63)   *a.* for which x_i, x a person, [the person that he_i likes]$_{j/i}$ insult x_i
     b. for which x_i, x a person, [his_i mother]$_{j/i}$ likes x_i

Another solution is to say that the pronoun cannot be to the left of its antecedent if the antecedent is a variable. This is the **Leftness Condition**.[13] But notice that this condition cannot apply at S-structure, because of the following.

(64)   whose$_i$ mother$_j$ does his$_i$ father like t$_j$

In order for the Leftness Condition to apply, there must first be recon-struction to

(65)   for which x_i, x_i a person [his_i mother likes x_i's father]

So if the Leftness Condition is correct, it appears to be an LF condition. Another possibility, if we assume the copying analysis of movement, is that it is an S-structure condition.

If weak crossover is ruled out by a condition at LF, we would expect that it would also apply to (*a*) quantifiers that are moved at LF and (*b*) *wh*-phrases that are moved at LF. The first is confirmed by (66).

(66)   *a.* *The person that he_i likes insulted everyone$_i$.
     b. *His$_i$ mother likes everyone$_i$.
     c. *His$_i$ father likes every boy$_i$'s mother.

Compare (66) with (67).

(67)   *a.* Everyone$_i$ was insulted by the person that he_i likes.
     b. Everyone$_i$ likes his$_i$ mother.
     c. Every boy$_i$'s mother likes his$_i$ father.

These examples are thematically equivalent to those in (66) but gram-matical.

Unmoved *wh*-phrases in English also produce weak crossover viola-tions at LF, as expected.

(68) *a.* Which newpaper$_i$ reported that it$_i$s editors liked which
         candidate.
      b. *Which newspaper reported that her$_i$ mother liked which
         candidate$_i$.

Recall now that the LF rule QR moves a quantifier to sentence-initial
position, leaving behind a variable. Consider the LF of (66*b*). If we do not
replace the pronoun with a variable, we have

(69) for all x$_i$, his$_i$ mother likes x$_i$

and the Leftness Condition applies to this expression. It rules it out
because the pronoun is to the left of the variable that is its antecedent.
But suppose that we translate *his* into a variable, also.

(70) for all x$_i$, x$_i$'s mother likes x$_i$

Now we cannot apply the Leftness Condition. Suppose that the problem
with this sentence is that the operator 'for all x$_i$' binds two variables,
neither of which binds the other; this is essentially the Bijection Principle
of Koopman and Sportiche (1983). Of course, this solution is unavailable
to us if there is no translation of the pronoun into a variable at LF, as we
suggested earlier in connection with the application of Condition C. On
the other hand, we would not have to make this restriction if we adopted
the notion that traces are copies of fronted constituents. As already noted,
this assumption would allow us to maintain the Leftness Condition.

In Chapter 8, § 4, we discussed the superiority effect and the proposal
that D-linking obviates this effect. In this chapter we have discussed weak
crossover, which bears (at least) a superficial resemblance to superiority.
There appears to be a D-linking effect with weak crossover.[14] DPs that are
more 'determinate' more readily act as antecedents for pronouns to their
left, e.g.

(71) *a.* He was the type of man with whom$_i$ his$_i$ work would always
         come first.
      b. He was the kind of man who$_i$ when he$_i$ loses his$_i$ collar stud
         bellows the house down.
      c. How many [copies of Aspects]$_i$ does your friend who collects
         them$_i$ own?
      d. Which well-known actor did the policeman who$_i$ arrested
         him$_i$ accuse of being drunk.

The idea here is that *who, what,* etc. are relatively 'indeterminate,' while relative pronouns with fairly specific antecedents, *how many, which,* and so on are relatively 'determinate'. Why this difference should be relevant is unclear if weak crossover is a strictly LF phenomenon. However, if 'D-linked' *wh*-phrases are not interpreted as quantifiers, it is possible that the weak crossover phenomenon is sensitive to the quantificational status of the antecedent of the pronoun. What this might mean in practical terms is unclear, however, because the relative clause would seem to have the same status internally regardless of the status of the DP that it modifies with respect to D-linking. None the less, we see that there are relative clauses that show a somewhat stronger weak crossover effect than the grammatical cases in (71).

(72)   *a.* ?I met a lawyer who$_i$ his$_i$ wife was planning to divorce.
       b. ?A person to whom$_i$ you introduced his$_i$ fiancée should be very grateful.

There is growing interest in the contribution of discourse to the interpretation of anaphora, and it is reasonable to expect that the contribution on discourse to WCO and similar configurations will become clearer as research progresses.

EXERCISES

9-1. Explain the ungrammaticality of each of the following sentences in terms of the account given in the text. To do this, you must say what the structure is (including the traces) and indicate which principle or principles are violated. If there is no such account, show why.

(1)   *a.* *Who$_i$ do you think he$_i$ claimed would win?
      b. *Which children$_i$ did the teachers that they$_i$ offended report to the principal?
      c. *To whom$_i$ did she$_i$ believe you were going to give the book?
      d. *On his$_i$ desk I had placed everyone$_i$'s final exam.
      e. *After everyone$_i$ went home, I figured out her$_i$ grade.

9-2. Consider the following examples.

(1)   *a.* *The pictures of John$_i$ that he$_i$ saw in the bookstore should make you very proud.

b. *Whichever picture of John$_i$ he$_i$ buys, it will be a nice one.

c. *A nice picture of John$_i$ would be a very pleasant thing for him$_i$ to show to you.

(2)　a. The picture of John$_i$ that you showed to him$_i$ should make you very proud.

b. Whichever picture of John$_i$ you show to him$_i$, it will be a nice one.

c. A nice picture of John$_i$ would be a very pleasant thing for you to show to him$_i$.

(3)　a. The pictures that John$_i$ bought that he$_i$ had seen in the bookstore should make you very proud.

b. Whichever picture that John$_i$ sees he$_i$ happens to buy, it will be a nice one.

c. A nice picture that John$_i$ painted would be a very pleasant thing for him$_i$ to show to you.

What do examples such as these suggest about the representation and analysis of anti-reconstruction phenomena?

[§ 1.1]

*9-3. The following sentences illustrate an anti-reconstruction effect different from the one discussed in the text and in Exercise 9-2.

(1)　a. *He$_i$ never admitted that John$_i$ had seen the movie.

b. That John$_i$ had seen the movie, he$_i$ never admitted.

How can the grammaticality of (1b) be reconciled with any of the accounts of reconstruction explored in the text? As possibly relevant additional data, consider also the following.

(2)　a. Everyone freely admits that we will win.

b. That we will win, everyone freely admits.

(3)　a. Everyone$_i$ freely admits that he$_i$ will win.

b. *That he$_i$ will win, everyone$_i$ freely admits.

[§ 1.1]

*9-4. Discuss the relevance of the following cases to the analysis of reconstruction.

(1)　a. Everyone$_i$ ate a slice of cake after he$_i$ sat down.

b. After he$_i$ sat down, everyone$_i$ ate a slice of cake.

(2)　a. I interviewed everyone$_i$ after he$_i$ sat down.

b. *After he$_i$ sat down, I interviewed everyone$_i$.

(3)　a. Who$_i$ ate a slice of cake after he$_i$ sat down?

b. After he$_i$ sat down, who$_i$ ate a slice of cake?

(4) *a.* Who$_i$ did you interview after he$_i$ sat down?
      b. After he$_i$ sat down, who$_i$ did you interview?

[§ 1.3]

*9-5. Extending your answers to Exercises 9-3 and 9-4, consider the following data.

(1) *a.* Everyone$_i$'s mother freely admits that he$_i$ will not win.
      b. That he$_i$ will not win, everyone$_i$'s mother freely admits.
(2) *a.* Everyone$_i$'s mother arrived just before he$_i$ called.
      b. *Just before he$_i$ called, everyone$_i$'s mother arrived.
(3) *a.* I will interview every contestant$_i$'s father after she$_i$ wins her$_i$ race.
      b. *After she$_i$ wins her$_i$ race, I will interview every contestant$_i$'s father.

*9-6. The following sentences are problematic for the approach to reconstruction proposed by Lebeaux [§ 2.4]. Explain why.

(1) *a.* *I told her$_i$ you were hoping to buy this picture of Mary$_i$.
      b. *I persuaded him$_i$ not to invite John$_i$'s sister to the party.
      c. *I convinced her$_i$ not to mention to anyone the fact that Mary$_i$ had won.
(2) *a.* This picture of Mary$_i$, I told her$_i$ you were hoping to buy.
      b. John$_i$'s sister, I persuaded him$_i$ not to invite to the party.
      c. The fact that Mary$_i$ had won, I convinced her$_i$ not to mention to anyone.

[Based on Postal 1993.]
[§ 2]

9-7. Weak crossover does not appear to work the same way in French as it does in English. Consider the following examples.

(1) *a.* sa   femme
          his wife
      b. la   femme du   médecin
          the wife   of the doctor
      c. le   médecin$_i$ que sa$_i$ femme a   présenté t$_i$ à cette infirmière
          the doctor   who his wife   has introduced to that   nurse
          charmante
          charming
          '*the doctor$_i$ who$_i$ his$_i$ wife introduced to that charming nurse'

    d. *le médecin$_i$ dont$_i$ la femme t_i l'$_i$ a présenté à cette
       the doctor   of-whom the wife   him has introduced to that
       infirmière charmante
       nurse   charming
       'the doctor whose wife introduced him to that charming nurse'

(2) *a.* *Sa jambe fait   mal.
       his leg   makes pain
       'His leg hurts.'
    b. La jambe lui   fait   mal.
       the leg   to-him makes pain
       'His leg hurts.'
    c. un homme$_i$ à qui sa$_i$ jambe fait   mal t_i.
       a   man   to whom his leg   makes pain
       'a man whose leg hurts'
    d. *un homme$_i$ dont$_i$ la jambe t_i lui$_i$ fait   mal
       a   man   of-whom the leg   to-him makes pain
       'a man whose leg hurts'

Explain the difficulty that these examples raise for the analysis of weak crossover.
[Postal 1993]
[§ 2]

**9-8. 1. Consider the following sentences.

(1) *a.* I introduced to every student$_i$ her$_i$ immediate neighbor.
    b. I would reveal to every woman$_i$ the person that she$_i$ was most
       concerned about.
(2) *a.* I introduced t_i to her$_i$ immediate neighbor [every woman in the
       room that I had met]$_i$.
    b. I would reveal t_i to her$_i$ enemies [no woman whose safety I was
       concerned about]$_i$.

What do these sentences suggest about the relationship between S-structure, LF
and quantifier scope?
    2. It is typically claimed that A'-movements undergo reconstruction at LF, so
that a pronoun moved out of the c-command domain of a quantifier at S-
structure acts as though it is in the c-command domain of the quantifier at LF.

(3) *a.* [to his$_i$ neighbor]$_j$, everyone$_i$ gave a present t_j
    b. [her$_i$ mother]$_j$, every student$_i$ loves t_j

Discuss the status of Heavy Shift, illustrated in (2), in relation to reconstruction and binding. Does the evidence suggest that it is an A-movement or an
A'-movement?

*9-9. Consider the following sentences.

(1)   *a.* His$_i$ paycheck, everyone$_i$ should give me t.
      b. *His$_i$ paycheck, you should give everyone$_i$ t.
      c. You should give everyone$_i$ his$_i$ paycheck.
(2)   *a.* *A picture of him$_i$ shaving, you should show no one$_i$ t.
      b. *His$_i$ partner, I managed to introduce no one$_i$ to t on time.
      c. *The person that wrote it$_i$, I agreed to give every book$_i$ back to t at
          no charge.

What do these sentences suggest about the binding relationships that hold within
the VP?

*9-10. In Exercise 9-8 we introduced the notion that A′-movements undergo
reconstruction at LF prior to the determination of quantifier binding. What do
the following examples suggest in this context?

(1)   At his$_i$ parties, no one$_i$ should smoke pot t.
(2)   *a.* *At his$_i$ parties you should give no one$_i$ pot t.
      b. *At his$_i$ parties you should talk to everyone$_i$ t.
      c. *To his$_i$ mother you should introduce everyone$_i$ t.

FURTHER READING

The original work on crossover phenomena is Postal (1971). Wasow (1979) was
the first to use traces to account for strong crossover phenomena. Koopman
and Sportiche's (1983) article on the Bijection Principle is widely cited and is
required reading for any study of crossover.

Lasnik and Stowell (1991) argue that there are certain constructions that should
produce weak crossover violations but do not; they attribute the exceptional
behavior of these constructions to the existence of an empty epithet. Postal (1993)
draws out a number of interesting and novel distinctions among sentences that
exemplify crossover, and finds the classical accounts wanting. Bresnan (1994)
argues that an account of weak crossover must be formulated in terms of linear
precedence.

Crossover is touched on in many works on scrambling, since weak crossover
violations are produced by A′-movements, while scrambling appears to have
properties of A-movement. See, for example, Bayer and Kornfilt (1991), Fanselow
(1990), Saito and Hoji (1983), and Webelhuth (1989).

Head Movement and Minimalism

1. Properties of head movement

For the most part we have focused in this book on the movement of phrasal constituents, a phenomenon that is central to both A-movement (e.g. NP movement) and A′-movement (e.g. *wh*-Movement*)*. In this chapter we turn to the movement of X^0 categories, which is usually referred to as **head movement**.

A prototypical case of head movement is English Subject Aux Inversion (SAI), illustrated in (1).

(1) *a.* What will you read?
     b. Which of these books have you read?
     c. What did you read?
(2) *a.* Will you read this book?
     b. Have you read this book?
     c. Did you read this book?

As discussed in Chapter 5, § 3.1, an analysis of SAI that is fully consistent with X′-theory is one in which the head of IP moves to the head of CP, as illustrated in (3).

(3)

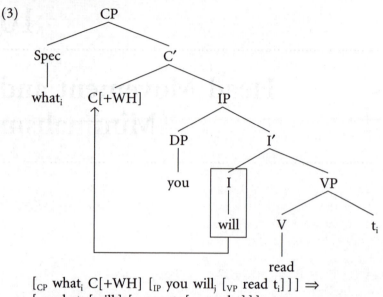

$[_{CP}$ what$_i$ C[+WH] $[_{IP}$ you will$_j$ $[_{VP}$ read t$_i]]] \Rightarrow$
$[_{CP}$ what$_i$ [will$_j$] $[_{IP}$ you t$_j$ $[_{VP}$ read t]]]

This movement has two salient properties. First, it is structure-preserving, in the sense that the movement does not build new structure or create novel configurations. SAI is substitution of Infl for C, so that the output structure is configurationally the same as the input structure. Since the input structure is consistent with X'-theory, so is the output structure. There are logically possible alternatives; for example, Infl could be adjoined to IP or to C', as in (4).

(4)

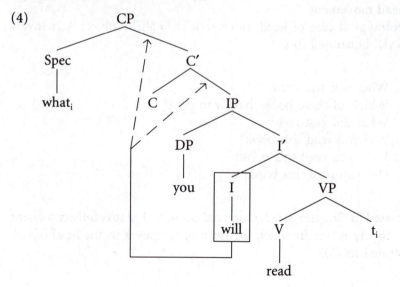

It is natural to suppose that the structure-preserving property is not peculiar to head movement. Let us assume as a simplifying assumption that Move α is always structure-preserving. In general, heads will move to head positions and phrases to phrasal positions as provided by X'-theory. The correctness of such a principle is predicated on the absence of evidence for non-structure-preserving adjunctions of heads (such as the one illustrated in (4)). In the absence of such evidence, it is legitimate to rule out such adjunctions entirely, since doing so reduces the class of possible languages and in part allows us to explain how language learners are able to settle on the correct analysis immediately upon exposure to the language.[1] This reasoning is the same as that used in Chapter 5, Appendix A, to argue for constraints on the type of branching allowed in the representation of syntactic structure.

A second property of head movement is that it is local, in the sense that a head adjoins to the head that governs its projection. For example, in (3) Infl moves to the C, which governs its maximal projection IP. The locality of head movement is sometimes referred to as the **Head Movement Constraint** (Travis 1984). It can be derived from the ECP, if we extend the requirement of proper government to the trace of the moved head. Since the head is not lexically governed, it must be antecedent governed. Movement of a head over the head that governs its projection produces a configuration in which the trace is not antecedent governed, because the projection of the intermediate head is a barrier by Minimality (Chapter 7, § 5). An illustration is given in (5).

(5)

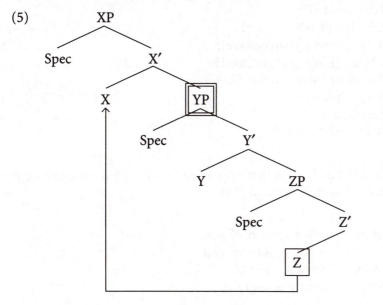

Here, Y is the closer governor of the trace of Z, blocking antecedent government of the trace by Z itself. The same result follows from Relativized Minimality (Chapter 7, § 7).[2]

2. Head movement to Infl

Pollock's (1989) analysis of the auxiliary system of English and French is an influential application of head movement. We consider it in some detail in this section.

The crucial assumptions in Pollock's proposal are that a verb and its inflection are distinct heads in D-structure, and that the verb may raise to adjoin to its inflection prior to S-structure. Pollock makes the standard assumption that at D-structure in English (and in other languages), Tense is in Infl, the head of IP, while V is the head of VP. The morpheme denoting negation (e.g. *not* in English and *ne . . . pas* in French) is assumed to originate in a position between Infl and V. Evidence from SAI and negation shows that the English auxiliary verbs *have* and *be* raise to Infl in the derivation of S-structure while main verbs do not.

(6)　*a.* Mary has left.
　　　b. Has Mary left?
　　　c. Mary hasn't left.
(7)　*a.* Mary is {leaving/angry/here}.
　　　b. Is Mary {leaving/angry/here}?
　　　c. Mary isn't {leaving/angry/here}.
(8)　*a.* Mary left.
　　　b. *Left Mary?
　　　c. *Mary left {not/n't}.

Auxiliary verbs in English may appear either to the left or to the right of adverbs, as shown in (9) and (10).

(9)　　*a.* Mary has often spoken of you.
　　　　b. Mary often has spoken of you.
(10)　*a.* Mary is frequently angry.
　　　　b. Mary frequently is angry.

Typically an adverb does not appear to the right of a main verb, unless the constituent that canonically is adjacent to the verb undergoes movement to the right, as in Heavy Shift. The examples in (11) and (12) illustrate.

(11)   *a.* Mary speaks French well.
      b. *Mary speaks well French.
      c. Mary speaks well all of the languages of Europe.
(12)   *a.* Mary often speaks French.
      b. *Mary speaks often French.

    Pollock makes two crucial assumptions regarding the position of adverbs. First, he assumes that adverbs do not move from one position to another. Second, he assumes that there is a unique position for adverbs at D-structure. From these two assumptions it follows that in sentences such as (9a) and (10a), the auxiliary verb moves to the left of the adverb. Example (12b) suggests that a main verb does not undergo such movement.

    Compare now the English pattern with that of French. In French, *ne . . . pas* denotes negation. Auxiliaries in French infinitives (notated as V[-fin]) display a pattern similar to auxiliaries in English finite clauses; that is, French *ne pas V[-fin]* . . . alternates with *ne V[-fin] pas* just in case the V is auxiliary, i.e. *être* and *avoir*.

(13)   *a.* ne pas   être   heureux . . .
          NE NEG to-be happy
          'not to be happy'
      b. n'être   pas   heureux . . .
          NE-to-be NEG happy
          'not to be happy'
(14)   *a.* ne pas   avoir   de voiture . . .
          NE NEG to-have of car
          'not to have a car'
      b. n'avoir   pas   de voiture . . .
          NE-to-have NEG of car
          'not to have a car'
(15)   *a.* ne pas   sembler heureux . . .
          NE NEG to-seem happy
          'not to seem happy'
      b. *ne sembler pas   heureux . . .
          NE to-seem NEG happy

This alternation, like the English alternation in (9)–(10), can be accounted for if the auxiliary verb in French optionally moves to the left. Call this movement **V-raising**.

(16)

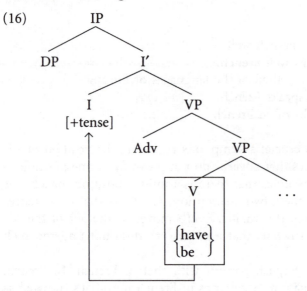

Compare now the behavior of main verbs in French and English. We saw that in English, only auxiliary verbs undergo V-raising, as indicated by the position of negation and adverbs and inversion. But in French all verbs appear to the left of negation, undergo inversion, and appear to the left of adverbs.

(17) a. Marie ne {regarde pas/*pas   regarde} la télévision.
         Marie NE {look-at NEG/NEG look-at} the television
         'Marie isn't watching television.'
      b. Marie {n'est pas/*ne   pas   est} heureuse.
         Marie {NE-is NEG/NE NEG is}   happy
         'Marie isn't happy.'
      c. Marie {n'a   pas/*ne pas a}   de voiture.
         Marie {NE-has NEG/NE NEG has} of car
         'Mary doesn't have a car.'
      d. Marie {mange souvent/*souvent mange} du   gâteau.
         Mary {eat   often/often   eat}   of-the cake
         'Mary often eats cake.'

Thus it appears that the parametric difference between French and English is that in French main verbs may raise to Infl, while in English, only auxiliary verbs may raise to Infl. Noting that main verbs are θ-assigners while auxiliaries are not, Pollock suggests that the reason for the difference may be that in French inflection is 'strong' enough to allow θ-roles to be transmitted at S-structure (satisfying the Projection Principle), while in English inflection is not 'strong' enough. Hence main verbs cannot raise to Infl in English.

Recall now that in infinitives in French, only auxiliary verbs move to the left of negation. Pollock suggests that there are really two parts to V-raising in French. The first moves any verb out of VP to the left of an adverb adjoined to VP. The second moves a verb to the left of negation when tense is finite, but only auxiliary verbs to the left of negation when tense is non-finite. If we assume that head movements are structure-preserving, it follows that there must be two distinct head positions, one to the left of Neg and one to the left of Adv. Pollock proposes that one such head is Tense and the other is Agr for 'agreement'.

(18)   [Tense [Neg [Agr [Adv [$_{VP}$ V ...]]]]]]

The core idea is then that in French, all verbs will move to Agr, all verbs will move to finite Tense, and only auxiliary verbs will move to non-finite Tense. *Ne* too is a head, as shown in (19).

(19)

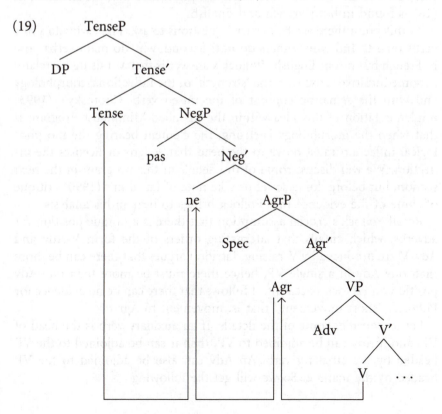

(20)   Marie Present pas ne Agr (souvent) regarde la télévision   ⇒
       Marie Present pas ne regarde+Agr (souvent) t la télévision   ⇒
       Marie Present pas ne+regarde+Agr t (souvent) t la télévision ⇒
       Marie ne+regarde+Agr+Present pas t t (souvent) t la télévision
       = Marie ne regarde pas (souvent) la télévision

In English there is a difference in infinitives between the movement of auxiliary verbs and lexical verbs that parallels the French pattern for all verbs.

(21)   *a.* to almost forget one's name
       b. *to forget almost one's name
(22)   *a.* to almost have forgotten one's name
       b. to have almost forgotten one's name
(23)   *a.* to seldom be angry
       b. to be seldom angry

The analysis for English would then be that auxiliary verbs undergo movement to Agr and to Tense in both finite and non-finite cases, while main verbs do not move at all. Note the assumption here that the structure in (18) is found in both French and English.

At this point there are two crucial questions to ask. First, why do some verbs raise to Infl while others do not? Second, why do main verbs raise in French but not in English? Pollock's answer is that V-raising correlates in some intuitive sense with the 'strength' of the inflectional morphology and with the semantic content of the raised verb. Chomsky's (1993) implementation of this idea within the so-called Minimalist Program is that when the morphology is strong, the element bearing the morphological inflection must move to the head that assigns or licenses the inflection. We will discuss some of the details of this program in the next section, but before doing so let us take note of Iatridou's (1990) critique of some of the evidence that Pollock brings to bear in his analysis.

Recall Pollock's crucial assumption that there is a unique position for adverbs, which entails that alternating orders of the form V-Adv and Adv-V are produced by V-raising. Iatridou argues that there can be more than one Adv in a single VP, hence there must be more than one Adv position on Pollock's account. It follows that there can be no evidence for Pollock's 'short movement,' that is, movement to Agr.

Let us consider some of the details. If an auxiliary verb is the head of VP, and if Adv can be adjoined to VP, then it can be adjoined to the VP headed by the auxiliary verb. An Adv can also be adjoined to the VP headed by the main V. So we will get the following.

(24) *a.* to [(frequently) be [(rudely) criticizing]]
      b. to [(rudely) be [(frequently) criticizing]]

If there is more than one position, there is no argument for movement of the auxiliary verb, since each V must be the head of its own VP. So in the case in which the auxiliary precedes the adverb (e.g. *to be frequently criticizing*), the adverb can be analyzed as adjoined at D-structure to the lower VP. Similarly, when there is a predicate, we get the Adv on *be* or on the predicate.

(25) *a.* to often be sarcastic
      b. to be often sarcastic
      c. I consider him very often sarcastic.

Again, there is no argument for movement of the V in the infinitive if there are two positions for Adv.

For French, Iatridou suggests that there could be an underlying [$_{VP}$ [V Adv] DP] order (see Di Sciullo and Williams 1987), or that V+Adv is a complex V. Either would yield the following, again without movement of V.

(26) *a.* embrasser souvent les enfants, . . .
          to-kiss   often   the children
      b. oublier   presque son nom, . . .
          to-forget almost   his name

Another problem for Pollock, according to Iatridou, is the following.

(27) Pierre a à peine vu Marie.
(28) Pierre a vu à peine Marie.

How do we get (28), where the adverb intervenes between the direct object and the non-finite, past participial, form of the verb? It is impossible to appeal in this case to movement of the inflected verb *a* to Agr and Infl. Pollock proposes that there are two Agr's, one for each V, and two VPs.

(29) Pierre Tense Agr$_1$ [$_{VP}$ a Agr$_2$ [$_{VP}$ [$_{Adv}$ à peine] vu Marie]]

But if there are two VPs, one for each of the Agr/V pairs, and if there is an Adv position in the lower VP, then the aspectuals must be able to originate to the left of the Adv, as in (29). Once again we conclude that aspectuals do not have to undergo short movement in order to get to the left of the Adv. In order to derive (28) the main verb must undergo short movement, or V+Adv must be a D-structure option, as suggested above.

Another problem for Pollock's analysis of French occurs when there are two adverbs and one verb.

(30) *a.* souvent mal faire   ses   devoirs
          often   badly to-make one's homework
      b. faire souvent mal   ses   devoirs
          to-do often   badly one's homework
      c. souvent faire mal   ses   devoirs
          often   to-do badly one's homework

Example (30*a*) shows that there can be two adverbs adjoined to VP. Example (30*b*) shows that the verb can move over both of them, presumably to Agr in the configuration (31).

(31)   Agr [$_{VP}$ souvent [$_{VP}$ mal [$_{VP}$ faire ses devoirs]]]

But then the question arises, how is (30*c*) derived? There does not appear to be a landing site between the two adverbs for the verb.

While Iatridou's critique makes some telling points, the general framework proposed by Pollock has become more or less accepted in the Principles and Parameters framework. Note that while Iatridou shows that parts of Pollock's analysis do not go through, she does not show that the analysis is not possible in principle. In fact there are quite different motivations for the approach in more recent work; we turn to some of them next.

3. The Minimalist Program

The Minimalist Program (MP) of Chomsky (1993; 1994; 1995) incorporates a version of Pollock's head movement account into a more general framework of assumptions about the nature of phrase structure and the nature of movement. We will begin with a summary of some of the core ideas of the general framework, illustrate their application to head movement, and then consider the consequences in other areas of the grammar. Throughout this discussion it should be kept in mind that many of the features of this program are not motivated through empirical considerations, but on the basis of intuitive notions of the 'simplicity' or 'naturalness' of the formal system.

It should also be noted that the Minimalist Program is intended to be a significant departure from what has gone before. MP takes as its point of departure the hypothesis that D-structure, S-structure, the government relation, the X' schema, and referential indices play no essential role in syntactic theory and must be dispensed with. Taking this step places a great burden on the theory and on the theorist, given the central role that these concepts have played in earlier work. Whether the MP approach is on the right track will only become clear after some time has passed; our goal here is simply to convey some of the basic concepts and to point to some likely directions of future research.

3.1. *Economy conditions*

The approach of MP is to account for the structure of language as the consequence of what are assumed to be intuitively natural 'economy conditions' on the computational mechanisms that comprise grammars. There are essentially two such mechanisms, phrase structure, which falls under X'-theory in the Principles and Parameters framework, and movement, which is characterized by Move α in the Principles and Parameters framework. We will discuss in § 5 a number of proposals for simplifying X'-theory and reducing it to its bare essentials; first we focus on the working out of the MP for Move α.

It is important to recognize the extent of the methodological shift implicit in the MP. In Principles and Parameters theory and much of the work leading up to it, a major driving force is the Uniformity Principle. On this view, grammars are more highly valued to the extent that they conform closely to general configurational and derivational patterns. However, in the MP there is a strong principle of structural and computational simplicity: grammars are more highly valued to the extent that they minimize structure and derivations. The full implications of this shift have yet to be realized, but it will become clear that many analyses in the PPT framework are not viable under the assumptions of the MP. Nevertheless, the goal is to determine how many of the results of PPT (and of GB theory) can be captured using a significantly reduced formal apparatus.

Let us begin with one instantiation of the notion of 'intuitively natural economy conditions' with respect to movement.[3] The basic principle motivating the MP is that other things being equal, the more economical derivation is preferred. Consider for example movement from A to B to a more distant C. If A to B is a legitimate movement, then the additional movement to C is a further operation, adding complexity to the derivation. One interpretation of economy is that the shorter derivation is preferred over the longer one, and blocks the longer derivation.

However, taking this idea literally in its most simplistic form would suggest that no movement is possible, since the absence of movement is maximally economical. What is necessary in order to make the idea of economy more realistic is to consider alternative movements where the outcome of the alternatives is independently required, so that the option of no movement at all is not available. Thus we must consider *why* movement takes place, as well.

Consider movement just from A to B. It is natural to think of the most economical way of going from A to B to be the path that involves the fewest steps. For example, in a tree such as (32) a single movement to B might appear to be most economical.

(32)

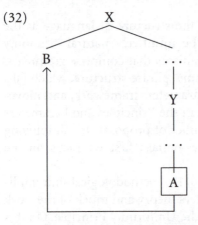

On the other hand, the length of each step might enter into the computation of economy. It is difficult to see how a movement from A to B that employs many steps of minimal length would be more or less economical than the movement illustrated in (32) without some stipulation. Again, to resolve this matter, it is necessary to consider not only what kind of movement is involved, but also why the movement takes place. Simply preferring a stepwise derivation of the movement from A to B will not entail an empirical difference with a single movement from A to B, since the same structure is derived in both cases. One way that the notion of economy can in principle have some empirical consequences is if in certain cases, non-movement and movement are valued differently, as long as there is a fixed reason for why movements occur. For example, as we just discussed in connection with movement from A to B to C, suppose that the shorter derivation blocks the longer one. Under such circumstances, the two derivations will give rise to different derived structures, yielding empirical differences. Chomsky (1993) proposes the following principles that give substance to this idea.

(33) **GREED:** A constituent does not move unless it has to in order to satisfy some requirement that it has.

(34) **PROCRASTINATE:** Movement occurs as late as possible in the derivation.

PROCRASTINATE can be motivated in terms of economy if we assume that early movements are more costly, in computational terms, than late movements, in particular, LF movements.

To illustrate, consider the feature of [Case]. Let us suppose that every DP possesses such a feature, and that in order to be licensed, a DP with this feature must appear in the specifier position of a Case assigner (call it Agr) that possesses this feature. This relationship is an instance of **feature checking**. Assume furthermore that a feature that is not licensed produces ungrammaticality; we will have more to say about this in a moment. Now, since the feature [Case] must be licensed, it must move to [Spec, AgrP].

(35)

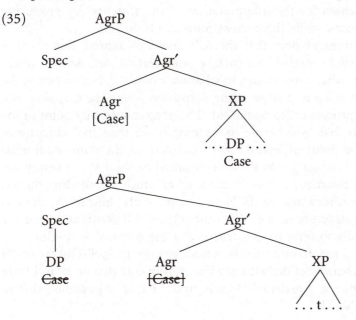

We have indicated feature checking by striking out the features in the derived structure. We say that the feature is 'discharged' through Spec-head agreement.

Once again the question arises as to how the notion of economy can produce any real linguistic consequences, given that everything that has to move does move, and nothing moves until the last possible moment. The key is in our understanding of 'last possible moment,' or 'Last Resort.' The idea here is that for each feature there is a structure of Last Resort, such that the feature must be checked at some point in the derivation no later than that structure. PROCRASTINATE together with Last Resort will produce the result that the feature will not be checked before this structure is derived.

Let us suppose that for some features, the structure of Last Resort is the equivalent of S-structure, that is, the structure that corresponds to the perceived order of constituents. In this case, the movement will produce some reordering of constituents. Let us suppose that for some other features, the structure of Last Resort is LF. In this case, the movement will occur and the feature will be licensed, but the movement will produce no superficial effects. In other words, it will have no consequences for 'phonetic form' (PF). Here we recall the major motivation for LF in Chapter 8, which is that it allows for movements that do not correlate with S-structure reorderings. The difference between the current use of LF and the original motivation for LF is that originally LF movements had consequences for the interpretation of the sentence, by producing scope differences, while the current movements do not.

It is important to note that the MP does not assume that there is actually a distinct level of S-structure with certain well-defined properties. Rather, what corresponds to what we would call S-structure is the structure that exists at a stage of the derivation where the mapping into PF occurs, a process called **Spell-Out**. This stage can be any point in the derivation, so that 'S-structure' is nothing more than the structure as it exists at the point of Spell-Out. In contrast, in the more traditional approach, the mapping into PF is determined by the independently defined level of S-structure, that is, the level at which the Binding theory, agreement requirements, the ECP, and so on apply. Effectively, there is no level of S-structure in the MP, although we will continue to use the term informally to refer to the structure at the point of Spell-Out.

As suggested earlier, movements that occur prior to Spell-Out are costly in terms of economy of derivation, while movements that occur in LF are cost-free. Hence, it is preferable to wait until LF if at all possible—that is, PROCRASTINATE.

Returning to our illustration, let us consider what features force movement before Spell-Out/S-structure and which features do not. As sketched out briefly in § 1, Chomsky adapts Pollock's distinction between strong and weak morphology. A strong feature is one that must be licensed at S-structure, prior to Spell-Out, while a weak feature is one that need be licensed only at LF. Crucially, the same feature may be weak in one language and strong in another, a difference that produces differences in constituent order assuming precisely the same underlying phrase structure. Continuing our example of Case features, suppose that ACCUSATIVE is strong in one language and weak in another, and suppose furthermore that the underlying structure is that of (36).

(36) ... AgrP

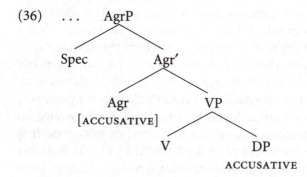

Assume that uniformly, agreement holds between a head and its specifier. When this feature is strong, the DP will move to [Spec, AgRP] prior to S-structure, producing an ordering in which the object precedes the V.[4] In a language in which the feature is weak, the DP moves at LF and the order of constituents is unchanged; the object follows the V. Assuming that there are no other movements, we thus reduce the Head Parameter to the relative strength of the object Case morphology. In languages in which the subject proceeds the verb, it is plausible to suppose that the NOMINATIVE feature is strong and that the subject moves to [Spec, AgrSP] prior to S-structure.

There are three cautions that must be raised in regards to the approach just sketched out. First, simply stipulating a feature in order to trigger movement is not a satisfactory answer to the question of why movement occurs in a particular construction. The feature is a device for expressing the fact that movement occurs. Unless it is independently motivated in some way (e.g. through overt inflectional morphology), the feature is nothing more than a formal descriptive device.

Second, stipulating that a language A has a weak variant of a feature that is strong in another language B in order to account for the fact that movement occurs in B but not in A is also nothing more than a way of encoding this difference between languages, unless some morphological or other linguistically meaningful correlate can be found. The fact that movement occurs allows us to hypothesize the existence of a strong feature, but it by no means constitutes evidence for the existence of this feature.

Third, it is very much an open question how to account on this approach for the relative position of adjuncts with respect to the verb, since adjuncts are not assigned Case. Of course, we could hypothesize a feature that will trigger the movement, but that returns us to the first caution.

Let us return to the question of whether a single long movement or a succession of short movements is more economical. The movement from A to B must be licensed, and can only occur if the position B is a checking position for A, that is, a position in which the features of A can be licensed. Therefore, there can be no question of two alternative methods of moving from A to B; if each of the individual short movements is not independently motivated by GREED, there is only one way to get from A to B. On the other hand, the empirical evidence suggests for the most part that true long movements in general do not occur; they are derived through the formation of chains.[5] Chomsky (1993) therefore proposes that the long distance movement from A to B be accomplished in a single operation that involves the creation of a chain with links of minimal length. In this way we have an account, for example, of why *wh*-Movement to a higher [Spec, CP] that is marked [+wh] must pass through the lower [Spec, CP], as in (37).

(37) $[_{CP}$ who$_i$ C[+wh] you think $[_{CP}$ $[_{Spec}$ $t_i'$$]$ that $[_{IP}$ I saw $t_i$$]$$]$$]$

The lower C is not marked [+wh], and hence the independent movement to the lower [Spec, CP] is not licensed on this approach. In fact, if it were, there would be no further movement to the higher [Spec, CP], since the feature [+wh] would be discharged at the lower [Spec, CP] and would lack the feature for subsequent movements. But the formation of a chain through the lower [Spec, CP] is possible as part of the movement into the higher [Spec, CP]. This is a crucial departure from the Move α perspective, where movements are optional and the derived structures are ruled in or out through the application of licensing conditions.

Chomsky (1995: chapter 4) marks an important variant of the minimalist approach. Recall the notion that we have been entertaining that more complex movements are ruled out by simpler movements. While this intuition may be a natural one, it is difficult to see how to demonstrate, for any given derivation, that all 'comparable' derivations are both more complex and impossible. In fact, it is not clear how to designate the set of derivations 'comparable' to a given derivation in the intended sense. Partly in response to these difficulties, Chomsky (1995) moves to a conception of economy where in effect the result of the comparison is built into the characterization of Move. On this view, Move has the following properties.

- Whenever a strong feature [F] is introduced into the derivation, it must be immediately checked off (by Move).

This requirement replaces the earlier GREED and Last Resort. Notice that on this formulation, GREED is a property of the strong feature on the target of movement, not of the constituent that is moved, as in the earlier formulation.

- If α and β both can check off the feature [F], the closer one is the one that moves (the 'Minimal Link Condition').

This requirement replaces the earler notion of 'shortest movement.' Notice that under this revised formulation there is no general sense of comparing the complexity of alternative derivations; only one movement is possible, by definition, and hence there is only one possible derivation.

- What undergoes movement is, strictly speaking, not a constituent but a feature. At LF features can move freely, but prior to Spell-Out movement of features produces Pied Piping for reasons of convergence at PF (a theory of which is yet to be formulated).

This requirement explains why GREED, which is formulated in terms of the checking of features, appears to be producing the movement of constituents.

- Features that are 'interpretable' (i.e. that have some semantic content) are not erased when they check off a strong feature, and can successively check off more than one strong feature in a single derivation.

This formulation allows the replacement of the complex chain formation operation with successive cyclic movement, where a feature on the moved constituent (e.g. *wh*) checks off the feature [*wh*] of successive complementizers. The successive cyclic movement analysis reduces all movements to a single step, once again. In the absence of evidence for multiple complementizers all of which share the same feature, apparent long movements will be analyzed as single step long movements, on this approach. So the analysis of *who did you say that you saw* will be one of the following, depending on independent empirical and theoretical considerations.

(38)   *a.* who$_i$ wh you say [t$_i$ wh/that you saw t$_i$]
       b. who$_i$ wh you say [that you saw t$_i$]

For a fuller exposition of these ideas and exploration of the details, see Chomsky (1995).

3.2. *Bare phrase structure*

Our customary way of thinking of the relationship between phrase markers and Move α is that we first construct the tree and then apply Move α to it. Chomsky reintroduces a device first proposed in Chomsky (1955) called the Generalized Transformation (GT) whose function is to map sets of one or more phrase markers into single phrase markers (see Chapter 9, § 1.4). If the set consists of two or more phrase markers, these are composed into a single phrase marker in a way that conforms to X'-theory. An example is given in (39).

(39)   PM1:   PM2:

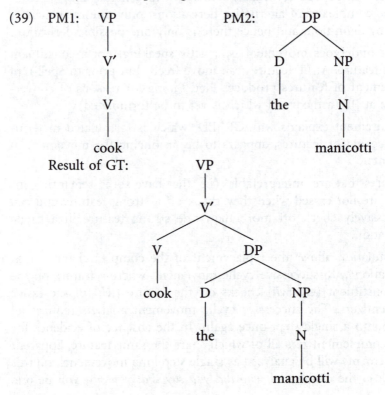

Crucially, the set that GT applies to may consist of a single tree, and one possible function of GT is to remove a part of the tree and put it somewhere else. GT is constrained in such a way that it must extend the tree, so that the result is in some sense larger than the input. This is the first principle that must be independently assumed. An illustration would be movement of a *wh*-phrase from its argument position into [Spec, CP], for example.

Chomsky (1994; 1995) proposes to do away with the notions of X′-theory entirely. To see how this could be done, note that X′-theory has two major functions, as shown by the X′ schema, which is repeated here from Chapter 5.

(40)

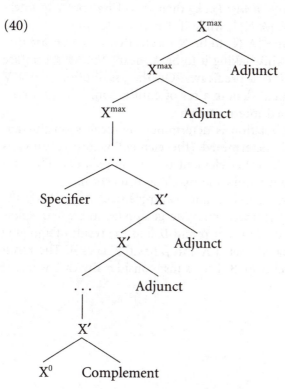

First, the X′ schema stipulates that XP must dominate X′ and X′ must dominate X. Second, it stipulates that the complement is adjoined to the head and that the specifier is adjoined to the result. Suppose that we simply abandon the notion that phrasal categories are distinguished by their level; on such a view heads and maximal projections are all of the same category, and they are distinguished by where they appear in the structure. An X that does not branch is a head; an X that does not have an X above it and that has a path of nodes only of category X down to a head of category X is a maximal projection.[6]

The concatenation of two categories $\{\alpha, \beta\}$ must have a label δ. Concatenation is the creation of a new category, an operation called Merge. (Merge is the name given in the MP to the Generalized Transformation discussed earlier.) While it is logically possible that δ be fixed for all α, β or random, the only language-like system that makes sense would be one in which δ is either α or β, so that the result of Merge is a projection. The minimalist assumption is that both are possible in principle; an incorrect assignment would theoretically be filtered out by the impossibility of interpreting the result in a larger structure. For instance, if $\{A, N\}$ is categorized as N (e.g. *heavy book*) then it will be correctly interpreted in the structure [V [A N]], while if it is characterized as A it will not be. Taking the structure [A N] to be N means that it is a phrase that denotes a set of entities, while taking it to be A means that it is a phrase that denotes a property (i.e. a predicate). On the assumption that a V requires that its complement denote a set of entities, only the first possibility yields a well-formed interpretation.

The head-complement relation is determined by locality on this approach; once the head is determined (the element whose category is assigned to the phrase), the other element is the complement. The specifier is a non-complement within the maximal projection.[7]

The difference between a specifier and a complement depends on the properties of the category formed when Merge applies to create a single syntactic object out of two. Consider α and β, and the result of applying Merge. Suppose that α has the label A and β has the label B. The result γ will have either the label A or B. Let us just consider the case where it has the label B.

(41)

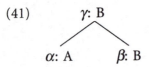

$$\gamma: B$$
$$\alpha: A \qquad \beta: B$$

Recall now the concept of segment. Two nodes are considered to be segments of a single projection if neither is an independent projection. In the MP, whether the two Bs in (41) are segments or distinct projections is an optional matter. If we choose the segment option, then α is an adjunct. If we choose the option under which the Bs are distinct projections, then α is a specifier.

3.3. Some consequences

Let us pursue the idea that the most economical movement from A to B involves the formation of a chain, each of whose links is of minimal length. This formulation is reminiscent of Subjacency, where each link in the chain must be minimal in the sense that it crosses at most one barrier, in the framework of Chomsky (1986*b*), or perhaps even no barriers, in some alternative framework. A desirable consequence of the MP would be to derive the content of the Subjacency condition from economy considerations without any stipulations about the presence or absence of barriers.

Recall some of the main effects of Subjacency: the Complex NP Constraint and the *wh*-island Condition. In both cases, there is a filled specifier that forces the moved constituent to cross over a barrier, in the framework of Chomsky (1986*b*). For instance, the typical derivation of a *wh*-island violation is as in (42).

(42)   *what$_i$ did you wonder [$_{CP}$ where$_j$ C [$_{IP}$ we put t$_i$ t$_j$]]]
        *where$_j$ did you wonder [$_{CP}$ what$_i$ C [$_{IP}$ we put t$_i$ t$_j$]]]
        *who$_j$ did you wonder [$_{CP}$ what$_i$] C [$_{IP}$ I gave t$_i$ to t$_j$]]

The interpretation of the violation in terms of economy is that the higher *wh*-phrase was prevented from making the shorter movement because the lower [Spec, CP] is filled. In some sense (which is not made precise by Chomsky 1993), the logical possibility of the shorter movement (since the actual possibility does not exist) should be sufficient to render the longer movement ungrammatical in the MP.

A similar notion holds for the Head Movement Constraint, which earlier we attributed to the ECP or Relativized Minimality. In this case, a head moves over one head and adjoins to a higher head. Again, the potential availability of the nearer head as a landing site should block the longer movement.

More generally, economy considerations appear to straightforwardly yield the results of Relativized Minimality discussed in Chapter 7 (§ 7). Consider the movement of α in (43) to the empty position [e].

(43)   [e] ... α' ... α

In each case of A'-, A-, or head movement, an intervening element α' of the same type is in some sense the 'closest' landing site of the movement.

However, since this position is occupied, movement must skip it, which is a non-minimal movement, and therefore ruled out.

Manzini (1994) provides a formalization of this approach and develops its consequences for the theory of locality. The notion of locality is expressed in terms of the minimal domain of a head X, defined as follows. (X) abbreviates 'minimal domain.'

(44)   The minimal domain (X) of a head X consists of all and only the elements that are immediately contained by, and do not immediately contain, a projection of X.

(45)   The domain of a head X consists of (X) and of all the elements that the members of (X) contain.

The locality of two minimal domains is given by the following definition.

(46)   (X) and (Y) are adjacent if and only if there is no (Z) such that some member of (Z) contains (X) and does not contain (Y), or vice versa.

That is, two minimal domains are adjacent to one another if there is no third minimal domain that contains one and not the other.

Movement is only possible between adjacent domains. The following illustrates.

(47)

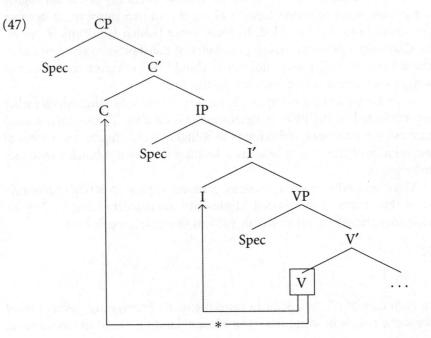

The formal statement of the locality condition for dependent elements such as the trace of an antecedent is given in (48).

(48) Locality: For all i, let A_i be in (X_i). Given a dependency $(A_1, \ldots, A_n)$, for all i, (X_i) and (X_{i+1}) are adjacent.

To see how this constraint applies to (47), consider the movement of V to C. A_1 is the moved V, while A_2 is its trace. The trace is dependent on V, but the minimal domain of V is CP, while the minimal domain of the trace is VP. There is another minimal domain, IP, that contains VP but not CP. Hence the two domains are not adjacent, and the dependency is not local. Thus Locality produces the effect of Relativized Minimality.

With a crucial modification, the Locality constraint of (48) may be extended not only to the standard Relativized Minimality cases but to CED cases involving extraction from adjunct.[8] An example is given in (49).

(49) *Who$_i$ did you visit London [$_{CP}$ after you got to know t$_i$]?

The key property of this sentence for present purposes is that the adjunct is not dominated by all projections of V, as shown in (50).

(50)

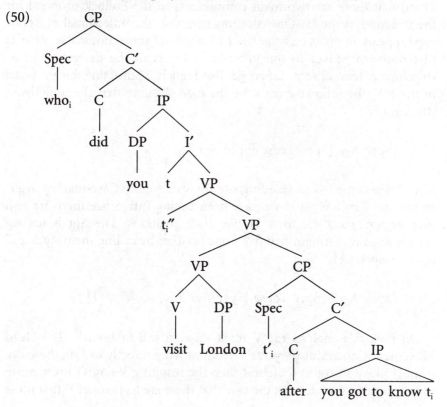

Let us say that (Y) is 'superior' to (X) if and only if all of the nodes in (Y) dominate some node in (X). It is clear that (V) in (50) is not superior to the lower (C) headed by *after*. We now define dependency so that it incorporates the notion of superiority in this sense.

(51)   For all i, let A_i be in (X_i), $(A_1, \ldots, A_n)$ is a dependency only if for all i, (X_i) is superior to (X_{i+1}).

In (50) the chain $(who_i, t_i'', t_i', t_i)$ is not a dependency under the definition in (51). On the other hand, if we move directly from the lower CP to the higher CP without adjoining to VP, Locality is violated.

4. Minimalism and head movement

Recall that there are two main components to the Pollock proposal for the structure of the IP. One component is that the inflectional morphology appears in syntax as the head of maximal projections; the other is that the verb moves to the inflectional heads in the derivation of S-structure, at least in some languages like French. Translating this proposal in the MP, the following must be the case. Assume that the underlying structure is

(52)   [Spec Agr [Spec Tense [Spec Agr [$_{VP}$ ... V ...]]]]

where [Spec, Agr] is the landing site for structurally Case-marked arguments and Tense is what we have been calling Infl. Since there are two such arguments, there must be two such positions. The Agr heads are conventionally distinguished from one another by calling them AgrS and AgrO, respectively.

(53)   [Spec AgrS [Spec Tense [Spec AgrO [$_{VP}$ ... V ...]]]]

On Pollock's analysis the V must raise to Infl in French. The Head Movement Constraint prevents V from moving directly to Infl; therefore it must move to AgrO first, and then the resulting V+AgrO must move to Infl. It must therefore be the case that there are features of V that must be discharged; the need to discharge these features forces the movement. Suppose that V has the feature G. (54) illustrates.

(54)

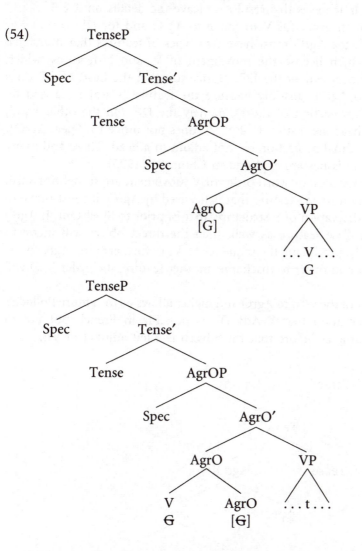

Notice that when we shift from talking about movement of a phrase to a specifier to talking about adjunction of a head to another head, we are no longer able to characterize feature checking as always occurring in a Spec-head configuration. On the other hand, it is possible to define the relationship between the adjoined head (e.g. V) and the head to which it adjoins (e.g. AgrO) in such a way that it has the essential configurational properties of the Spec-head relation. In a sense, the adjoined V bears a non-complement relation to AgrO, since only a sister of a head is a com-plement.[9] Chomsky (1993) provides a formal definition of the **checking domain** which achieves this result; we leave the details until § 5.

Notice that in order for V to move to AgrO and for DP to move to [Spec, AgrO], the AgrO must have two types of features that it assigns: V-features, which license the movement of V, and N-features, which license the movement of the DP. Notice too that the head of DP does not adjoin to AgrO, possibly because the feature [Case] is carried by the maximal projection of the D, namely the DP. On the other hand, the VP may bear the feature G, but VP does not move to [Spec, AgrO], because a maximal projection cannot adjoin to a head. These and many other technical issues are explored in Chomsky (1995).

The consequences for word order of V movement are straightforward. If the verb has a strong feature that is licensed by AgrO, it must move to AgrO in the derivation of S-structure, that is, prior to Spell-Out. If AgrO has a strong Case feature as well, then the direct object will move to [Spec, AgrOP], producing the sequence O-V. If, furthermore, AgrO must move to Tense in order to discharge another feature, the order V-O will be derived.

Movement of the verb to AgrO and higher allows us to capture Pollock's original observation that V-Adv-DP is possible in French but not in English. Assume as before that the adverb is a left adjunct of VP.

(55)

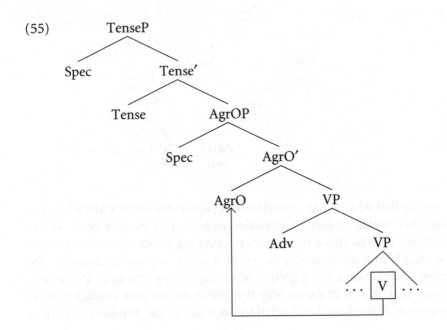

Crucially, V has a feature that is strong in French but weak in English, which forces the raising of V in French prior to S-structure. Because of PROCRASTINATE, V-raising also occurs in English, but at LF.[10]

The question now arises (once again) as to why the auxiliary verbs raise in English. Recall that in Pollock's proposal this was due to the fact that the morphology in French is strong and allows the assignment of θ-roles after V-raising. Auxiliary verbs do not assign θ-roles and so may raise to the weak English morphology. The counterpart in the MP is to say that the auxiliary verbs in English are semantically empty and as a consequence are not interpretable at LF. If they have not raised before LF then they cannot raise after Spell-Out, and their features will not be checked. It should be clear that this proposal, no less than Pollock's, rests on a complex web of assumptions whose consequences and foundations have yet to be fully explored.

At this point we eliminate a simplification that we have been making for the sake of exposition. Chomsky (1993) proposes that Case is not actually assigned on the basis of Agr, but by V and Tense. However, in order to be able to assign Case, V and Tense must be adjoined to Agr. Therefore, the feature G in the preceding illustrations is actually the Case feature of V which is not checked off by Agr, but enabled in virtue of the adjunction of V to Agr. (Similarly for the assignment of Case by Tense.) The intuition is that it is only through agreement that Case is assigned; that is, the DP that receives Case is in the specifier of Agr.

On the other hand, through a more extended consideration of the role of Agr, Chomsky (1995: 351 f.) concludes that the only purpose of Agr is to bear a strong feature that triggers movement prior to Spell-Out. There is no evidence for Agr with the corresponding weak feature. The same effect can now be achieved by locating the strong feature on Tense (for NOMINATIVE) and V (for ACCUSATIVE). Given this, it is straightforward, and in fact desirable given minimalist assumptions, to eliminate Agr entirely, except when it appears overtly in some language. The upshot is that for Chomsky (1995), the analysis of the inflectional system is 'something like the analysis that was conventional before Pollock's (1989) highly productive split-I theory' (377).

Continuing with the earlier proposal, let us consider the interaction between V-raising and the movement of DPs. Assuming VP-internal subjects and Agr, the full structure is that of (56).

(56)

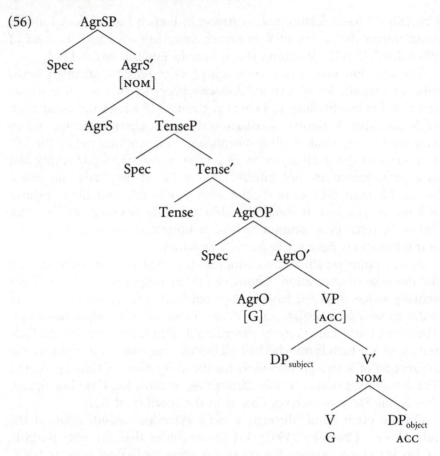

If the Case features are weak and G is strong, V moves to AgrO and produces a VSO order. If NOM is strong as well, then SVO is derived. There are in fact several other ways to derive each of the various word orders, as explored in Exercise 10-1.

5. Head movement in VP: Larsonian shells

In this section we consider some arguments that not only do verbs adjoin to functional heads that license inflectional morphology, but there is also movement within complex VPs from one V-head position to another.

As noted in Chapter 5, Appendix A, it follows from the assumption that the VP has binary branching that a constituent to the right c-commands everything to the left of it, as in (57).

(57)

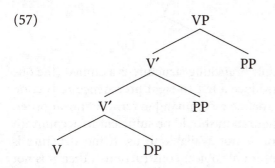

The facts that are indicative of the c-command relations suggest that quite the opposite is the case, however. To take the clearest case, consider the following asymmetries in double object constructions.[11]

(58)   *a.* Mary sent Kim a gift.
       b. I promised Mary a special present.

The evidence from binding suggests that the direct object can be bound by the indirect object, but not vice versa.

(59)   *a.* I showed Mary$_i$ herself$_i$.
       b. *I showed herself$_i$ Mary$_i$.
(60)   *a.* I gave every worker$_i$ her$_i$ paycheck.
       b. *I gave its$_i$ owner every paycheck$_i$.

Weak crossover (Chapter 9, § 2) suggests that the indirect object bears the same relationship to the direct object as a subject bears to an object.

(61)   *a.* ?Which worker$_i$ did you send her$_i$ paycheck?[12]
       b. *Whose$_i$ paycheck did you send her$_i$ mother?

The superiority effect (Chapter 8, § 5) suggests that the indirect object c-commands the direct object.

(62)   *a.* ?Who did you give which paycheck?
       b. *Which paycheck did you give whom?

On the view that binding, WCO, and superiority are sensitive to c-command relations, neither of the two most plausible structures gives the correct predictions.

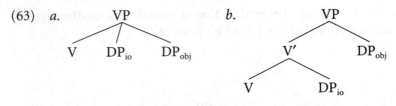

Notice that if the flat multiple branching structure is assumed (the one in (63a)) we will have to introduce a left-to-right precedence restriction on these binding relations, or define c-command in terms of linear order. On the assumption that configuration should be sufficient to account for syntactic relations, this option is not available to us. If the structure is that of (63b) (or (57) for non-double object constructions), then it is not clear what definition of c-command will allow the constituents to the left to c-command those to the right, but not vice versa.

Larson (1988; 1991) therefore hypothesizes that neither of these structures is correct. Rather, the constituent that binds is the constituent that c-commands, on the standard definition of c-command. On this approach, the structure must be one in which constituents to the left are actually higher than those to the right, as illustrated in (64), corresponding to (57).

(64)

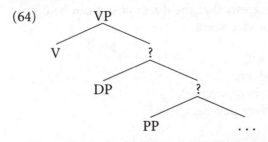

One obvious question to ask here is, what are the '?' categories? Suppose that in fact all complements and adjuncts in VP are actually specifiers or complements of some V, as in the following elaboration of (64).

(65)

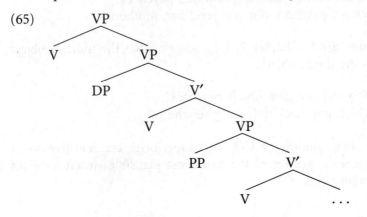

Now, plainly, if there is only one overt V in a VP like *toss the banana into the sink with a slingshot*, all of the lower Vs in (65) must be empty at S-structure. But if the lower Vs are empty at D-structure as well, it is not clear how to impose the selectional requirements of V on the lower constituents of VP. Larson suggests, in fact, that the higher Vs are empty, and that the lowest V is the true V.[13] This verb raises into the higher V slots, as illustrated in (66). The higher VPs with empty heads are called VP-shells.

(66)

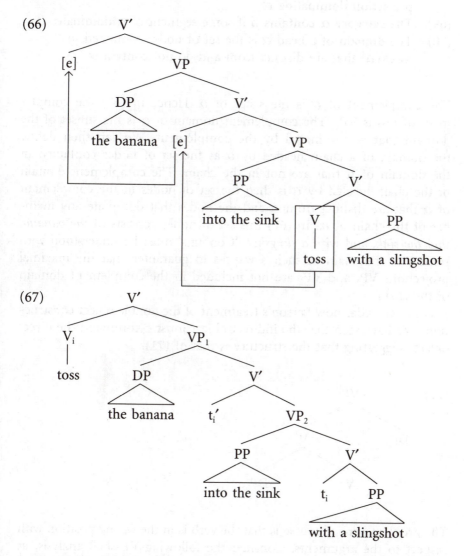

(67)

It should be clear from this illustration that the selectional restrictions of the V can in principle be satisfied in terms of the V-chain produced by the movement of the V to the highest slot; what is essential is that the notion of **complement domain** be defined so that the PP *with a slingshot,* for example, counts as a complement of *toss* in virtue of its relationship to the trace t_i of *toss.* The following definitions are intended to do this.[14]

(68) For a head α, **MAX(α)** is the least full-category maximal projection dominating α.

(69) The category α **contains** β if some segment of α dominates β.

(70) The **domain** of a head α is the set of nodes contained in MAX(α) that are distinct from and do not contain α.

The complement of α is the sister of α. Hence in (67) the complement of *toss* is VP_1. The complement domain of α is the subset of the domain that is dominated by the complement. We can then define the domain of a chain headed by α as the set of nodes contained in the domain of α that are not in the chain. The complement domain of the chain headed by α is then the set of nodes in the complement of α that are distinct from α and the nodes that dominate any member of the chain of α. In (67) this set of nodes consists of *the banana, into the sink,* and *with a slingshot.* 'Contains' must be understood with respect to the chain in such a way as to guarantee that the maximal projections VP_1 and VP_2 are not included in the complement domain of the chain.

Let us consider now Larson's treatment of the double object construction. We have seen that the indirect object must c-command the direct object, suggesting that the structure is that of (71).

(71)

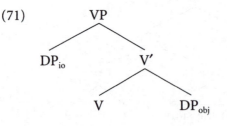

The problem here of course is that the verb is in the wrong position with respect to the arguments. Consider the following VP-shell analysis, as illustrated in (72).

(72)

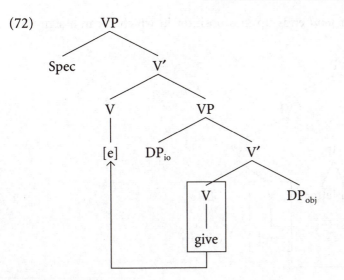

In order to derive the sequence V-DP$_{io}$-DP$_{obj}$, we raise the verb to the empty V position, as shown.

The problem with this analysis is that it appears to assign a radically different D-structure to *give John the book* and *give the book to John*. Evidence from binding and weak crossover suggests that the direct object c-commands the indirect object in this configuration, rather than the other way around as in (72).

(73)   *a.* I showed John$_i$ to himself$_i$.
       b. *Who$_i$se friend did you give his$_i$ paycheck to?

Suppose, therefore, that the underlying structure for the double object construction is the same as that of the V-DP-PP construction, i.e.

(74)

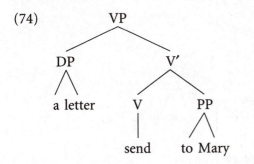

Kim a letter send to Mary is not a grammatical sentence in English. Since V governs to the right in English, this structure must be embedded in a

VP-shell, so that *send* ends up in a position in which it can assign Case to *letter*.

(75)

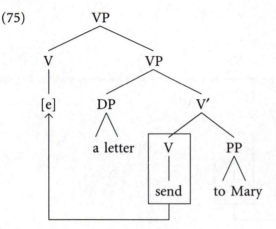

The verb moves into the empty V slot, assigning Case to *letter* across the lower VP node.

Now what about the double object construction? Consider the possibility that this construction is similar to the passive construction, in that the 'subject' appears in an adjunct to VP, while the direct object undergoes NP movement into specifier position. In order for such an analysis to work for the double object construction, the structure must be the following. Note that the indirect object lacks a preposition, so that it is not assigned Case and must undergo movement in order to get Case.

(76)

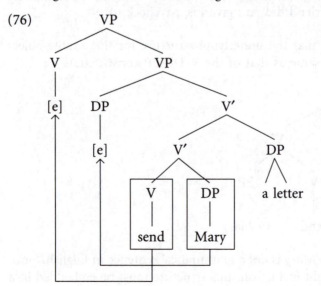

Mary moves into [Spec, VP], and V moves into the empty V position. V therefore assigns Case to the indirect object, and the indirect object c-commands the direct object. The DP *letter* in fact has a different status in the two constructions in this analysis. In the case of the DP-PP construction, *letter* is the specifier. In the case of the double object construction, *letter* bears the same relationship to the VP as does the *by* phrase in the passive. That is, it acquires the θ-role that would be assigned to the specifier, but it is not in specifier position.

If the verb is passive, it cannot assign Case to the indirect object in [Spec, VP]. In (77), then, *Mary* would have to move to the lowest position in which it could receive Case, [Spec, IP].

(77)   Mary was sent a letter.

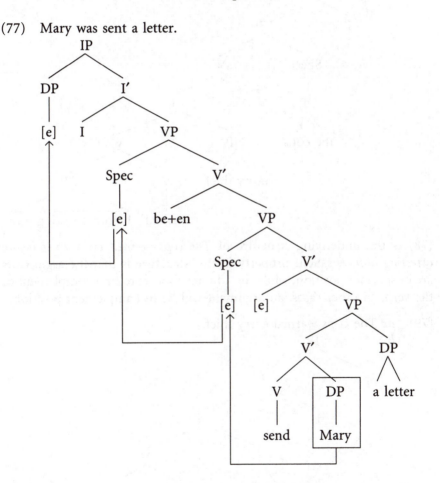

As suggested above, the only possible formulation of this sequence of movements in the MP is that there is a single chain formed that puts

Mary into [Spec, IP]. The formation of such a chain is triggered by the need to assign Case to the chain prior to Spell-Out.

It can be seen that the VP-shell analysis is strongly driven by the desire to correlate the binding properties of constituents with their configurational properties. An interesting consequence is that adjuncts are lower in the tree than the arguments that bind into them. In (78), for example, the direct object c-commands the temporal adjunct.

(78)

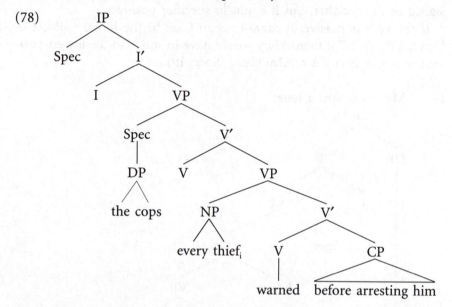

(78) is the underlying structure of *The cops warned every thief before arresting him*. A salient property of this structure is that the arguments are in specifier position, while the adjunct appears to be a complement of the verb. In other cases, an argument will be in complement position.

(79)   a. The cops warned every thief.
       b.

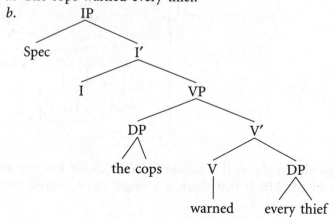

It therefore does not appear to be possible to implement the argument/adjunct distinction on this approach in terms of configurational properties.

6. Antisymmetry

Reformulation of X′-theory in the MP has the goal of reducing the theory of phrase structure to its barest essentials. This is done, in principle at least, by eliminating any stipulations, so that all independently attested properties of phrase structure follow from the smallest possible number of independent principles. To date there have been two main attempts along these lines, that of Chomsky (1993; 1994; 1995), which we have discussed already, and that of Kayne (1994). Both proposals are preliminary, and many of their consequences have yet to be determined. We summarize Kayne's proposal here, leaving it to the reader to follow the development of this area of research as it takes shape in the literature.

6.1. Asymmetric c-command

Kayne (1994) seeks to eliminate statements about left-to-right order entirely from the theory of phrase structure. We can understand this goal as a consequence of the Configuration assumption noted in Chapter 1. Under this approach, the hierarchical relations in a syntactic structure should be sufficient to account for all of its properties.

At first sight this goal seems unrealistic, in view of the fact that when A dominates B and C, there is nothing in the hierarchical structure that tells us what the ordering is between B and C. But Kayne proposes that phrase structures are legitimate only if the hierarchical structure entails a unique linear ordering. Intuitively, if A c-commands B but B does not c-command A, then there is an asymmetry in the hierarchical structure that can be utilized for this purpose. Specifically, we would say that when A asymmetrically c-commands B, every node that A dominates must precede (or follow) every node that B dominates.[15] Call the terminal nodes dominated by A the image of A, represented as d(A). Then the principle may be formulated as follows.

(80) **Asymmetry Principle:** For all non-terminal nodes A, B such that A asymmetrically c-commands B, then for all pairs (a, b) such that $a \in$ d(A) and $b \in$ d(B), a precedes b.[16]

Crucially, this principle applies only to asymmetric c-command. There is no ordering relation on constituents that c-command one another.

Consider the application of principle (80) to the tree in (81).

(81)

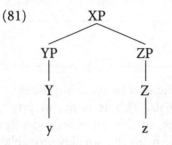

Here, YP asymmetrically c-commands Z, and ZP asymmetrically c-commands Y. So d(YP), which is y, precedes d(Z), which is z. But by the same token, z precedes y. But this is impossible in a single sentence, so there must be something wrong with the structure in (81). In fact, an examination of this structure shows that XP lacks a head. If XP had a head, as in (82), ZP could not asymmetrically c-command Y.

(82)

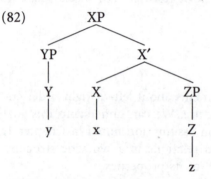

Thus, from the requirement that asymmetric c-command must map into a unique linear order, Kayne derives the property that every phrase must have a head. Moreover, a phrase cannot have more than one head; consider (83).[17]

(83)

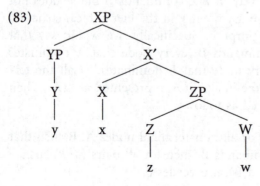

Since YP asymmetrically c-commands Z and W, y precedes z and y precedes w. But there is no non-terminal node that dominates just z but not w, or vice versa. Therefore there is no ordering between z and w. It is reasonable to require not only that each element of the sentence have some unique ordering with respect to every other element, but also that the ordering be consistent over the entire set of elements in the sentence. (83) fails to satisfy the second requirement.

6.2. Deriving word order

There are a number of other consequences of Kayne's proposal, some of which are explored in the exercises. We focus here on just one, which concerns the direction of branching. Notice that from the formulation of the requirement of asymmetric c-command it follows that the specifier and the complement must be on opposite sides of the head. Consider (84).

(84)

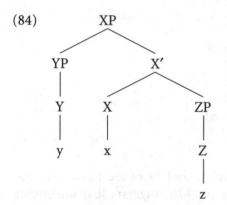

From asymmetric c-command we derive the orderings (y, z), (y, x) and (x, z). That is, specifier precedes head and head precedes complement. Because of the fact that x asymmetrically c-commands z it is impossible for x to follow z, unless of course the correlate of asymmetric c-command is 'follows' instead of 'precedes.' In that case, the specifier follows the head, and the complement must precede the head.

It follows directly that there cannot be any languages (in this framework of assumptions) in which all of the arguments precede the verb at D-structure. Languages that appear to be V-final (such as Japanese, Korean, German, and Dutch) must be derived from a structure in which the specifier is on the opposite side of the phrase from the complement. Hence in this framework, as in the MP, all superficial differences in word order must be attributed to movement from an essentially uniform D-structure.

This conclusion may be correct for Dutch, as argued by Zwart (1993); it is somewhat less than clearly correct for Japanese, Korean, and other head-final languages. Crucially, in Dutch the surface order of verbs can be the same as it is in English, even though a verb typically appears in final position; the exception is that the tensed verb appears in second position in a main clause. Here are some examples to illustrate.[18]

(85) *a.* Jan zal Marie kussen.
     John will Mary kiss
     'John will kiss Mary.'
    b. *Jan zal kussen Marie.
(86) *a.* * ... dat Jan kust Marie.
        that John kisses Mary
    b. ... dat Jan Marie kust.
        that John Mary kisses
     '... that John kisses Mary.'
(87) *a.* ... dat Jan Marie gekust heeft.
        that Jan Marie kissed has
     '... that John kissed Mary.'
    b. ... dat Jan Marie heeft gekust.
        that Jan Marie has   kissed
     '... that John kissed Mary.'

While the full range of data is complex, and there are numerous dialectal differences, the grammaticality of (87*b*) suggests that underlying Dutch word order may not be the standard one in (88*a*), but the one in (88*b*).

(88) *a.* $[_{VP} [_{VP} \text{ DP } V_2] V_1]$
    b. $[_{VP} V_1 [_{VP} V_2 \text{ DP}]]$

In order for the second possibility to be correct, the DP must move to the left, e.g. to [Spec, AgrOP]. Furthermore, the possibility of the order DP-V_2-V_1 means that there would also have to be an optional movement of the lower verb to the left. These movements are illustrated in (89).

(89)

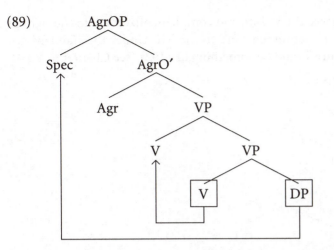

What is the evidence that the DP is moving from a postverbal position? It turns out that in Dutch it is possible for non-DPs to follow the verb. CPs must be extraposed.

(90)　*a.* . . . dat Jan zal verteld   dat hij Marie gekust heeft.
　　　　　　that John will have told that he Marie kissed has
　　　　　'. . . that John will have told that he kissed Mary.'
　　　b. *dat Jan [dat hij Marie gekust heeft] zal verteld

PPs may extrapose.

(91)　*a.* . . . dat Jan een boek geeft aan Marie.
　　　　　　that John a   book gives to   Mary
　　　　　'. . . that John gives a book to Mary.'
　　　b. . . . dat Jan een boek aan Marie geeft.
　　　　　　that John a   book to   Mary gives
　　　　　'. . . that John gives a book to Mary.'

Zwart proposes that the constituents that appear to the right are in fact generated to the right in D-structure. They do not move to the left because they do not need to, an explanation that is familiar from the earlier Case theory accounts of A-movement and adapted in the MP. A DP, which must receive Case, must move to the left of the verb into a Case position. The fact that a PP may appear on either side of the verb would suggest on this approach that PP may have a 'strong' feature that is discharged in the specifier position of some functional category.

While an argument can be made for Dutch being V-initial, it is somewhat less straightforward to account in this framework for languages that are strictly left-branching. Kayne points out, for example, that in a language like Japanese the V, Infl, and complementizers are to the right in S-structure, while the arguments are to the left. Under the standard approach, the structure would be something like (92) (see Chapter 5, § 3.4).

(92)

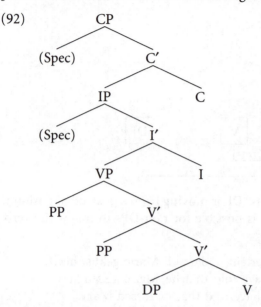

But on Kayne's approach the structure must be the mirror image of this as far as the X′ categories are concerned. Kayne suggests that the way that the branching structure in (92) can be derived is by moving IP into [Spec, CP] and VP into [Spec, IP], as illustrated in (93). Let us assume for simplicity that the arguments of the verb have already been moved to the left.

(93)

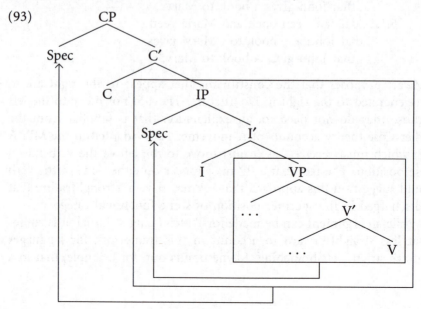

Kayne offers some suggestive evidence that this analysis may be on the right track; the most striking generalization is that in languages that are strictly head-final, there is no overt *wh*-Movement. Such a consequence follows directly if *wh*-Movement involves movement to [Spec, CP], a position which is filled in these languages by IP.[19] Of course, it is an open question why IP should move to [Spec, CP] in the first place.

6.3. *Leftward and rightward movement*

An important consequence of Kayne's proposal is that there is no rightward movement if there is a uniform right branching structure. To see this, consider the structure in (94).

(94)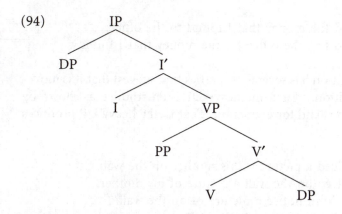

For the sake of illustration we are taking PP to be the specifier of VP. Suppose that we were to move PP to the right of VP and adjoin it to a new segment, as in (95).

(95)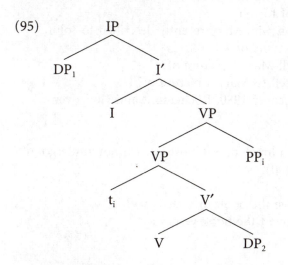

Kayne assumes that adjunction produces a segmented category. An adjunct does not c-command a category if it is dominated by one of its segments, as is the case in (95). As a consequence of the right adjunction, an ordering is produced in which VP asymmetrically dominates PP and therefore precedes it; PP asymmetrically c-commands DP_2 and therefore precedes it. But VP contains DP_2, so there is a contradiction. In general, right adjunction is impossible in a right-branching structure in this framework, regardless of whether the right adjunction is produced by movement or is base-generated.

The conclusion that there is no rightward movement in a right-branching language (of which English is a typical case) is problematic, given that there appear to be several constructions that might plausibly be produced by rightward movement. One example is Heavy Shift, illustrated in (96).

(96) a. I returned the money that I found to the office.
      b. I returned t to the office [DP the money that I found].

In fact this construction has several properties that suggest that it is movement to an A′-position.[20] First, the heavy DP is an adjunct, as shown by the fact that it is an island for extraction. That is, the heavy DP produces a typical CED effect.

(97) a. John noticed a picture of his mother on the wall.
      b. John noticed on the wall a picture of his mother.
      c. Who did John notice a picture of on the wall?
      d. *Who did John notice on the wall a picture of?
(98) a. Mary described several appealing traits of Susan to John.
      b. Mary described to John several appealing traits of Susan.
      c. Susan is a person who Mary recently described several
          appealing traits of to John.
      d. *Susan is a person who Mary recently described to John
          several appealing traits of.
(99) a. Who did John sell Mary a picture of?
      b. *Who did John sell to Mary a picture of?[21]
          (Wexler and Culicover 1980; Rochemont and Culicover
          1990)

Second, a *wh*-phrase in indirect object position cannot undergo A′-movement, as shown in (100).

(100) a. Who did Bill give the book to t yesterday?
       b. ?Who did Bill give t the book yesterday?

But a DP in this position can undergo A-movement.

(101)   Bill was given the book.

A DP in the indirect object position cannot undergo Heavy Shift, suggesting that Heavy Shift, like *wh*-Movement, is A′-movement.

(102)   *a.* Bill gave John t yesterday the book that he was looking for.
        b. What did Bill give John t yesterday.
        c. *Bill gave t the book yesterday anyone who wanted it.

Third, in Heavy Shift, the heavy DP licenses a parasitic gap, which suggests that it is in an A′-position (see Chapter 6, § 7).[22]

(103)   I filed t_i without reading e_i [all of the reports that you gave me]$_i$.

A general strategy for producing the order B-A from underlying A-B when one constituent cannot move for some reason is to move the other constituent. So, while it appears that the heavy DP is moving to the right of the VP, if this movement is ruled out, it is natural to seek a derivation in which the VP moves to the left of the heavy DP. But if the VP moves to the left of this DP, we must explain how it is that this DP gets to the left of the VP in the first place. Rochemont and Culicover (to appear) discuss two options. One, due to Larson (1988), is that the DP originates in a specifier position and the V′ moves to the empty V of a VP-shell.

(104)

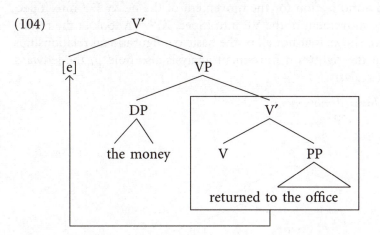

The basic difficulty with this analysis is that the direct object is not moved to an A′-position, and hence it is not clear how to capture the properties noted above.

Another, more radical, approach is first to move the heavy DP to a specifier position, and then to move the entire VP to the left of it, as illustrated in (105).

(105)

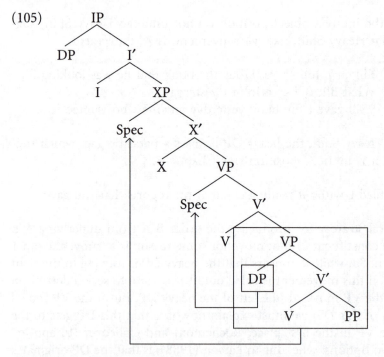

It is of course necessary on such an approach to justify the XP projection, and to find a motivation for the movement of the heavy DP into [Spec, VP] and the movement of the VP into [Spec, XP].[23] A look at the resulting structure shows that not all of the basic configurational relationships that hold in the rightward movement analysis also hold in the leftward movement analysis.

(106)   *Rightward movement:*

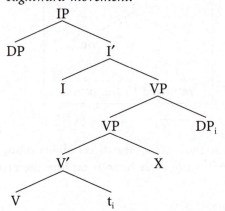

(107) *Leftward movement:*

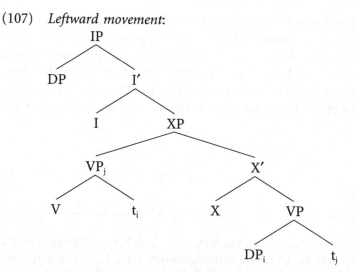

The leftward movement analysis does capture the A′ status of the heavy DP, but not the fact that the heavy DP c-commands its trace at S-structure. This problem can be remedied in several ways. First, we could hypothesize that the binding relationship does not hold at S-structure, but at LF, at a point at which the moved VP is 'reconstructed' into the position occupied by t_j. At this point, DP_i would c-command t_i. (For more on reconstruction, see Chapter 9.) Second, we could hypothesize that the VP is not moved to a specifier higher than DP_i, but is adjoined to DP_i directly, as in (108).

(108)

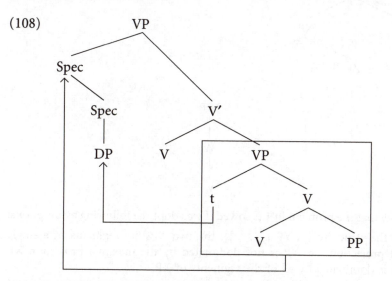

In summary, it appears that at least for the A′-movements, it is possible to produce the desired c-command relations through either leftward movement or rightward movement, if particular assumptions are made about the original structure. Whether these assumptions can be independently justified is of course a crucial question. But putting this issue aside, what appears to have empirical significance here is not the direction of movement *per se*, but the configurations that are produced as a consequence of the sequence of movements between D-structure and S-structure.

EXERCISES

10-1. Assuming structure (56) in the text, show how many different ways the following constituent orders can be derived. Assume that DP$_{subject}$ can only move to [Spec, AgrSP] and DP$_{object}$ can only move to [Spec, AgrOP].

1. SVO
2. SOV
3. VSO

*10-2. Assume the principle of asymmetric c-command in (80) in the text.

1. Show that it follows that adjoined structures cannot be of the form in (1), where each XP is a distinct maximal projection.

(1)

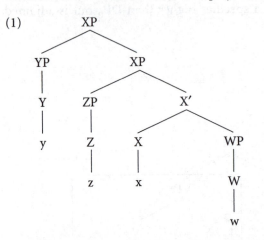

2. Show that the problem in 1 is solved if we adopt the following assumptions:

(i) In the structure [$_{XP}$ YP [$_{XP}$ ...]], the two XPs are segments of a single maximal projection. i.e. YP is not dominated by the maximal projection XP unless it is dominated by all of the segments of XP.

(ii) α c-commands β iff no segment of α dominates β and every node that dominates α dominates β.

10-3. Assume the notion of segment and the definition of c-command in Exercise 10-2. Show that there can be at most one adjunction to a maximal projection on this account.

*10-4. In the text we discussed the fact that the indirect object appears to c-command (or m-command) the direct object, but not vice versa. Without mentioning linear order, how would you revise c- or m-command so as to make DP_1 bind DP_2 in the VP but not vice versa?

**10-5. Assuming the correlation between asymmetric c-command and linear order, explain whether or not Kayne's theory of movement allows adjunction to a specifier.

**10-6. In Chapter 2 we discussed the phenomenon of Exceptional Case Marking (ECM) in English, whereby the subject of an infinitive behaves as though it is the direct object of a higher verb. An example is given in (1).

(1)   I believe [$_{IP}$ John to be intelligent].

The standard GB device for accounting for the behavior of the subject of the infinitive is to say that it is governed by the higher verb, in this case *believe*. The alternative, that the subject is raised into the VP, is not attractive from the GB perspective, since there is no landing site in VP.

Show how this objection to the raising account can be avoided if the subject raises to [Spec, AgrO]. Work out the derivation of (1), and indicate any problems or questions that have to be resolved on such an approach.

*10-7. What would the analysis of a conjoined DP like *Mary and John* have to be under Kayne's assumptions? Explain your answer.

FURTHER READING

The study of verb movement has produced a considerable literature, one that is too vast to summarize here comprehensively. Briefly, there are three basic lines of research. One concerns the movement of V out of VP into second position, perhaps into C or I. The second concerns the movements of V to higher Vs, sometimes called clause union, and producing verb clusters. Larsonian shells involve a special case of such verb raising. The third concerns adjunction to functional heads that may not be reflected in superficial word order. For some representative approaches to these types of V movement, see, among many others, Den Besten (1983), Den Besten and Moed-van Walraven (1986),

Diesing (1990), Evers (1975), Haegeman (1988), Haegeman (1992), Haegeman and van Riemsdijk (1986), Haider (1991), Haider and Prinzhorn (1986), Heycock and Kroch (1993), Heycock and Santorini (1992), Kathol (1990), Koopman (1983), Rizzi (1982), Travis (1991), Weerman (1989), and the papers in Hornstein and Lightfoot (1994).

Jackendoff (1990) is a critique of Larson (1988). Jackendoff argues that the prominence of the indirect object over the direct object for binding and other phenomena should be taken as evidence that linear precedence is relevant to Binding theory, not that the syntactic structures need to be radically revised in order to achieve the desired c-command relations. For additional criticisms, see Williams (1994).

An important precursor to the theory of Kayne (1994) is Kayne (1991); Kayne argues that clitics are always moved to the left and always adjoin to the left of a functional head, e.g. Agr or Tense. But see Zwart (1993) for arguments that clitic movements might not be subsumable under the general framework for phrasal and head movement of Kayne (1994).

APPENDIX 1
GB THEORY ROADMAP

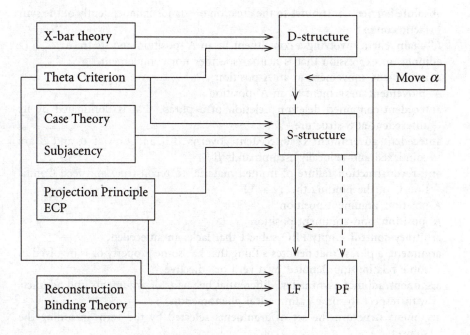

GLOSSARY OF TERMS

absolute barrier contributes to the creation of islands independently of the syntactic context

A'-chain chain involving a constituent in an A'-position and its trace

adjunct an expression that is neither specifier nor complement

A-movement movement to an A-position

A'-movement movement to an A'-position

antecedent-contained deletion deletion of a phrase that is dominated by its antecedent at S-structure

antecedent government α antecedent governs β if and only if α and β are coindexed and α locally c-commands β

anti-reconstruction failure of fronted material to reconstruct and feed Condition C of the Binding theory at LF

A-position argument position

A'-position non-argument position

arbitrary control empty PRO subject that lacks an antecedent

argument a phrase that denotes a thing that has some property or is involved in some relationship denoted by a verb or adjective

argument/adjunct asymmetry differential behavior of arguments and adjuncts with respect to some grammatical phenomenon

argument structure the set of arguments selected by the verb, including the subject

asymmetric c-command α c-commands β and β does not c-command α

Asymmetry Principle for all non-terminal nodes A,B such that A asymmetrically c-commands B, then for all pairs (a, b) such that $a \in d(A)$ and $b \in d(B)$, a precedes b.

autonomy the principles and primitives that make up one component of a grammar are unique to that component

barrier α is a barrier for β iff (i) α is a blocking category for β and α is not IP or (ii) α immediately dominates γ, a blocking category for β

binding conditions (a) an anaphor must be bound within its governing category; (b) a pronominal must be free within its governing category; (c) an R-expression must be free

binds α binds β iff (i) α c-commands β and (ii) α and β are coindexed

blocking category γ is a blocking category (BC) for β iff γ is not L-marked and γ dominates β

bounding node a node that contributes to the blocking of extraction

BT-compatibility α under the indexing I is BT-compatible in the local domain β if (*a*) α is an anaphor and is bound in β under this indexing; (*b*) α is a pronominal and is free in β under this indexing; (*c*) α is an R-expression and is free in β under this indexing

Case marking that indicates the grammatical function of an argument

Case assignment assignment of a Case feature to an argument

Case checking licensing of a Case feature borne by an argument

Case Filter every NP must be assigned Abstract Case

Case-Resistance Principle Case may not be assigned to a category bearing a Case-assigning feature

c(ategory)-selection satisfaction by a complement of syntactic requirements of a head

c-command α c-commands β iff the lowest branching node that immediately dominates α also dominates β

chain [final version] $C = (\alpha_1, \alpha_2, \ldots, \alpha_n)$ is a chain iff, for $1 \le i \le n$, α_i is the local binder of α_{i+1}

chain composition if $C = (\alpha_1, \ldots, \alpha_n)$ is the chain of the real gap, and $C' = (\beta_1, \ldots, \beta_m)$ is the chain of the parasitic gap, then the 'composed chain' $(C, C') = (\alpha_1, \ldots, \alpha_n, \beta_1, \ldots, \beta_m)$ is the chain associated with the parasitic gap construction and yields its interpretation

checking domain region of a phrase marker in which checking features are checked

Clausal Principle any part of a sentence that has a complete propositional interpretation is represented as a clause at some level of syntactic representation

competence the idealized linguistic knowledge of a native speaker

complement the sister of the head

complement domain [MP] the complement domain of α is the subset of the domain that is dominated by the complement

Complex NP Constraint [Ross] no element contained in a sentence dominated by a noun phrase with a lexical head noun may be moved out of that noun phrase by a transformation

COMP-to-COMP movement through intermediate [Spec, CP] positions

Condition on Extraction Domains extraction from adjuncts is ungrammatical

Configuration (Primacy of) the assumption that all syntactic phenomena can be accounted for in terms of the minimal configurational properties of the syntactic structure

conjunctive ECP ECP that applies if both of two conditions are satisfied

contains [MP] the category α contains β if some segment of α dominates β (To avoid circularity, dominates must be taken to be not defined in terms of contain.)

control relationship between an empty PRO subject and its antecedent

coreference situation where two NPs refer to the same thing

discourse anaphor anaphor that gets its reference from discourse and not from the sentence that contains it

disjunctive ECP ECP that applies if one of two possible conditions is satisfied

D-linking partial determination of the reference of logical elements through a connection with discourse

domain [of binding] the set of categories (i.e. IP and NP) for which binding of anaphors is constrained; [MP] the domain of a head α is the set of nodes contained in MAX(α) that are distinct from and do not contain α

dominates one constituent α of a sentence dominates another constituent β if β is contained in α

Empty Category Principle (ECP) an empty category must be properly governed; [Relativized Minimality] an empty category must be properly head governed

empty operator an operator that undergoes Move α to [Spec, CP] but lacks phonetic form

endocentric the category of the phrase is the same as the category of the head

Exceptional Case Marking (ECM) a verb governs and assigns (ACCUSATIVE) Case to the subject of its complement

expletive an element that has a syntactic category and a grammatical function but no independent meaning

Extended Projection Principle requirement that every clause have a subject

external θ-role θ-role assigned to the subject

extraction islands syntactic domains, extraction from which produces ungrammaticality

feature checking a head α licenses the feature [F] on β in its checking domain

feature discharge checking off and neutralization of a feature. Same as feature checking

floated quantifier quantifier that does not appear within the NP that it modifies

functional category non-lexical category, often but not always corresponding to overt morphological inflection

governing category (GC) the governing category for α is the minimal clause or NP containing α, a governor for α, and a SUBJECT accessible to α

government α governs β if (i) α is a head, (ii) α m-commands β, (iii) there is no barrier γ between α and β

GREED [MP] a constituent does not move unless it has to in order to satisfy some requirement that it has

head zero-level projection

head movement movement of an X^0 category

Head Movement Constraint constraint that guarantees the locality of head movement

Head Parameter parameter that determines direction of government (right or left)

Identification [Relativized Minimality] an empty category must be antecedent governed or bound

indexing a notational device that correlates an NP with what it refers to

Infl abstract head of which the sentence (subject and predicate) is a projection

Inherent Case Assignment Inherent Case is a realization of θ-role

internal θ-role θ-role assigned to an argument within VP

i-within-i Condition Agr is not accessible if changing the index of AGR and the index of the subject to the index of the anaphor would yield a situation in which the anaphor and the NP that contains it have the same index

landing site destination of a movement

Left Branch Condition [Ross] no NP which is the leftmost constituent of a larger NP can be reordered out of this NP by a transformational rule

Leftness Condition stipulation that a pronoun cannot be to the left of its antecedent at S-structure if the antecedent is a variable

lexical categories the categories N, V, A, and P

lexical entry itemization of the information associated with a lexical item

lexical government α lexically governs β if and only if α governs β and α is lexical

lexical item essentially, a word

Lexicon the component of the grammar that contains all linguistic information associated with lexical items

L-marking a head α L-marks β if α is lexical and θ-governs β

locative inversion English construction in which the subject appears after the main verb and a locative or directional adverb appears in initial position in the clause

Logical Form (LF) level of syntactic representation that maps into semantic interpretation

logophoricity the influence of speaker point-of-view on the interpretation or well-formedness of a sentence

long distance anaphor anaphor that does not have to have a local antecedent

long movement a phrase moves out of its clause in a single step

MAX(α) [MP] for a head α, MAX(α) is the least full-category maximal projection dominating α

maximal projection the highest phrasal node in a series of projections of a head

m-command α m-commands β iff for all γ, γ a maximal projection that dominates α, γ dominates β

middle construction in which the subject is the *PATIENT* and the verb is active and intransitive

minimality barrier [Barriers] barrier for government created by the presence of a closer governor

negative inversion construction in English that moves the tensed auxiliary to the left of the subject in the presence of a fronted negative constituent

null operator see empty operator

o-command Y o-commands Z just in case Y locally o-commands X dominating Z. Y locally o-commands Z just in case Y is higher on the obliqueness hierarchy than Z

parasitic gap a gap that is licensed by another gap in the same sentence

performance what a native speaker does in processing language

φ-features φ-features are those that must be satisfied through agreement in the course of a derivation, e.g. person, number

phonetic form (PF) phonetic representation of a sentence

Pied Piping movement of α in the structure $[_\beta \ldots \alpha \ldots]$ causes movement of β

PROCRASTINATE [MP] movement occurs as late as possible in the derivation

Projection Principle the selectional requirements of a lexical item are projected onto every level of syntactic representation

proper government α properly governs β if and only if (i) α lexically governs β or (ii) α antecedent governs β

PRO Theorem the argument that PRO is ungoverned

Pruning deletion of a CP node

Quantifier Raising (QR) application of Move α to a quantifier phrase (QP)

reconstruction a fronted *wh*-phrase is moved to the position of its trace ('reconstructed'), and the *wh*-operator is moved to sentence-initial position at LF to indicate its scope in LF

reference relationship between an NP and an object (or objects) in the world

rigid minimality minimality that is not sensitive to the type of governor. See minimality barrier

scrambling the apparently free reordering of constituents of a phrase

segments parts of a single category in phrase structure formed by adjunction

Sentential Subject Constraint [Conditions] no element dominated by an S may be moved out of that S if that node S is dominated by an NP which itself is immediately dominated by S

short movement a phrase moves to the initial position of the CP that contains its D-structure position

sisters constituents immediately dominated by the same node

sloppy identity identity of form without identity of reference

small clause a phrase that has a clausal (or propositional) interpretation, but lacks the full inflectional morphology of a sentence

Spec-head agreement specifier and head agree on the value of a feature

Specified Subject Condition [Conditions] no rule can involve X, Y in the structure $\ldots X \ldots [_\alpha \ldots Z \ldots -WYV \ldots] \ldots$ where Z is the specified subject of WYV in α

specifier sister of X' that is immediately dominated by XP

Spell-Out process of mapping from syntactic representation to PF

s-selection satisfaction by a complement of semantic requirements of a head

strong crossover a pronoun c-commands the trace of its antecedent which appears to the left of it (in S-structure)

structural Case Case assigned to A-positions

Structural Case Assignment a Case assigner α assigns Case to β iff α governs β and α and β are adjacent

structure-preserving principle syntactic structures must satisfy X'-theory at all levels of representation

Subjacency [Conditions] movement cannot cross more than one bounding node, where the bounding nodes are IP and NP; [Barriers] α is subjacent to β if there is no more than 1 barrier between α and β

SUBJECT the SUBJECT of a clause is AGR if there is one, otherwise the [Spec, IP] or [Spec, NP]

subject/object asymmetry differential behavior of subjects and objects with respect to some grammatical phenomenon

subset relation one language is properly included within another language

superior α is superior to β if every maximal projection dominating α dominates β but not conversely

superiority condition constraint against movement of a *wh*-phrase over another *wh*-phrase that is superior to it

Syntacticization the strategy of taking every phenomenon that is conceivably tied to syntactic structure and characterizing it in syntactic terms

target constituent that undergoes movement

Tensed S Condition [Conditions] no rule can involve X, Y in the structure ... X ... $[_\alpha$ ... Y ...] ... where α is a tensed S

that-t **Filter** statement that the sequence *that-t* is ungrammatical

Thematic Case Thesis the thesis that Abstract Case is a realization of θ-role assignment

θ-**Criterion** [chain version] a chain has at most one θ-position; a θ-position is visible in its maximal chain; [argument version] (*a*) every argument must receive a θ-role; (*b*) every θ-role must be assigned to an argument

θ-**government** α θ-governs β iff α and β are sisters and α assigns a θ-role to β

θ-**role** syntactic representation of the semantic role of an argument

topicalization movement of a constituent to a clause-initial A$'$-position

trace empty copy of a moved constituent

Trace Principle all movements leave traces. Also see Projection Principle

unaccusativity where an NP in argument position lacks (ACCUSATIVE) Case

unergative surface intransitive verb that lacks an underlying direct object

Uniformity the general view that two phenomena that share some properties are the same phenomenon, in part at least, at some level of analysis

unlearnability the learner cannot determine the correct grammar in a finite amount of time

verb second (V2) verb appears in clause-second position

Visibility Condition in order to receive a θ-role, an NP must have Case

VP-Internal Subject Hypothesis hypothesis that $NP_{subject}$ is in [Spec, VP] at D-structure

V-raising movement of V to a functional head

weak crossover a pronoun c-commands the trace of a constituent that appears to the left of it and that contains its antecedent

wh-in-situ *wh*-phrase that does not undergo movement prior to S-structure

wh-**islands** embedded *wh*-questions that block extraction

X$'$ schema characterization of possible structure within a phrase regardless of categories

SOLUTIONS AND HINTS TO SELECTED EXERCISES

CHAPTER 2

2-1.
1. N^{10}, PP^{11}, P^{12}, NP^{13}
2. Adj^6
3. N'^7, N'^4, N'^3, NP^1
4. NP^1
5. PP^5
6. Det^2
7. PP^{11}
8. Det^2, N'^3

2-2.
1. PP^{11}, P^{12}, NP^{13}
2. N'^4, Adj^6, N'^7, N^{10}, PP^{11}, P^{12}, NP^{13}
3. All the nodes dominated by NP^1 except N^{10}.
4. All the nodes dominated by NP^1 except PP^5 and the nodes dominated by PP^5.

2-3.
(1)   *a.* NOMINATIVE Case is assigned to the subject by Infl, using the m-command definition of government.

      b. ACCUSATIVE Case is assigned to the direct object by V, using the m-command definition of government.

      c. ACCUSATIVE Case is assigned to *Mary* by the preposition *to*, using the m-command definition of government.

      d. *Gave* governs and is adjacent to *Mary* and can therefore assign ACCUSATIVE Case; *a book* is not adjacent to the verb and so assignment of Case to it is a problem.

(2)   *a.* NOMINATIVE Case is assigned to the subject by Infl, using the m-command definition of government. *Mary* and *I* must be assigned Case in virtue of being constituents of a conjoined NP to which Case has been assigned.

      b. NOMINATIVE Case is assigned to an NP that is apparently not governed by Infl.

   c. There is no Infl here; hence *me* gets assigned default ACCUSATIVE Case.

   d. There must be phonetically empty Case assigners in the second conjunct.

(3) *a.* There must be a phonetically empty Case assigner (a tensed form of *be* perhaps) that assigns NOMINATIVE to the subject; the predicate agrees in Case with the subject.

   b. Here is the overt version of the Case assigner in (3*a*).

(4) *a.* The ERGATIVE Case is assigned to the entire NP but appears only on the last word.

   b. The constituents of the NP are separated; they each show the same Case, suggesting that the Case is assigned to the full NP, then the constituents are optionally moved, and then the Case is realized overtly.

(5) *a.* We can assume that Japanese has the mirror image structure of English, and that ACCUSATIVE Case is assigned to the left by the verb. NOMINATIVE Case is assigned by Infl, as in English.

   b. What is strange here is that the direct object gets NOMINATIVE instead of ACCUSATIVE Case. Suppose that this is an optional realization of the same Abstract Case.

   c. Same as *a.*

   d. Same as *b.*

   e. GENITIVE Case is assigned to the subject of an NP.

   f. Apparently, NOMINATIVE Case can also be assigned to the subject of an NP.

2-4. Hints:

1. What is the difference between the NPs that are coindexed with *there* in (1)? Can the same difference hold in comparable examples?

2. What is the syntactic difference between the grammatical (2*d*) and the ungrammatical (2*b*)?

3. Look at the trees corresponding to the grammatical and ungrammatical sentences in (3) and (4) and try to determine what structural differences can be correlated with the differences in grammaticality.

2-5. One possibility is that the ACCUSATIVE Case is assigned not by V, but by the node that dominates V and the indirect object. Such an analysis satisfies government and adjacency, but allows non-heads to be Case assigners. Another approach would be to define 'adjacency' in such a way that the direct object is adjacent to the verb even if there is an intervening indirect object.

2-7. It looks from the examples in (1)–(3) that French lacks ECM, but has Case assignment across a maximal projection into small clauses. But example (4) suggests that the ECM construction is possible just in case the subject of the infinitive is relativized and hence moved out of its clause.

CHAPTER 3

3-1.

(1)   *a.* John considers [himself intelligent].
   b. I imagined [myself singing in French].
   c. I insisted [(that) *myself be allowed to speak].

These judgements suggest that small clauses and gerundives are untensed, like infinitives, while subjunctives are tensed, in effect.

3-2.

(1*a*)   The binding conditions apply correctly. The infinitive is the governing category for the pronominals and anaphors. *Himself* (out by Condition A) and *him* (in by Condition B) are free; *herself* (in by Condition A) and *her* (out by Condition B) are bound.

(2*a*)   *His* does not c-command and hence does not bind *John*; Condition C is not violated.

(2*b*)   If the structure is [NP *not even he*] then *he* does not c-command *John* and it is not clear why this sentence is ruled out by Condition C.

(2*c*)   Here it appears that exactly the opposite judgement holds for the sentence (2*b*).

(3*a*)   *Themselves* is not bound by either NP. Condition A applies correctly.

(3*b*)   Condition A should rule this one out.

(4*a*)   The reflexive lacks an antecedent that binds it.

(4*c*)   The reflexive has an antecedent, but the antecedent does not c-command the reflexive.

(5*b*)   The antecedent of the reciprocal appears to be outside of the governing category.

(6*b*)   Condition A should rule in the reflexive and Condition B should rule out the pronoun, but the opposite judgements hold.

3-3. Hint: Can a pronominal subject be referentially dependent on a direct object?

3-5. Hint: Which binding condition(s) appear to be operating here?

*3-6. Hint: The definition of *bind* requires that the antecedent c-command the dependent. To what extent do the required c-command relations hold in these examples? What are the structural assumptions that must be made, and are they plausible?

3-10. In order to account for (1) and (2) we could assume that there are two verbs *want* and two verbs *expect*. One verb takes an IP complement and allows for ECM, the other takes a CP complement and permits ungoverned PRO in the subject.

CHAPTER 4

4-1. Consider the following data. Explain how these data constitute evidence that there is a lexical (that is, an adjectival) passive and a syntactic (that is, a verbal) passive.

(1) shows that true adjectives appear with *act* etc. Passive participles do too, while progressive participles do not.

(2) shows that adjectives can appear with *very*, while verbs require *very much*. Passive participles appear to be both.

4-2.

(1) *a.* Mary was insulted by Susan.

D-structure: e Past be [$_{IP}$ e -en [$_{VP}$ insult Mary [by Susan]]]
Lower -*en*: e Past be [$_{IP}$ e [$_{VP}$ insult+en Mary [by Susan]]]
Move NP: Mary$_i$ Past be [$_{IP}$ t$'_i$ [$_{VP}$ insult+en t$_i$ [by Susan]]]

   b. Mary was expected to win the election.

D-structure: e Past be [$_{IP}$ e -en [$_{VP}$ expect [$_{IP}$ Mary to win election]]]
Lower -*en*: e Past be [$_{IP}$ e [$_{VP}$ expect+en [$_{IP}$ Mary to win election]]]
Move NP: Mary$_i$ Past be [$_{IP}$ t$'_i$ [$_{VP}$ expect+en [$_{IP}$ t$_i$ to win election]]]

(2) *a.* Mary seemed angry.

D-structure: e Past seem [$_{XP}$ Mary angry]
Move NP: Mary$_i$ Past seem [$_{XP}$ t$_i$ angry]

4-3.
1. *un-* goes on adjectives, so it looks like passives are adjectival.
3. The subject of which the *un*-adjective is predicated must be able to appear as the single argument of the passive.

4-4. After the object NP moves into subject position, the resulting chain will have two θ-roles assigned to it, in violation of the θ-Criterion.

4-5. Hint: What are some other consequences of assuming that the complement is CP?

4-6.

(1*a*) *Mary* lacks Case, *Susan* lacks a θ-role.
(1*c*) *Susan* lacks Case.

4-8. Assume that the CP is a complement of the verb. Since it does not get Case, it can appear immediately after the passive verb. NPs cannot, since they require Case. (3*a*) appears to be a problem since it looks like the CP is moving to get Case. But a CP does not need to get Case.

4-9.

1. *there* cannot be a thematic argument, so it cannot be the direct object of *persuade* in the structure [$_{VP}$ *persuade there* [$_{CP}$ *PRO to VP*]].

2. The examples in (1) follow since the subject of the infinitive in each instance lacks Case. The examples in (2) follow if the small clause construction in (2*c*) requires a true subject-predicate relation between the NP (*Susan*) and the predicate (*in the next room*). Since *there* is not referential, nothing can be predicated of it, so (2*d*) is ruled out.

3. Both CP and an *it*...CP chain can function as the subject in the small clause construction (while *there*...NP cannot).

*4-14. Hint: Consider the possibility that there are two verbs *seem* that take different types of complements.

CHAPTER 5

5-1.

(1*b*)   Lexical heads: *England, go, head-to-head, with, Brazil, in, final, match.*
        Functional heads: empty C, *will, the.*
(1*c*)   Lexical heads: *Mary, suggestion, we, quit, was, well-received.*
        Functional heads: D in *Mary's suggestion, that, should.*

5-2.

(1*a*)   Specifier: *our*
        Complement: *(for) our discomfort*
(1*c*)   Specifier: *John*
        Complement: *Mary*
        Adjunct: *deeply*
(1*e*)   Specifier: *this*

5-3.

1. In general English specifiers appear to the left of the head; this particular construction is exceptional and should be treated as such. For example, the subject of a sentence must appear to the left of the predicate, the subject of a small clause must appear to the left of the predicate, the subject of an infinitival must appear to the left, and so on.

2. Hint: One analysis would derive *a book of Bill's* from **a book of Bill's books*. Another would derive *a book of Bill's* from *one/*a [e] of Bill's book(s)*.

5-5.

1. Hint: What mechanisms determine the distribution of NPs?

5-7.

1. At first glance these examples should be grammatical. The fact that they are not poses a problem. Perhaps we could say that DP must dominate N.

2. These examples suggest that sometimes DP need not dominate N, or that in some cases there can be an empty N. But what are the conditions under which this empty N can occur?

5-10. Hint: Does visibility require that an NP with Case have a θ-role?

CHAPTER 6

6-1. In (1) the assumption that there is a trace of *wh* allows us to capture the fact that even when it is moved, *advantage* forms an idiomatic construction with the verb *take*. In (2) the assumption that there is a trace of *wh* allows selectional requirements of the verb *word* to be satisfied configurationally. In (3) the assumption that there is a trace of *wh* (in fact a *wh*-chain) allows us to explain why the fronted *wh*-phrase has the Case assigned to direct object. In (4) the fronted *wh*-phrase acts as though it is in object position with respect to the binding of the reflexive, a fact that is captured by assuming a trace that has the properties of the fronted *wh*-phrase. In (5) the fronted *wh*-phrase acts as though it locally binds the pronominal or anaphor in the lower clause.

6-2.

(1*b*) $[_{CP} [_{Spec} \text{who}_i]$ did $[_{IP}$ you t $[_{VP}$ say $[_{CP} [_{Spec} t'_i] [_C e] [_{IP} \text{Susan will call } t_i]]]]]$

6-4.

(1*a*) *what$_i$* is extracted from a *wh*-island, which is a Subjacency violation. In addition, the subject trace is not properly governed, so there is an ECP violation as well.

(1*c*) *where$_i$* is extracted from an NP complement, which is a Subjacency violation. Its trace is not antecedent governed. Furthermore, since *where$_i$* is an adjunct, its trace is not lexically governed, either, so there is an ECP violation.

(1*d*) *what$_i$* is extracted from a relative clause, which produces a Subjacency violation. There is no ECP violation, because the trace is lexically governed.

6-7. Hint: what are the possible relations between verbs and DPs?

CHAPTER 7

7-1. The BCs are marked with a single box, the barriers with a double box.

(1c)

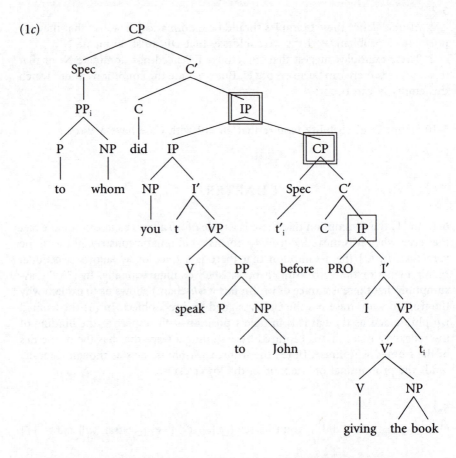

For the movement t_i to t'_i IP is a BC but not a barrier. For the movement t'_i to the higher [Spec, CP] the CP is a BC because it is not L-marked, and it is a barrier. The IP that dominates it is a barrier by inheritance. Hence this movement violates Subjacency. t_i is antecedent governed by t'_i, but t'_i is not antecedent governed by *to whom*, and it is not lexically governed. Hence t'_i is not properly governed and ECP is violated.

(1*h*)

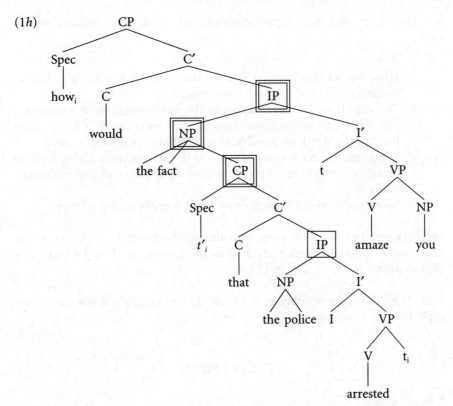

The lower IP is a BC, but not a barrier for the movement t_i to t'_i. The CP complement of *fact* is a barrier because it is not L-marked (by stipulation, since *fact* does assign a θ-role to its complement). The NP that dominates CP is a barrier by inheritance, as is the IP that dominates the NP. Thus the movement of *how*$_i$ to the higher [Spec, CP] violates Subjacency. t'_i is not lexically governed and because of the barriers, it is not antecedent governed either—hence there is an ECP violation.

7-2.

1. Hint: How would Subjacency rule out (1*b*)?

7-7. Hint: Assume that there is an empty complementizer that must be both antecedent governed and lexically governed.

CHAPTER 8

8-1.

(1*a*) [$_{CP}$ [[how many bananas]$_j$ who$_i$]$_i$ [$_{IP}$ t_i bought t_j]]

(1*b*) [$_{CP}$ [$_{IP}$ everyone$_i$ [$_{IP}$ someone$_j$ [t_i loves t_j]]]]

[$_{CP}$ [$_{IP}$ someone$_j$ [$_{IP}$ everyone$_i$ [t_i loves t_j]]]]

8-2. Hint: Construct the LF representation and consider the binding possibilities.

8-8.

(1) *a.* John$_i$ was walking innocently down the street when a heavy picture of himself$_i$ came crashing to the pavement.

    b. The steps that Mary$_i$ has taken over the past few months will guarantee that if it is ever claimed that there are pictures of herself$_i$ for sale in the flea market, it will be possible to successfully bring suit for libel.

    c. Bill$_i$ suggested that it was not going to be easy for Susan and himself$_i$ to break the world's record given the poor equipment that had been made available.

    d. Nasty stories about herself$_i$ make Mary$_i$ feel like hiring a lawyer.

*8-9. Assume that the ECP account of the superiority effect is correct. Given this, what is the evidence that in LF quantifiers adjoin to IP in LF while *wh*-phrases adjoin to [Spec, CP] in LF?

8-10. Hint: move the *wh*-phrases at LF and determine which if any constraints apply to these movements.

CHAPTER 9

9-1.

(1*a*) is a strong crossover violation; it is ruled out by Condition C of the Binding theory, since *he*$_i$ c-commands the trace of *who*$_i$.

(1*b*) is a weak crossover violation.

(1*c*) is a strong crossover violation.

(1*d*) is not a strong crossover violation. It is not a weak crossover violation, either, because the PP *on his desk* is moved from the VP, where it is presumably within the scope of the quantifier.

(1*e*) is a failure of the quantifier to bind the pronoun due to lack of c-command at any level of representation.

9-3, 9-4, 9-5, 9-9. Hint: The data here point to the fact that in English, quantifiers in certain configurations may bind pronouns to the right that they do not c-command. In these cases, there does not appear to be reconstruction; when the pronoun is contained within a constituent that is moved to the left of such a quantifier, binding fails.

NOTES

CHAPTER 1

1. See Chomsky (1965).
2. Here and elsewhere we will ignore the situation in which two grammars generate exactly the same language. If such a situation is possible, then choosing either grammar for the language in question would count as 'learning' in the intended sense.
3. The discussion of this and the next learnability problem is based on Hamburger and Wexler (1973).
4. Technically, we say that the learning procedure *converges* for the class of grammars assumed by Theory of Grammar D.
5. Here we are echoing the sentiment of page 3 of *Syntactic Structures* (Chomsky 1957).
6. See, for example, the work in Generalized Phrase Structure Grammar (GPSG) of Gazdar *et al.* (1985).
7. An early version of this particular hypothesis is the so-called Katz–Postal Hypothesis (Katz and Postal 1964): *transformations do not change meaning*. Katz and Postal hypothesized that all aspects of meaning were determined by 'deep structure'; reordering of parts of this structure would produce particular word orders, but the meaning would not be affected.
8. See for example McCawley (1976).
9. See Chomsky (1970) for a critique.
10. One constituent α of a sentence dominates another constituent β if β is contained in α. So any phrase dominates all of the individual lexical items within it, as well as any phrases of which they are a part.
11. See Kayne (1994).

CHAPTER 2

1. An alternative analysis of the determiners is that they are heads; see Chapter 5 for discussion.
2. Sometimes a lexical item may not be a word; it may be a part of a word or an idiomatic expression consisting of more than one word. We will ignore the distinction here.
3. See Marantz (1984) and the papers in Cole and Sadock (1977) for studies of various case systems.

4. Examples (11*d*)–(11*i*) are from Neidle (1988). The letter *č* is pronounced 'ch' as in English 'chart', the letter *š* is pronounced 'sh' as in the English 'shark', and the letter *ž* is pronounced 'zh' as in the French and English 'azure'.

5. INSTR denotes the instrumental case.

6. For completeness, we note that there is another type of case-marking system: that of Margan^Y (Breen 1981, cited in Blake 1987).

(i)	NOMINATIVE	barri	stone
	ERGATIVE	barringgu	with a stone
	LOCATIVE	barringga	on a stone
	DATIVE	barringu	for a stone
	ALLATIVE	barridhadi	to a stone
	ABLATIVE	barrimundu	from a stone

The ergative case marks the subject of transitives, while nominative marks the subject of an intransitive and the direct object of a transitive.

7. The Case Filter conventionally applies to NPs that are phonetically realized, in contrast with those that are phonetically empty, such as *pro*, PRO, and *t*, all of which will be discussed in later chapters. For present purposes we state the Case Filter as a condition on all NPs.

8. Chomsky (1981).

9. On the other hand, in languages that have a well-developed case system, cases other than NOMINATIVE and ACCUSATIVE can apparently be assigned to subject and object position. We deal with a range of such cases in the Appendix to Chapter 4.

10. Here we draw upon some of the ideas developed in Safir (1985).

11. This analysis of *for* is problematic for those dialects of English in which *for* appears with the infinitive, as in *I want for to go*. In this case, we have a Case assigner without an overt NP or a trace to assign Case to. For discussion, see Henry (1992).

12. In languages such as German that are similar to English but have overt case marking, the indirect object *Susan* receives not ACCUSATIVE Case but DATIVE Case.

(i) *a.* Ich   gab meinem Bruder einen Buch
          I-NOM gave my-DAT brother a-ACC book
     b. *Ich gab meinen Bruder einen Buch
          I-NOM gave my-ACC brother a-ACC book

This overt case marking is a clue that the Abstract Case assigned to the indirect object should not be ACCUSATIVE. If it is not ACCUSATIVE Case, though, the question arises as to why it is not, and how to specify what the correct Case is. See Exercise 2-7.

13. Stowell (1983) has argued that the category of the small clause is the same as the category of the head.
14. The first two sentences in (77) are due to Paul Postal (1974).
15. Stowell (1981).
16. Koster (1978).
17. The grammar of Russian requires that the INSTRUMENTAL case be used when the property expressed by the adjective is not an inherent one.
18. In these Walbiri examples, the sign '-' is used to link an inflectional morpheme to the root, while '=' is used to link a non-inflectional clitic morpheme to another morphemic complex.

CHAPTER 3

1. This sentence is not as bad as (13a). To explore this fact, see Exercise 3-14.
2. For present purposes we may take a specified subject to be an overt lexical NP; Chomsky's original formulation is somewhat more complex.
3. By the same token, a pronoun can have an antecedent when it is in the subject position of a tensed S, while it cannot when it is in subject position of an infinitive or in the same clause as its antecedent. The technical device for achieving this result is to suppose that a pronoun and an NP are marked as disjoint in reference pairwise. This marking is blocked by TSC and SSC, so that we get the following.

   (i) *a.* *Mary$_i$ likes her$_i$.
        b. Mary$_i$ likes her$_j$.
        c. Mary$_i$ expects that she$_i$ will win.
        d. Mary$_i$ expects us to like her$_i$.

4. It also fails to m-command the anaphor. For simplicity we develop our account in terms of the narrower c-command relation.
5. Evans (1980) notes cases such as the following.

   (i) Few Congressmen$_i$ were at the party and they$_i$ were drunk.

   Here, the antecedent of the pronoun is a quantified NP, but there is co-reference, not binding. Here, the quantified NP is understood as denoting the same set as the pronoun.
6. Notice that these examples are also violations of the condition that an R-expression must be free.
7. We are assuming, of course, that there is no fundamental principle to the effect that a closer antecedent excludes a more distant one. If such a generalization is true, it follows in this theory from the way that the domain is defined in terms of government.

8. e.g. Jelinek and Demers (1994).

9. Strictly speaking we should distinguish between this coindexing and the coindexing that indicates coreference; see Borer (1986*b*).

10. In this regard, the treatment of Agr diverges from the analysis of agreement morphology as expressing the grammatical relations, since in English, at least, the grammatical relation of SUBJECT is expressed in a non-uniform fashion if we assume that Agr is a subject.

11. Chomsky (1981).

12. This approach is due to Chomsky (1986*b*) and based on Huang (1983).

13. Chomsky (1986*b*).

14. This statement is a close paraphrase of Chomsky's (1986*b*) formulation.

15. Chomsky (1986*b*) makes a proposal along these lines.

16. The application of Uniformity to subjects is called the **Extended Projection Principle**.

17. These examples are due to Lasnik and Uriagareka (1988).

CHAPTER 4

1. See Chomsky (1957; 1965; 1970; 1973; 1981).

2. We cannot rule out the possibility of a more elaborated lexical analysis that will account for the idiomatic interpretation, as has been proposed in Head-driven Phrase Structure Grammar, or HPSG (Pollard and Sag 1994). Such an analysis refers directly to the grammatical relations of the various arguments, a device that is not allowed in GB theory. On such an analysis, all of the properties of the object in the active can be associated with the subject of the passive, including the possibility of an idiomatic interpretation or its function as the subject of an ECM infinitive.

3. Again, an account that refers to the grammatical relations of the arguments can accommodate a lexical account.

4. For some speakers, sentences such as these are much improved when the indirect object is a pronoun, as in (i).

(i) ?The book was given her by John.

Why the pronoun is better than the full NP in this position is an open question.

5. This analysis of the passive in terms of Case is due to Jaeggli (1986).

6. The term 'rationale clause' is due to Faraci (1974).

7. These examples are adapted from Keyser and Roeper (1984).

8. It is to be understood here that the person doing the bribing is acting deliberately, not the bureaucrats.

9. This example is attributed by Keyser and Roeper to R. Manzini.

10. This analysis is due to Jaeggli (1986).
11. As proposed by Baker, Johnson, and Roberts (1989).
12. The following formulation is from Rizzi (1986).
13. Including LF (see Chapter 8).
14. The fact that *John washed* means *John washed himself* could be taken to be evidence that a single NP can have two θ-roles. See Exercise 4-7.
15. The formulation we are using here is due to Chomsky (1986*b*: 97).
16. Chomsky (1986*b*: 135).
17. Examples based on Radford (1988: 440).
18. These examples, in particular (38*b*), should not be confused with cases involving *as if, as though* and *like*, as in

    (i)   John seems $\begin{Bmatrix} \text{as if} \\ \text{as though} \\ \text{like} \end{Bmatrix}$ he is hungry.

    If *seem* in this case is a Raising verb, it constitutes a difficulty for our analysis (see Exercise 4-11). But there is evidence that this *seem* is not a Raising verb, and is closely related to verbs like *act, behave,* and *look* (see Exercise 4-12).
19. Chomsky (1982).
20. See Chapter 6, § 4.3.
21. There are other ways in which chains can be formed, also (e.g. Rizzi 1986 and Frampton 1990).
22. The terminology is due to Perlmutter (1978).
23. The data here are taken from Belletti and Rizzi (1981).
24. Some of the details here are assumed for convenience, in particular, that the derived subject actually moves to the VP, leaving a trace in subject position. For a detailed discussion of the phenomenon of postverbal subjects in Italian, see Rizzi (1982) and Burzio (1986).
25. Burzio (1986). The pattern captured by this generalization was first observed by Perlmutter (1978).
26. This biconditional form of Burzio's generalization as stated by Burzio is probably too strong. It claims that if a θ-role is assigned to the subject position, ACCUSATIVE Case is assigned to some other position. This appears to rule out the existence of simple intransitives, where the D-structure subject is assigned a θ-role and NOMINATIVE Case. A weaker and less uncontroversial statement is that a verb that assigns ACCUSATIVE Case to its object assigns a θ-role to its subject. There are clear counterexamples even to this weaker claim, as noted by Borer (1986*b*). Consider the following examples from Spanish.

    (i)   *a.* Hay　　montañas　en Sudamerica.
    　　　　exist-SG　mountains　in　South-America
    　　　　'There are mountains in South America.'

      b. Montañas bonita, las   hay en Sudamerica.
        mountains nice   them   exist in South-America
        'As for nice mountains, there are such in South America.'

Borer points out that the clitic *las* in (i.*b*) is evidence that the verb assigns ACCUSATIVE Case. There is no θ-role assigned to the subject, which is occupied by an empty expletive *pro.*

27. The following discussion is based in part on Tsujimura (1989) and on Nakayama (1991).
28. This proposal is due to Miyagawa (1989).
29. There are a number of ways of implementing this idea. Following May (1985), we could say that the adjoined constituent is not dominated by VP unless it is dominated by all segments of VP. So in (i), α is not dominated by VP, while β is.

(i)

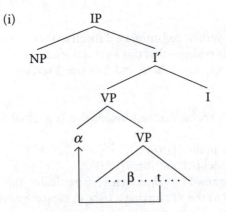

Then, taking c-command to be m-command, it follows that something adjoined to VP is dominated by exactly the maximal projections that dominate the subject, and hence the adjoined constituent c-commands the subject. For example, the only maximal projection that dominates α in (i) is IP, which also dominates NP. Hence α m-commands NP even though α is adjoined to VP.

    Miyagawa (1989) avoids this issue by assuming that the subject, the NQ, and the VP are sisters.

30. We ignore here the additional complication of the ergative case-marking pattern.
31. The discussion of Case in Russian draws heavily on the analysis in Neidle (1988).
32. Neidle (1988).
33. See Borras and Christian (1959).
34. This discussion of Icelandic is based on the analysis of Maling and Zaenen (1990*b*) and Zaenen, Maling, and Thráinsson (1990).

35. Zaenen, Maling, and Thráinsson (1990).
36. Zaenen, Maling, and Thráinsson (1990).
37. Unless the stories are Mary's stories, in which case the reflexive is grammatical.
38. See Grimshaw (1990) for discussion.
39. The analysis is essentially that of Belletti and Rizzi (1988).
40. See Belleti and Rizzi (1988) for elaboration of this analysis for Italian. For still another view, see Pesetsky (1987). For a very different view, in which the antecedent-anaphor relation is licensed in part by the θ-roles assigned to the two NPs, see Jackendoff (1972).

CHAPTER 5

1. See Kayne (1994).
2. See Greenberg (1963).
3. Greenberg (1963).
4. Jelinek and Demers (1994).
5. Lummi is a Straits Salish language. The Straits Salish languages are spoken in the Pacific Northwest of North America.
6. In these examples the symbol '=' is used to indicate a morpheme boundary.
7. If we consider *do* as a modal, then it is an exception to this statement.
8. Chomsky (1957).
9. The explanation will involve either raising of V and adjoining it to each of the morphological heads in turn, until it reaches C, or lowering each of the morphological heads onto V in an ordering that reflects the hierarchical structure. See Baker (1988) for discussion.
10. See Baker (1988), Chomsky (1993).
11. In fact, even if we do not assume movement, there must be positions for the clause-initial NP and for the inverted Infl that are distinct from their positions in non-interrogatives. This is because under X'-theory, a head must appear in a head position; it cannot be adjoined to a phrase.
12. For discussion of questions in Hibernian English, see McCloskey (1992).
13. It is worth noting that the negative focus follows the *that*-complementizer, while the embedded *wh*-phrase precedes it. There is no satisfactory account of this puzzle in the literature, although there have been many proposals. See Further Readings.
14. Earlier work in X'-theory proposed that VP assigns its external θ-role directly to [Spec, IP], under an extended definition of sister; see Chomsky (1986*b*).

    (i) α and β are sisters if all lexical categories that dominate one dominate the other.

    In the configuration in (ii), VP does not c-command [Spec, IP], but there is no lexical category that dominates only one and not the other, so VP and the subject are sisters under this definition.

(ii)

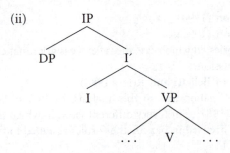

It is then possible to assign the external θ-role associated with the VP to the subject on the basis of the fact that the subject is the sister of the VP.

This extended definition of sister undermines the intention of the branching structure, which is that sisters are immediately dominated by the same node. Constituents adjoined to VP, I', or IP are all sisters of VP, on this extended definition, as well as of DP. While a solution in terms of an extended notion of sister may be technically workable, there may also be unintended consequences of using this definition of sister.

15. Proposed on the basis of different considerations by Kitagawa (1986), Kuroda (1988), Koopman and Sportiche (1991), and others.

16. Sportiche (1988).

17. Diesing (1990).

18. This DP analysis was first proposed by Abney (1987). It is interesting to note the parallelism between (54) and (37). Both have a lexical projection as the complement of a functional head. We might speculate that this is the general pattern for all categories. For some discussion, see Grimshaw (1991).

19. Fukui (1986) proposes a mixed theory, in which functional categories have obligatory specifiers, while lexical categories only have specifiers when an appropriate constituent is adjoined in specifier position.

20. There is some minor evidence, though, that there is an empty complement even in the case of fully intransitive verbs. See Exercise 6-8.

21. This point is noted by Speas (1990).

22. Due to Speas (1990).

23. We have eliminated a systematic ambiguity in Speas's definition between the use of the variables X and G to refer to nodes in a tree and to refer to their labels.

24. The level called L(ogical) F(orm). We explore the properties of this level in Chapters 8 through 10.

25. Proposed by Fukui (1986).

26. Travis (1984).

27. This Agr may be different from the Agr introduced in the Binding theory in order to develop the notion of accessible SUBJECT. See Chapter 3.

28. The comma after *did* in this example and the other *b*-examples indicates that for the sentence to be grammatical, it must have slight emphasis on the auxiliary to the left of the comma and emphasis on what follows the comma.

Some speakers do not share this intuition, and find the *b*-examples to be ungrammatical.

29. We rule out the possibility that there is postposing out of the topicalized phrase, as illustrated in (i).

(i) ... and he did [drink the coffee hot] ⇒
    ... and [drink the coffee hot] he did ⇒
    ... and [drink the coffee t] he did, hot

The postposed constituent would have to be adjoined to CP, since it would be moving out of [Spec, CP]. Hence it would follow IP adjuncts.

(ii)

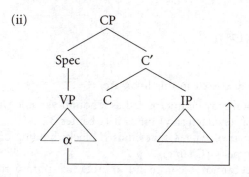

There is some evidence to support our decision to rule out this possibility. A *without*-clause is subject controlled, and can thus be argued to be adjoined only to IP and not to VP.

(iii) a. I lifted him without injuring myself.
     b. *I lifted him without injuring himself.

The following examples show that it is at best marginally grammatical to postpose a constituent of VP to the right of a *without*-clause.

(iv) a. ??He gave presents without embarrassing himself to his friends.
     b. ??Leslie put some money without hurting himself on the table.
     c. *Leslie gave Mary without embarrassing himself a book about ostriches.
     d. *Leslie drank the coffee without hurting himself hot.

Topicalization does not improve the postposing, suggesting that whatever postposing takes place is restricted to VP and cannot escape VP after VP has moved to [Spec, CP].

(v) a. ?? ... and give presents he did without embarrassing himself to his friends.

    b. ?? . . . and put some money Leslie did without hurting himself on
    the table.

    c. * . . . and give Mary Leslie did without embarrassing himself a
    book about ostriches.

    d. * . . . and drink the coffee Leslie did without hurting himself hot.

30. This constraint may explain why *do so* does not apply simply to a transitive
verb, as in

    (i)   *Leslie read the book and Mary did so the magazine.

31. Due to Kayne (1984).
32. See Barss and Lasnik (1986).
33. See Perlmutter and Postal (1983).
34. Bresnan (1982*a*).
35. Pollard and Sag (1994).
36. Other phenomena that are discussed in this book are:

- *Variable binding*: a pronoun may be interpreted as a bound variable with
respect to a quantifier that (syntactically) binds it (Chapter 3).
- *Relativized Minimality*: an α of type X that binds β blocks binding of β
by a more distant α' of type X (Chapter 7, § 7).
- *Superiority*: a *wh*-phrase cannot c-command another *wh*-phrase that
c-commands its trace (Chapter 8, § 5).
- *Weak crossover*: a *wh*-phrase or a quantifier cannot bind two variables
unless one variable binds the other (Chapter 9, § 2).
- *Parasitic gaps*: a true gap cannot bind a parasitic gap, and vice versa (Chapter 6, § 7).

37. Pollard and Sag (1992; 1994).
38. We adapt and simplify some of the HPSG terminology for ease of exposition.
39. Originally noted by Postal (1971).
40. Jackendoff (1972; 1992) offers a similar account of these data in terms of a
hierarchy stated over thematic relations, not grammatical relations.
41. The morphemes glossed as numerals identify particular noun classes.
42. Grimshaw (1979).

CHAPTER 6

1. A$'$ is read as 'A-bar'.
2. Pied Piping is discussed in Ross (1967); the relevant portion of Ross (1967)
appears in the excerpt in Harman (1974). Ross himself attributes the term
to Robin Lakoff. In the ancient story, the Pied Piper led all of the rats out
of the city of Hamelin after him, while he played his pipes. When the city
refused to pay for his services, he led out all the children, too.

3. We return to the issue raised here in Chapter 9 in connection with reconstruction phenomena.

4. Webelhuth (1989).

5. This formulation differs from the one introduced in Chapter 3 in that the current one does not require that each member of the chain be *locally* c-commanded. We will show in the course of the discussion why local c-command is also a requirement of chain links.

6. See Chomsky (1980).

7. The ungrammaticality of (21*c*) also follows if the trace of *wh* is pronominal. The trace is locally bound and hence would violate Condition B. However, the trace of *wh* cannot be pronominal in general because it does not predict the ungrammaticality of the following sentence.

   (i)   *Who$_i$ did he$_i$ think that you saw t$_i$?

   The trace is not locally bound by *he$_i$*, and therefore Condition B does not apply. Only Condition C of the Binding theory accounts for this example.

8. See Chapter 2, § 1.2.

9. May (1985); Rizzi (1991).

10. See Rudin (1988) for discussion.

11. Rudin adapts a proposal along the same lines by Lasnik and Saito (1984) for Polish.

12. Roughly speaking, a clitic is an element that is syntactically autonomous, but morphologically bound. Clitics frequently function as pronominals and cannot appear in argument position. The following examples show that in French, clitics must be adjoined to the left of the verb.

    (i)   *French*:
          a. Je vois Jean.
             I   see   Jean
             'I see Jean.'
          b. Je le   vois.
             I him see
             'I see him.'
          c. *Je vois le.
          d. *Je Jean vois.

13. May (1985).

14. Chomsky (1973). One of Ross's constraints, the Coordinate Structure Constraint, is not dealt with in the Conditions framework and in most subsequent work in GB.

    (i)   Coordinate Structure Constraint (CSC): In a coordinate structure, no conjunct may be moved, nor may any element contained in a conjunct be moved out of that conjunct. (Ross 1974: 181)

The constraint appears to fall into a different category than the other constraints, since it allows parallel extraction from conjoined structures but not single extraction from one conjunct.

(ii)   *a.* I washed my car and vacuumed my car.
   b. This is the car that I washed t and vacuumed t.
(iii)   *a.* I washed my motorcycle and vacuumed my car.
   b. *This is the car that I washed my motorcycle and vacuumed t.

For some attempts to derive the CSC from more general principles, see Gazdar *et al.* (1985) and Goodall (1984).

15. For discussion see Chomsky (1986*b*).
16. Not all embedded *wh*-questions constitute islands to extraction. Cf.

(i)   *a.* This is the car which$_i$ I was wondering whether or not to buy t$_i$.
   b. Of all the people I know, John is the only one who$_i$ I seriously wonder how I can avoid offending t$_i$.

Such examples clearly constitute counterexamples to any absolute characterization of *wh*-island. In Italian, simple extraction from a *wh*-question does not produce ungrammaticality. Rizzi (1982) proposed that the set of bounding nodes in Italian is different than in English. Chomsky (1981: 159) notes that the *wh*-island condition can be 'relaxed' in some cases in English, and suggests that the grammars of some speakers of English have the characterization of bounding nodes found in Italian. This still does not explain why some extractions are more grammatical than others, even for a single speaker. See also Chomsky's (1986*b*: 36–9) inconclusive speculations along the same lines within the *Barriers* framework. A non-transformational approach to the problems of Subjacency islands is pursued by Pollard and Sag (1994), who judge the extractions from *wh*-questions to be in general syntactically well formed but in some cases pragmatically anomalous.

17. If the subject CP of this sentence is exhaustively dominated by NP, as in (i), extraction from the sentential subject will violate Subjacency.

(i)   *[$_{CP}$ who$_i$ would [$_{IP}$ [$_{NP}$ [$_{CP}$ t′$_i$ that John saw t$_i$]] surprise Susan]]

However, this structure violates X′-theory, since NP lacks a head.

18. Proposed by Chomsky and Lasnik (1977). Chomsky and Lasnik did attempt to explain the filter in terms of psychologically motivated 'perceptual strategies.'
19. As noted by Pesetsky (1982*b*).
20. The assumption made here is that *whether* and *if* are complementizers, not *wh*-specifiers.
21. See Kayne (1980), Chomsky (1981).

22. Chomsky (1977) proposes that in topicalization the topic itself does not move. Rather, the topic is in a left-adjoined position, and an empty operator moves, as described in the next section.
23. The earliest proposal along these lines is that of Chomsky (1977).
24. See Chapter 7, § 2.
25. As Ross (1967) showed.
26. This construction is also called Heavy NP Shift.
27. See Rochemont and Culicover (1990).
28. Williams (1994) and Postal (1994) argue that what appears to be a parasitic gap in the case of Heavy NP Shift is actually produced by Right Node Raising, illustrated in (i).

    (i) John buys, and I like to cook, garbanzo beans.

    On this analysis, the shared constituent is in, or functions as though it is in, its original argument position. RNR is typically found in coordinate structures; the novelty of the Postal/Williams proposal is that it also is found in non-coordinate structures such as (ii).

    (ii) John bought without cooking the garbanzo beans now in the pantry.

29. Culicover and Rochemont (1990).
30. There are some relatively well-formed examples that appear to contradict the claim that the parasitic gap appears in a position that could not be produced by movement into the main clause.

    (i) *a.* This is a book which$_i$ you should never go anywhere without reading t$_i$
    b. This is the kind of meat that OP$_i$ Robin always gets sick after eating t$_i$.

31. As first shown by Kayne (1983).
32. Chomsky (1982).
33. Chomsky (1986*b*).
34. Chomsky (1986*b*).

CHAPTER 7

1. Huang (1982).
2. Aoun *et al.* (1987) argue that extraction of an adjunct across a *that*-complementizer produces a weak ungrammaticality effect, as illustrated in (i).

    (i) *a.* why do you believe John left
    b. why do you believe that John left

The claim is that while (i.*a*) is ambiguous, (i.*b*) is not. Many speakers apparently do not share these judgements. See Exercise 8-11 for further exploration of this issue.

3. This is a slight simplification of the formulation in Chomsky (1986*b*).

4. Chomsky (1981).

5. See Chomsky (1986*b*).

6. Bresnan (1977: 194 n. 6) judges cases such as these to be 'mildly awkward.' The theoretical importance of such cases is discussed by Culicover (1993).

7. See Chomsky (1986*b*).

8. The notion of segments of a projection is due to May (1985).

9. Noted by Rizzi (1990).

10. Ross (1983).

11. Following Jaeggli (1982).

12. A fact that is not accounted for in any of these treatments is the fact that except when what is extracted is a direct object, the presence of the *that*-complementizer usually introduces a very slight degree of ungrammaticality. Example (65) is better without *that* than with it. But see also note 2.

13. Here we adapt the analysis of Cinque (1990), which closely resembles that of Rizzi (1990) in a number of important respects.

14. CED effects do not follow from Relativized Minimality, but must be accounted for separately in this theory.

15. Cinque (1990) presents a somewhat different but related view, in which there are strong and weak barriers, with different effects on extraction.

16. Such an analysis is proposed by Frampton (1990), which we summarize here.

17. For a fuller discussion of canonical government, see § A.1.

18. The judgements shown here are the predicted ones. Some native speakers find examples such as those in (92) less than fully ungrammatical.

19. Such a notion has been suggested by Grimshaw in unpublished work.

20. Cinque uses the expression 'not distinct from [+V]' to cover the cases of selection by C and I.

21. The data here is from Cinque (1990). Similar constructions can be found in Dutch (Van Haaften, Smits, and Vat 1983) and Greek (Tsimpli 1995).

CHAPTER 8

1. The reading in (1*c*) is not possible in all languages. At the present time there is no satisfactory explanation for the fact that scope ambiguity occurs in some languages but not in others.

2. May (1985).

3. This conclusion assumes that either the stipulation in Chomsky (1986*b*) against adjunction to IP is invalid (as it is in Lasnik and Saito 1992) or that it does not apply at LF.

4. It is possible that some instances of empty operator movement must also be analyzed as adjunction to IP.
5. Lasnik and Saito (1992).
6. There are two other possibilities that also need to be considered, though. First, it is possible that there is an empty functional head T(opic) that licenses the movement of the topic, as illustrated in (i).

(i) I think $[_{CP}$ that $[_{TP} [_{Spec} [_{DP}$ bananas like these$]_i]$ T $[_{IP}$ you should never buy $t_i]]]$

Second, it is possible that CP can iterate, as in (ii).

(ii) I think $[_{CP}$ that $[_{CP} [_{Spec} [_{DP}$ bananas like these$]_i]$ C $[_{IP}$ you should never buy $t_i]]]$

We leave the choice open here.
7. The crucial examples and their import are taken from Kayne (1984: ch. 2).
8. The judgements reported here are less restrictive than those of Hornstein (1984; see also Hornstein and Weinberg 1990).
9. For discussion, see Fiengo and May (1994: ch. 5).
10. See Jackendoff (1972).
11. Fiengo and May (1994).
12. The terminology presumes the transformational approach, but the phenomenon is problematic for either a transformational or an interpretative account of ellipsis.
13. The term is due to Hornstein (1994).
14. Pointed out by Baltin (1987).
15. This argument is due to Hornstein (1994).
16. See Chapter 10, § 3.
17. These data are taken from Bondre (1993), and also are discussed in Manzini and Wexler (1987).
18. These data are from Manzini and Wexler (1987).
19. Examples taken from Manzini and Wexler (1987).
20. For discussion of this phenomenon, see Sells (1987) and references cited there.
21. See Everaert (1991) for discussion.
22. Suggested in recent work by Reinhart and Reuland (1991; 1993).
23. Assuming, by Uniformity, that the complementizer of a question in any language will be C[+wh].
24. The following discussion is based closely on the data and the analysis in Huang (1982).
25. Due to Baker (1970).
26. In Exercise 8-4 we consider whether LF extraction of *wh* in English multiple *wh*-questions obeys Subjacency.

27. Huang (1982).
28. This is a slight restatement of Chomsky's original formulation.
29. May (1985).
30. Pesetsky (1987).
31. Pesetsky attributes the superiority effect to the fact that the two lines of dependency cross, an approach that is further developed in May (1985). On this approach, the apparent ECP violation arises when the path from one *wh*-phrase to its trace is not contained entirely within the path from the other *wh*-phrase to its trace. The following illustrates for the sentence *what did who say*.

(i)   who$_j$ what$_i$ t$_j$ say t$_i$

CHAPTER 9

1. Or if it does, its effects can be undone later, at S-structure.
2. These terms are taken from Heim (1982).
3. For remarks along similar lines, see Chomsky (1993).
4. This approach is adapted from Barss (1986).
5. These arguments are adapted from Lasnik and Uriagareka (1988).
6. Van Riemsdijk and Williams (1981) suggest that there is a level of representation after move NP at which the Binding theory applies, called NP Structure.
7. Huang (1993).
8. See Diesing (1992) for such a claim in a different context.
9. Watanabe (1992); Chomsky (1993).
10. Here we are developing and modifying an idea of Lebeaux (1988).
11. Such a view was originally developed by Chomsky (1955).
12. Such a device is explored by Haïk (1984) for this and other cases.
13. Chomsky (1977).
14. As noted originally by Wasow (1972; 1979).

CHAPTER 10

1. This discussion presumes that there could in principle be empirical consequences of adjoining the head in different places in the structure. In the absence of such empirical consequences, the alternative adjunction sites would be equivalent, and there would be no learning problem; any choice would be equally empirically adequate.
2. For investigation of the possibility that there can be non-local head movement, see Lema and Rivero (1990; 1991) and Rivero (1991; 1994).

3. Here we are loosely following the ideas of Chomsky (1993) and Chomsky (1994).

4. Assuming, of course, that V does not independently move to the left of [Spec, AgrOP] prior to Spell-Out.

5. We say 'for the most part' because of the possibility that true long movements exist. See the discussion in Chapter 6 of the Relativized Minimality framework (§ 7) and weak and strong barriers (Appendix A). If such movements cannot be reanalyzed as sequences of maximally local short movements, then they constitute a problem for the version of the MP that we are currently entertaining.

6. These ideas are very close to those put forward by Speas (1990); see Chapter 5, § 3.4.

7. See Chomsky (1994: 11).

8. CED violations cannot be accounted for in terms of Chomsky's (1995) proposal.

9. Chomsky (1993; 1994).

10. This explanation is lost in the approach of Chomsky (1995: 332). On that approach, verbs in English undergo raising to a higher 'light' verb, which produces the order V-Adv-XP.

(i) v [Adv [V XP]] $\Rightarrow$
      V+v [Adv [t XP]]

(We discuss some of the motivations for this type of verb raising in § 5.) If XP is a DP, it cannot undergo movement to license Case because of the intervening Adv, on Chomsky's account. However, the same principle would appear to block the licensing of Case on the DP in French, as well, which is the incorrect result. V-Adv-NP is the only possible sequence in French.

11. Observed by Barss and Lasnik (1986).

12. For some speakers the movement of an indirect object to an A'-position produces ungrammaticality.

13. An alternative hypothesis is that the higher verb is 'light'; that is, it is a dummy verb that adds little if anything to the interpretation and nothing to the phonological output, but it is nevertheless a verb with a lexical entry.

14. These are adapted from Chomsky (1993).

15. Kayne (1994) formulates the relation derived from asymmetric c-command as that of a linear ordering, which is technically distinct from linear precedence. The linear ordering is then correlated with the 'precedes' relation. Since there appears to be no particular advantage in the more abstract formulation, our discussion directly correlates asymmetric c-command with linear precedence.

16. $a \in d(A)$ means that a is in the set of elements in d(A).

17. The situation is actually somewhat more complicated. The demonstration that every constituent has one and only one head follows if there is an

independent characterization of what the possible phrase markers are. But the definition of what the phrase markers are involves such notions as 'projection', 'complement', 'specifier', and 'head', so that it is not clear that there can be a projection without a head, quite independently of antisymmetry.

18. All of the examples are from Zwart (1993).

19. In such languages, LF *wh*-Movement cannot be substitution for [Spec, CP], but it could be adjunction to the IP in [Spec, CP].

20. The next few paragraphs follow closely the discussion in Rochemont and Culicover (to appear).

21. There are those who do not share our judgements about this example. To us the difference in grammaticality illustrated here is very sharp.

22. There is some evidence that these are not true parasitic gaps, as pointed out by Postal (1994) and Williams (1994). Note first that Heavy Shift out of PPs is impossible.

   (i) *I was talking to t_i last night [some people that I met at the concert]$_i$.

Compare this example with (ii).

   (ii) I was talking to __ last night without really convincing __ [some people that I met at the concert]

The relative acceptability of (ii) suggests that the apparent parasitic gaps are due not to A′-movement, but to a phenomenon known as Right Node Raising (RNR). RNR does not involve movement, but rather deletion of material under identity with material to the right of it. In (iii), for example, the deleted material appears in a relative clause, which would block extraction.

   (iii) I know people who like __, and Mary knows people who absolute adore, the Beatles.

23. Kayne (1994) proposes an alternative, in which everything in the VP independently moves to the left of the heavy DP and the V moves to a position in which it c-commands everything else. But this derivation suffers from the problem raised above that the heavy DP is *in situ* in argument position and therefore lacks the adjunct properties that we have identified.

REFERENCES

Note on availability of materials: To the greatest extent possible, references are limited to published materials. In some cases the source of unpublished materials is indicated. The addresses of two major sources are:

MIT Working Papers in Linguistics
Department of Linguistics and Philosophy
Room 20D-219
MIT
Cambridge, MA 02139
USA
email: MITWPL@mit.edu
phone: 617-253-7370
WWW: http://broca.mit.edu/mitwpl.web/WPL-volumes-files/WPL12.html

University of Massachusetts Graduate Student Linguistics Association
Department of Linguistics
South College Building
University of Massachusetts
Amherst, MA 01003
USA

ABNEY, STEVEN (1987), 'The Noun Phrase in its Sentential Aspect', unpublished doctoral dissertation, MIT, Cambridge, Mass. (available from MIT Working Papers in Linguistics).

ABRAHAM, WERNER (ed.) (1983), *On the Formal Syntax of the Westgermania*, John Benjamins, Amsterdam.

—— KOSMEIJER, WIM, and REULAND, ERIC (eds.) (1991), *Issues in Germanic Syntax*, Mouton de Gruyter, Berlin.

ACKEMA, PETER, and SCHOORLEMMER, MAAIKE (1995), 'Middles and Nonmovement', *Linguistic Inquiry*, 26: 173–97.

ADAMS, MARIANNE (1985), 'Government of Empty Subjects in Factive Clause Complements', *Linguistic Inquiry*, 16: 305–13.

AIKAWA, TAKAKO (1993), 'Reflexivity in Japanese and LF-Analysis of *zibun*-Binding', unpublished doctoral dissertation, The Ohio State University, Columbus, Oh. (available from MIT Working Papers in Linguistics).

ANDERSON, STEVEN, and KIPARSKY, PAUL (eds.) (1973), *Festschrift for Morris Halle*, Holt, Rinehart & Winston, New York.

AOUN, JOSEPH (1985), *A Grammar of Anaphora*, MIT Press, Cambridge, Mass.

AOUN, JOSEPH (1986), *Generalized Binding*, Foris Press, Dordrecht.

—— HORNSTEIN, NORBERT, LIGHTFOOT, DAVID, and WEINBERG, AMY (1987), 'Two Types of Locality', *Linguistic Inquiry*, 8: 537–77.

—— and LI, YEN-HUI AUDREY (1993), '*Wh*-Elements in Situ: Syntax or LF?', *Linguistic Inquiry*, 24: 199–238.

—— and SPORTICHE, DOMINIQUE (1983), 'On the Formal Theory of Government', *Linguistic Review*, 2: 211–36.

AUTHIER, J.-MARC (1991), 'V-Governed Expletives, Case Theory, and the Projection Principle', *Linguistic Inquiry*, 22: 721–40.

—— (1992), 'Iterated CPs and Embedded Topicalization', *Linguistic Inquiry*, 23: 329–36.

BABBY, LEONARD (1980), *Existential Sentences and Negation in Russian*, Karoma Publishers, Ann Arbor.

BACH, EMMON (1977), 'Review of Paul M. Postal, *On Raising*', *Language*, 53: 621–54.

BAKER, LEE (1970), 'Notes on the Description of English Questions: The Role of an Abstract Question Morpheme', *Foundations of Language*, 6: 197–219.

BAKER, MARK (1988), *Incorporation: A Theory of Grammatical Function Changing*, University of Chicago Press, Chicago.

—— JOHNSON, KYLE, and ROBERTS, IAN (1989), 'Passive Arguments Raised', *Linguistic Inquiry*, 20: 219–51.

BALTIN, MARK R. (1982), 'A Landing Site Theory of Movement Rules', *Linguistic Inquiry*, 13: 1–38.

—— (1987), 'Do Antecedent-Contained Deletions Exist?', *Linguistic Inquiry*, 18: 579–95.

—— and KROCH, ANTHONY S. (eds.) (1989), *Alternative Conceptions of Phrase Structure*, University of Chicago Press, Chicago.

BARSS, ANDREW (1986), 'Chains and Anaphoric Dependence: On Reconstruction and its Implications', unpublished doctoral dissertation, MIT, Cambridge, Mass.

—— and LASNIK, HOWARD (1986), 'A Note on Anaphora and Double Objects', *Linguistic Inquiry*, 7: 347–54.

BATES, DAWN (ed.) (1991), *Proceedings of the Tenth West Coast Conference on Formal Linguistics*, Center for the Study of Language and Information, Stanford, Calif.

BATTISTELLA, ED (1983), 'A Subjacency Puzzle', *Linguistic Inquiry*, 14: 698–704.

BAYER, JOSEF, and KORNFILT, JAKLIN (1991), 'Against Scrambling as Move-Alpha', in *Proceedings of the Twenty-First Annual Meeting of the North Eastern Linguistics Society*, University of Massachusetts, Amherst, Mass.: 1–16.

BELLETTI, ADRIANA (1988), 'The Case of Unaccusatives', *Linguistic Inquiry*, 19: 1–34.

—— BRANDI, L., and RIZZI, LUIGI (eds.) (1981), *Theory of Markedness in Generative Grammar*, Scuola Normale Superiore, Pisa.

—— and RIZZI, LUIGI (1988), 'Psych-Verbs and Th-Theory', *Natural Language and Linguistic Theory*, 6: 291–352.

BENNIS, HANS, and HAEGEMAN, LILIANE (1984), 'On the Status of Agreement and Relative Clauses in West-Flemish', Proceedings of the International Conference held at UFSAL, Brussels, June 1983, in Wim de Geest and Yvan Putseys (eds.), *Sentential Complementation*, Foris Publications, Dordrecht: 33–53.

—— and HOEKSTRA, TEUN (1984), 'Gaps and Parasitic Gaps', *Linguistic Review*, 4: 29–87.

BERWICK, ROBERT (1985), *The Acquisition of Syntactic Knowledge*, MIT Press, Cambridge, Mass.

BLAKE, BARRY (1987), *Australian Aboriginal Grammar*, Croom Helm, London.

BONDRE, PRIYA (1993), 'Parameter Setting and the Binding Theory: No Subset Problem', in Gisbert Fanselow (ed.), *The Parametrization of Universal Grammar*, John Benjamins, Amsterdam: 17–35.

BORER, HAGIT (ed.) (1986a), *Syntax and Semantics 19: The Syntax of Pronominal Clitics*, Academic Press, New York.

—— (1986b) 'I-Subjects', *Linguistic Inquiry*, 17: 375–416.

BORRAS, F. M., and CHRISTIAN, R. F. (1959), *Russian Syntax*, Oxford University Press, Oxford.

BOUCHARD, DENIS (1984), *On the Content of Empty Categories*, Foris Publications, Dordrecht.

—— (1985), 'PRO, Pronominal or Anaphor', *Linguistic Inquiry*, 16: 471–7.

BOUTON, LAWRENCE F. (1970), 'Antecedent-Contained Pro-forms', in Mary Ann Campbell *et al.* (eds.), *Papers from the Sixth Regional Meeting of the Chicago Linguistic Society*, University of Chicago, Chicago: 154–67.

BRECHT, RICHARD D., and LEVINE, JAMES S. (1986), *Case in Slavic*, Slavica Publishers, Columbus, Oh.

BREEN, J. G. (1981), 'Margan^y and Gunya', in R. M. W. Dixon and B. Blake (eds.), *The Handbook of Australian Languages*, vol. ii, ANU Press, Canberra: 274–393.

BRESNAN, JOAN (1976), 'Nonarguments for Raising', *Linguistic Inquiry*, 7: 485–501.

—— (1977), 'Variables in the Theory of Transformations', in Peter W. Culicover, T. Wasow, and Adrian Akmajian (eds.), *Formal Syntax*, Academic Press, New York: 157–96.

—— (ed.) (1982a), *The Mental Representation of Grammatical Relations*, MIT Press, Cambridge, Mass.

—— (1982b), 'The Passive in Grammatical Theory', in Joan Bresnan (ed.), *The Mental Representation of Grammatical Relations*, MIT Press, Cambridge, Mass.: 3–86.

—— (1994), 'Locative Inversion and the Architecture of Universal Grammar', *Language*, 70: 72–131.

—— and GRIMSHAW, JANE (1978), 'The Syntax of Free Relatives in English', *Linguistic Inquiry*, 19: 331–91.

BROWNING, MARGUERITE (1987), 'Null Operator Constructions', unpublished doctoral dissertation, MIT, Cambridge, Mass. (available from MIT Working Papers in Linguistics).

BROWNING, MARGUERITE (1989), 'ECP ≠ CED', *Linguistic Inquiry*, 20: 481–91.

BURTON, STRANG, and GRIMSHAW, JANE (1992), 'Coordination and VP-Internal Subjects', *Linguistic Inquiry*, 23: 305–12.

BURZIO, LUIGI (1983), 'Conditions on Representations and Romance Syntax', *Linguistic Inquiry*, 14: 193–221.

—— (1986), *Italian Syntax: A Government-Binding Approach*, Reidel, Dordrecht.

—— (1989), 'On the Non-existence of Disjoint Reference Principles', *Rivista di grammatica generativa*, 14: 3–27.

—— (1991), 'The Morphological Basis of Anaphora', *Journal of Linguistics*, 27: 81–105.

CAMPOS, HECTOR (1986), 'Indefinite Object Drop', *Linguistic Inquiry*, 17: 354–9.

CARLSON, GREG N. (1987), 'Same and Different', *Linguistics and Philosophy*, 10: 531–65.

CARRIER, JILL, and RANDALL, JANET H. (1992), 'The Argument Structure and Syntactic Structure of Resultatives', *Linguistic Inquiry*, 23: 173–234.

CHIERCHIA, GENNARO (1992), 'Anaphora and Dynamic Binding', *Linguistics and Philosophy*, 15: 111–83.

CHOMSKY, NOAM (1955), *The Logical Structure of Linguistic Theory*, published in 1975, Plenum, New York.

—— (1957), *Syntactic Structures*, Mouton, The Hague.

—— (1965), *Aspects of the Theory of Syntax*, MIT Press, Cambridge, Mass.

—— (1968), *Language and Mind*, Harcourt, Brace & World, New York.

—— (1970), 'Remarks on Nominalizations', in Richard Jacobs and Peter Rosenbaum (eds.), *Readings in English Transformational Grammar*, Ginn & Co., Waltham, Mass.: 184–221.

—— (1973), 'Conditions on Transformations', in Steven Anderson and Paul Kiparsky (eds.), *Festschrift for Morris Halle*, Holt, Rinehart & Winston, New York: 232–86.

—— (1975), *Reflections on Language*, Pantheon, New York.

—— (1977), 'On Wh Movement', in Peter W. Culicover, Thomas Wasow, and Adrian Akmajian (eds.), *Formal Syntax*, Academic Press, New York: 71–132.

—— (1980), 'On Binding', *Linguistic Inquiry*, 11: 1–46.

—— (1981), *Lectures on Government and Binding*, Foris Publications, Dordrecht.

—— (1982), *Some Concepts and Consequences of the Theory of Government and Binding*, MIT Press, Cambridge, Mass.

—— (1986a), *Knowledge of Language: Its Nature, Origin, and Use*, Praeger, New York.

—— (1986b), *Barriers*, MIT Press, Cambridge, Mass.

—— (1991), 'Linguistics and Adjacent Fields: A Personal View', in Asa Kasher (ed.), *The Chomskyan Turn*, Blackwell, New York: 3–25.

—— (1993), 'A Minimalist Program for Linguistic Theory', in Kenneth Hale and Samuel Jay Keyser (eds.), *The View from Building Twenty*, MIT Press, Cambridge, Mass.: 1–52.

—— (1994), 'Bare Phrase Structure', *MIT Working Papers in Linguistics Occasional Papers*, MIT, Cambridge, Mass.

—— (1995), *The Minimalist Program*, MIT Press, Cambridge, Mass.

—— and LASNIK, HOWARD (1977), 'Filters and Control', *Linguistic Inquiry*, 8: 425–504.

—— —— (1991), 'Principles and Parameters Theory', in J. Jacobs, A. von Stechow, and T. Vennemann (eds.), *Syntax: An International Handbook of Contemporary Research*, Walter de Gruyter, Berlin. Reprinted in Noam Chomsky (1995), *The Minimalist Program*, MIT Press, Cambridge, Mass.: 13–127.

CHUNG, SANDRA (1994), '*Wh*-Agreement and "Referentiality" in Chamorro', *Linguistic Inquiry*, 25: 1–44.

—— and McCLOSKEY, JAMES (1987), 'Government, Barriers and Small Clauses in Modern Irish', *Linguistic Inquiry*, 18: 173–237.

CINQUE, GUGLIELMO (1990), *Types of Ā-Dependencies*, MIT Press, Cambridge, Mass.

COLE, PETER, HERMON, GABRIELLA, and SUNG, LI-MAY (1990), 'Principles and Parameters of Long-Distance Reflexives', *Linguistic Inquiry*, 21: 1–22.

—— and MORGAN, JERRY L. (eds.) (1975), *Syntax and Semantics 3: Speech Acts*, Academic Press, New York.

—— and SADOCK, JERROLD M. (eds.) (1977), *Syntax and Semantics 8: Grammatical Relations*, Academic Press, New York.

CONTRERAS, HELAS (1984), 'A Note on Parasitic Gaps', *Linguistic Inquiry*, 5: 704–13.

—— (1991), 'On the Position of Subjects', in Susan Rothstein (ed.), *Perspectives on Phrase Structure: Heads and Licensing*, Academic Press, San Diego: 63–79.

COOPMANS, PETER (1987), 'Where Stylistic and Syntactic Processes Meet: Inversion in English', *Language*, 65: 728–51.

—— BORDELOIS, IVONNE, and DOTSON, B. (eds.) (1986), *Formal Parameters of Generative Grammar*, ii: *Going Romance*, Foris Publications, Dordrecht.

CULICOVER, PETER W. (1992), 'A Note on Quantifier Binding', *Linguistic Inquiry*, 23: 659–63.

—— (1993), 'Evidence against ECP Accounts of the *That-t* Effect', *Linguistic Inquiry*, 24: 557–61.

—— and JACKENDOFF, RAY (1995), '*Something Else* for the Binding Theory', *Linguistic Inquiry*, 26: 249–75.

—— and ROCHEMONT, MICHAEL S. (1990), 'Extraposition and the Complement Principle', *Linguistic Inquiry*, 21: 23–48.

—— —— (1992), 'Adjunct Extraction from NP and the ECP', *Linguistic Inquiry*, 23: 496–501.

—— WASOW, THOMAS, and AKMAJIAN, ADRIAN (eds.) (1977), *Formal Syntax*, Academic Press, New York.

—— and WILKINS, WENDY (1984), *Locality in Linguistic Theory*, Academic Press, New York.

DAVIS, LORI (1986), 'Remarks on the θ-Criterion and Case', *Linguistic Inquiry*, 17: 564–8.

—— (1987), 'Remarks on Government and Proper Government', *Linguistic Inquiry*, 18: 311–21.

DELAHUNTY, GERALD P. (1982), 'Subject Sentences Do Exist', *Linguistic Analysis*, 12: 379–98.

DEN BESTEN, HANS (1983), 'On the Interactions of Root Transformations and Deletive Rules', in Werner Abraham (ed.), *On the Formal Syntax of the Westgermania*, John Benjamins, Amsterdam: 47–131.

—— and MOED-VAN WALRAVEN, CORRETJE (1986), 'The Syntax of Verbs in Yiddish', in Hubert Haider and Martin Prinzhorn (eds.), *Verb Second Phenomena in Germanic Languages*, Foris, Dordrecht: 111–35.

—— and WEBELHUTH, GERT (1990), 'Stranding', in Gunther Grewendorf and Wolfgang Sternefeld (eds.), *Scrambling and Barriers*, Linguistik Aktuell 5, Benjamins, Amsterdam: 77–92.

DEPREZ, VIVIAN (1991), 'WH-Movement: Adjunction and Substitution', in Dawn Bates (ed.), *Proceedings of the Tenth West Coast Conference on Formal Linguistics*, Center for the Study of Language and Information, Stanford, Calif.: 103–14.

DIESING, MOLLY (1990), 'Verb Movement and the Subject Position in Yiddish', *Natural Language and Linguistic Theory*, 8: 41–79.

—— (1992), 'Bare Plural Subjects and the Derivation of Logical Representations', *Linguistic Inquiry*, 23: 353–80.

DI SCIULLO, ANNA MARIA, and WILLIAMS, EDWIN (1987), *On the Definition of Word*, MIT Press, Cambridge, Mass.

DIXON, R. M. W., and BLAKE, B. (eds.) (1981), *The Handbook of Australian Languages*, vol. ii, ANU Press, Canberra.

DRUBIG, H. BERNHARD (1992), 'On Topicalization and Inversion', in Rosemarie Tracy (ed.), *Who Climbs the Grammar Tree*, Linguistische Arbeiten 281, Max Niemeyer, Tübingen: 375–422.

EMONDS, JOSEPH (1979), 'Appositive Relatives Have no Properties', *Linguistic Inquiry*, 10: 211–43.

ENÇ, MURVET (1989), 'Pronouns, Licensing and Binding', *Natural Language and Linguistic Theory*, 7: 51–92.

ENGDAHL, ELISABET (1983), 'Parasitic Gaps', *Linguistics and Philosophy*, 6: 5–34.

EVANS, GARETH (1980), 'Pronouns', *Linguistic Inquiry*, 11: 337–62.

EVERAERT, M. (1986a), *The Syntax of Reflexivization*, Foris Publications, Dordrecht.

—— (1986b), 'Long Reflexivization and Obviation in the Romance Languages', in Peter Coopmans, Ivonne Bordelois, and B. Dotson (eds.), *Formal Parameters of Generative Grammar*, ii: *Going Romance*, Foris Publications, Dordrecht: 51–72.

—— (1991), 'Contextual Determination of the Anaphor/Pronominal Distinction', in Jan Koster and Eric Reuland (eds.), *Long Distance Anaphora*, Cambridge University Press, Cambridge: 77–118.

EVERS, ARNOLD (1975), 'The Transformational Cycle in Dutch and German', unpublished doctoral dissertation, University of Utrecht.

FANSELOW, GISBERT (1990), 'Scrambling as NP-Movement', in Günther

Grewendorf and Wolfgang Sternefeld (eds.), *Scrambling and Barriers*, John Benjamins, Amsterdam: 113–40.

—— (ed.) (1993), *The Parametrization of Universal Grammar*, John Benjamins, Amsterdam.

FARACI, ROBERT (1974), 'Aspects of the Grammar of Infinitives and For-Phrases', unpublished doctoral dissertation, MIT, Cambridge, Mass.

FARLEY, A., FARLEY, P., and McCULLOGH, K.-E. (eds.) (1986), *Papers from the Parasession on Pragmatics and Grammatical Theory, 22nd Regional Meeting, Chicago Linguistic Society*, Chicago.

FARMER, ANN K. (1987), 'They Held Each Other's Breath and Other Puzzles for the Binding Theory', *Linguistic Inquiry*, 8: 57–163.

FIENGO, ROBERT, and MAY, ROBERT (1994), *Indices and Identity*, MIT Press, Cambridge, Mass.

FRAMPTON, JOHN (1990), 'Parasitic Gaps and the Theory of Wh-Chains', *Linguistic Inquiry*, 21: 49–78.

FREIDIN, ROBERT (ed.) (1990), *Current Issues in Comparative Grammar*, Kluwer Academic Publishers, Dordrecht.

—— (ed.) (1991), *Principles and Parameters in Comparative Grammar*, MIT Press, Cambridge, Mass.

FUKUI, NAOKI (1986), 'A Theory of Category Projection and its Applications', unpublished doctoral dissertation, MIT, Cambridge, Mass. (available from MIT Working Papers in Linguistics).

GAZDAR, GERALD, KLEIN, EWAN, PULLUM, GEOFFREY, and SAG, IVAN (1985), *Generalized Phrase Structure Grammar*, Harvard University Press, Cambridge, Mass.

GEEST, W. DE, and PUTSEYS, Y. (eds.) (1984), *Sentential Complementation*, Proceedings of the International Conference held at UFSAL, Brussels, June 1983, Foris Publications, Dordrecht.

GIORGI, ALESSANDRA (1984), 'Toward a Theory of Long Distance Anaphors: A GB Approach', *Linguistic Review*, 3: 307–62.

GOLD, E. MARK (1967), 'Language Identification in the Limit', *Information and Control*, 10: 447–74.

GOLDSMITH, JOHN (1985), 'A Principled Exception to the Coordinate Structure Constraint', in William Eilfort, Paul Kroeber, and Karen Peterson (eds.), *Papers from the 21st Regional Meeting of the Chicago Linguistics Society*, Chicago Linguistics Society, Chicago: 133–43.

GOODALL, GRANT (1984), 'Parallel Structures in Syntax', unpublished doctoral dissertation, University of California, La Jolla, Calif.

—— (1991), 'Spec of IP and Spec of CP in Spanish Wh-Questions', in Dawn Bates (ed.), *Proceedings of the Tenth West Coast Conference on Formal Linguistics*, Center for the Study of Language and Information, Stanford, Calif.: 175–82.

GREENBERG, JOSEPH (1963), *Universals of Language*, MIT Press, Cambridge, Mass.

GREWENDORF, GÜNTHER, and STERNEFELD, WOLFGANG (eds.) (1990), *Scrambling and Barriers*, John Benjamins, Amsterdam.

GRIMSHAW, JANE (1979), 'Complement Selection and the Lexicon', *Linguistic Inquiry*, 10: 279–326.

—— (1990), *Argument Structure*, MIT Press, Cambridge, Mass.

—— (1991), 'Extended Projection', unpublished MS, Brandeis University, Waltham, Mass.

GROSU, ALEXANDER (1975), 'The Position of Fronted *Wh* Phrases', *Linguistic Inquiry*, 6: 588–99.

GUÉRON, JACQUELINE, and POLLOCK, JEAN-YVES (eds.) (1989), *Linguistique comparée et théorie de liage*, Foris, Dordrecht.

HAAFTEN, TON VAN, SMITS, RIK, and VAT, JAN (1981), 'Left Dislocation, Connectedness, and Reconstruction', in W. Abraham (ed.), *On the Formal Syntax of the Westgermania: Papers from the 3rd Groningen Grammar Talks*, John Benjamins, Amsterdam: 133–54.

HAEGEMAN, LILIANE (1988), 'Verb Projection Raising and the Multidimensional Analysis: Some Empirical Problems', *Linguistic Inquiry*, 19: 671–83.

—— (1992), *Theory and Description in Generative Syntax: A Case Study in West Flemish*, Cambridge University Press, Cambridge.

—— and VAN RIEMSDIJK, HENK (1986), 'Verb Projection Raising, Scope and the Typology of Rules Affecting Verbs', *Linguistic Inquiry*, 17: 417–66.

HAIDER, HUBERT (1990), 'Topicalization and Other Puzzles of German Syntax', in Gunther Grewendorf and Wolfgang Sternefeld (eds.), *Scrambling and Barriers*, Linguistik Aktuell 5, John Benjamins, Amsterdam: 93–112.

—— (1991), 'The Germanic Verb-Second Puzzle', *Linguistics: An Interdisciplinary Journal of the Language Sciences*, 29: 703–17.

—— and PRINZHORN, MARTIN (eds.) (1986), *Verb Second Phenomena in Germanic Languages*, Foris, Dordrecht.

HAÏK, ISABEL (1984), 'Indirect Binding', *Linguistic Inquiry*, 15: 185–224.

HALE, KENNETH (1973), 'Person Marking in Walbiri', in Stephen R. Anderson and Paul Kiparsky (eds.), *Festschrift for Morris Halle*, Holt, Rinehart & Winston, New York: 308–44.

—— JEANNE, LAVERNE, and PLATERO, PAUL (1977), 'Three Cases of Overgeneration', in Peter W. Culicover, Thomas Wasow, and Adrian Akmajian (eds.), *Formal Syntax*, Academic Press, New York: 379–416.

—— and KEYSER, SAMUEL JAY (eds.) (1993), *The View from Building Twenty*, MIT Press, Cambridge, Mass.

HAMBURGER, HENRY, and WEXLER, KENNETH (1973), 'Identifiability of a Class of Transformational Grammars', in K. J. J. Hintikka, J. M. E. Moravcsik, and P. Suppes (eds.), *Approaches to Natural Language*, Reidel, Dordrecht: 153–66.

—— —— (1975), 'A Mathematical Theory of Learning Transformational Grammar', *Journal of Mathematical Psychology*, 12: 137–77.

HARMAN, GILBERT (ed.) (1974), *On Noam Chomsky: Critical Essays: Excerpts from 'Constraints on Variables in Syntax'*, Anchor Press/Doubleday, Garden City, NY.

HEIM, IRENE (1982), 'The Semantics of Definite and Indefinite Noun Phrases', unpublished doctoral dissertation, University of Massachusetts, Amherst, Mass.

(available from the University of Massachusetts Graduate Student Linguistics Association).

HELLAN, LARS (1986), 'On Anaphora and Predication in Norwegian', in Lars Hellan and K. Koch Christensen (eds.), *Topics in Scandinavian Syntax*, Reidel, Dordrecht: 103–24.

—— (1988), *Anaphora in Norwegian and the Theory of Grammar*, Foris, Dordrecht.

—— (1991), 'Containment and Connectedness Anaphors', in Jan Koster and Eric Reuland (eds.), *Long Distance Anaphora*, Cambridge University Press, Cambridge: 27–48.

—— and CHRISTENSEN, K. KOCH (eds.) (1986), *Topics in Scandinavian Syntax*, Reidel, Dordrecht.

HENDRICK, RANDALL (1988), *Anaphora in Celtic and Universal Grammar*, Kluwer, Dordrecht.

HENRY, ALISON (1992), 'Infinitives in a For-To Dialect', *Natural Language and Linguistic Theory*, 10: 279–302.

HESTVIK, ARILD (1992), 'LF Movement of Pronouns and Antisubject Orientation', *Linguistic Inquiry*, 23: 557–94.

HEYCOCK, CAROLINE, and KROCH, ANTHONY (1993), 'Verb Movement and the Status of Subjects: Implications for the Theory of Licensing', *Groninger Arbeiten zur germanistischen Linguistik*, 36: 75–102.

—— and SANTORINI, BEATRICE (1992), 'Head Movement and the Licensing of Nonthematic Positions', in J. Mead (ed.), *Proceedings of the Eleventh West Coast Conference on Formal Linguistics*, Center for the Study of Language and Information, Stanford, Calif.: 262–76.

HIGGINBOTHAM, JAMES (1980), 'Pronouns and Bound Variables', *Linguistic Inquiry*, 1: 679–708.

—— (1982), 'Reciprocal Interpretation', *Journal of Linguistic Research*, 1: 97–117.

—— (1985), 'On Semantics', *Linguistic Inquiry*, 16: 547–94.

HINTIKKA, JAAKO, MORAVCSIK, JULIUS M. E., and SUPPES, PAT (eds.) (1973), *Approaches to Natural Language*, Reidel, Dordrecht: 167–79.

HOEKSTRA, TEUN, and MULDER, RENÉ (1990), 'Unergatives as Copula Verbs: Location and Existential Predication', *Linguistic Review*, 7: 1–79.

—— and ROBERTS, IAN (1993), 'Middle Constructions in Dutch and English', in Eric Reuland and Werner Abraham (eds.), *Knowledge and Language*, ii: *Lexical and Conceptual Structure*, Kluwer, Dordrecht: 183–220.

HORNSTEIN, NORBERT (1984), *Logic as Grammar*, MIT Press, Cambridge, Mass.

—— (1994), 'An Argument for Minimalism: the case of antecedent-contained deletion', *Linguistic Inquiry*, 26: 455–80.

—— and LIGHTFOOT, DAVID (eds.) (1994), *Verb Movement*, Cambridge University Press, Cambridge.

—— and WEINBERG, AMY (1990), 'The Necessity of LF', *Linguistic Review*, 7: 129–67.

HUANG, C.-T. JAMES (1982), 'Move *Wh* in a Language without *Wh*-Movement', *Linguistic Review*, 1: 369–416.

HUANG, C.-T. JAMES (1983), 'A Note on the Binding Theory', *Linguistic Inquiry*, 14: 554–61.

—— (1993), 'Reconstruction and the Structure of VP: Some Theoretical Consequences', *Linguistic Inquiry*, 24: 103–38.

IATRIDOU, SABINE (1986), 'An Anaphor not Bound in its Governing Category', *Linguistic Inquiry*, 17: 766–72.

—— (1990), 'About Agr(P)', *Linguistic Inquiry*, 21: 551–77.

INOUE, K. (1976), 'Reflexivization: An Interpretive Approach', in M. Shibatani (ed.), *Syntax and Semantics 5: Japanese Generative Grammar*, Academic Press, New York.

JACKENDOFF, RAY (1972), *Semantic Interpretation in Generative Grammar*, MIT Press, Cambridge.

—— (1977), *X-Bar Syntax: A Study of Phrase Structure*, MIT Press, Cambridge, Mass.

—— (1983), *Semantics and Cognition*, MIT Press, Cambridge, Mass.

—— (1990), *Semantic Structures*, MIT Press, Cambridge, Mass.

—— (1992), 'Babe Ruth Homered his Way into the Hearts of America', in Timothy Stowell and Eric Wehrli (eds.), *Syntax and Semantics 26: Syntax and the Lexicon*, Academic Press, New York: 155–78.

—— (1993), *Patterns in the Mind*, New York, Harvester Wheatsheaf.

JACOBS, RICHARD, and ROSENBAUM, PETER (eds.) (1970), *Readings in English Transformational Grammar*, Ginn & Co., Waltham, Mass.

JAEGGLI, OSWALDO (1982), *Topics in Romance Syntax*, Foris Publications, Dordrecht.

—— (1986), 'Passive', *Linguistic Inquiry*, 17: 587–622.

JELINEK, ELOISE, and DEMERS, RICHARD A. (1994), 'Predicates and Pronominal Arguments in Straits Salish', *Language*, 70: 697–736.

JOHNSON, KYLE (1984), 'Some Notes on Subjunctive Clauses and Binding in Icelandic', *MIT Working Papers in Linguistics*, 6: 102–37.

—— (1985), 'A Case for Movement', unpublished doctoral dissertation, MIT, Cambridge, Mass.

KASHER, ASA (ed.) (1991), *The Chomskyan Turn*, Basil Blackwell, New York.

KATADA, FUSA (1991), 'The LF Representation of Anaphors', *Linguistic Inquiry*, 22: 287–313.

KATHOL, ANDREAS (1990), 'A Uniform Approach to V2 in German', in *Proceedings of the Twentieth Meeting of the North East Linguistics Society*: 244–54.

KATZ, JEROLD J., and POSTAL, PAUL M. (1964), *Toward an Integrated Theory of Linguistic Descriptions*, MIT Press, Cambridge, Mass.

KAYNE, RICHARD (1975), *French Syntax*, MIT Press, Cambridge, Mass.

—— (1980), 'Extensions of Binding and Case-Marking', *Linguistic Inquiry*, 20: 75–96.

—— (1983), 'Connectedness', *Linguistic Inquiry*, 24: 223–49.

—— (1984), *Connectedness and Binary Branching*, Foris Publications, Dordrecht.

—— (1991), 'Romance Clitics, Verb Movement, and PRO', *Linguistic Inquiry*, 22: 647–86.

—— (1994), *The Antisymmetry of Syntax*, MIT Press, Cambridge, Mass.

KEYSER, SAMUEL J. (ed.) (1978), *Recent Transformational Studies in European Languages*, Linguistic Inquiry Monograph 3, MIT Press, Cambridge, Mass.

—— and ROEPER, THOMAS (1984), 'On the Middle and Ergative Constructions in English', *Linguistic Inquiry*, 15: 381–416.

—— —— (1992), 'Re: The Abstract Clitic Hypothesis', *Linguistic Inquiry*, 23: 89–125.

KIMBALL, JOHN (ed.) (1975), *Syntax and Semantics 4*, Academic Press, New York.

KISS, KATALIN E. (ed.) (to appear), *Discourse Configurationality*, Oxford University Press, Oxford.

KITAGAWA, YOSHIHISA (1986), 'Subjects in Japanese and English', unpublished doctoral dissertation, University of Massachusetts, Amherst (available from the University of Massachusetts Graduate Student Linguistics Association).

KOOPMAN, HILDA (1983), *The Syntax of Verbs*, Foris Publications, Dordrecht.

—— and SPORTICHE, DOMINIQUE (1982), 'Variables and the Bijection Principle', *Linguistic Review*, 2: 139–60.

—— —— (1991), 'The Position of Subjects', *Lingua*, 85: 211–58.

KOSTER, JAN (1978), 'Why Subject Sentences Don't Exist', in Samuel J. Keyser (ed.), *Recent Studies in Transformational Grammars of European Languages*, MIT Press, Cambridge, Mass.: 53–64.

—— (1984), 'On Binding and Control', *Linguistic Inquiry*, 5: 417–59.

—— (1987), *Domains and Dynasties: The Radical Autonomy of Syntax*, Foris Publications, Dordrecht.

—— and REULAND, ERIC (eds.) (1991), *Long Distance Anaphora*, Cambridge University Press, Cambridge.

KREIMAN, J., and OJEDA, ALMERINDO E. (eds.) (1980), *Papers from the Parasession on Pronouns and Anaphora, Chicago Linguistics Society*, Chicago Linguistics Society, Chicago.

KUNO, SUSUMO (1973), *The Structure of the Japanese Language*, MIT Press, Cambridge, Mass.

KURODA, S.-Y. (1988), 'Whether we Agree or Not', in William Poser (ed.), *Papers from the Second International Workshop on Japanese Syntax*, Center for the Study of Language and Information, Stanford University: 103–43.

LAKOFF, GEORGE (1986), 'Frame Semantic Control of the Coordinate Structure Constraint', in A. Farley, P. Farley, and K.-E. McCullogh (eds.), *Papers from the Parasession on Pragmatics and Grammatical Theory, Twenty Second Regional Meeting, Chicago Linguistic Society*, Chicago Linguistics Society, Chicago: 152–67.

LARSON, RICHARD K. (1987), '"Missing Prepositions" and the Analysis of English Free Relative Clauses', *Linguistic Inquiry*, 18: 239–66.

—— (1988), 'On the Double Object Construction', *Linguistic Inquiry*, 19: 335–91.

—— (1991), '*Promise* and the Theory of Control', *Linguistic Inquiry*, 22: 103–39.

—— IATRIDOU, SABINE, LAHIRI, UTPAL, and HIGGINBOTHAM, JAMES (1992), *Control and Grammar*, trans. BostonKluwer Academic Publishers, Dordrecht.

LARSON, RICHARD K. and MAY, ROBERT (1990), 'Antecedent-Contained Deletion or Vacuous Movement: Reply to Baltin', *Linguistic Inquiry*, 21: 103–22.

LASNIK, HOWARD (1976), 'Remarks on Coreference', *Linguistic Analysis*, 2: 1–22.

—— (1992*a*), 'Two Notes on Control and Binding', in Richard Larson, James Higginbotham, Sabine Iatridou, and Utpal Lahiri (eds.), *Control and Grammar*, Kluwer Academic Publishers, Dordrecht: 235–53.

—— (1992*b*), 'Case and Expletives: Notes toward a Parametric Account', *Linguistic Inquiry*, 23: 381–405.

—— and SAITO, MAMORU (1984), 'On the Nature of Proper Government', *Linguistic Inquiry*, 5: 235–89.

—— —— (1992), *Move Alpha*, MIT Press, Cambridge, Mass.

—— and STOWELL, TIM (1991), 'Weakest Crossover', *Linguistic Inquiry*, 22: 687–720.

—— and URIAGAREKA, JUAN (1988), *A Course in GB Syntax*, MIT Press, Cambridge, Mass.

LEBEAUX, DAVID (1988), 'Language Acquisition and the Form of the Grammar', unpublished doctoral dissertation, University of Massachusetts, Amherst, Mass. (available from the University of Massachusetts Graduate Student Linguistics Association).

LEMA, JOSE, and RIVERO, MARÍA-LUISA (1990), 'Long Head Movement: ECP vs. HMC', *Cahiers linguistiques d'Ottawa*, 18: 61–78.

—— —— (1991), 'Types of Verbal Movement in Old Spanish: Modals, Futures, and Perfects', *Probus*, 3: 237–78.

LEVIN, BETH, and RAPPAPORT, MALKA (1986), 'The Formation of Adjectival Passives', *Linguistic Inquiry*, 17: 623–62.

—— —— (1988), 'Non-event -*er* Nominals: A Probe into Argument Structure', *Linguistics*, 26: 1067–83.

—— —— (1995), *Unaccusativity: At the Syntax–Lexical Semantics Interface*, MIT Press, Cambridge, Mass.

LEVINE, ROBERT D. (1989), 'On Focus Inversion: Syntactic Valence and the Role of a SUBCAT List', *Linguistics*, 17: 1013–55.

LEVINSON, STEPHEN C. (1991), 'Pragmatic Reduction of the Binding Conditions Revisited', *Journal of Linguistics*, 27: 107–61.

LIGHTFOOT, DAVID (1976), 'The Theoretical Implications of Subject Raising', *Foundations of Language*, 14: 257–86.

—— (1982), *The Language Lottery: Toward a Biology of Grammars*, MIT Press, Cambridge, Mass.

—— (1991), *How to Set Parameters: Arguments from Language Change*, MIT Press, Cambridge, Mass.

LONGOBARDI, GIUSEPPE (1985), 'Connectedness, Scope and C-command', *Linguistic Inquiry*, 16: 163–92.

LUST, BARBARA (ed.) (1986), *Studies in the Acquisition of Anaphora*, i, D. Reidel, Dordrecht.

MCCAWLEY, JAMES D. (ed.) (1976), *Syntax and Semantics 7: Notes from the Linguistic Underground*, Academic Press, New York.

McCloskey, James (1992), 'Adjunction, Selection and Embedded Verb Second', unpublished MS, University of California, Santa Cruz.

McDonough, J., and Plunkett, B. (eds.) (1987), *Proceedings of NELS 7*, GLSA, University of Massachusetts, Amherst, Mass. (available from the University of Massachusetts Graduate Student Linguistics Association).

McNally, Louise (1992), 'VP Coordination and the VP-Internal Subject Hypothesis', *Linguistic Inquiry*, 23: 336–41.

Mahajan, Anoop (1990), 'The A/Ā Distinction and Movement Theory', unpublished doctoral dissertation, MIT, Cambridge, Mass. (available from MIT Working Papers in Linguistics).

Maling, Joan (1984), 'Non-clause Bounded Reflexives in Icelandic', *Linguistics and Philosophy*, 7: 211–41.

—— and Zaenen, Annie (eds.) (1990a), *Syntax and Semantics 24: Modern Icelandic Syntax*, Academic Press, New York.

—— —— (1990b), 'Unaccusative, Passive and Quirky Case', in Joan Maling and Annie Zaenen (eds.), *Syntax and Semantics 24: Modern Icelandic Syntax*, Academic Press, New York: 137–52.

Manzini, Maria Rita (1992), *Locality*, MIT Press, Cambridge, Mass.

—— (1994), 'Locality, Minimalism and Parasitic Gaps', *Linguistic Inquiry*, 25: 481–508.

—— and Wexler, Kenneth (1987), 'Parameters, Binding Theory, and Learnability', *Linguistic Inquiry*, 18: 413–44.

Marantz, Alec (1984), *On the Nature of Grammatical Relations*, MIT Press, Cambridge, Mass.

May, Robert (1985), *Logical Form*, MIT Press, Cambridge, Mass.

Miyagawa, Shigeru (1989), *Syntax and Semantics 22: Structure and Case Marking in Japanese*, Academic Press, New York.

Moltmann, Friederike (1992), 'Reciprocals and *Same/Different*: Towards a Semantic Analysis', *Linguistics and Philosophy*, 15: 411–62.

Morgan, James (1986), *From Simple Input to Complex Grammars*, MIT Press, Cambridge, Mass.

Müller, Gereon, and Sternefeld, Wolfgang (1993), 'Improper Movement and Unambiguous Binding', *Linguistic Inquiry*, 24: 461–507.

Nakayama, Mineharu (1991), 'Japanese Motion Verbs and Probe Recognition', Paper presented to the Workshop on Japanese Syntax, Rochester, NY, Apr. 1991.

Napoli, Donna Jo (1979), 'Reflexivization across Clause Boundaries in Italian', *Journal of Linguistics*, 5: 1–27.

Neidle, Carol (1988), *The Role of Case in Russian Syntax*, Kluwer Academic Publishers, Dordrecht.

Osherson, Daniel, Stob, M., and Weinstein, Scott (1986), 'Systems that Learn', MIT Press, Cambridge, Mass.

Partee, Barbara (1989), 'Binding Implicit Variables in Quantified Contexts', in *Chicago Linguistics Society 25*, Chicago Linguistics Club, Chicago: 342–65.

PERLMUTTER, DAVID (1978), 'Impersonal Passives and the Unaccusative Hypothesis', in Jeri J. Jaeger *et al.* (eds.), *Proceedings of the Fourth Annual Meeting of the Berkeley Linguistics Society*, Berkeley: 157–89.

—— (ed.) (1983), *Studies in Relational Grammar*, University of Chicago Press, Chicago.

—— and POSTAL, PAUL M. (1983), 'Toward a Universal Characterization of Passivization', in David M. Perlmutter (ed.), *Studies in Relational Grammar*, University of Chicago Press, Chicago: 1–29.

PESETSKY, DAVID (1982a), 'Paths and Categories', unpublished doctoral dissertation, MIT, Cambridge, Mass. (available from MIT Working Papers in Linguistics).

—— (1982b), 'Complementizer-Trace Phenomena and the Nominative Island Condition', *Linguistic Review*, 1: 297–343.

—— (1987), 'Wh-in-situ: Movement and Unselective Binding', in Eric J. Reuland and Alice G. B. ter Meulen (eds.), *The Representation of (In)definiteness*, MIT Press, Cambridge, Mass.: 98–130.

PICA, PIERRE (1987), 'On the Nature of the Reflexivization Cycle', in J. McDonough and B. Plunkett (eds.), *Proceedings of the Seventh Annual Meeting of the North East Linguistics Society*, GLSA, University of Massachusetts, Amherst, Mass.: 483–99 (available from the University of Massachusetts Graduate Student Linguistics Association).

PINKER, STEVEN (1989), *Learnability and Cognition*, MIT Press, Cambridge, Mass.

—— (1994), *The Language Instinct*, W. Morrow & Co., New York.

POLLARD, CARL, and SAG, IVAN (1992), 'Anaphors in English and the Scope of Binding Theory', *Linguistic Inquiry*, 23: 261–303.

—— —— (1994), *Head-Driven Phrase Structure Grammar*, University of Chicago Press, Chicago.

POLLOCK, JEAN-YVES (1989), 'Verb Movement, Universal Grammar and the Structure of IP', *Linguistic Inquiry*, 20: 365–424.

POSER, WILLIAM (ed.) (1988), *Papers from the Second International Workshop on Japanese Syntax*, Center for the Study of Language and Information, Stanford University, Calif.

POSTAL, PAUL (1971), *Crossover Phenomena*, Holt, Rinehart & Winston, New York.

—— (1974), 'On Certain Ambiguities', *Linguistic Inquiry*, 5: 367–424.

—— (1977), 'About a "Nonargument" for Raising', *Linguistic Inquiry*, 8: 141–54.

—— (1986), *Studies of Passive Clauses*, State University of New York Press, Albany, NY.

—— (1993), 'Remarks on Weak Crossover Effects', *Linguistic Inquiry*, 24: 539–56.

—— (1994), 'Parasitic and Pseudo-parasitic Gaps', *Linguistic Inquiry*, 25: 63–117.

—— and PULLUM, GEOFFREY K. (1988), 'Expletive Noun Phrases in Subcategorized Positions', *Linguistic Inquiry*, 19: 635–70.

PROGOVAC, LJILJANA (1992), 'Relativized SUBJECT: Long-Distance Reflexives without Movement', *Linguistic Inquiry*, 23: 671–80.

RADFORD, ANDREW (1988), *Transformational Grammar: A First Course*, Cambridge University Press, Cambridge.

RAPOSO, EDUARDO, and URIAGEREKA, JUAN (1990), 'Long-Distance Case Assignment', *Linguistic Inquiry*, 21: 505–37.

RAPPOPORT, G. C. (1986), 'On Anaphoric Binding in Russian', *Natural Language and Linguistic Theory*, 4: 97–120.

REINHART, TANYA (1983), *Anaphora and Semantic Interpretation*, University of Chicago Press, Chicago.

—— and REULAND, ERIC (1991), 'Anaphors and Logophors: An Argument Structure Perspective', in Jan Koster and Eric Reuland (eds.), *Long Distance Anaphora*, Cambridge University Press, Cambridge: 283–321.

—— —— (1993), 'Reflexivity', *Linguistic Inquiry*, 24: 657–720.

REULAND, ERIC, and ABRAHAM, WERNER (eds.) (1993), *Knowledge and Language*, ii: *Lexical and Conceptual Structure*, Kluwer, Dordrecht.

—— and KOSTER, JAN (1991), 'Long Distance Anaphora: An Overview', in Jan Koster and Eric Reuland (eds.), *Long Distance Anaphora*, Cambridge University Press, Cambridge: 1–25.

—— and TER MEULEN, ALICE G. B. (eds.) (1987), *The Representation of (In)-definiteness*, MIT Press, Cambridge, Mass.

RIEMSDIJK, HENK VAN, and WILLIAMS, EDWIN (1981), 'NP Structure', *Linguistic Review*, 1: 171–217.

RIVERO, MARÍA-LUISA (1980), 'On Left-Dislocation and Topicalization in Spanish', *Linguistic Inquiry*, 11: 363–93.

—— (1991), 'Long Head Movement and Negation: Serbo-Croatian vs. Slovak and Czech', *Linguistic Review*, 8: 319–51.

—— (1994), 'Clause Structure and V-Movement in the Languages of the Balkans', *Natural Language and Linguistic Theory*, 12: 63–120.

RIZZI, LUIGI (1978), 'A Restructuring Rule in Italian Syntax', in Samuel J. Keyser (ed.), *Recent Transformational Studies in European Languages*, Linguistic Inquiry Monograph 3, MIT Press, Cambridge, Mass.: 113–58.

—— (1982), *Issues in Italian Syntax*, Foris Publications, Dordrecht.

—— (1986), 'On Chain Formation', in Hagit Borer (ed.), *Syntax and Semantics 19: The Syntax of Pronominal Clitics*, Academic Press, New York: 65–95.

—— (1990), *Relativized Minimality*, MIT Press, Cambridge, Mass.

—— (1991), 'Residual Verb Second and the Wh-Criterion', Technical Reports in Formal and Computational Linguistics, No. 2, Faculté des Lettres, Université de Genève.

ROBERTS, IAN (1986), *The Representation of Implicit and Dethematized Subjects*, Foris, Dordrecht.

ROCHEMONT, MICHAEL S. (1989), 'Topic Islands and the Subjacency Parameter', *Canadian Journal of Linguistics*, 34: 145–70.

—— and CULICOVER, PETER W. (1990), *English Focus Constructions and the Theory of Grammar*, Cambridge University Press, Cambridge.

—— —— (to appear), 'Deriving Dependent Right Adjuncts in English', in Henk van Riemsdijk, David LeBlanc, and Dorothee Beermann (eds.), *Rightward Movement*, John Benjamins, Amsterdam.

ROEPER, THOMAS, and WILLIAMS, EDWIN (eds.) (1987), *Parameter Setting*, Reidel, Dordrecht.

ROSS, JOHN R. (1967), 'Constraints on Variables in Syntax', unpublished doctoral dissertation, MIT, Cambridge, Mass.

—— (1974), *Excerpts from 'Constraints on Variables in Syntax'*, in Gilbert Harman (ed.), *On Noam Chomsky: Critical Essays*, Anchor Press/Doubleday, Garden City, NY: 165–200.

—— (1983), 'Inner Islands', unpublished MS, MIT, Cambridge, Mass.

ROTHSTEIN, SUSAN (ed.) (1991), *Perspectives on Phrase Structure: Heads and Licensing*, Academic Press, San Diego.

—— (1992), 'Case and NP Licensing', *Natural Language and Linguistic Theory*, 10: 119–39.

RUDIN, CATHERINE (1988), 'On Multiple Questions and Multiple *Wh* Fronting', *Natural Language and Linguistic Theory*, 6: 445–501.

SAFIR, KENNETH (1983), 'On Small Clauses as Constituents', *Linguistic Inquiry*, 14: 730–5.

—— (1985), *Syntactic Chains*, Cambridge University Press, London.

—— (1986), 'Relative Clauses in a Theory of Binding and Levels', *Linguistic Inquiry*, 17: 663–89.

SAG, IVAN (1976), 'Deletion and Logical Form', unpublished doctoral dissertation, MIT, Cambridge, Mass. (available from Garland Press).

SAITO, MAMORU, and HOJI, HAJIME (1983), 'Weak Crossover and Move α in Japanese', *Natural Language and Linguistic Theory*, 1: 245–59.

SAXON, LESLIE (1984), 'Disjoint Anaphora and the Binding Theory', in Mark Cobler *et al.* (eds.), *Proceedings of the Fourth West Coast Conference on Formal Linguistics*, Stanford Linguistics Association, Stanford, Calif.: 242–51.

SCHMERLING, SUSAN (1975), 'Asymmetric Conjunction and Rules of Conversation', in Peter Cole and Jerry L. Morgan (eds.), *Syntax and Semantics 3: Speech Acts*, Academic Press, New York: 211–31.

SELLS, PETER (1987), 'Aspects of Logophoricity', *Linguistic Inquiry*, 18: 445–79.

SHIBATANI, M. (ed.) (1976), *Syntax and Semantics 5: Japanese Generative Grammar*, Academic Press, New York.

SMITS, R. J. C. (1989), *Eurogrammar: The Relative and Cleft Constructions of the Germanic and Romance Languages*, Foris Publications, Dordrecht.

SPEAS, MARGARET (1990), *Phrase Structure in Natural Language*, Studies in Natural Language and Linguistic Theory 21, Kluwer Academic Publishers, Dordrecht.

SPORTICHE, DOMINIQUE (1988), 'A Theory of Floating Quantifiers and its Corollaries for Constituent Structure', *Linguistic Inquiry*, 19: 425–49.

STEENBERGEN, MARLIES (1991), 'Long-Distance Binding in Finnish', in Jan Koster and Eric Reuland (eds.), *Long Distance Anaphora*, Cambridge University Press, Cambridge: 231–44.

STOWELL, TIMOTHY (1981), 'Origins of Phrase Structure', unpublished doctoral dissertation, MIT, Cambridge, Mass. (available from MIT Working Papers in Linguistics).

—— (1983), 'Subjects across Categories', *Linguistic Review*, 2: 285–312.

—— (1989), 'Subjects, Specifiers and X-bar Theory', in Mark Baltin and Anthony Kroch (eds.), *Alternative Conceptions of Phrase Structure*, University of Chicago Press, Chicago: 232–62.

—— and WEHRLI, ERIC (eds.) (1992), *Syntax and Semantics 26: Syntax and the Lexicon*, Academic Press, New York.

STROIK, THOMAS (1992), 'Middles and Movement', *Linguistic Inquiry*, 23: 127–37.

TAKAHASHI, DAIKO (1993), 'Movement of *Wh*-phrases in Japanese', *Natural Language and Linguistic Theory*, 11: 655–78.

TARALDSEN, KNUT TARALD (1981), 'The Theoretical Interpretation of a Class of Marked Extractions', in Adriana Belletti, L. Brandi, and Luigi Rizzi (eds.), *Theory of Markedness in Generative Grammar*, Scuola Normale Superiore, Pisa: 475–516.

TRACY, ROSEMARIE (ed.) (1992), *Who Climbs the Grammar Tree*, Linguistische Arbeiten 281, Max Niemeyer, Tübingen.

TRAVIS, LISA DEMENA (1984), 'Parameters and Effects of Word Order Variation', unpublished doctoral dissertation, MIT, Cambridge, Mass.

—— (1991), 'Parameters of Phrase Structure and Verb-Second Phenomena', in Robert Freidin (ed.), *Principles and Parameters in Comparative Grammar*, MIT Press, Cambridge, Mass.: 339–64.

TSIMPLI, IANTHI MARIA (1995), 'Focussing in Modern Greek', in Katalin È. Kiss (ed.), *Discourse Configurational Languages*, Oxford University Press, New York: 176–206.

TSUJIMURA, NATSUKO (1989), 'Unaccusative Mismatches in Japanese', in *Proceedings of ESCOL*, Columbus, Oh., Department of Linguistics, The Ohio State University: 264–76.

WASOW, THOMAS (1972), 'Anaphoric Relations in English', unpublished doctoral dissertation, MIT, Cambridge, Mass. (available from MIT Working Papers in Linguistics).

—— (1977), 'Transformations and the Lexicon', in Peter W. Culicover, Thomas Wasow, and Adrian Akmajian (eds.), *Formal Syntax*, Academic Press, New York: 327–60.

—— (1979), *Anaphora in Generative Grammar*, E. Story-Scientia, Ghent.

WATANABE, AKIRA (1992), 'Subjacency and S-Structure Movement of Wh-in-situ', *Journal of East Asian Linguistics*, 1: 255–91.

—— (1993), '*Wh*-in situ, Subjacency and Chain Formation', *MIT Working Papers in Linguistics Occasional Papers, 2*, MIT, Cambridge, Mass.

WEBELHUTH, GERT (1989), 'Syntactic Saturation Phenomena and the Modern Germanic Languages', unpublished doctoral dissertation, University of Massachusetts, Amherst, Mass. (available from University of Massachusetts Graduate Student Linguistics Association).

WEERMAN, FRED (1989), *The V2 Conspiracy*, Foris Publications, Dordrecht.

WEXLER, KENNETH, and CULICOVER, PETER W. (1980), *Formal Principles of Language Acquisition*, MIT Press, Cambridge, Mass.

—— and HAMBURGER, HENRY (1973), 'On the Insufficiency of Surface Data for the Learning of Transformation', in Jaako Hintikka, Julius M. E. Moravcsik, and Pat Suppes (eds.), *Approaches to Natural Language*, Reidel, Dordrecht: 167–79.

—— and MANZINI, MARIA RITA (1987), 'Parameters and Learnability in Binding Theory', in Thomas Roeper and Edwin Williams (eds.), *Parameter Setting*, Reidel, Dordrecht: 41–89.

WILLIAMS, EDWIN (1975), 'Small Clauses in English', in John Kimball (ed.), *Syntax and Semantics 4*, Academic Press, New York: 249–73.

—— (1983), 'Against Small Clauses', *Linguistic Inquiry*, 14: 287–308.

—— (1989), 'The Anaphoric Nature of θ-roles', *Linguistic Inquiry*, 20: 425–56.

—— (1994), *Thematic Structure in Syntax*, MIT Press, Cambridge, Mass.

WOODBURY, ANTHONY C. (1977), 'Greenlandic Eskimo, Ergativity and Relational Grammar', in Peter Cole and Jerrold M. Sadock (eds.), *Syntax and Semantics 8: Grammatical Relations*, Academic Press, New York: 307–36.

WOOLFORD, ELLEN (1991), 'VP-Internal Subjects in VSO and Nonconfigurational Languages', *Linguistic Inquiry*, 22: 503–40.

ZAENEN, ANNIE, MALING, JOAN, and THRÁINSSON, HOSKILDUR (1990), 'Case and Grammatical Functions: The Icelandic Passive', in Joan Maling and Annie Zaenen (eds.), *Syntax and Semantics 24: Modern Icelandic Syntax*, Academic Press, New York: 95–136.

ZWART, C. JAN-WOUTER (1993), 'Dutch Syntax and the Minimalist Program', unpublished doctoral dissertation, University of Groningen, Groningen.

INDEX